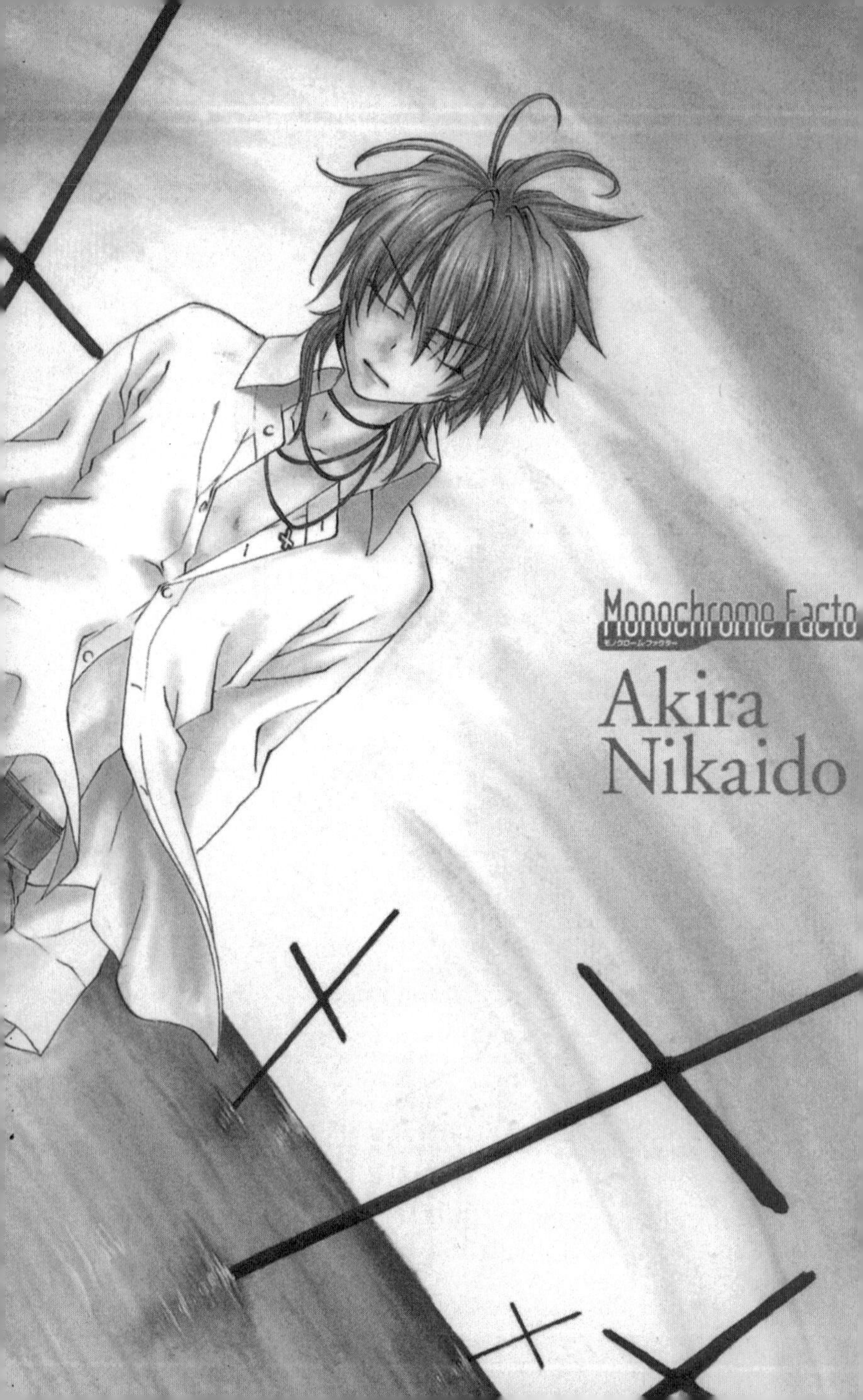
Monochrome Facto
モノクローム・ファクター
Akira
Nikaido

Monochrome Factor Volume 1
Created By KAILI SORANO

Translation - Takae Brewer
English Adaptation - Laura Wyrick
Associate Editor - Stephanie Duchin
Retouch and Lettering - Star Print Brokers
Production Artist - Michael Paolilli
Graphic Designer - Anne Marie Horne

Editor - Peter Ahlstrom
Digital Imaging Manager - Chris Buford
Pre-Production Supervisor - Erika Terriquez
Production Manager - Elisabeth Brizzi
Managing Editor - Vy Nguyen
Creative Director - Anne Marie Horne
Editor-in-Chief - Rob Tokar
Publisher - Mike Kiley
President and C.O.O. - John Parker
C.E.O. and Chief Creative Officer - Stuart Levy

A **TOKYOPOP** Manga

TOKYOPOP Inc.
5900 Wilshire Blvd. Suite 2000
Los Angeles, CA 90036

E-mail: info@TOKYOPOP.com
Come visit us online at www.TOKYOPOP.com

ISBN: 978-1-4278-0069-5

First TOKYOPOP printing: January 2008

10 9 8 7 6 5 4 3 2 1

Printed in the USA

Monochrome Factor

Vol. 1

by Kaili Sorano

TOKYOPOP

HAMBURG // LONDON // LOS ANGELES // TOKYO

1 01010101010

CONTENTS

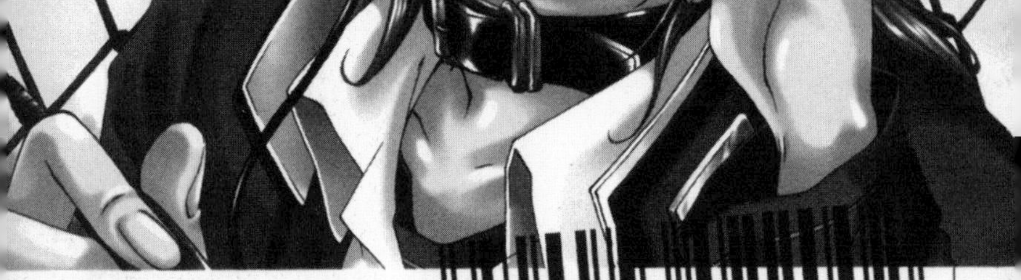
1 01010101010

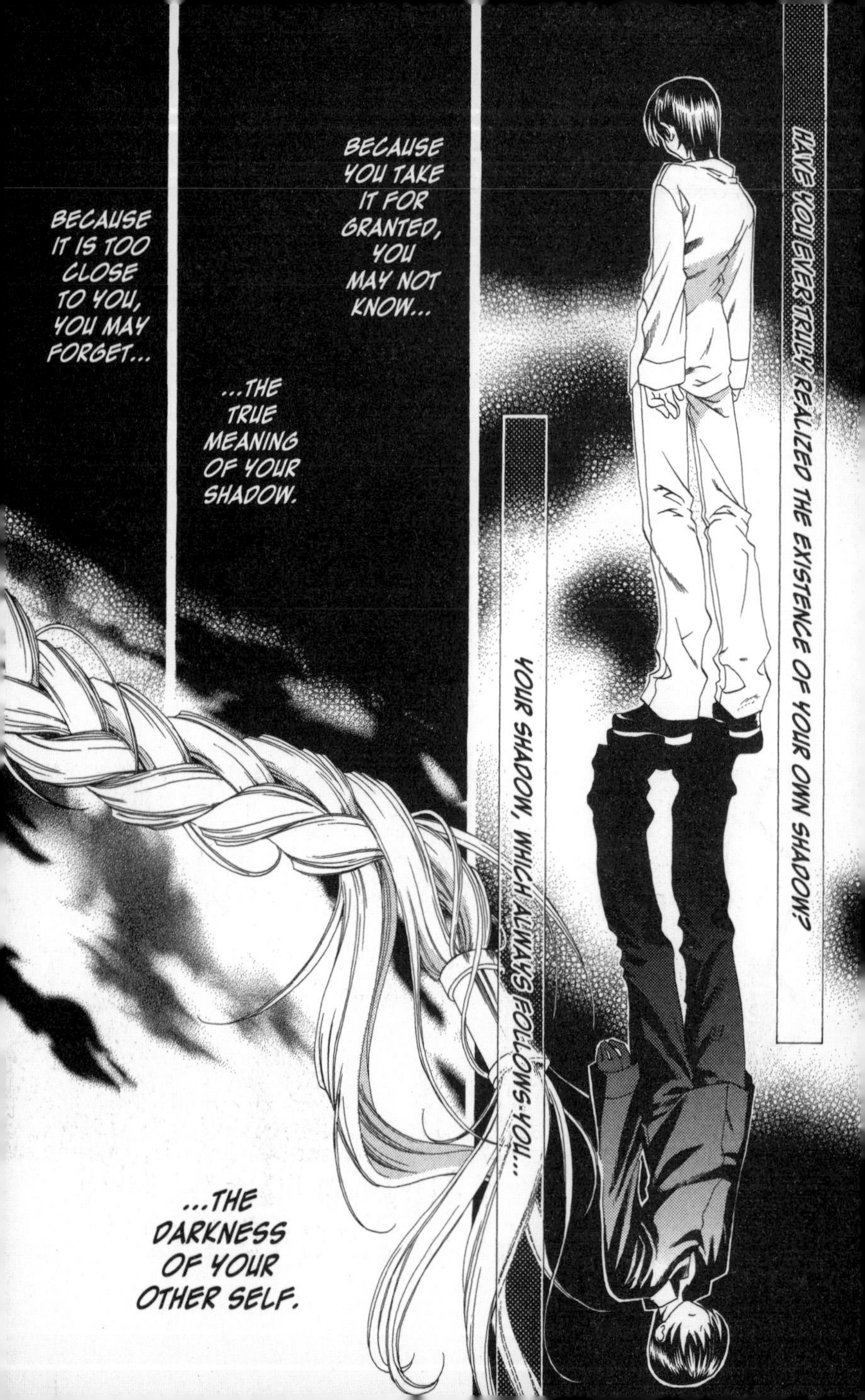
HAVE YOU EVER TRULY REALIZED THE EXISTENCE OF YOUR OWN SHADOW?
BECAUSE YOU TAKE IT FOR GRANTED, YOU MAY NOT KNOW...
...THE TRUE MEANING OF YOUR SHADOW.
BECAUSE IT IS TOO CLOSE TO YOU, YOU MAY FORGET...
YOUR SHADOW, WHICH ALWAYS FOLLOWS YOU...
...THE DARKNESS OF YOUR OTHER SELF.

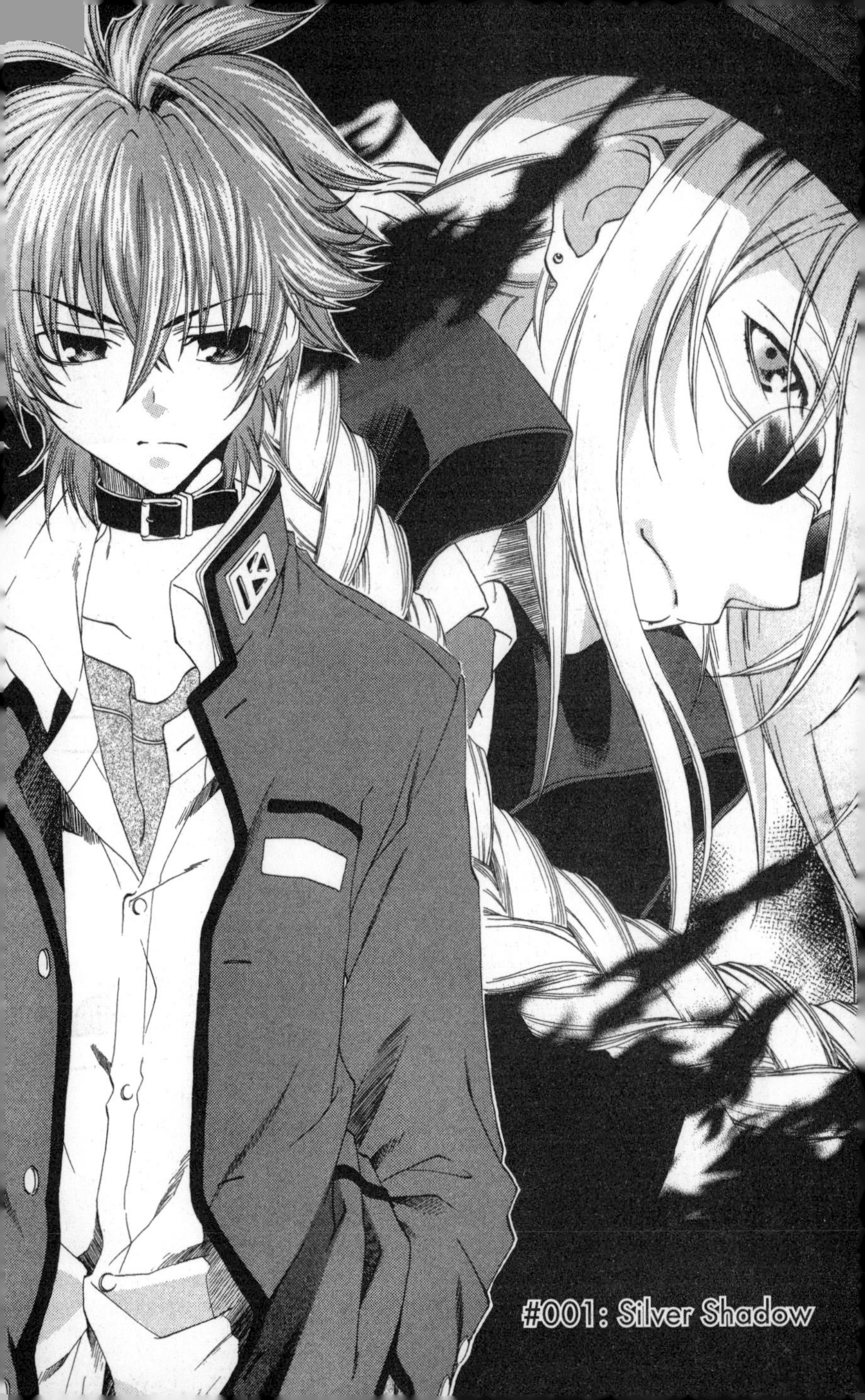
#001: Silver Shadow

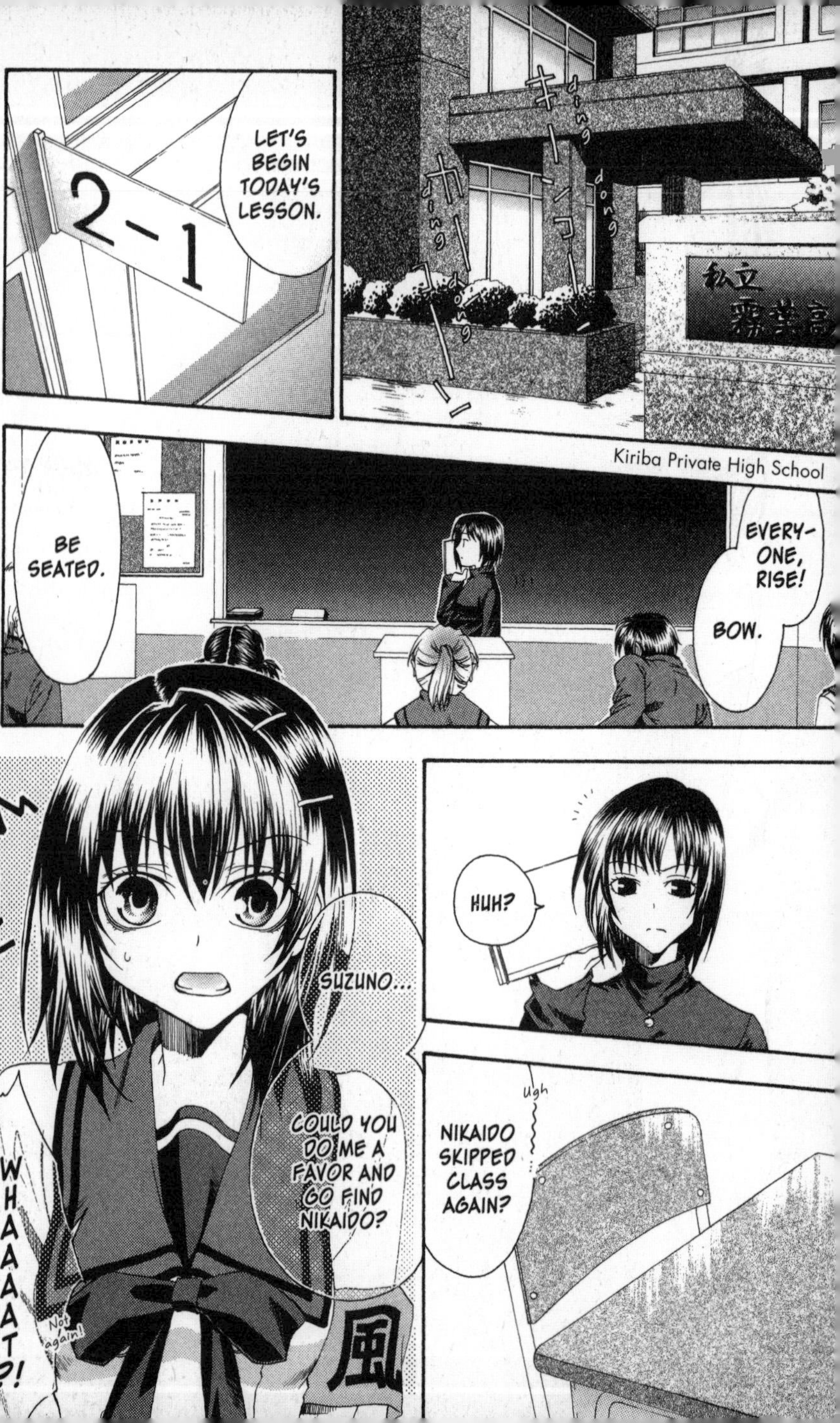
ding dong ding dong
私立
Kiriba Private High School
LET'S BEGIN TODAY'S LESSON.
EVERY-ONE, RISE!
BOW.
BE SEATED.
HUH?
Ugh
NIKAIDO SKIPPED CLASS AGAIN?
SUZUNO...
COULD YOU DO ME A FAVOR AND GO FIND NIKAIDO?
WHAAAAAT?!
Not again!
風

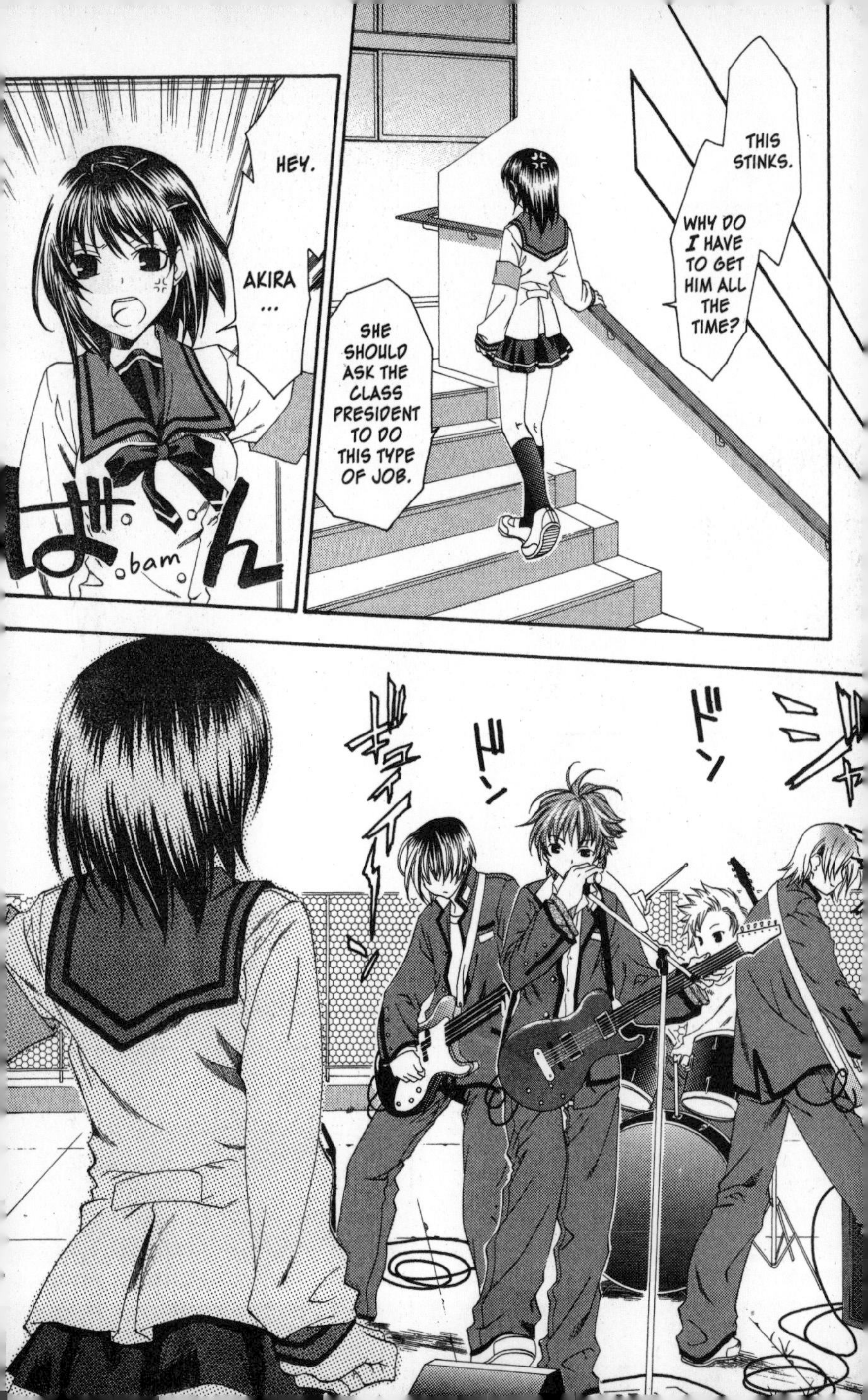
THIS STINKS.
WHY DO I HAVE TO GET HIM ALL THE TIME?
SHE SHOULD ASK THE CLASS PRESIDENT TO DO THIS TYPE OF JOB.
HEY.
AKIRA ...
ばん
bam
ドン

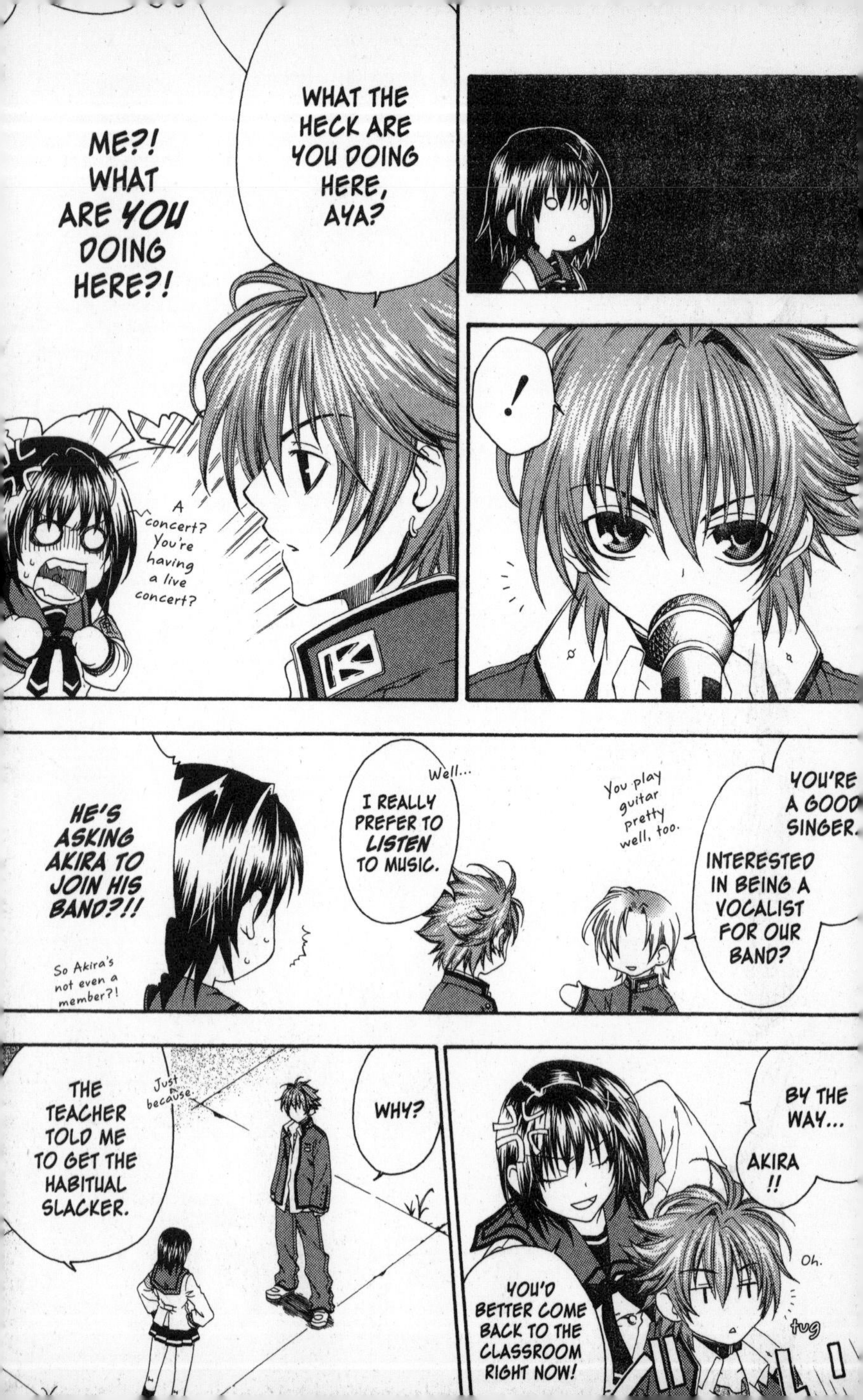
!
WHAT THE HECK ARE YOU DOING HERE, AYA?
ME?! WHAT ARE YOU DOING HERE?!
A concert? You're having a live concert?
YOU'RE A GOOD SINGER.
INTERESTED IN BEING A VOCALIST FOR OUR BAND?
You play guitar pretty well, too.
Well...
I REALLY PREFER TO LISTEN TO MUSIC.
HE'S ASKING AKIRA TO JOIN HIS BAND?!!
So Akira's not even a member?!
BY THE WAY...
AKIRA !!
Oh.
tug
YOU'D BETTER COME BACK TO THE CLASSROOM RIGHT NOW!
WHY?
Just because.
THE TEACHER TOLD ME TO GET THE HABITUAL SLACKER.

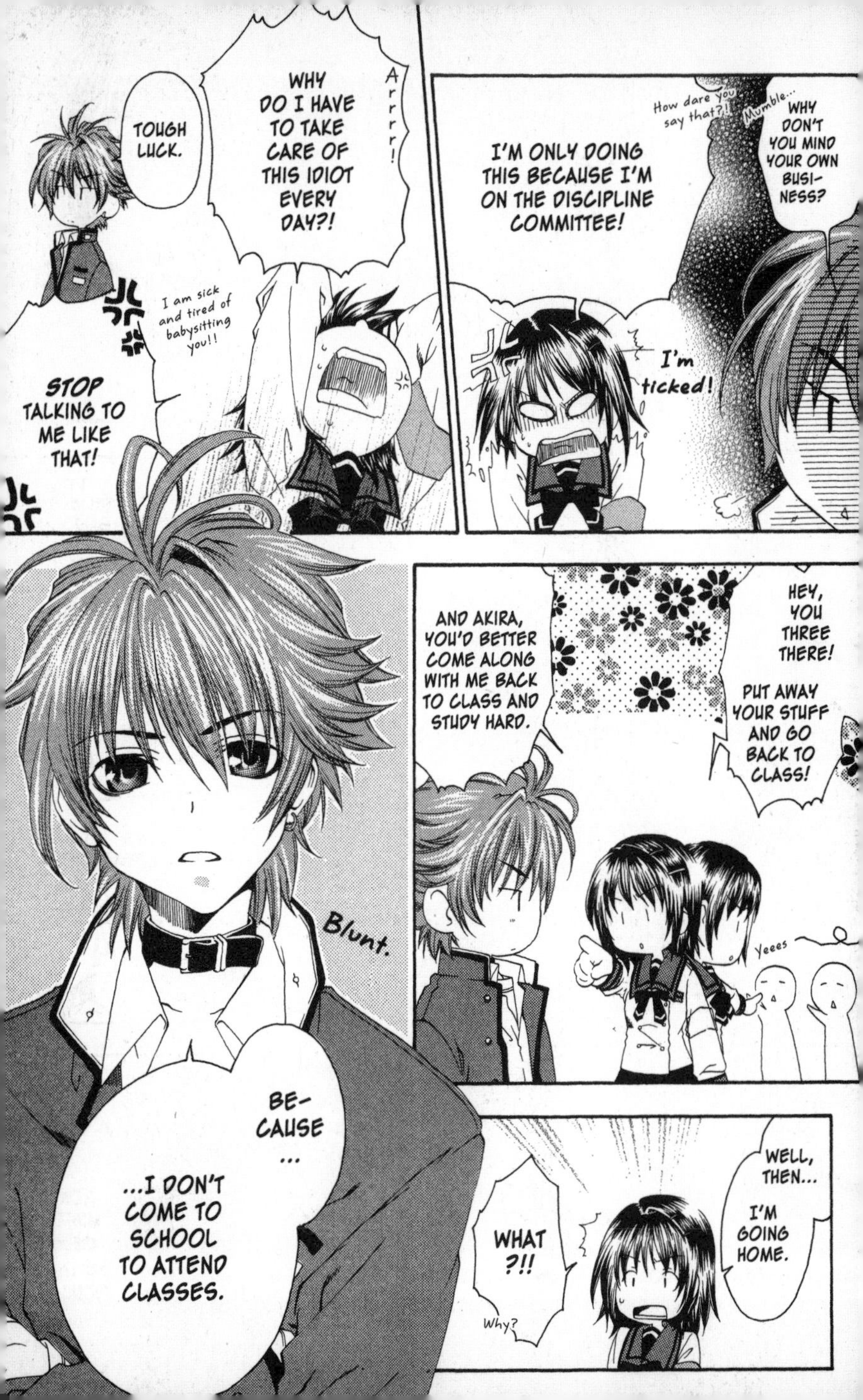

Mumble...
WHY DON'T YOU MIND YOUR OWN BUSI-NESS?
How dare you say that?!
I'M ONLY DOING THIS BECAUSE I'M ON THE DISCIPLINE COMMITTEE!
I'm ticked!
Arrrr!
WHY DO I HAVE TO TAKE CARE OF THIS IDIOT EVERY DAY?!
TOUGH LUCK.
I am sick and tired of babysitting you!!
STOP TALKING TO ME LIKE THAT!
HEY, YOU THREE THERE!
PUT AWAY YOUR STUFF AND GO BACK TO CLASS!
AND AKIRA, YOU'D BETTER COME ALONG WITH ME BACK TO CLASS AND STUDY HARD.
Yeees
WELL, THEN...
I'M GOING HOME.
WHAT ?!!
Why?
Blunt.
BE-CAUSE ...
...I DON'T COME TO SCHOOL TO ATTEND CLASSES.

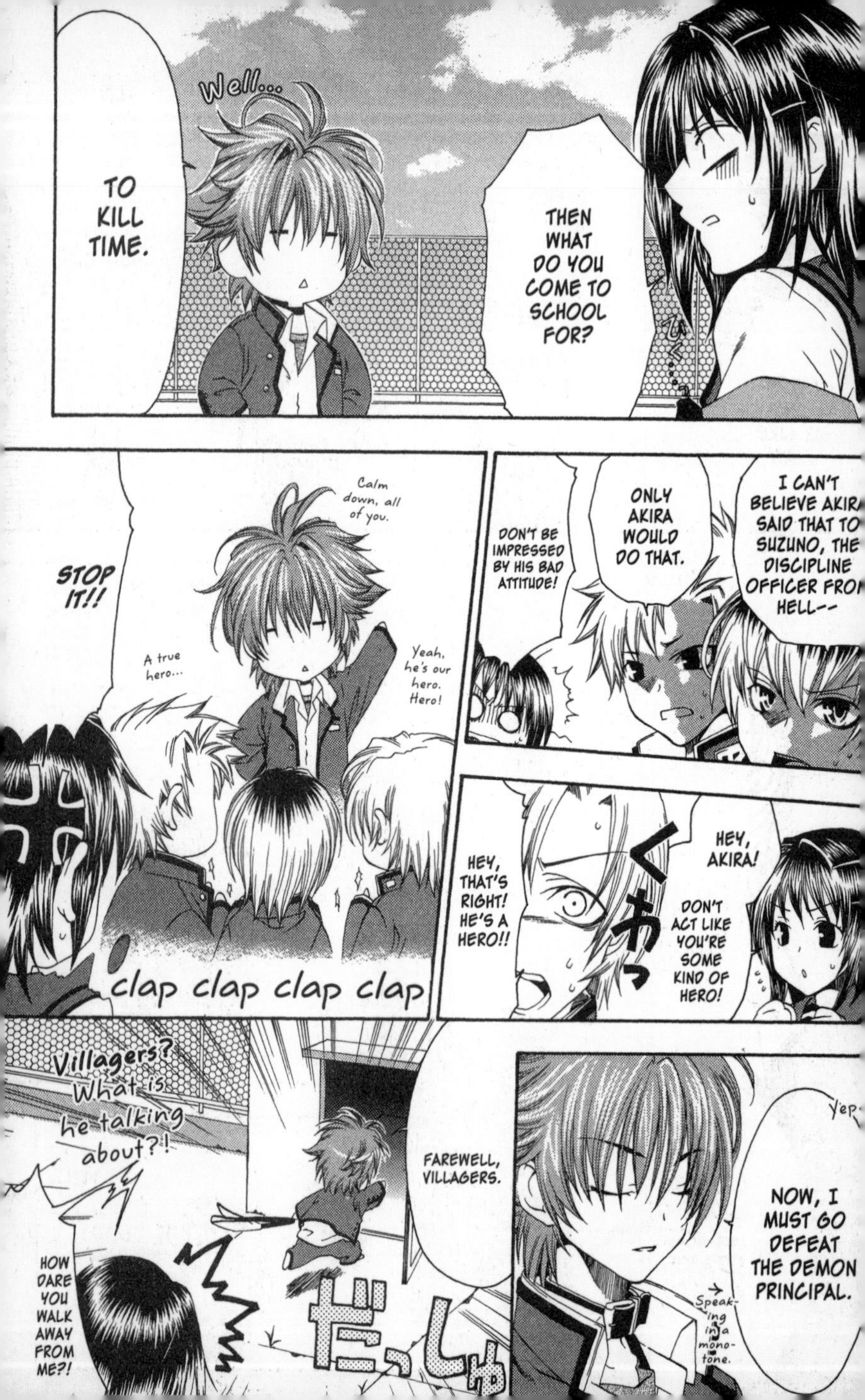
THEN WHAT DO YOU COME TO SCHOOL FOR?
Well...
TO KILL TIME.
I CAN'T BELIEVE AKIR SAID THAT TO SUZUNO, THE DISCIPLINE OFFICER FRO HELL--
ONLY AKIRA WOULD DO THAT.
DON'T BE IMPRESSED BY HIS BAD ATTITUDE!
HEY, AKIRA!
DON'T ACT LIKE YOU'RE SOME KIND OF HERO!
くわっ
HEY, THAT'S RIGHT! HE'S A HERO!!
Calm down, all of you.
Yeah, he's our hero. Hero!
A true hero...
STOP IT!!
clap clap clap clap
Yep.
NOW, I MUST GO DEFEAT THE DEMON PRINCIPAL.
→ Speaking in a monotone.
FAREWELL, VILLAGERS.
Villagers? What is he talking about?!
だっしゅ
HOW DARE YOU WALK AWAY FROM ME?!

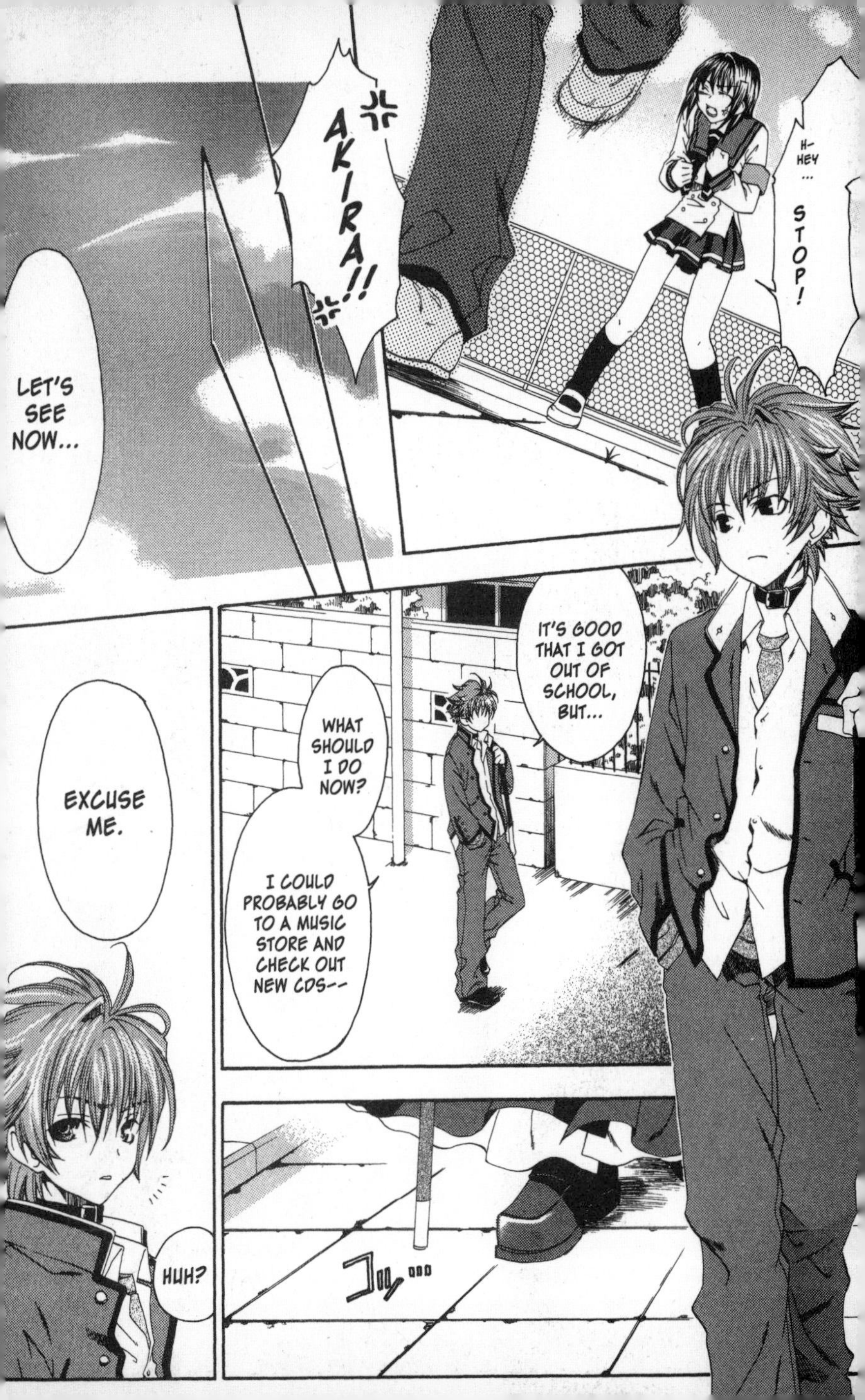
H-HEY... STOP!
AKIRA!!
LET'S SEE NOW...
IT'S GOOD THAT I GOT OUT OF SCHOOL, BUT...
WHAT SHOULD I DO NOW?
I COULD PROBABLY GO TO A MUSIC STORE AND CHECK OUT NEW CDS--
EXCUSE ME.
HUH?

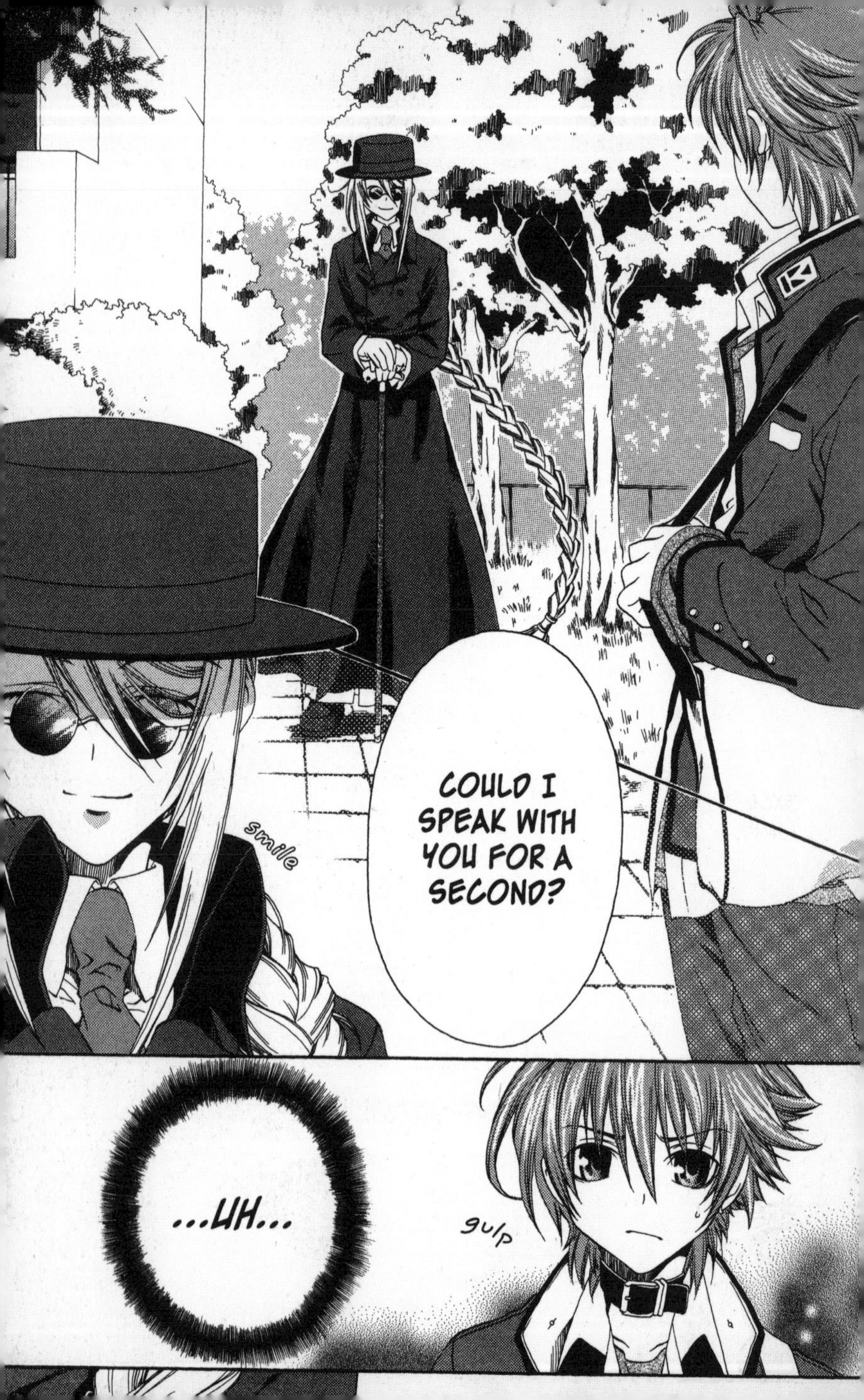
COULD I SPEAK WITH YOU FOR A SECOND?
smile
gulp
...UH...

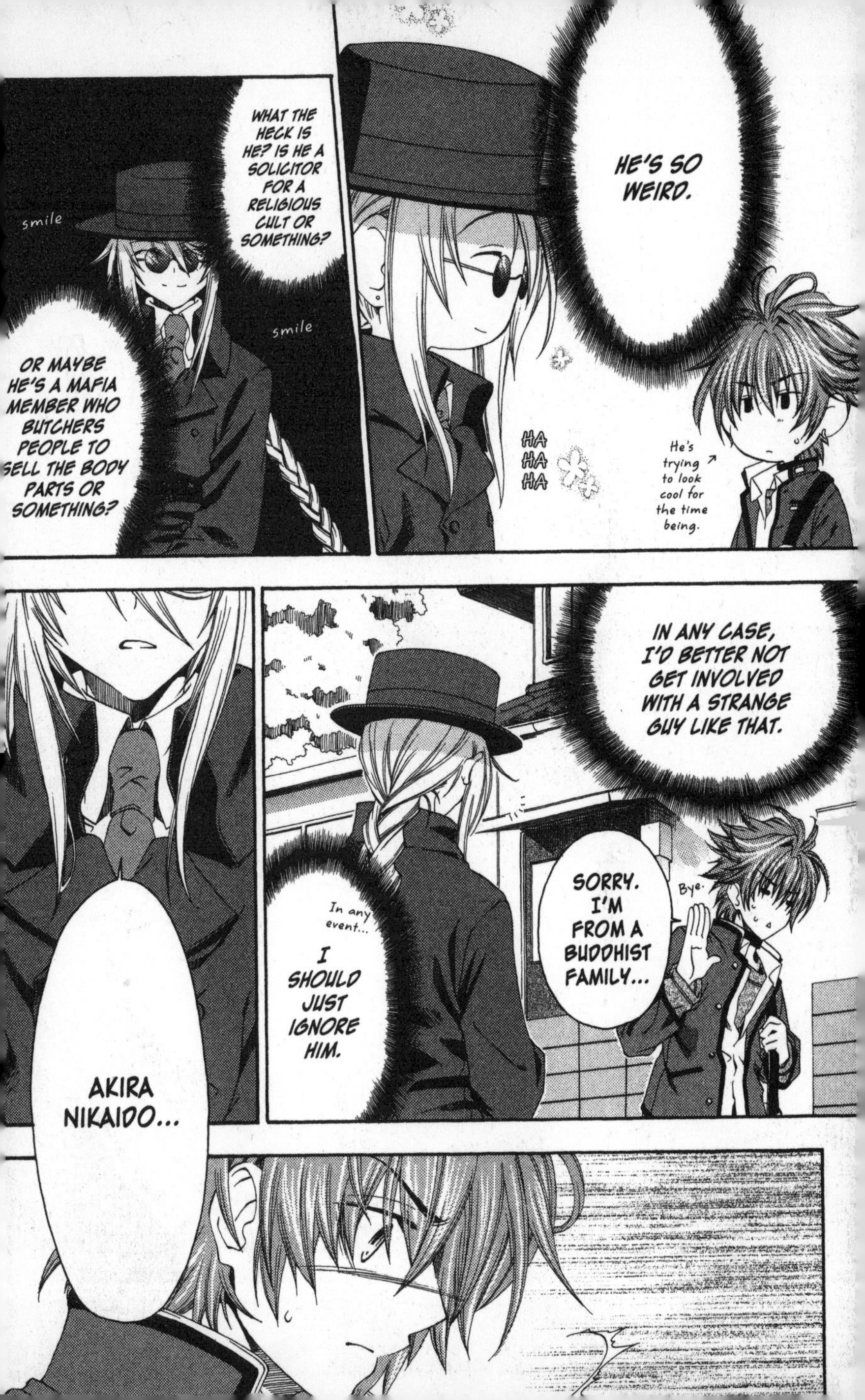
HE'S SO WEIRD.
HA HA HA
He's trying to look cool for the time being.
WHAT THE HECK IS HE? IS HE A SOLICITOR FOR A RELIGIOUS CULT OR SOMETHING?
smile
smile
OR MAYBE HE'S A MAFIA MEMBER WHO BUTCHERS PEOPLE TO SELL THE BODY PARTS OR SOMETHING?
IN ANY CASE, I'D BETTER NOT GET INVOLVED WITH A STRANGE GUY LIKE THAT.
SORRY. I'M FROM A BUDDHIST FAMILY...
Bye.
In any event...
I SHOULD JUST IGNORE HIM.
AKIRA NIKAIDO...

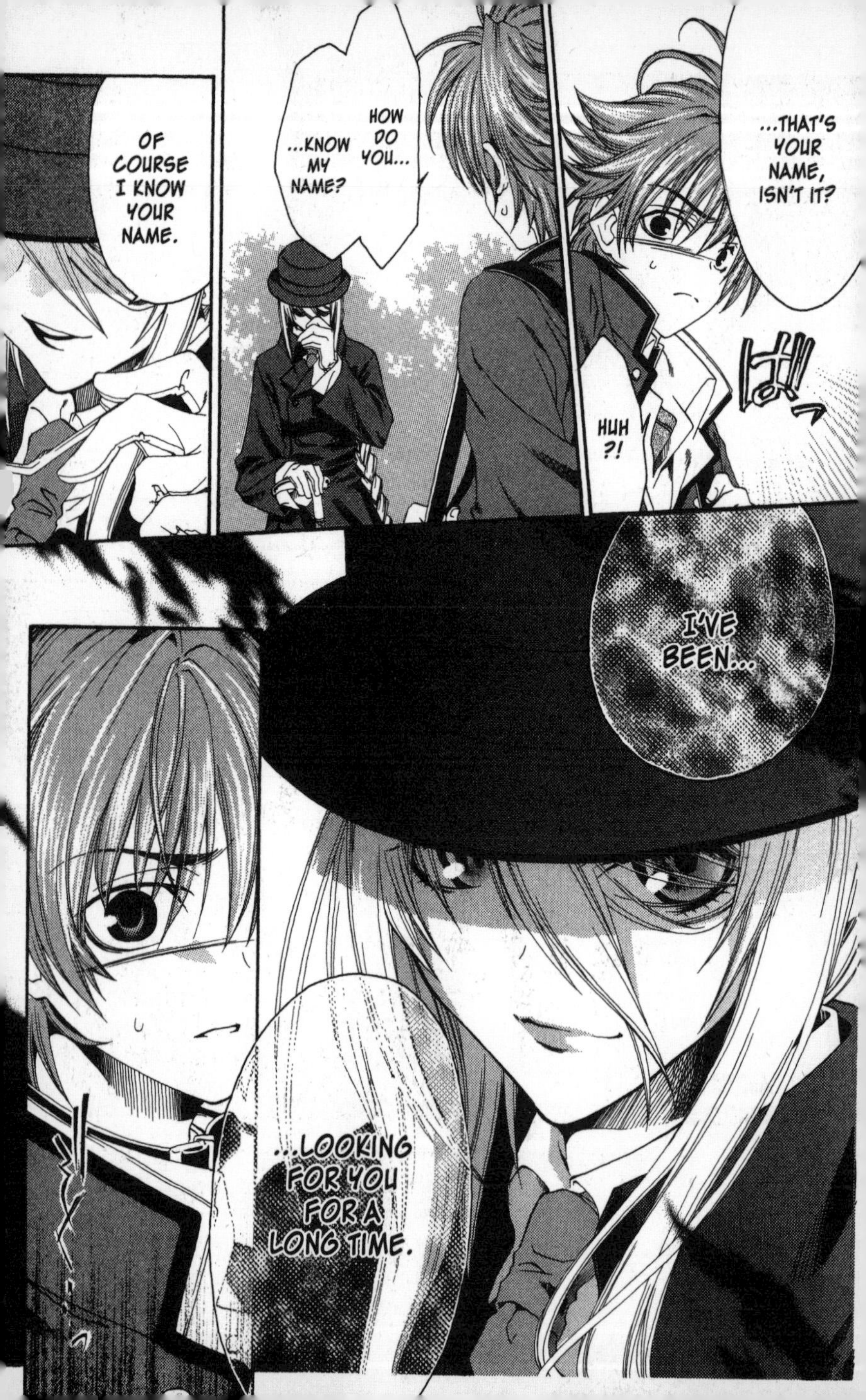
...THAT'S YOUR NAME, ISN'T IT?
HUH?!
HOW DO YOU...
...KNOW MY NAME?
OF COURSE I KNOW YOUR NAME.
I'VE BEEN...
...LOOKING FOR YOU FOR A LONG TIME.

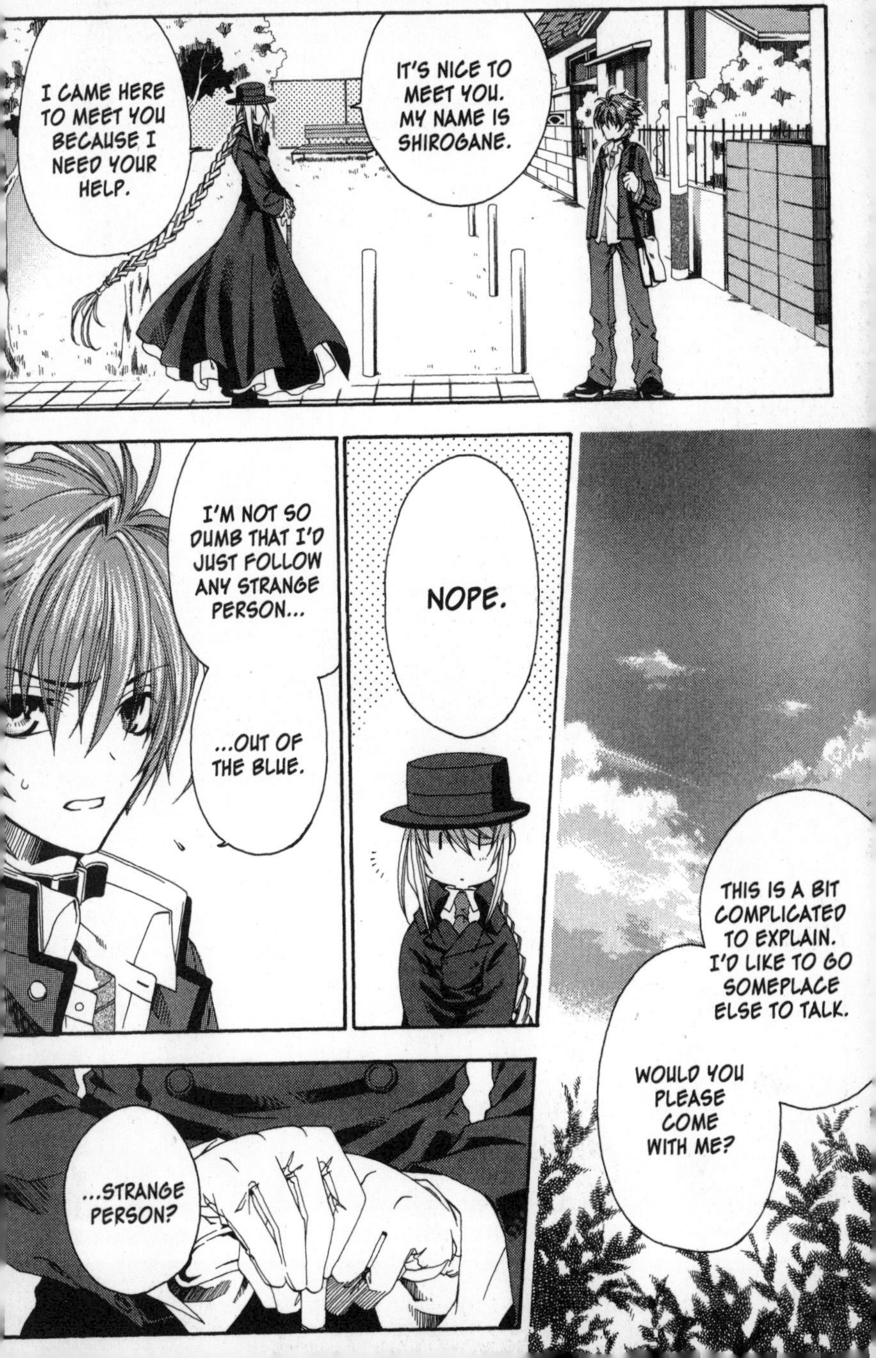
IT'S NICE TO MEET YOU. MY NAME IS SHIROGANE.
I CAME HERE TO MEET YOU BECAUSE I NEED YOUR HELP.
THIS IS A BIT COMPLICATED TO EXPLAIN. I'D LIKE TO GO SOMEPLACE ELSE TO TALK.
WOULD YOU PLEASE COME WITH ME?
NOPE.
I'M NOT SO DUMB THAT I'D JUST FOLLOW ANY STRANGE PERSON...
...OUT OF THE BLUE.
...STRANGE PERSON?

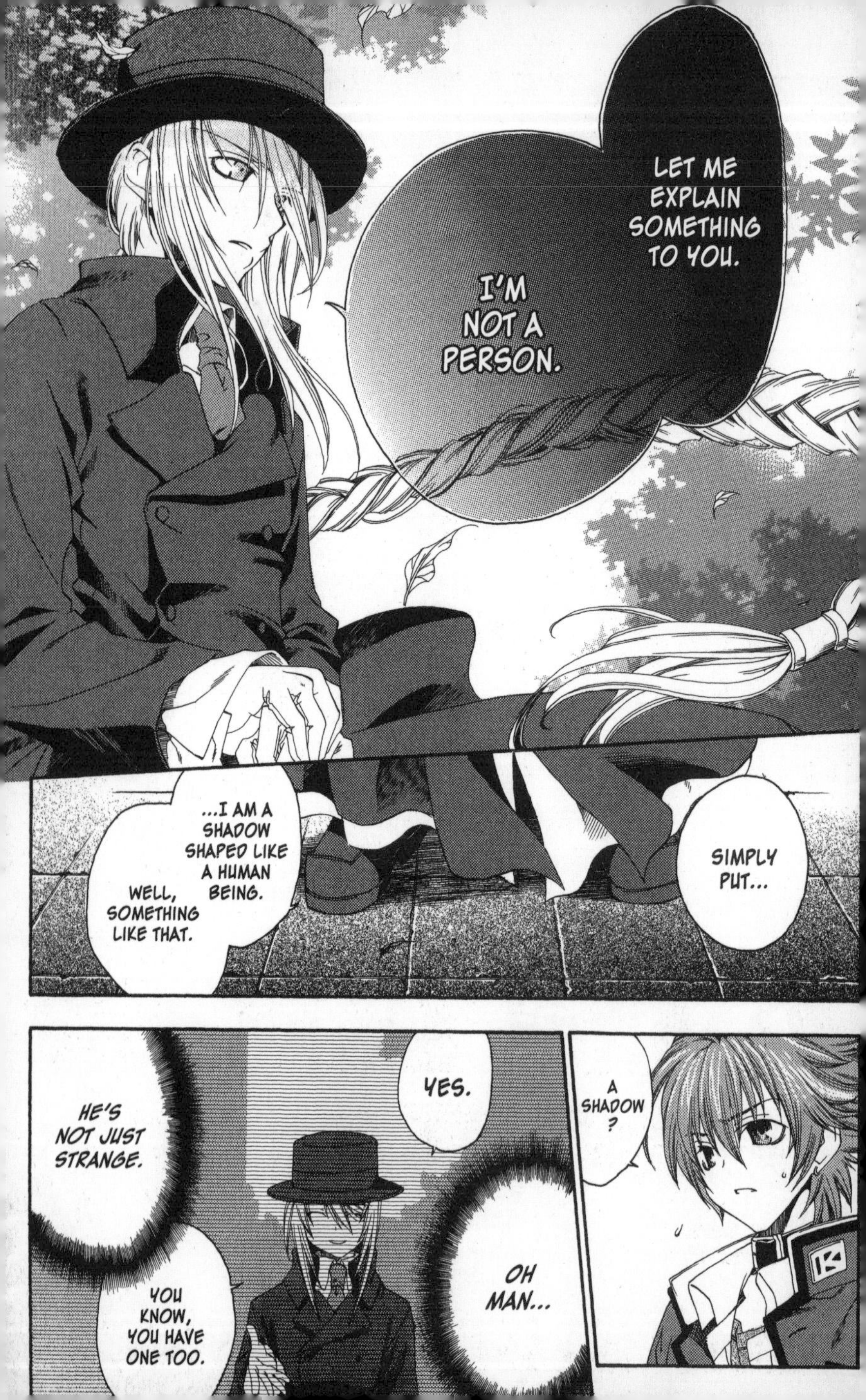
LET ME EXPLAIN SOMETHING TO YOU.
I'M NOT A PERSON.
SIMPLY PUT...
...I AM A SHADOW SHAPED LIKE A HUMAN BEING.
WELL, SOMETHING LIKE THAT.
A SHADOW?
YES.
HE'S NOT JUST STRANGE.
OH MAN...
YOU KNOW, YOU HAVE ONE TOO.

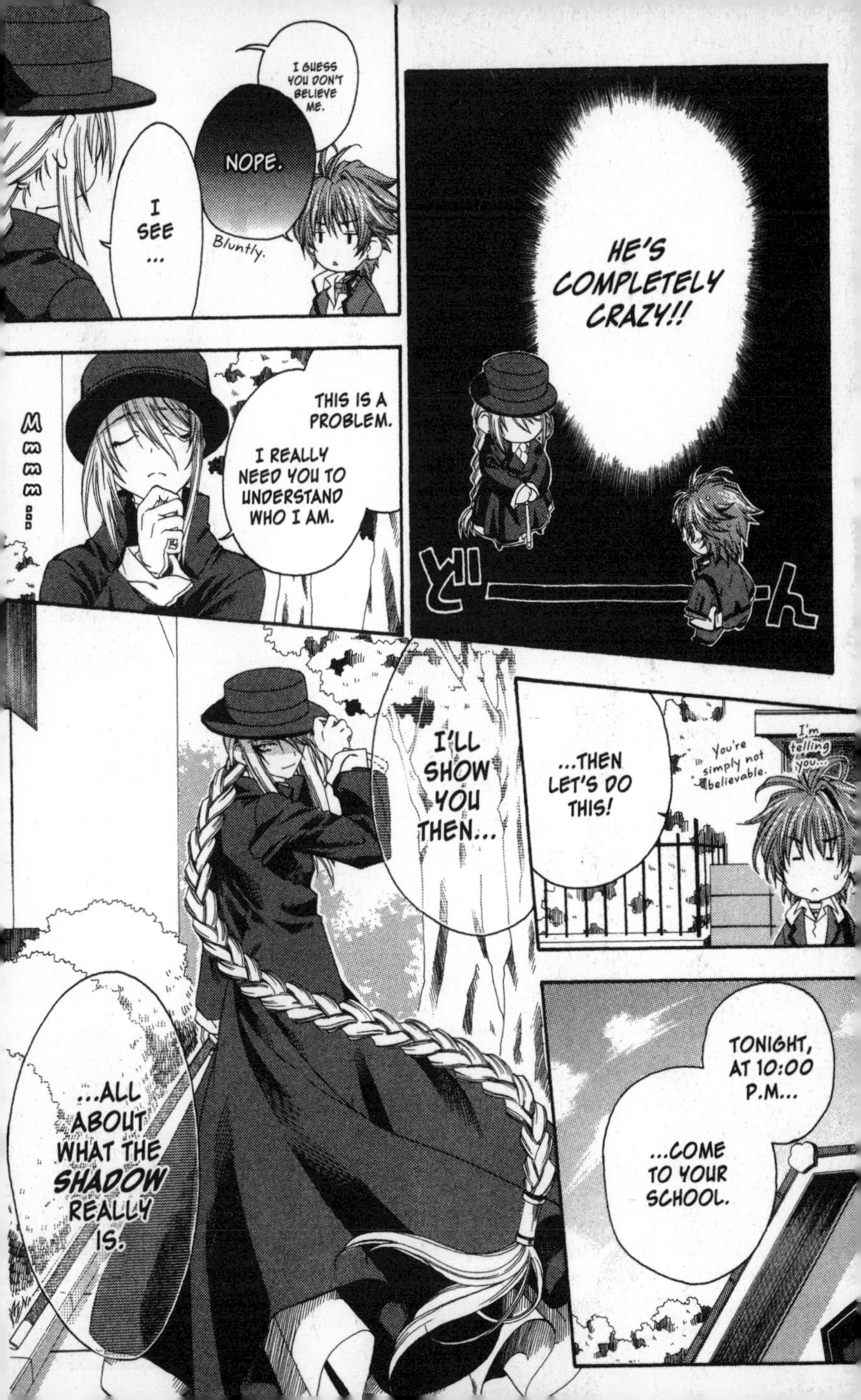
HE'S COMPLETELY CRAZY!!
どーーーん
I GUESS YOU DON'T BELIEVE ME.
NOPE.
Bluntly.
I SEE ...
THIS IS A PROBLEM.
I REALLY NEED YOU TO UNDERSTAND WHO I AM.
Mmmm...
I'm telling you...
You're simply not believable.
...THEN LET'S DO THIS!
TONIGHT, AT 10:00 P.M...
...COME TO YOUR SCHOOL.
I'LL SHOW YOU THEN...
...ALL ABOUT WHAT THE SHADOW REALLY IS.

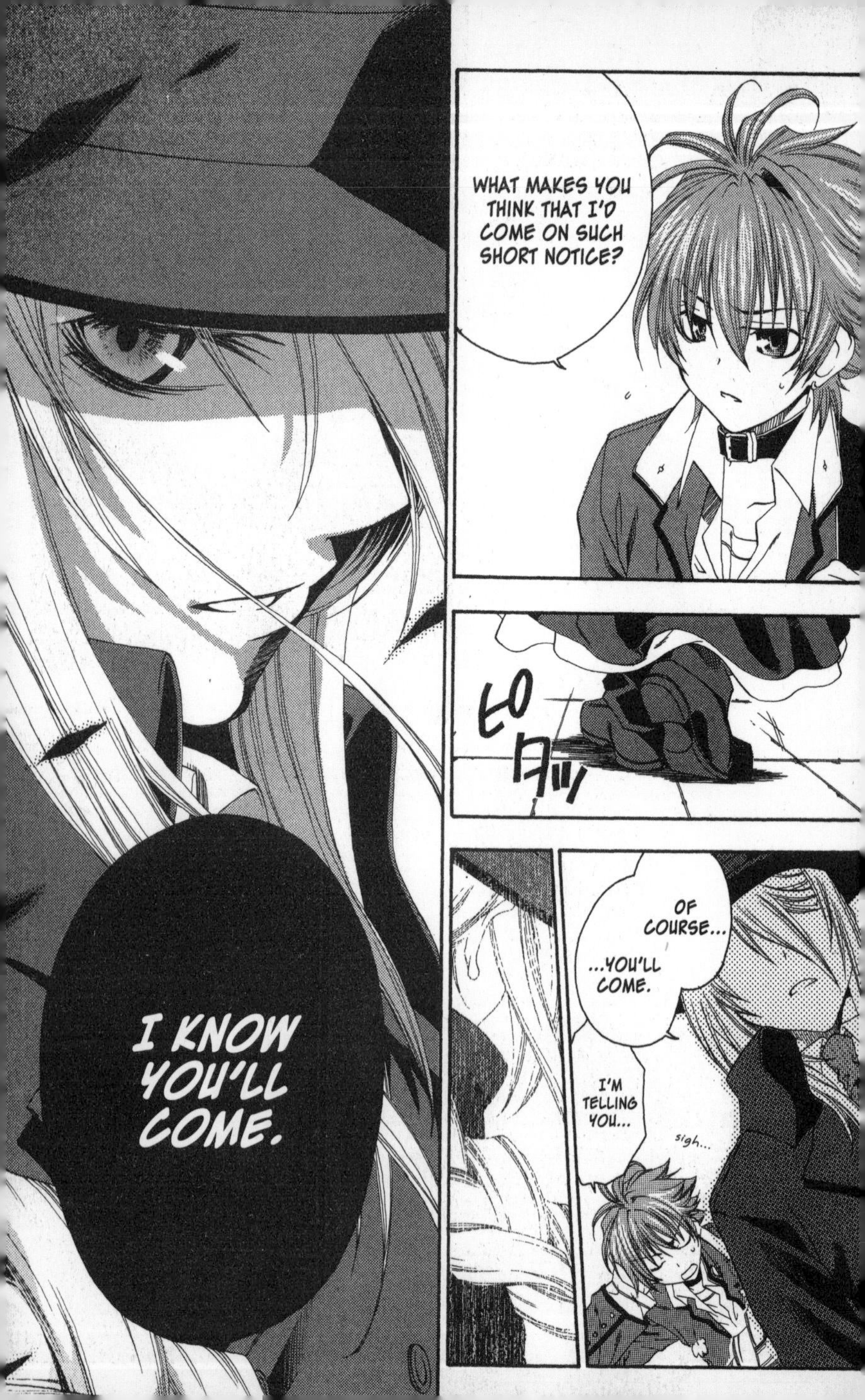
WHAT MAKES YOU THINK THAT I'D COME ON SUCH SHORT NOTICE?
ピタッ
OF COURSE... ...YOU'LL COME.
I'M TELLING YOU...
sigh...
I KNOW YOU'LL COME.

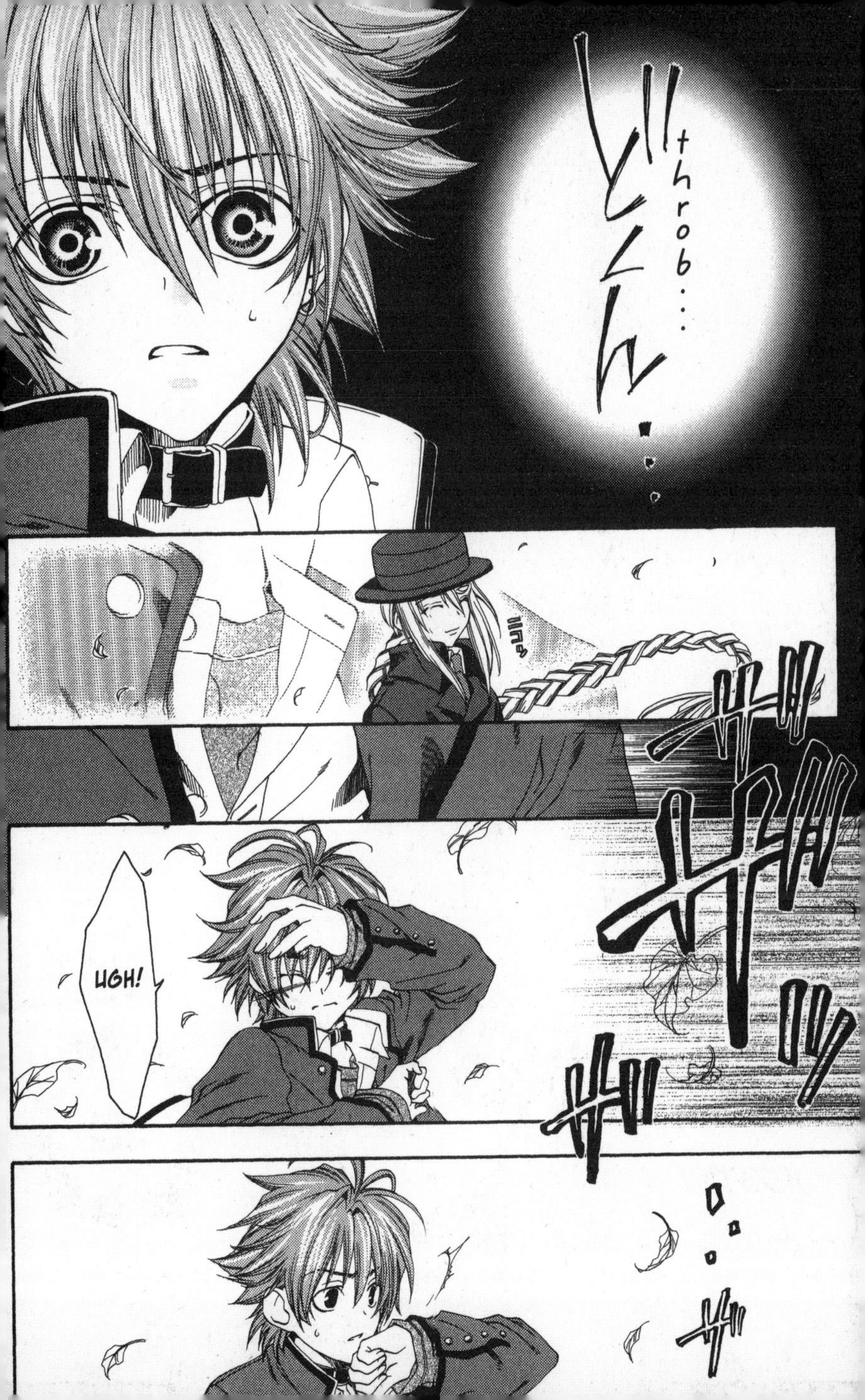
どくん…
throb...
UGH!

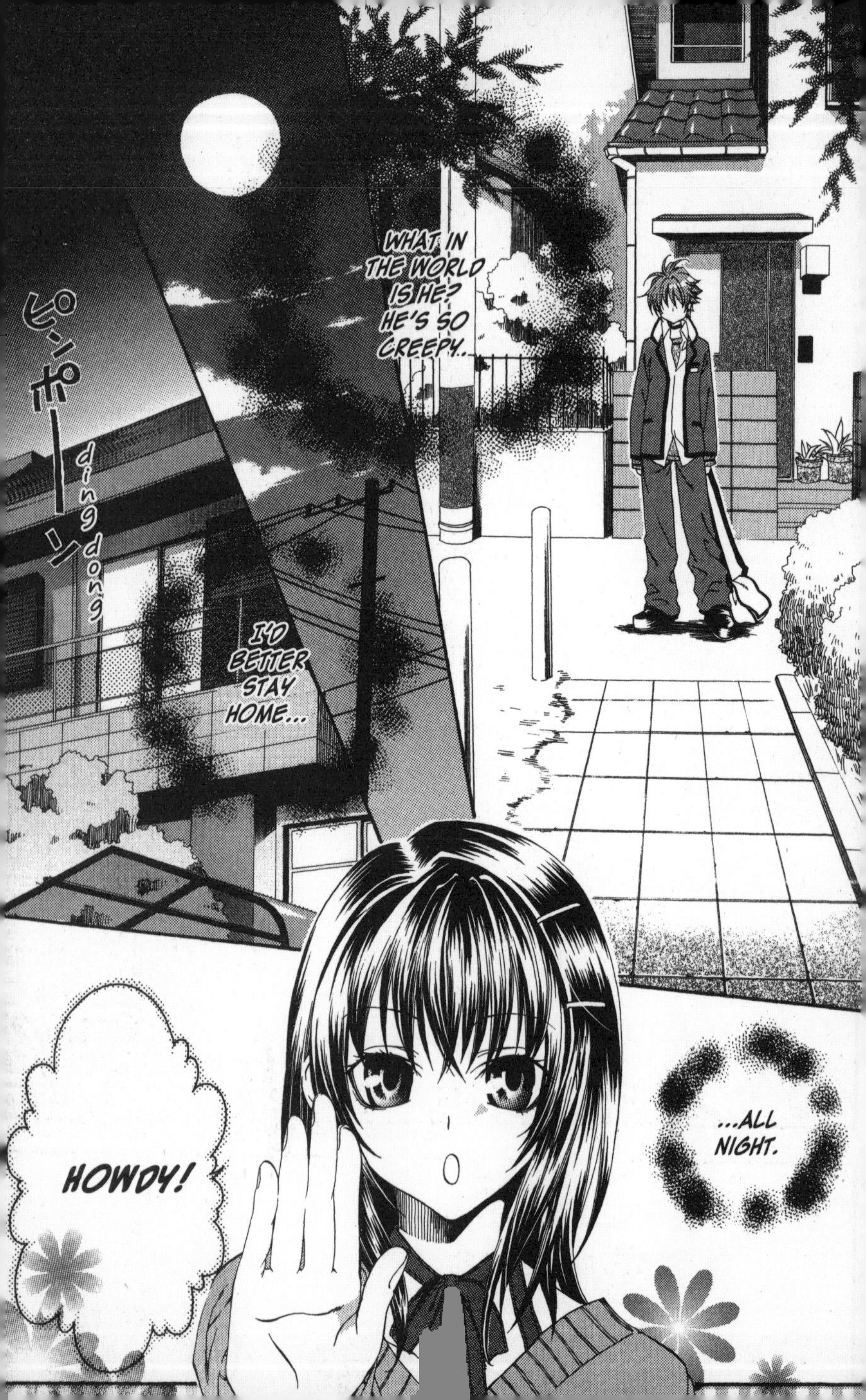
WHAT IN THE WORLD IS HE? HE'S SO CREEPY..
I'D BETTER STAY HOME...
ピンポーン
ding dong
...ALL NIGHT.
HOWDY!

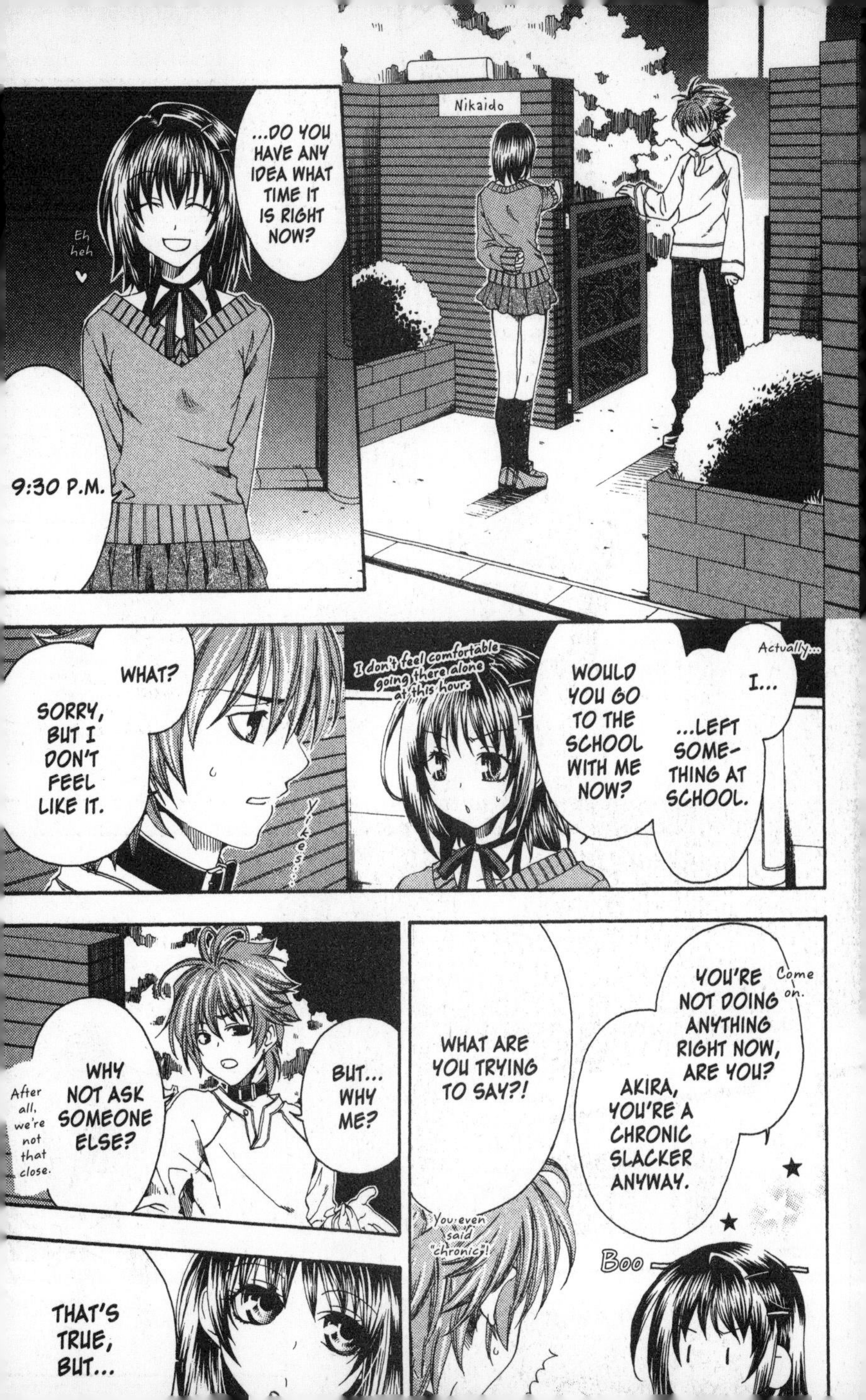
Nikaido
...DO YOU HAVE ANY IDEA WHAT TIME IT IS RIGHT NOW?
Eh heh
9:30 P.M.
Actually...
I...
...LEFT SOMETHING AT SCHOOL.
WOULD YOU GO TO THE SCHOOL WITH ME NOW?
I don't feel comfortable going there alone at this hour.
WHAT?
SORRY, BUT I DON'T FEEL LIKE IT.
yikes...
YOU'RE NOT DOING ANYTHING RIGHT NOW, ARE YOU?
Come on.
AKIRA, YOU'RE A CHRONIC SLACKER ANYWAY.
WHAT ARE YOU TRYING TO SAY?!
You even said "chronic"!
Boo
BUT... WHY ME?
WHY NOT ASK SOMEONE ELSE?
After all, we're not that close.
THAT'S TRUE, BUT...

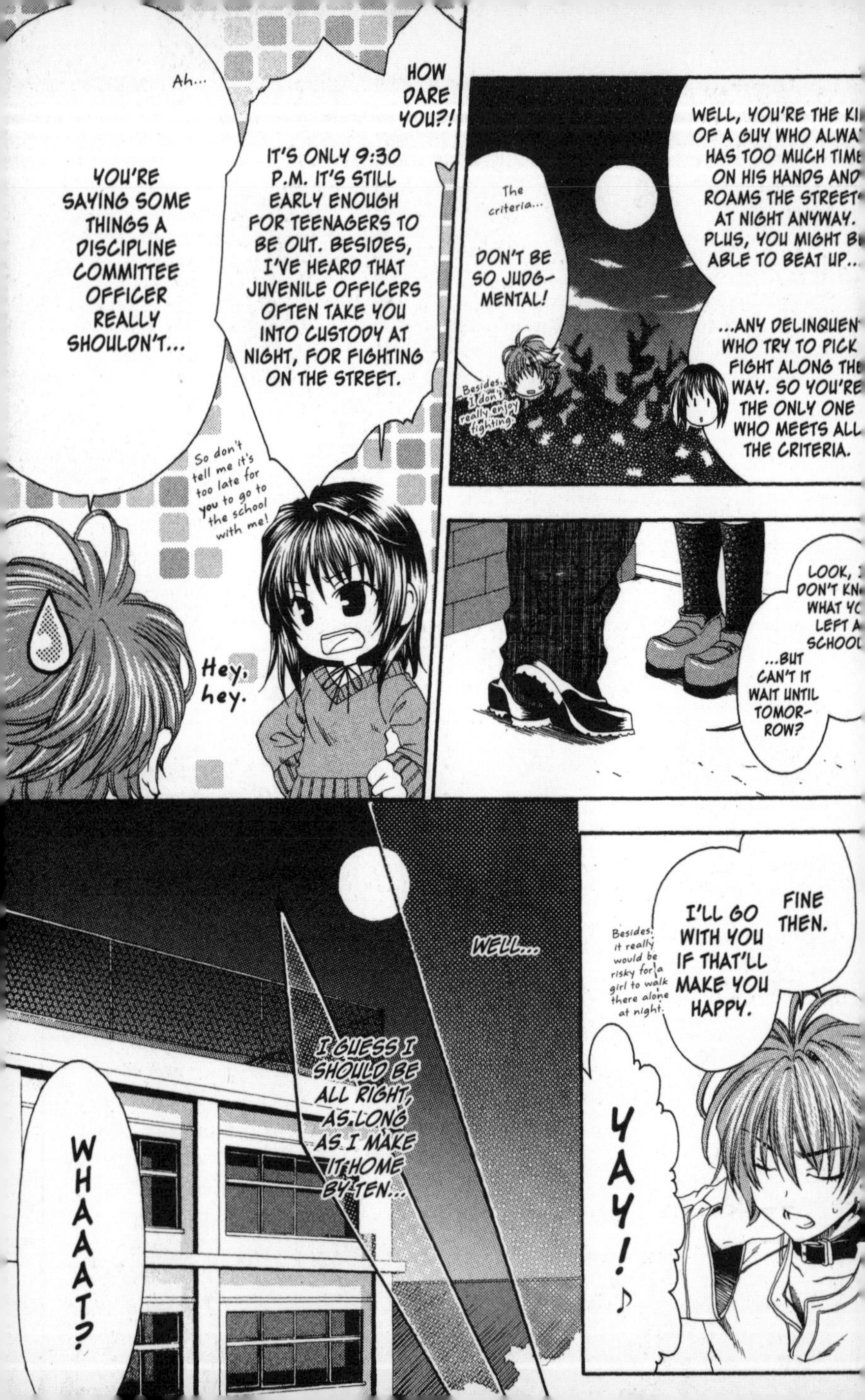
WELL, YOU'RE THE KI
OF A GUY WHO ALWA
HAS TOO MUCH TIME
ON HIS HANDS AND
ROAMS THE STREET
AT NIGHT ANYWAY.
PLUS, YOU MIGHT B
ABLE TO BEAT UP...
...ANY DELINQUEN
WHO TRY TO PICK
FIGHT ALONG THE
WAY. SO YOU'RE
THE ONLY ONE
WHO MEETS ALL
THE CRITERIA.
The criteria...
DON'T BE SO JUDG-MENTAL!
Besides, I don't really enjoy fighting.
LOOK, I DON'T KN WHAT YO LEFT A SCHOOL
...BUT CAN'T IT WAIT UNTIL TOMOR-ROW?
HOW DARE YOU?!
IT'S ONLY 9:30 P.M. IT'S STILL EARLY ENOUGH FOR TEENAGERS TO BE OUT. BESIDES, I'VE HEARD THAT JUVENILE OFFICERS OFTEN TAKE YOU INTO CUSTODY AT NIGHT, FOR FIGHTING ON THE STREET.
Ah...
YOU'RE SAYING SOME THINGS A DISCIPLINE COMMITTEE OFFICER REALLY SHOULDN'T...
So don't tell me it's too late for you to go to the school with me!
Hey, hey.
FINE THEN.
I'LL GO WITH YOU IF THAT'LL MAKE YOU HAPPY.
Besides, it really would be risky for a girl to walk there alone at night.
YAY!♪
WELL...
I GUESS I SHOULD BE ALL RIGHT, AS LONG AS I MAKE IT HOME BY TEN...
WHAAAAT?

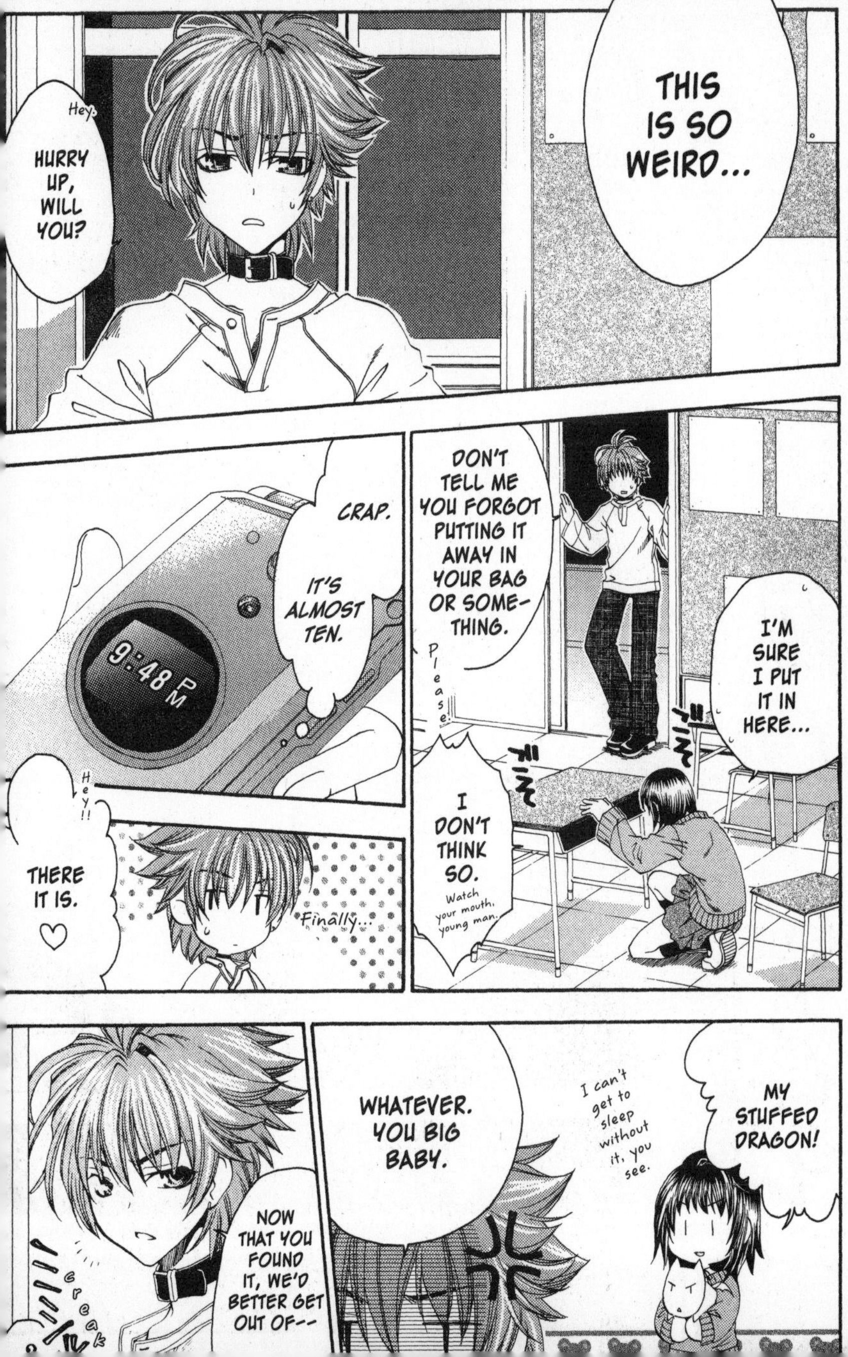
THIS IS SO WEIRD...
Hey.
HURRY UP, WILL YOU?
I'M SURE I PUT IT IN HERE...
DON'T TELL ME YOU FORGOT PUTTING IT AWAY IN YOUR BAG OR SOMETHING.
Please!
I DON'T THINK SO.
Watch your mouth, young man.
CRAP.
IT'S ALMOST TEN.
9:48 PM
Hey!!
THERE IT IS. ♡
Finally...
MY STUFFED DRAGON!
I can't get to sleep without it, you see.
WHATEVER. YOU BIG BABY.
NOW THAT YOU FOUND IT, WE'D BETTER GET OUT OF--
creak

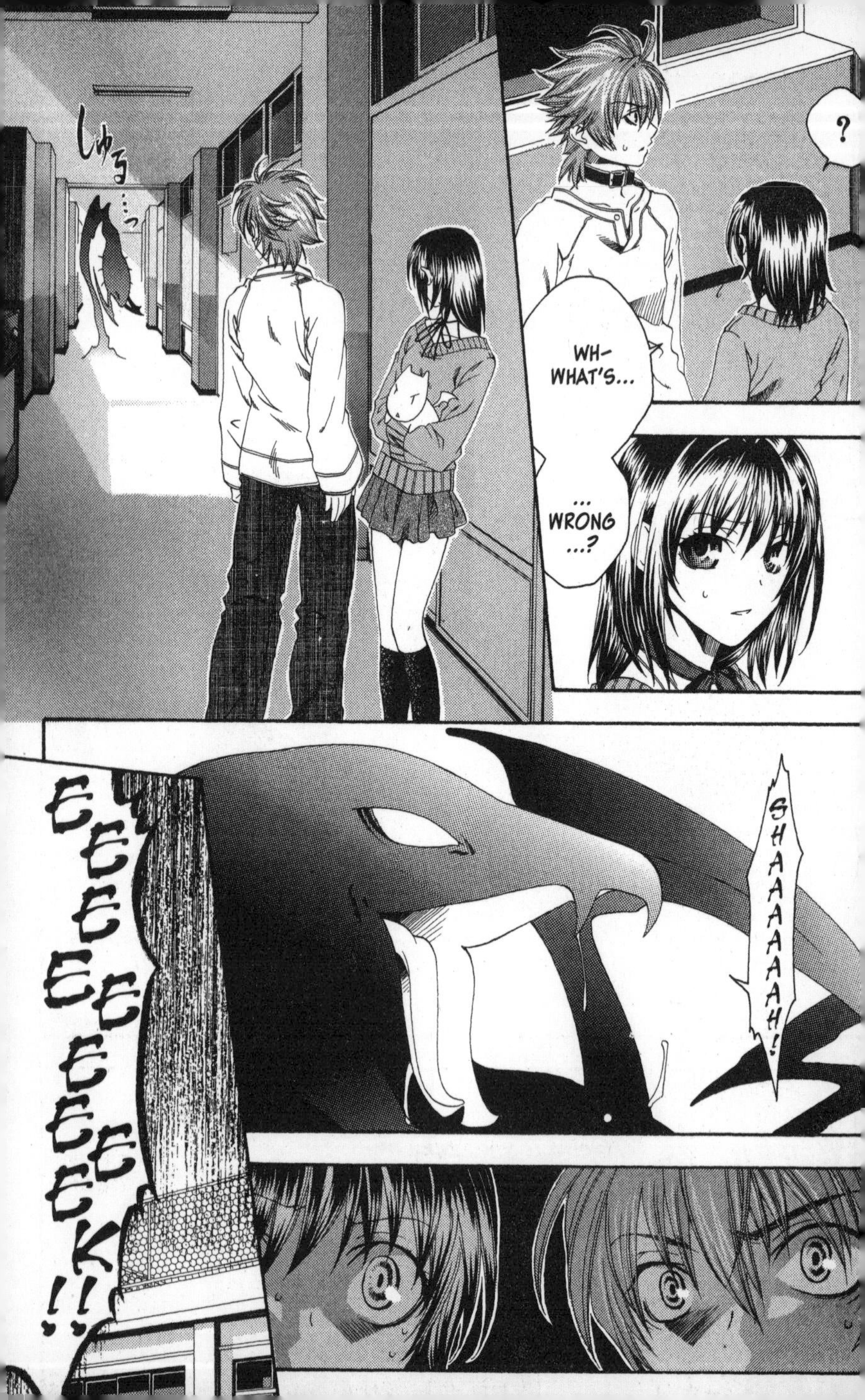
?
WH- WHAT'S...
... WRONG ...?
しゅる…っ
SHAAAAAAAH!
EEEEEEEEEEEK!!

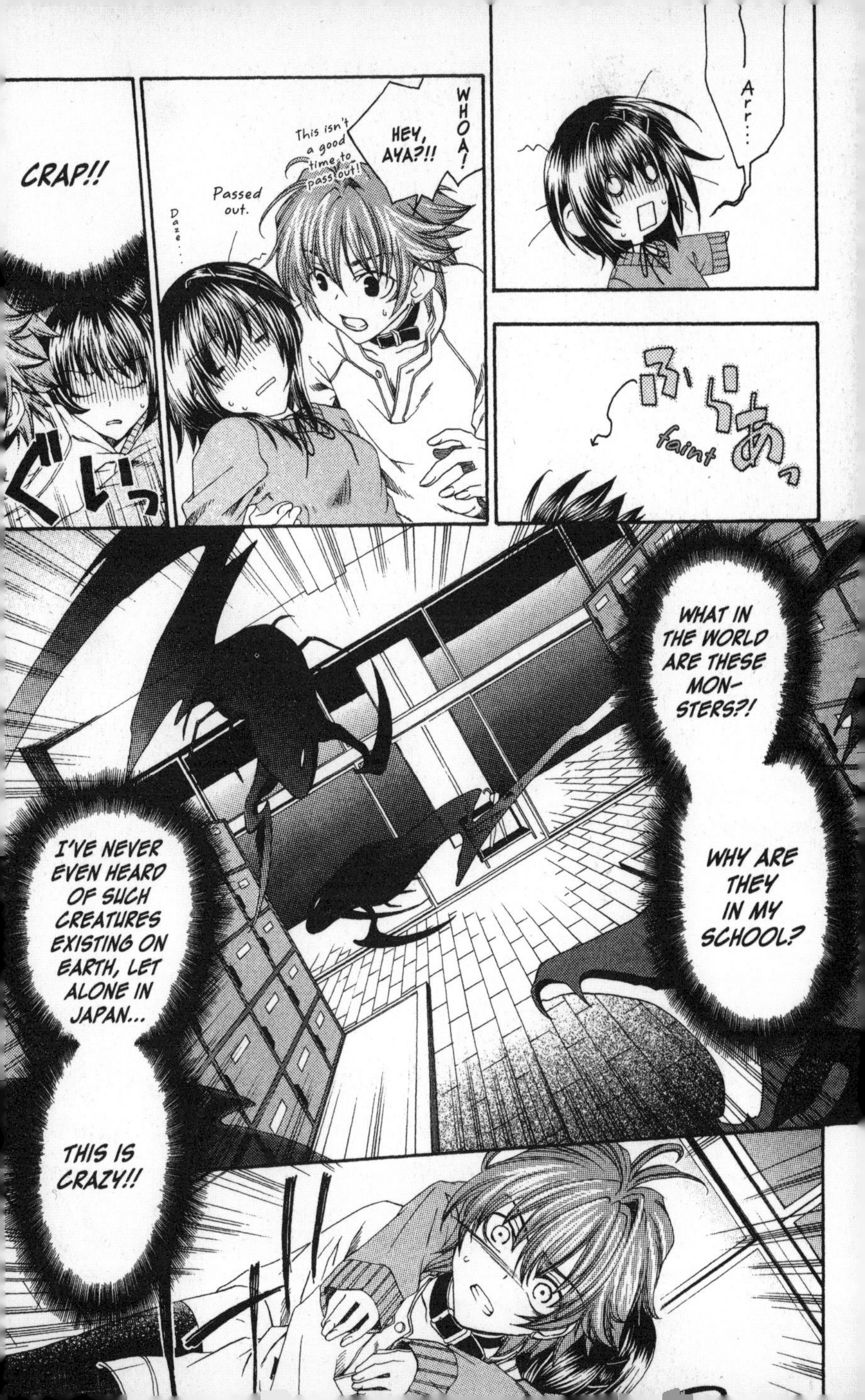
Arr...
ふらあっ
faint
WHOA!
HEY, AYA?!!
This isn't a good time to pass out!!
Passed out.
Daze...
CRAP!!
ぐいっ
WHAT IN THE WORLD ARE THESE MON-STERS?!
WHY ARE THEY IN MY SCHOOL?
I'VE NEVER EVEN HEARD OF SUCH CREATURES EXISTING ON EARTH, LET ALONE IN JAPAN...
THIS IS CRAZY!!

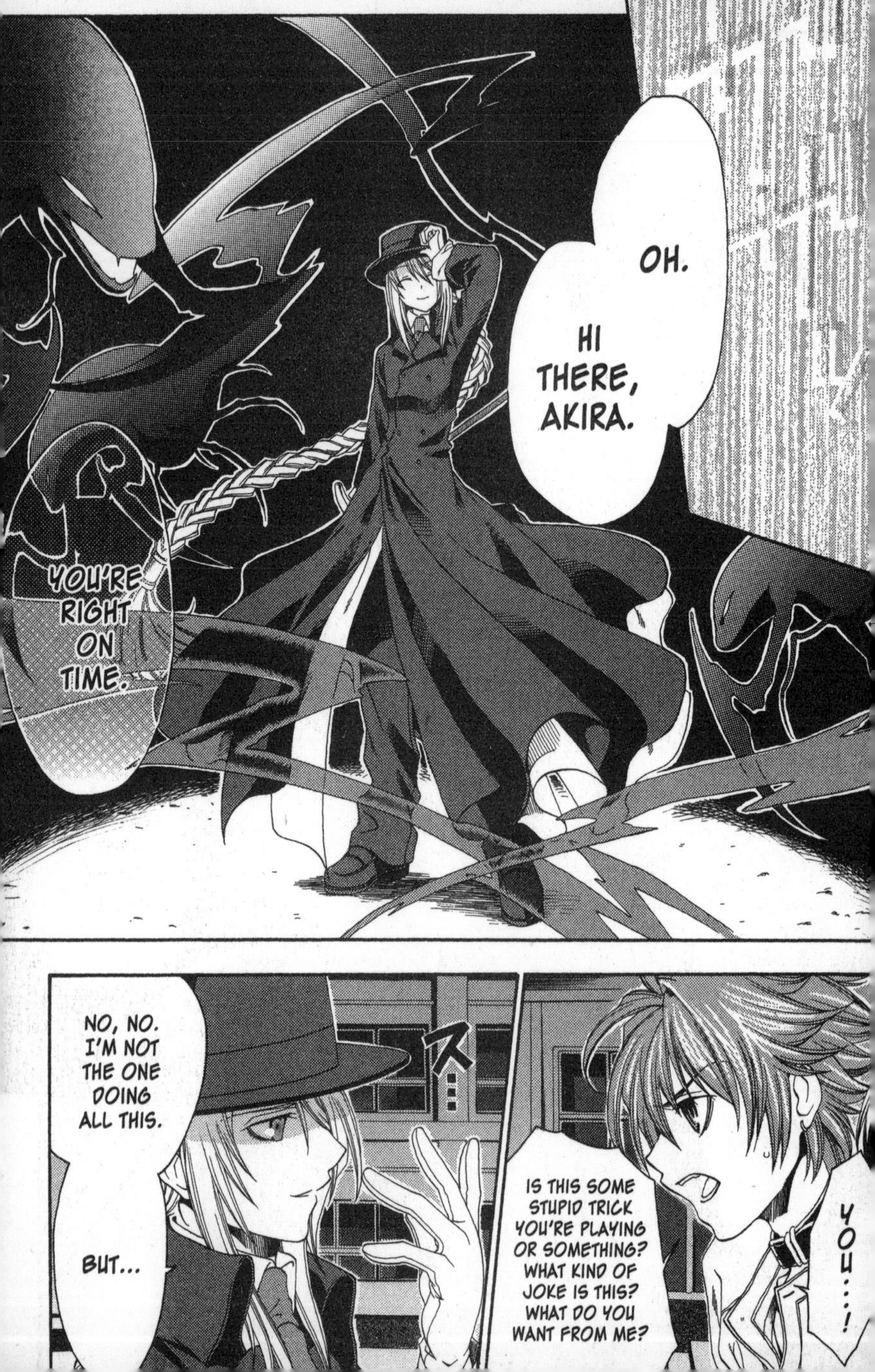
OH.
HI THERE, AKIRA.
YOU'RE RIGHT ON TIME.
YOU...!
IS THIS SOME STUPID TRICK YOU'RE PLAYING OR SOMETHING? WHAT KIND OF JOKE IS THIS? WHAT DO YOU WANT FROM ME?
ス...
NO, NO. I'M NOT THE ONE DOING ALL THIS.
BUT...

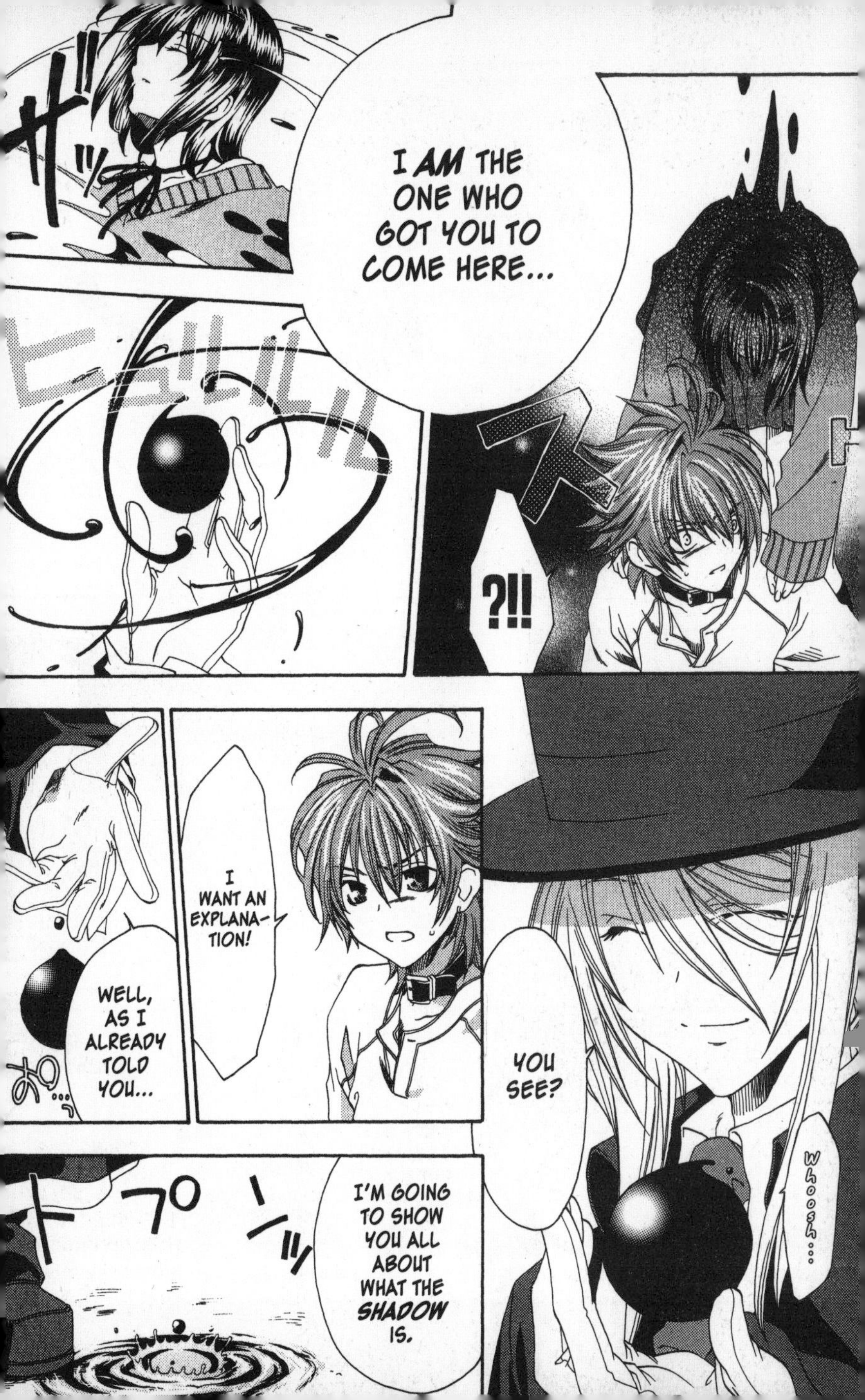
I AM THE ONE WHO GOT YOU TO COME HERE...
?!!
I WANT AN EXPLANATION!
WELL, AS I ALREADY TOLD YOU...
YOU SEE?
Whoosh...
I'M GOING TO SHOW YOU ALL ABOUT WHAT THE SHADOW IS.

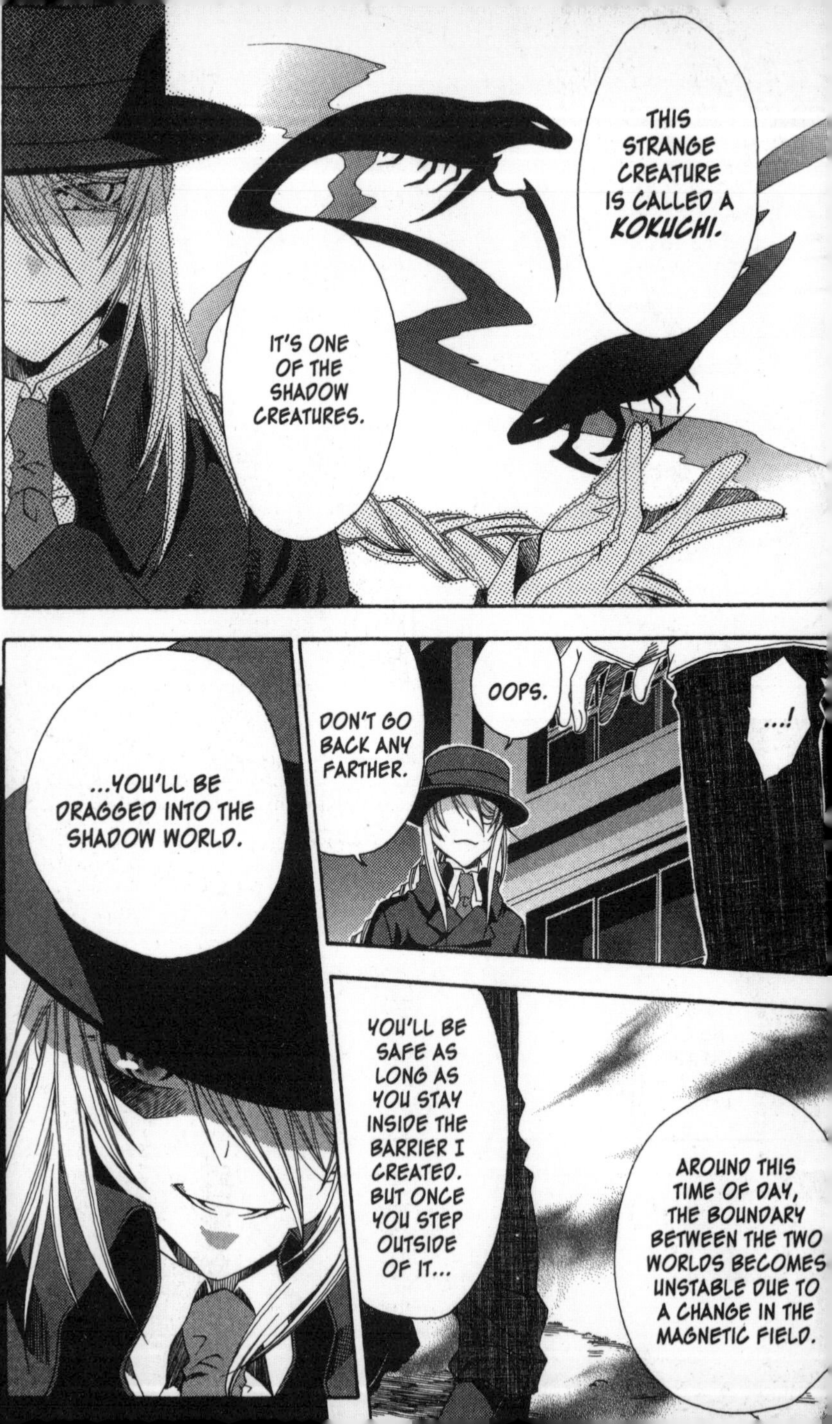
THIS STRANGE CREATURE IS CALLED A *KOKUCHI.*
IT'S ONE OF THE SHADOW CREATURES.
...!
OOPS.
DON'T GO BACK ANY FARTHER.
AROUND THIS TIME OF DAY, THE BOUNDARY BETWEEN THE TWO WORLDS BECOMES UNSTABLE DUE TO A CHANGE IN THE MAGNETIC FIELD.
YOU'LL BE SAFE AS LONG AS YOU STAY INSIDE THE BARRIER I CREATED. BUT ONCE YOU STEP OUTSIDE OF IT...
...YOU'LL BE DRAGGED INTO THE SHADOW WORLD.

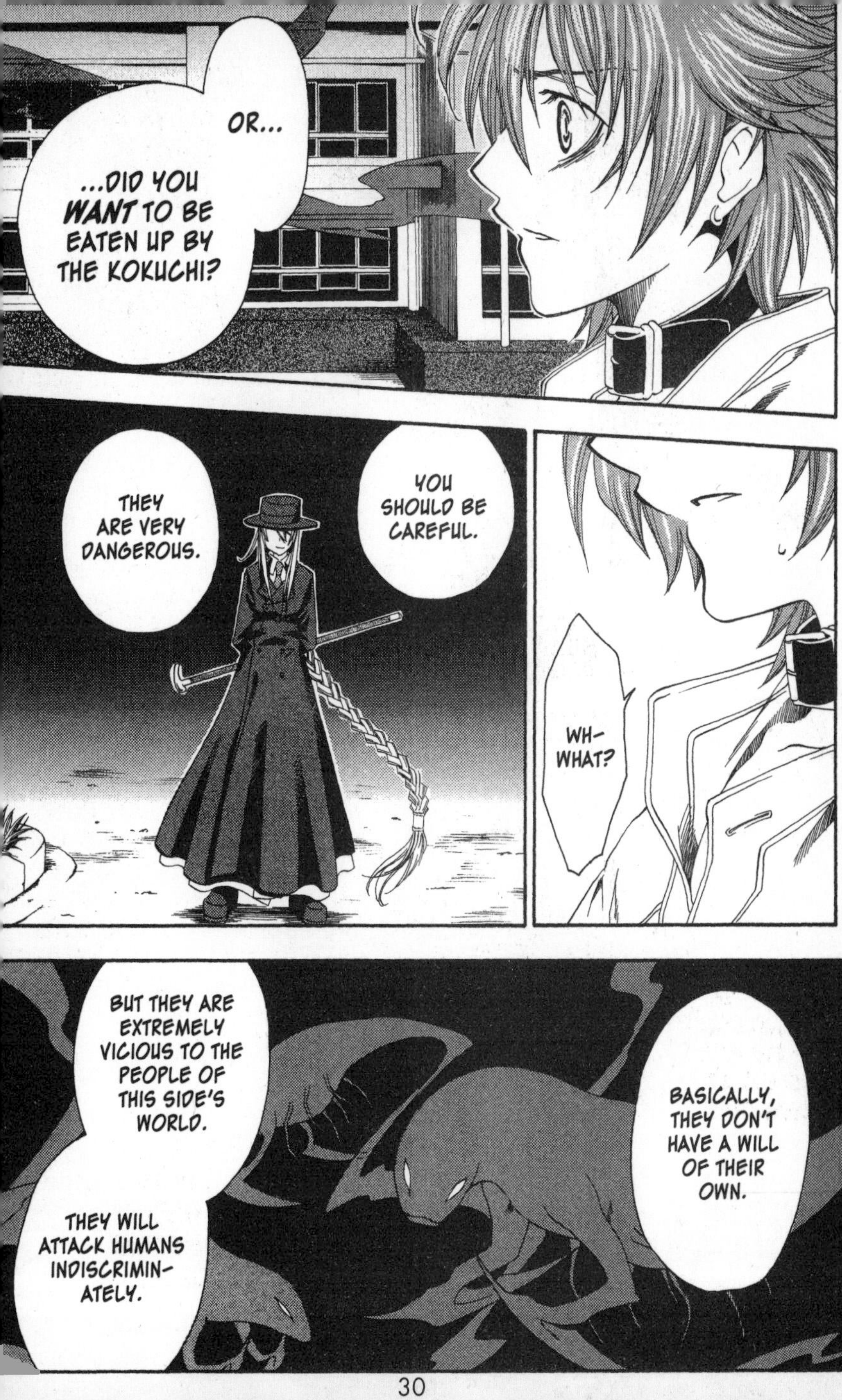
OR...
...DID YOU WANT TO BE EATEN UP BY THE KOKUCHI?
WH-WHAT?
YOU SHOULD BE CAREFUL.
THEY ARE VERY DANGEROUS.
BASICALLY, THEY DON'T HAVE A WILL OF THEIR OWN.
BUT THEY ARE EXTREMELY VICIOUS TO THE PEOPLE OF THIS SIDE'S WORLD.
THEY WILL ATTACK HUMANS INDISCRIMIN-ATELY.

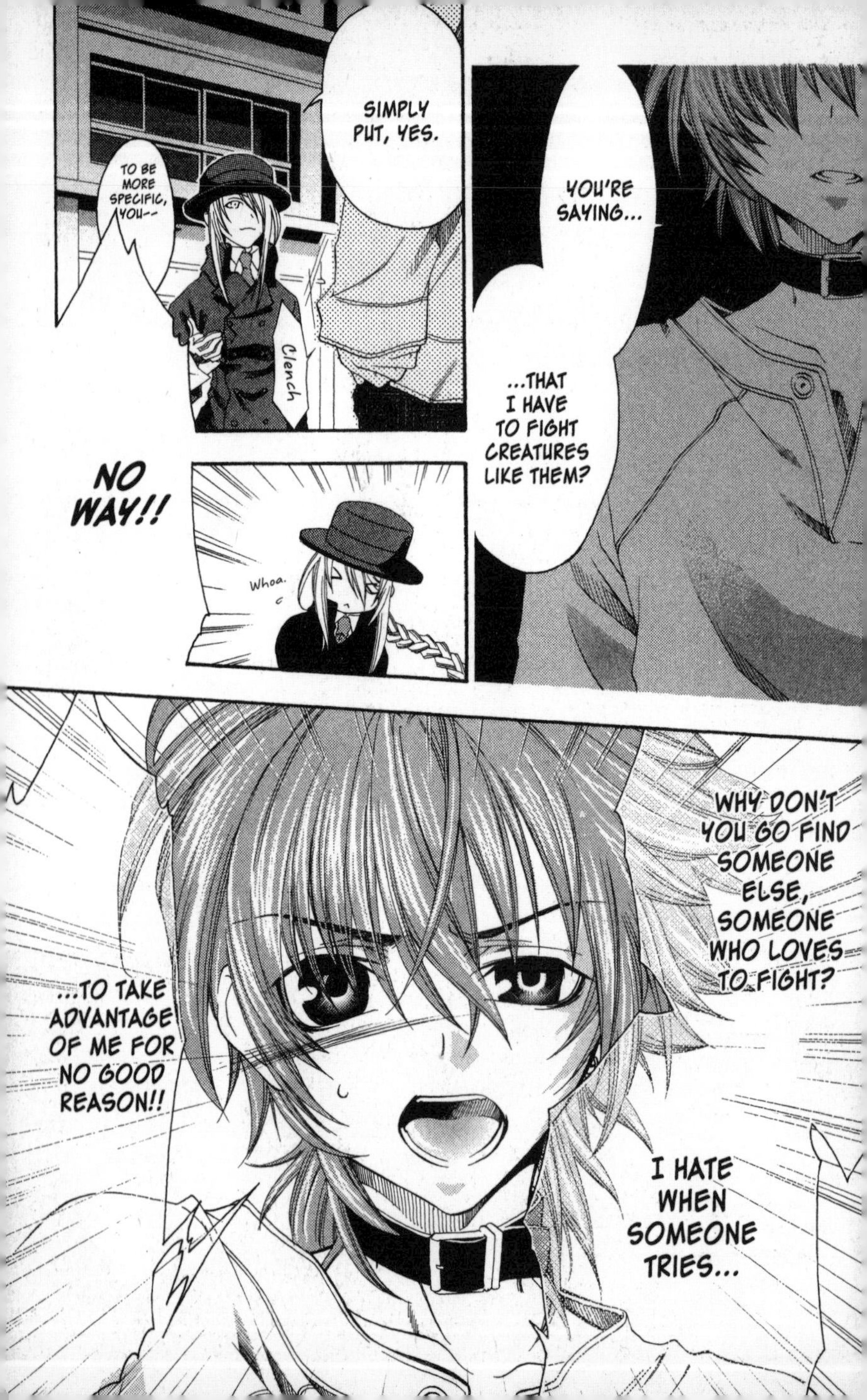
YOU'RE SAYING...
...THAT I HAVE TO FIGHT CREATURES LIKE THEM?
SIMPLY PUT, YES.
TO BE MORE SPECIFIC, YOU--
Clench
NO WAY!!
Whoa.
WHY DON'T YOU GO FIND SOMEONE ELSE, SOMEONE WHO LOVES TO FIGHT?
I HATE WHEN SOMEONE TRIES...
...TO TAKE ADVANTAGE OF ME FOR NO GOOD REASON!!

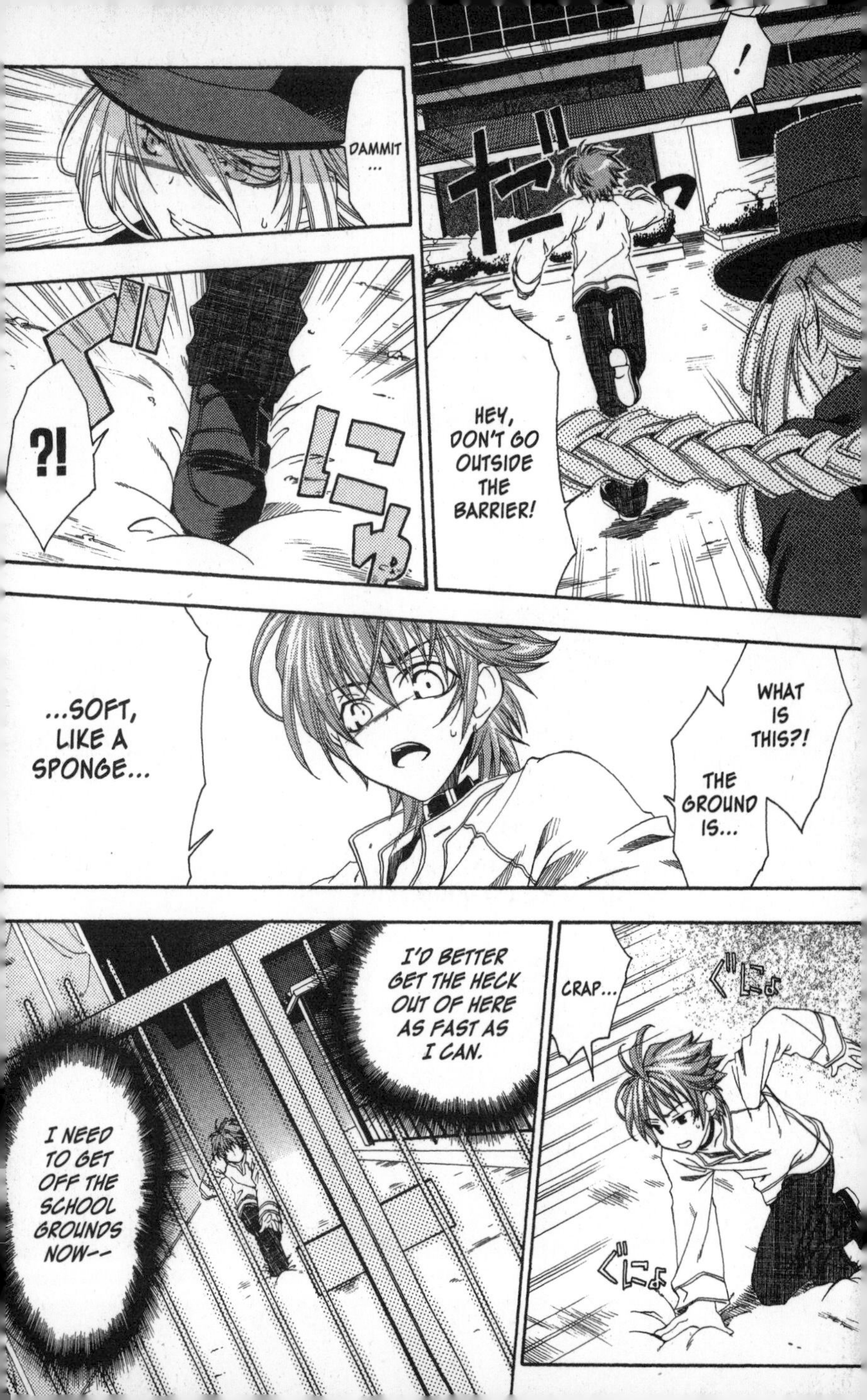
!
HEY, DON'T GO OUTSIDE THE BARRIER!
DAMMIT ...
?!
WHAT IS THIS?! THE GROUND IS...
...SOFT, LIKE A SPONGE...
CRAP...
I'D BETTER GET THE HECK OUT OF HERE AS FAST AS I CAN.
I NEED TO GET OFF THE SCHOOL GROUNDS NOW--

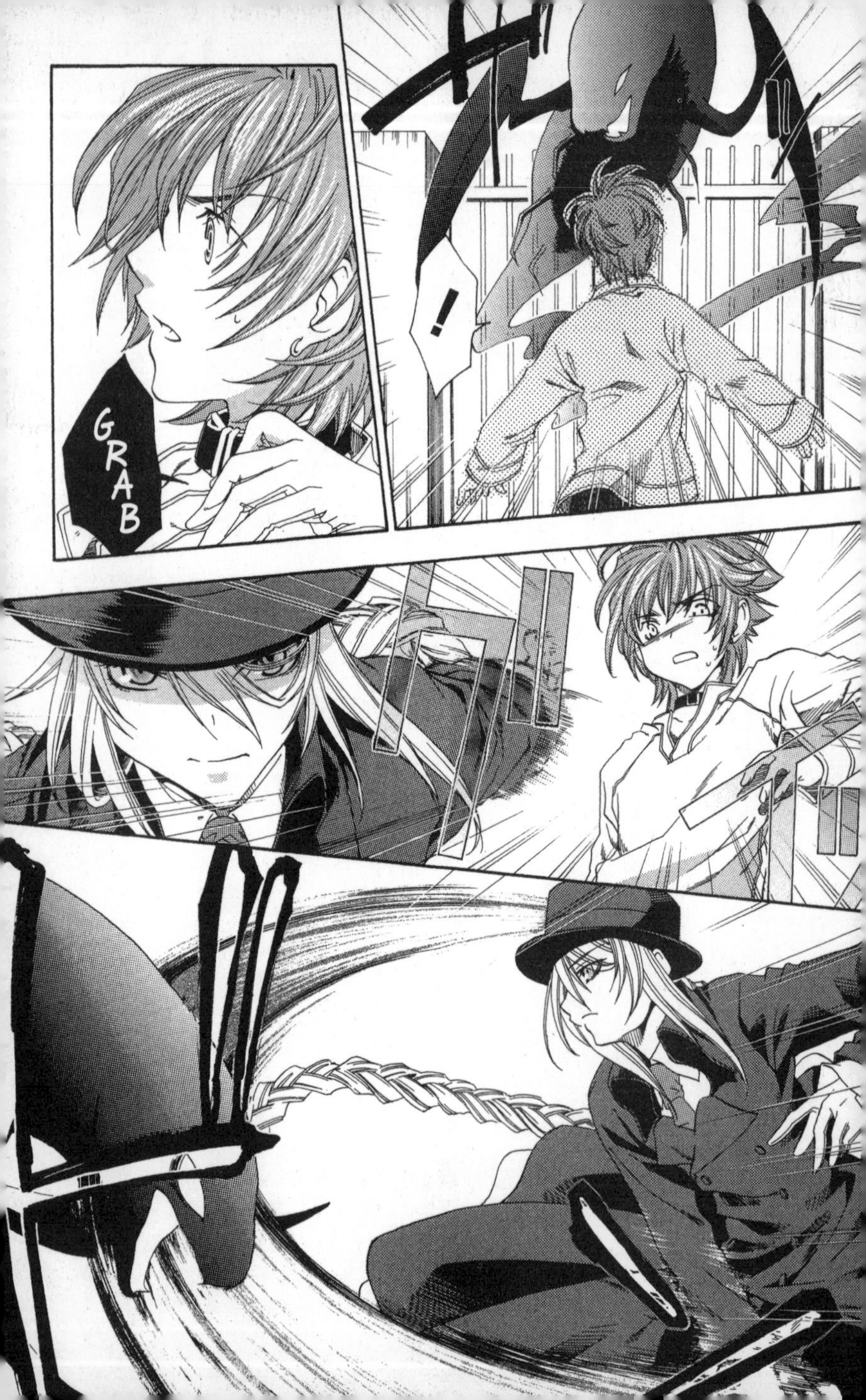
!
GRAB

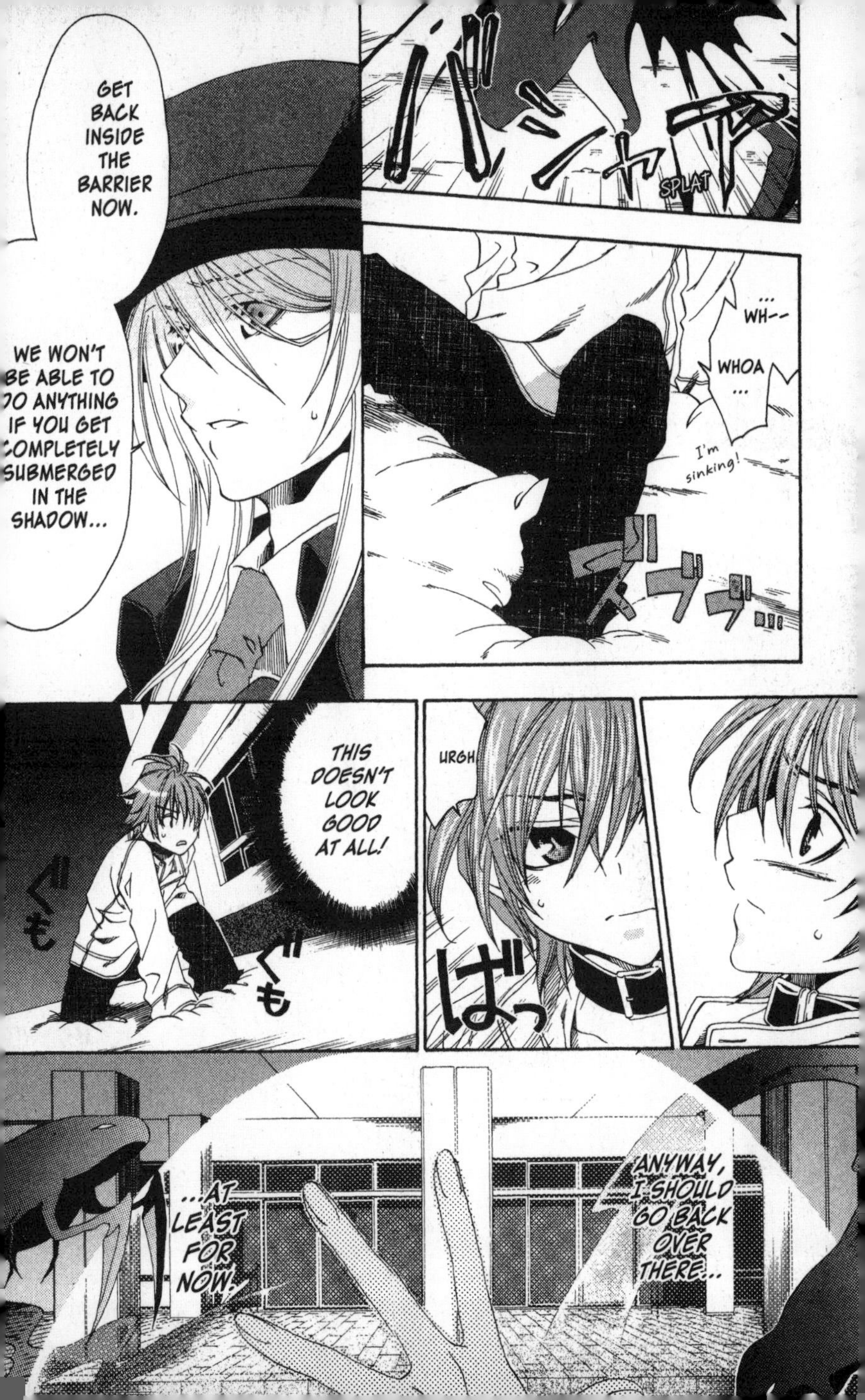
SPLAT
...WH--
WHOA...
I'm sinking!
GET BACK INSIDE THE BARRIER NOW.
WE WON'T BE ABLE TO DO ANYTHING IF YOU GET COMPLETELY SUBMERGED IN THE SHADOW...
URGH
THIS DOESN'T LOOK GOOD AT ALL!
ANYWAY, I SHOULD GO BACK OVER THERE...
...AT LEAST FOR NOW.

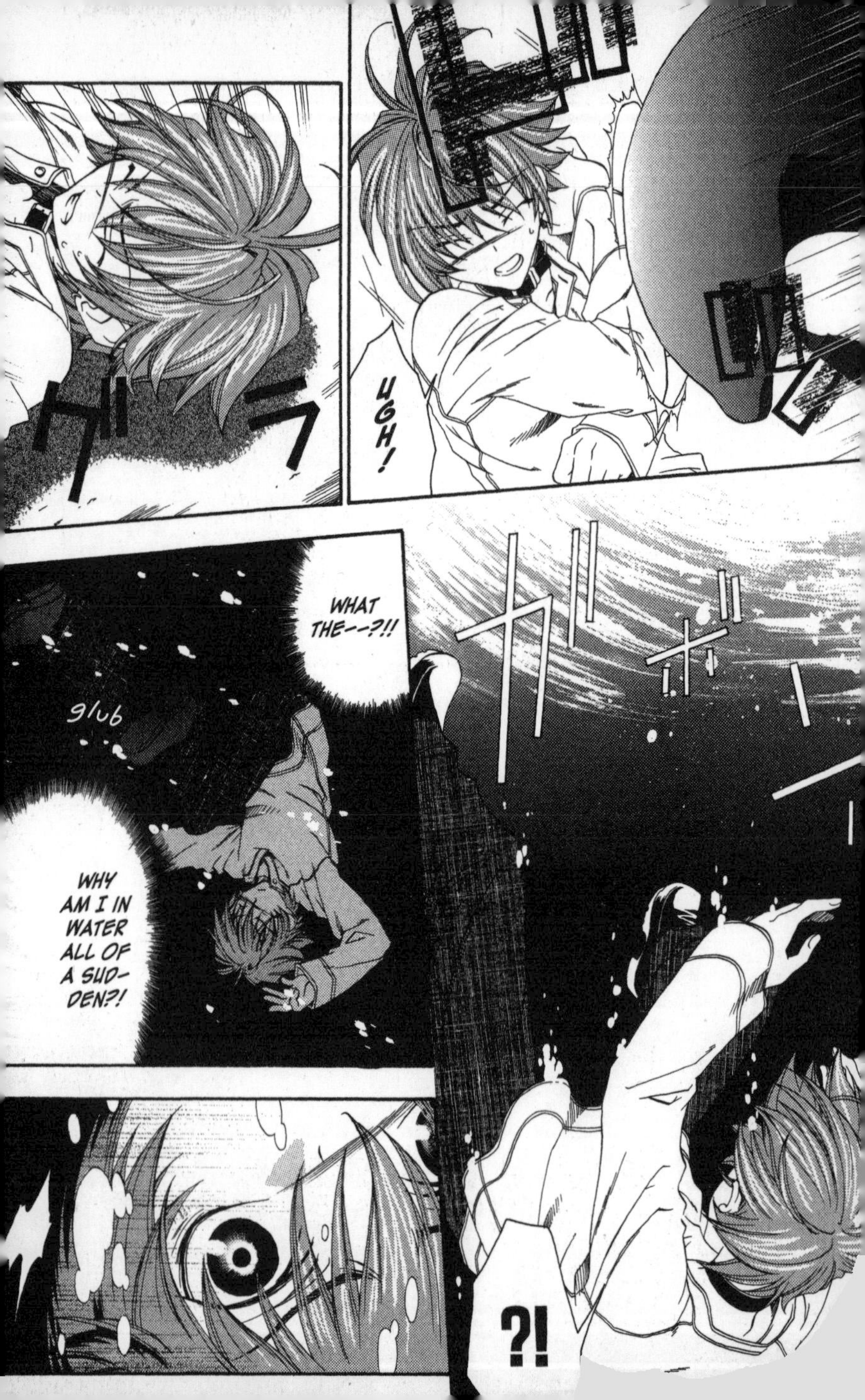

UGH!
?!
WHAT THE--?!!
glub
WHY AM I IN WATER ALL OF A SUDDEN?!

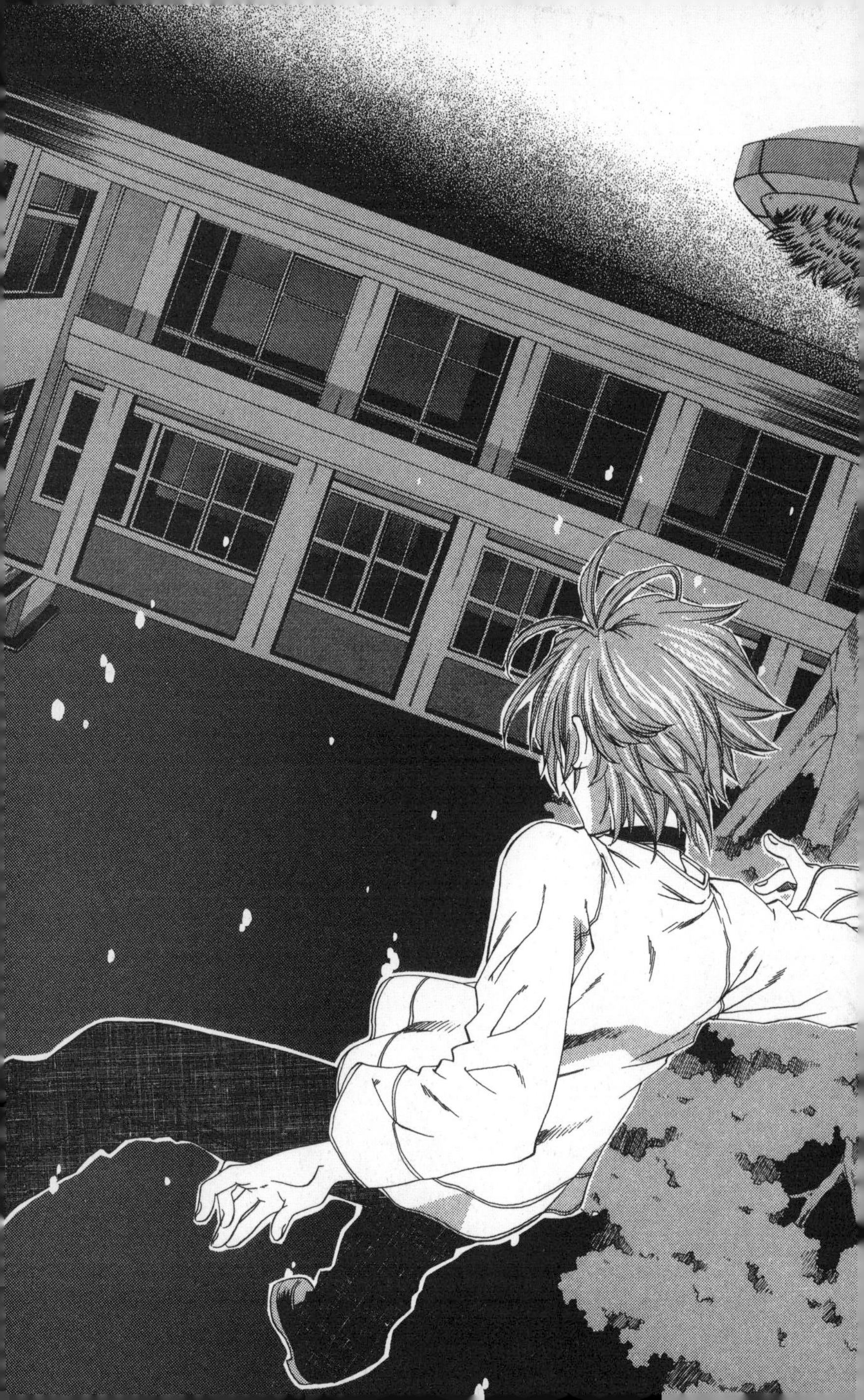

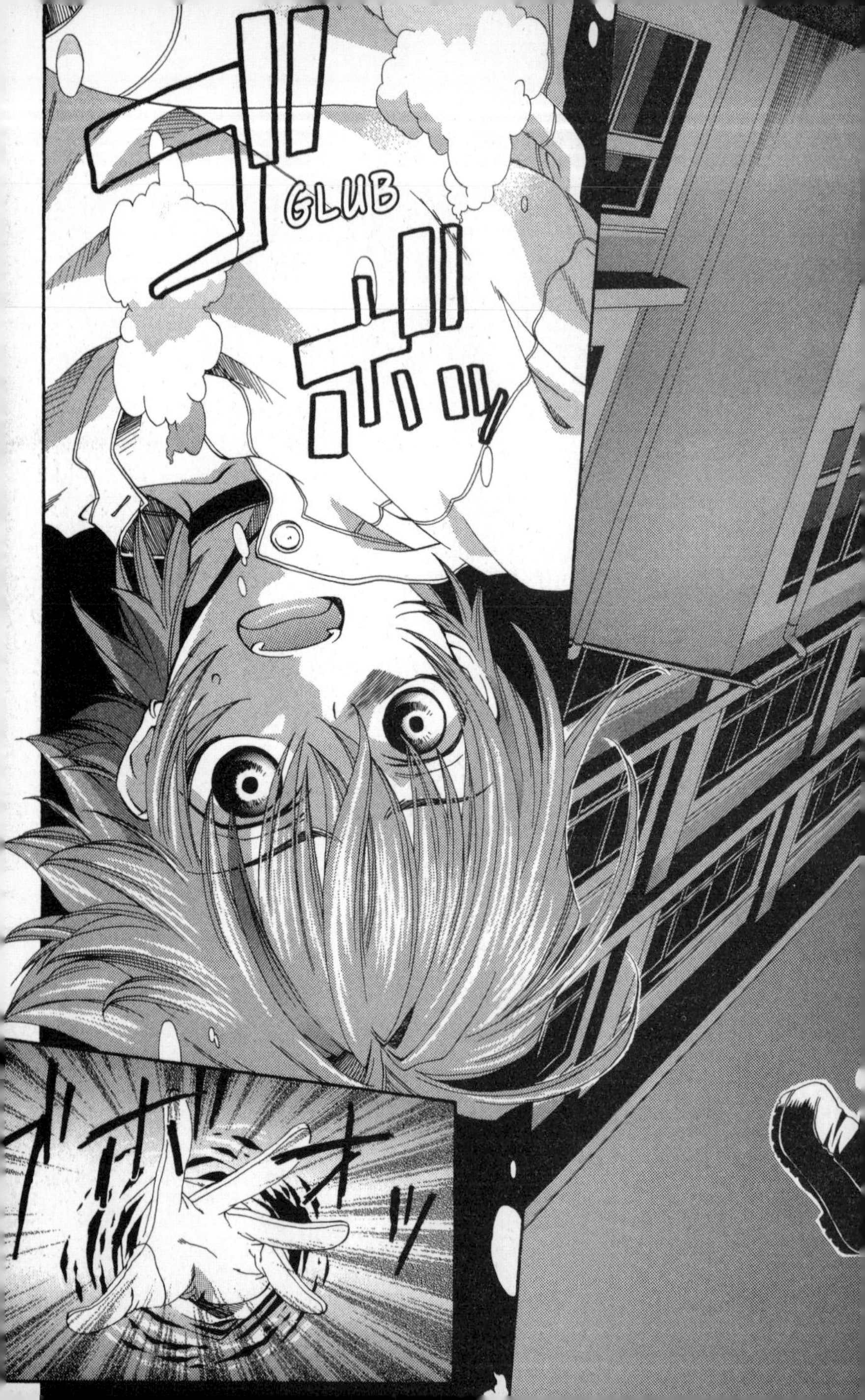
GLUB

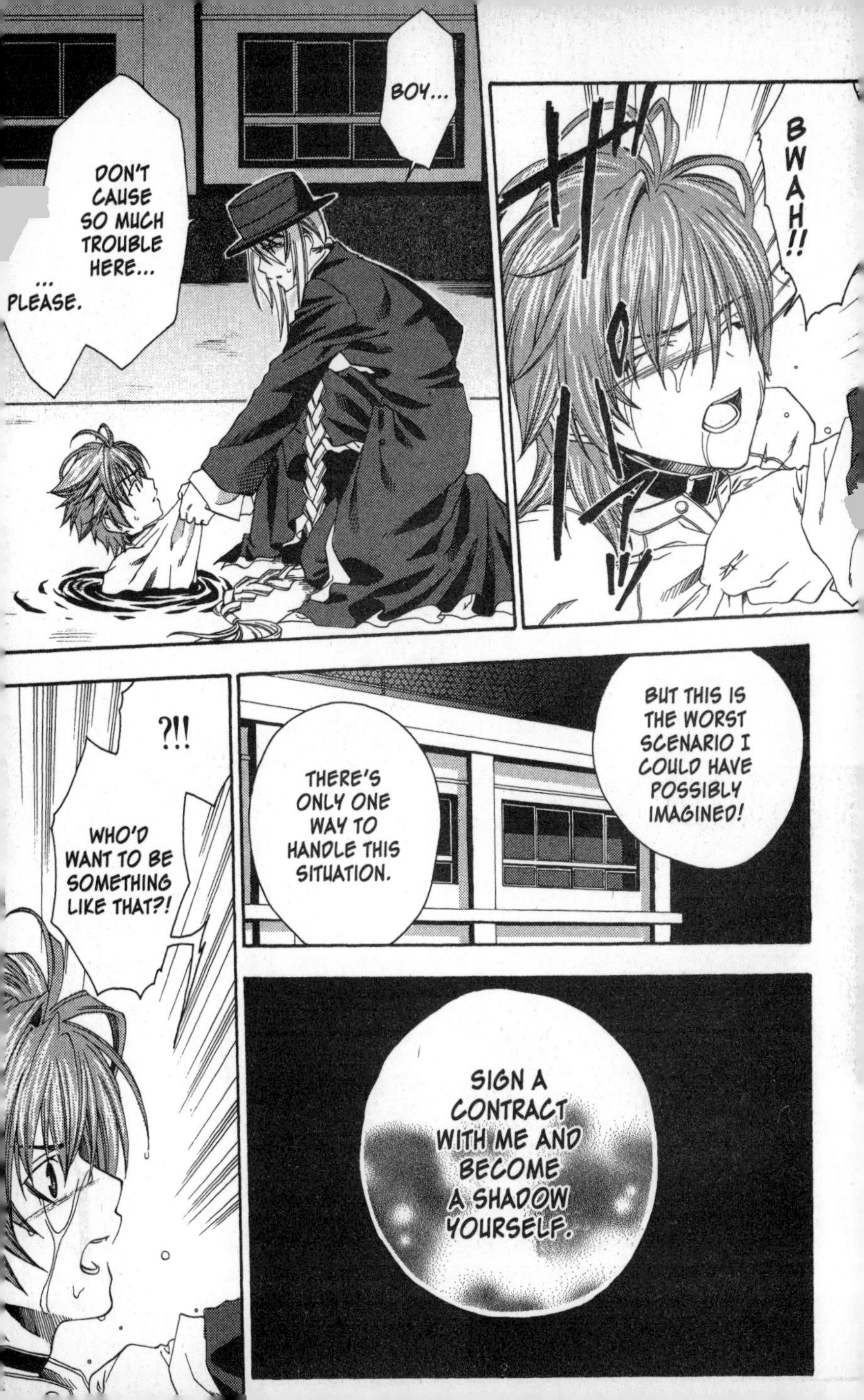
BWAH!!
BOY...
DON'T CAUSE SO MUCH TROUBLE HERE...
...PLEASE.
BUT THIS IS THE WORST SCENARIO I COULD HAVE POSSIBLY IMAGINED!
THERE'S ONLY ONE WAY TO HANDLE THIS SITUATION.
SIGN A CONTRACT WITH ME AND BECOME A SHADOW YOURSELF.
?!!
WHO'D WANT TO BE SOMETHING LIKE THAT?!

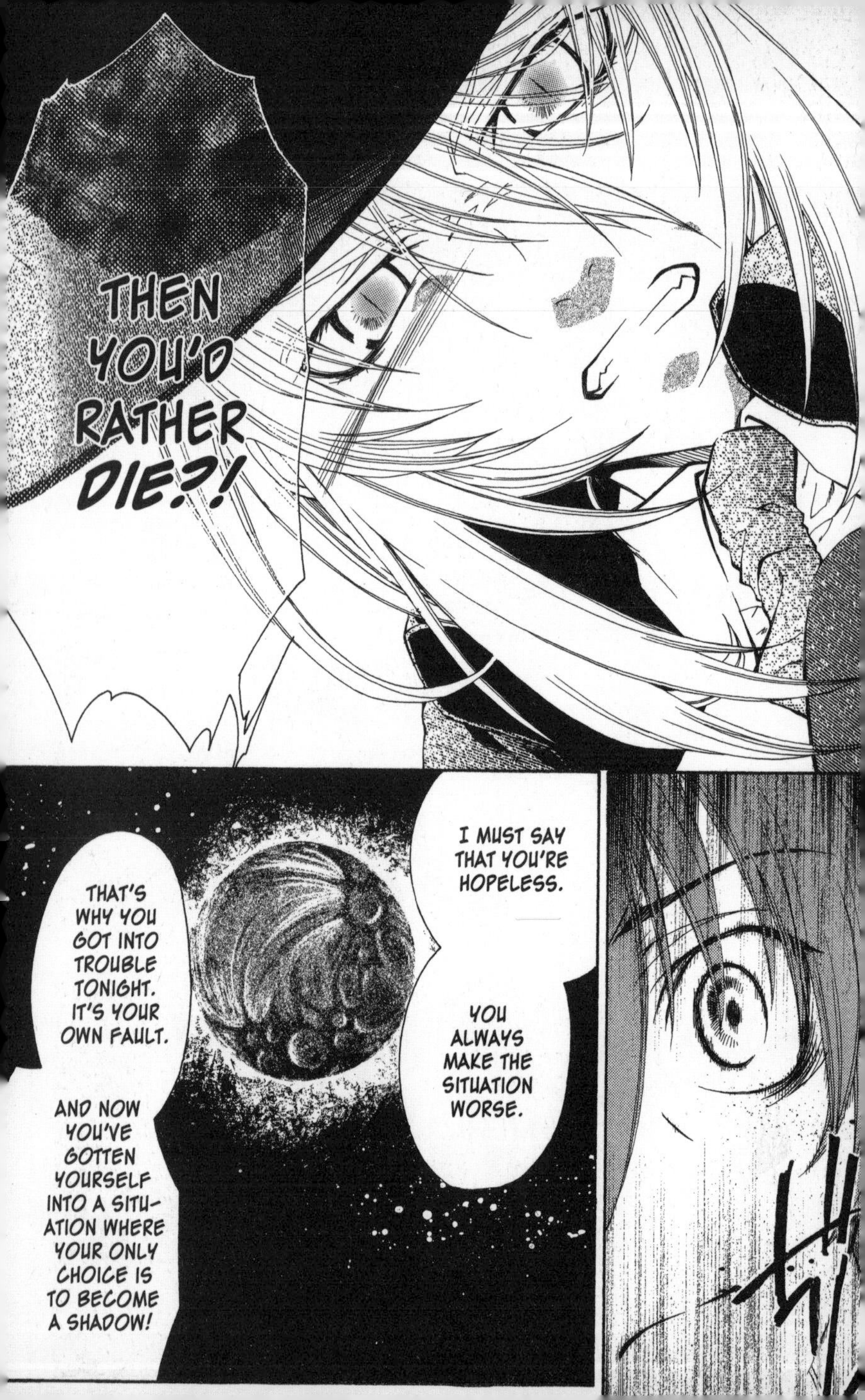
THEN YOU'D RATHER DIE?!
I MUST SAY THAT YOU'RE HOPELESS.
YOU ALWAYS MAKE THE SITUATION WORSE.
THAT'S WHY YOU GOT INTO TROUBLE TONIGHT. IT'S YOUR OWN FAULT.
AND NOW YOU'VE GOTTEN YOURSELF INTO A SITU-ATION WHERE YOUR ONLY CHOICE IS TO BECOME A SHADOW!

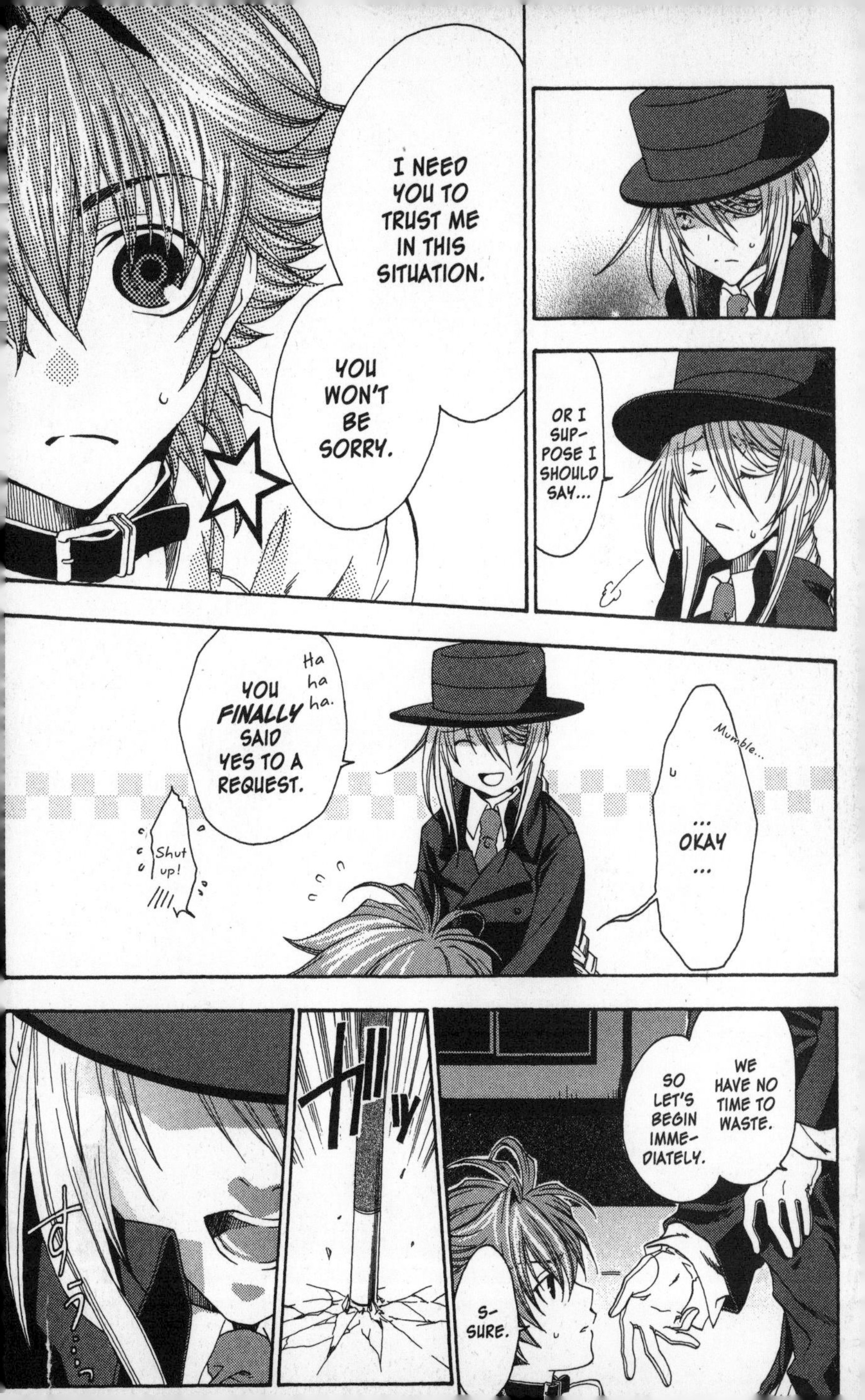
OR I SUP-POSE I SHOULD SAY...
I NEED YOU TO TRUST ME IN THIS SITUATION.
YOU WON'T BE SORRY.
Mumble...
... OKAY ...
Ha ha ha.
YOU *FINALLY* SAID YES TO A REQUEST.
Shut up!
WE HAVE NO TIME TO WASTE.
SO LET'S BEGIN IMME-DIATELY.
S-SURE.

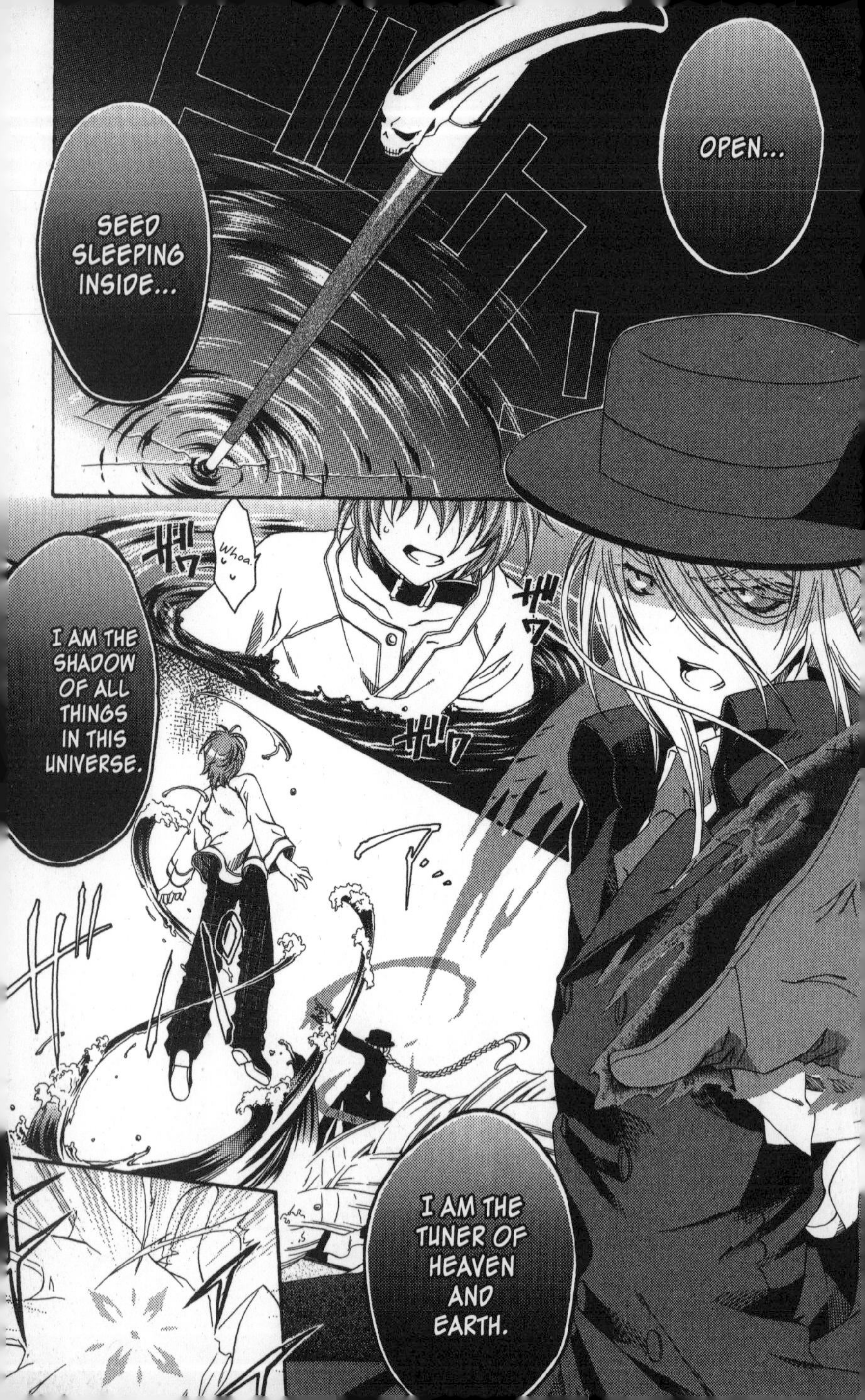
OPEN...
SEED SLEEPING INSIDE...
Whoa!
I AM THE SHADOW OF ALL THINGS IN THIS UNIVERSE.
I AM THE TUNER OF HEAVEN AND EARTH.

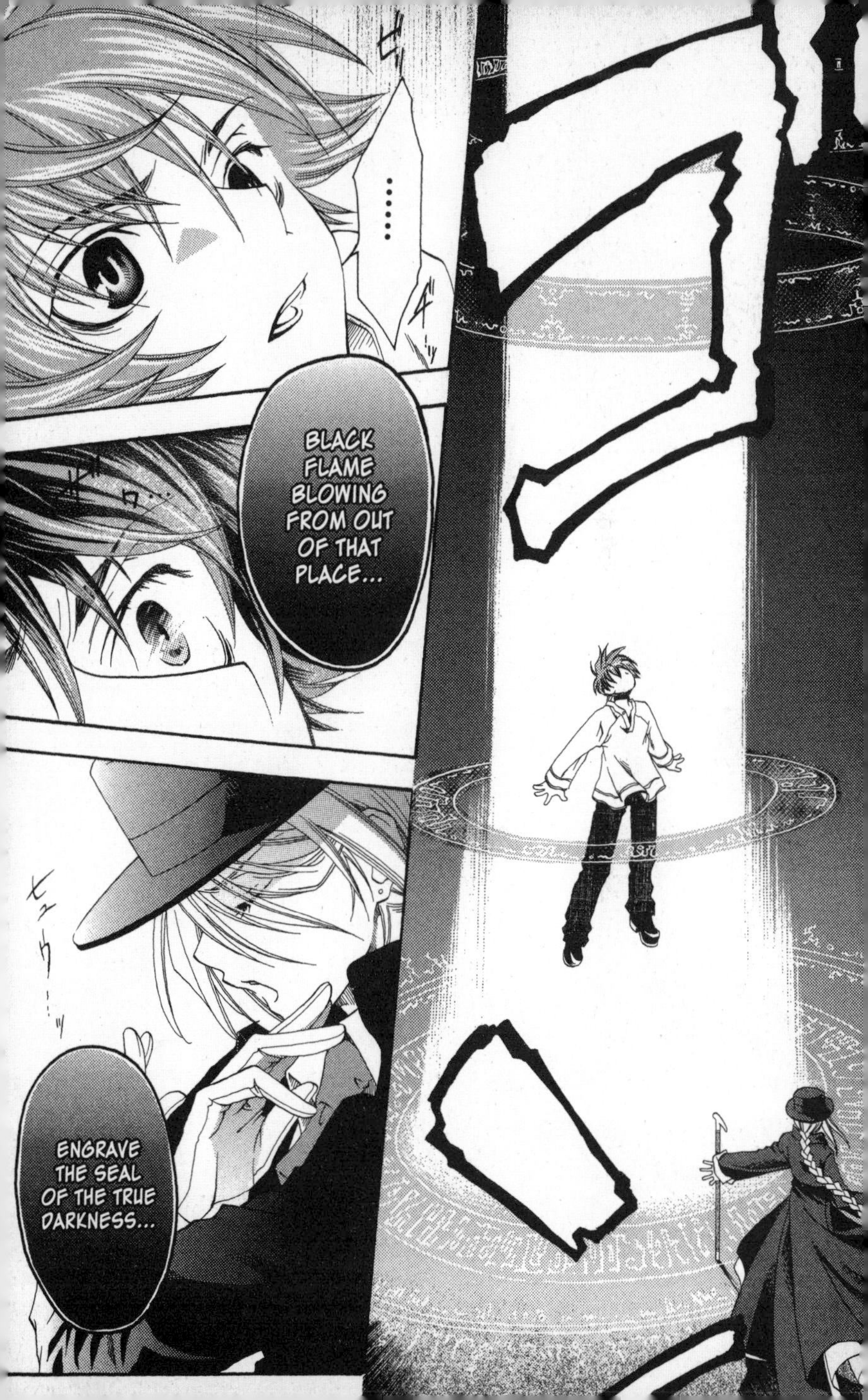
......
BLACK FLAME BLOWING FROM OUT OF THAT PLACE...
ENGRAVE THE SEAL OF THE TRUE DARKNESS...

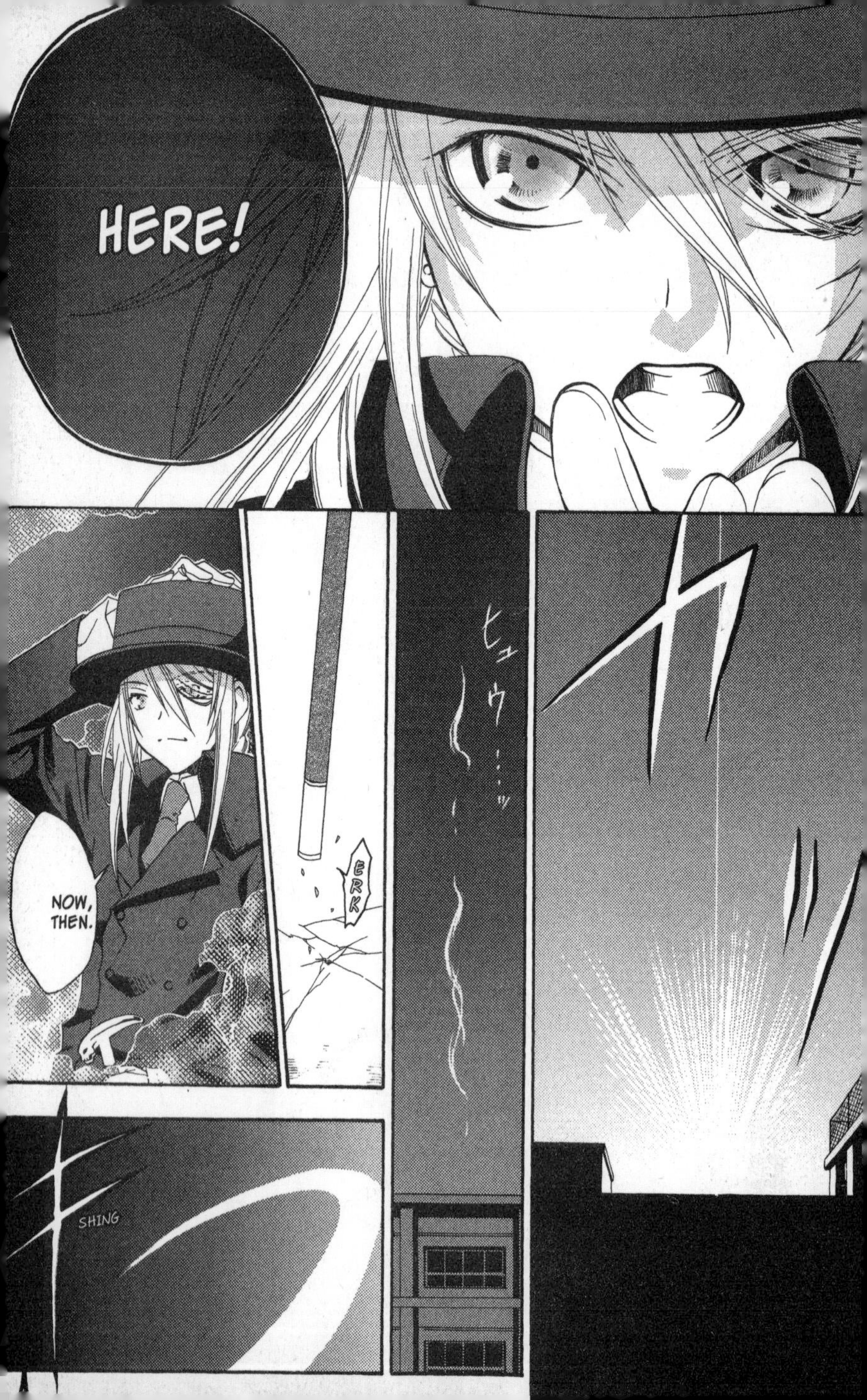
HERE!
ヒュウ…ッ
ERK
NOW, THEN.
SHING

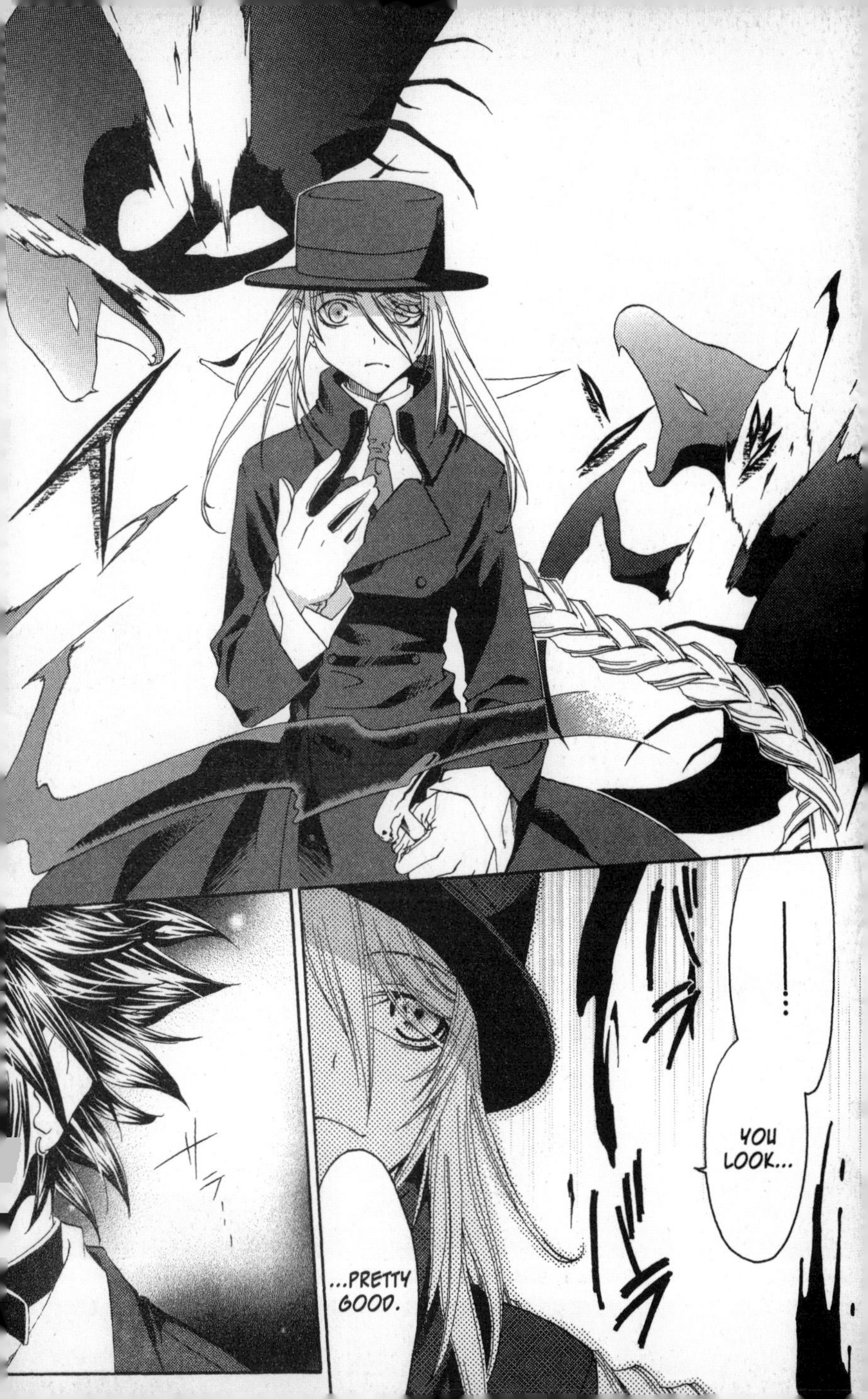
YOU LOOK...
...PRETTY GOOD.

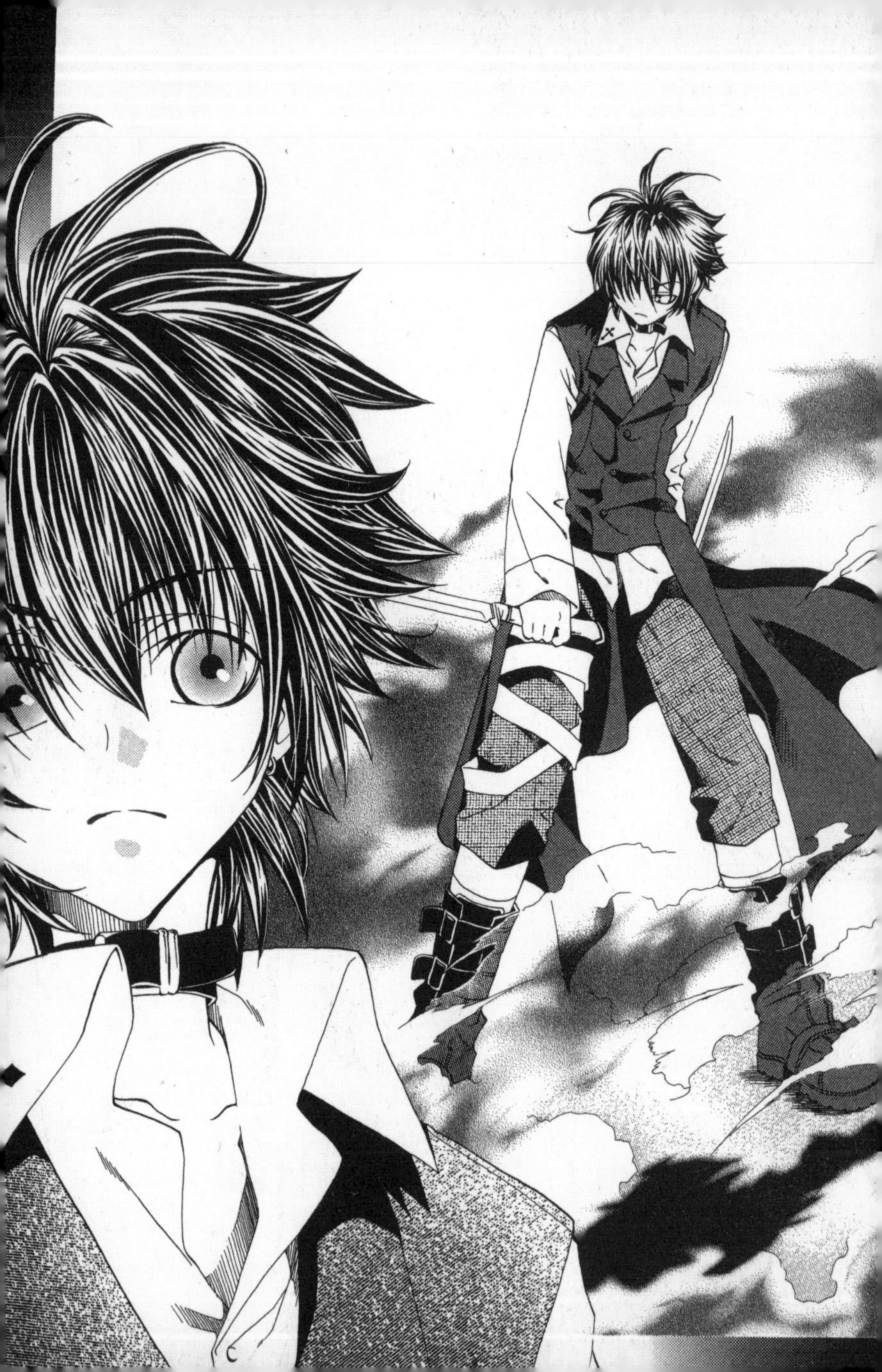

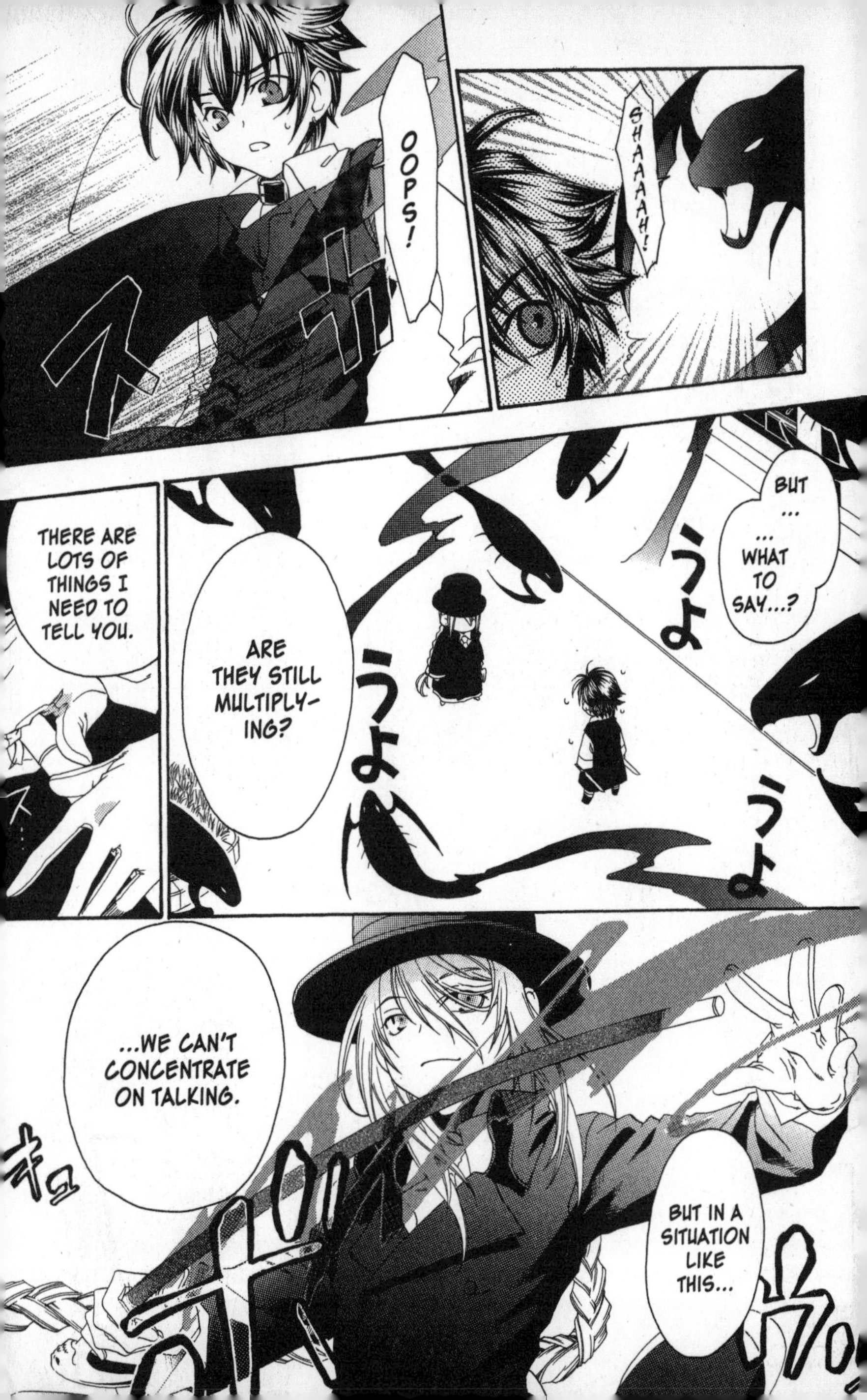
SHAAAAH!
OOPS!
スッ
BUT... ...WHAT TO SAY...?
うよ
うよ
うよ
ARE THEY STILL MULTIPLYING?
THERE ARE LOTS OF THINGS I NEED TO TELL YOU.
BUT IN A SITUATION LIKE THIS...
...WE CAN'T CONCENTRATE ON TALKING.

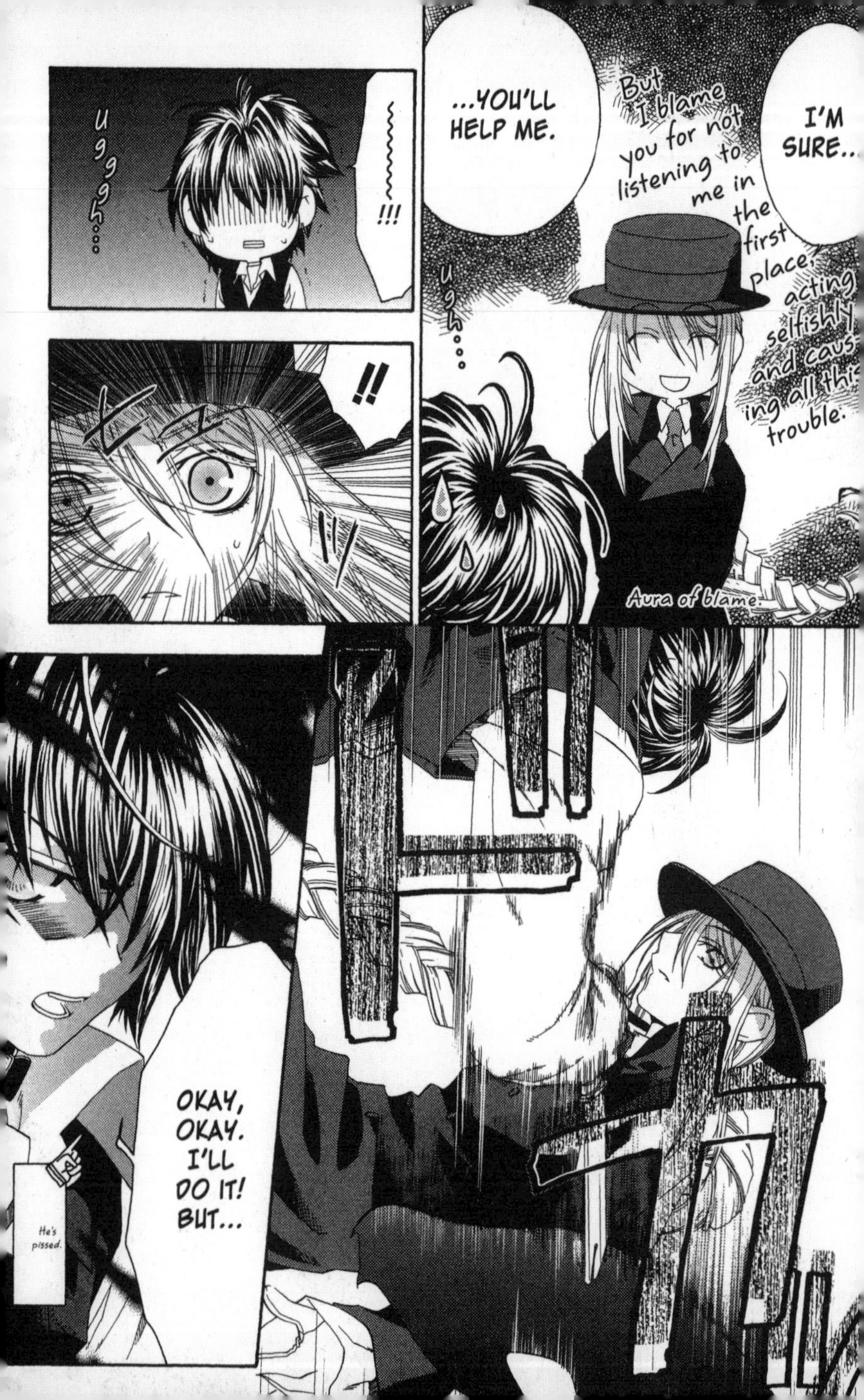
I'M SURE...
...YOU'LL HELP ME.
But I blame you for not listening to me in the first place, acting selfishly, and causing all this trouble.
Ugh...
Aura of blame.
Ugggh...
~~~~!!!
!!
OKAY, OKAY. I'LL DO IT! BUT...
He's pissed.
~~~~

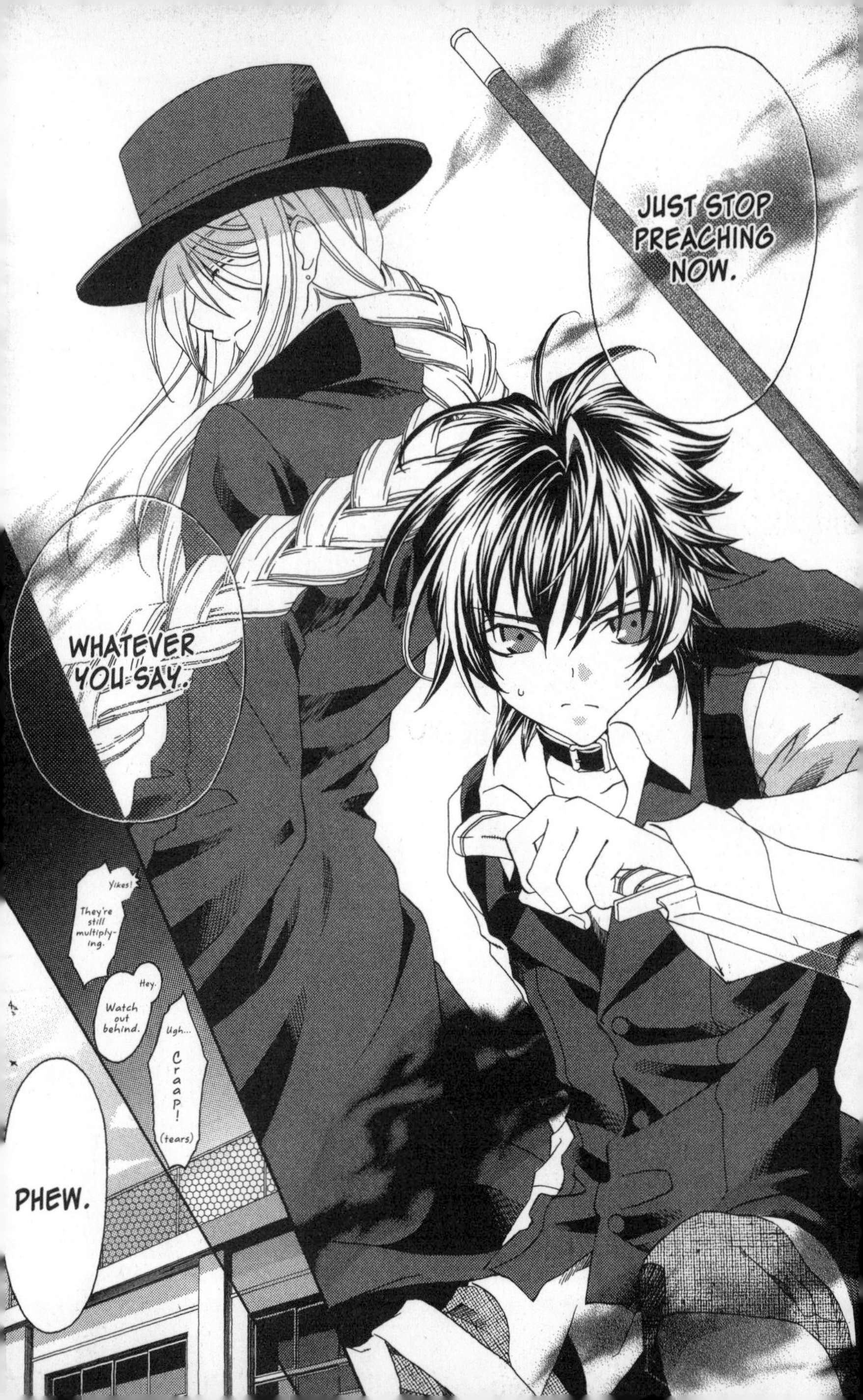
JUST STOP PREACHING NOW.
WHATEVER YOU SAY.
Yikes!
They're still multiplying.
Hey.
Watch out behind.
Ugh...
Craap!
(tears)
PHEW.

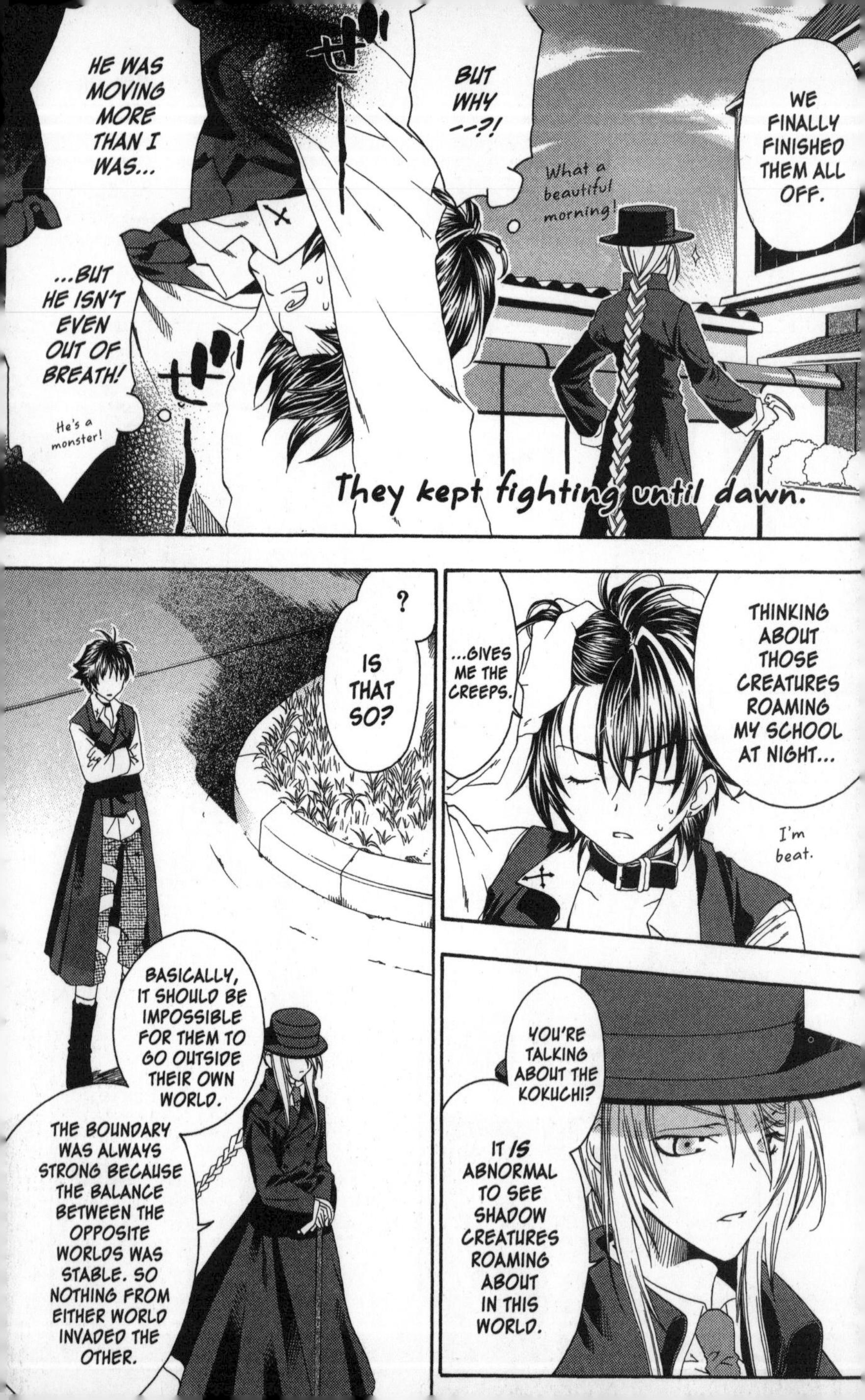
WE FINALLY FINISHED THEM ALL OFF.
What a beautiful morning!
BUT WHY --?!
HE WAS MOVING MORE THAN I WAS...
...BUT HE ISN'T EVEN OUT OF BREATH!
He's a monster!
They kept fighting until dawn.
THINKING ABOUT THOSE CREATURES ROAMING MY SCHOOL AT NIGHT...
...GIVES ME THE CREEPS.
I'm beat.
YOU'RE TALKING ABOUT THE KOKUCHI?
IT IS ABNORMAL TO SEE SHADOW CREATURES ROAMING ABOUT IN THIS WORLD.
?
IS THAT SO?
BASICALLY, IT SHOULD BE IMPOSSIBLE FOR THEM TO GO OUTSIDE THEIR OWN WORLD.
THE BOUNDARY WAS ALWAYS STRONG BECAUSE THE BALANCE BETWEEN THE OPPOSITE WORLDS WAS STABLE. SO NOTHING FROM EITHER WORLD INVADED THE OTHER.

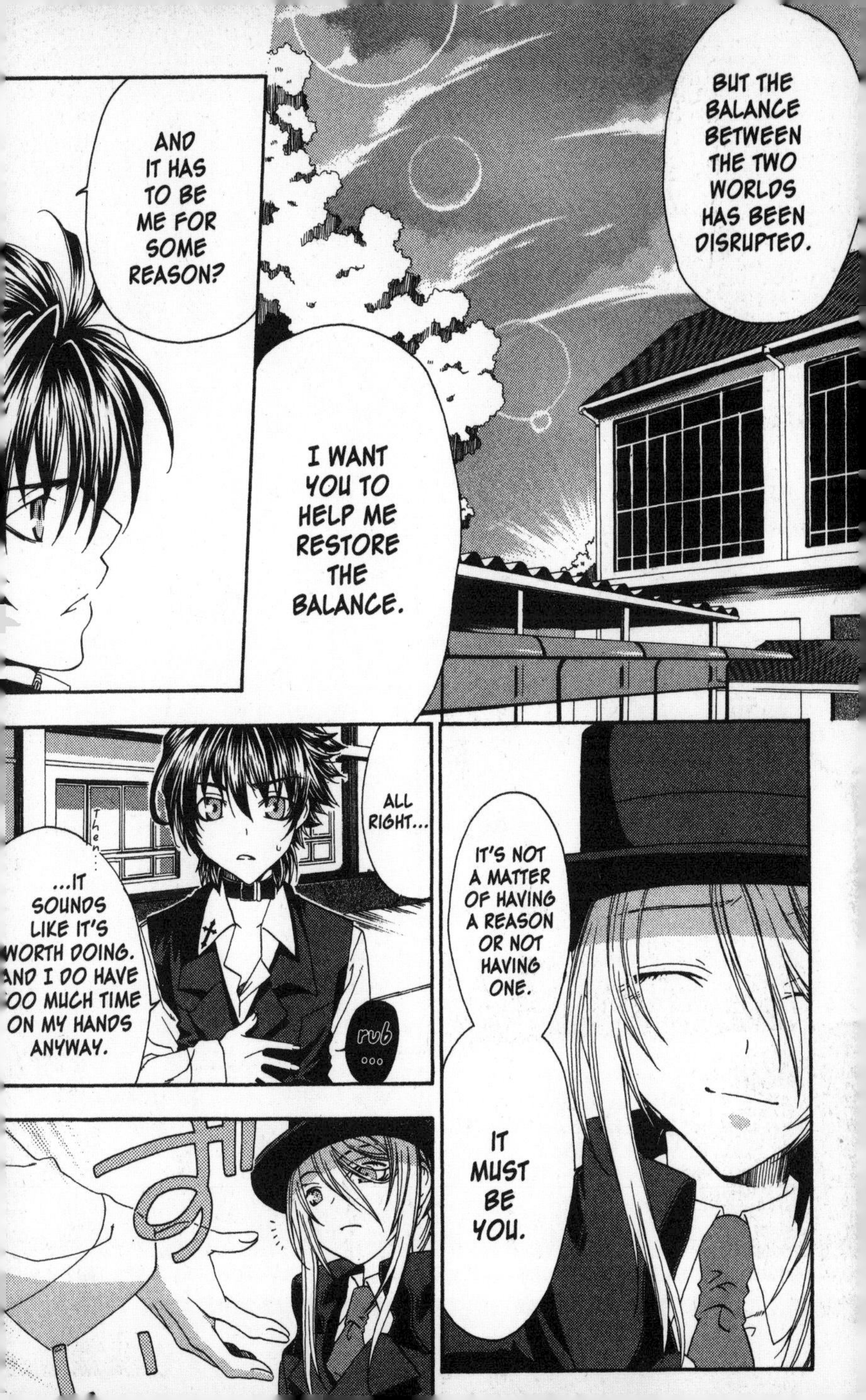
BUT THE BALANCE BETWEEN THE TWO WORLDS HAS BEEN DISRUPTED.
I WANT YOU TO HELP ME RESTORE THE BALANCE.
AND IT HAS TO BE ME FOR SOME REASON?
IT'S NOT A MATTER OF HAVING A REASON OR NOT HAVING ONE.
IT MUST BE YOU.
ALL RIGHT...
Then...
...IT SOUNDS LIKE IT'S WORTH DOING. ND I DO HAVE OO MUCH TIME ON MY HANDS ANYWAY.
rub

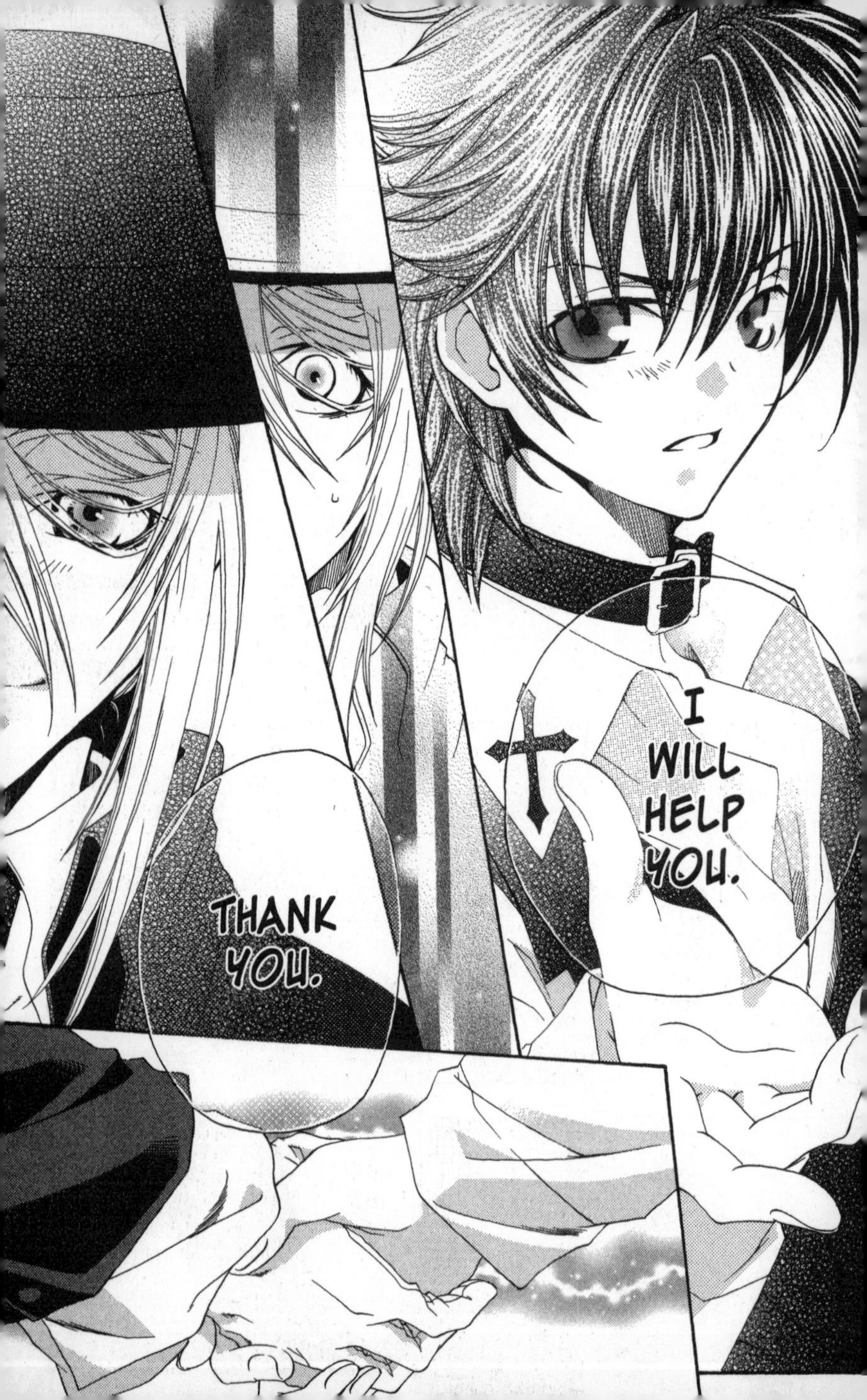
I WILL HELP YOU.
THANK YOU.

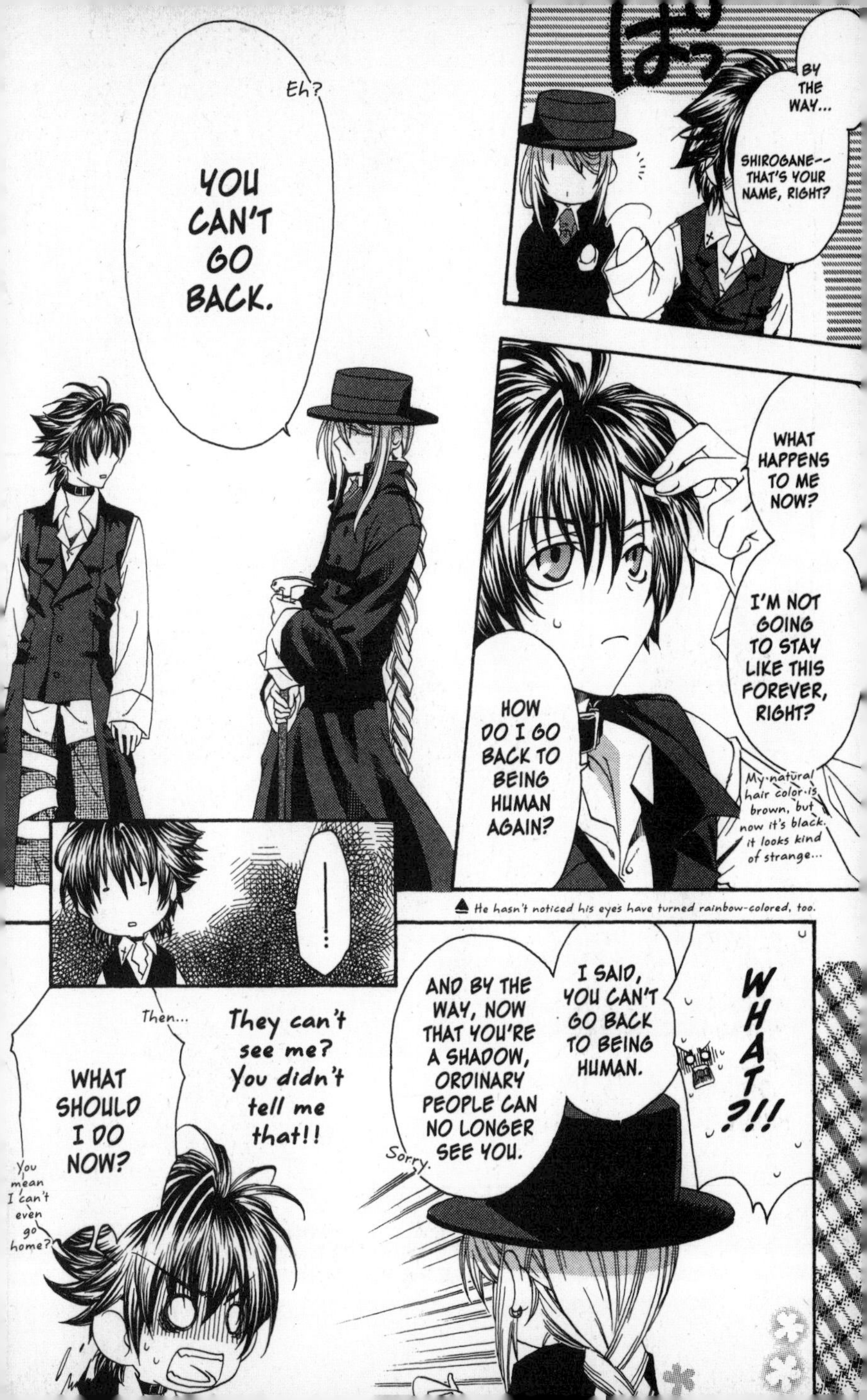
ぱっ
BY THE WAY...
SHIROGANE--THAT'S YOUR NAME, RIGHT?
WHAT HAPPENS TO ME NOW?
I'M NOT GOING TO STAY LIKE THIS FOREVER, RIGHT?
HOW DO I GO BACK TO BEING HUMAN AGAIN?
My natural hair color is brown, but now it's black. It looks kind of strange...
YOU CAN'T GO BACK.
Eh?
...!
I SAID, YOU CAN'T GO BACK TO BEING HUMAN.
AND BY THE WAY, NOW THAT YOU'RE A SHADOW, ORDINARY PEOPLE CAN NO LONGER SEE YOU.
Sorry.
WHAT?!!
They can't see me? You didn't tell me that!!
Then...
WHAT SHOULD I DO NOW?
You mean I can't even go home?
▲ He hasn't noticed his eyes have turned rainbow-colored, too.

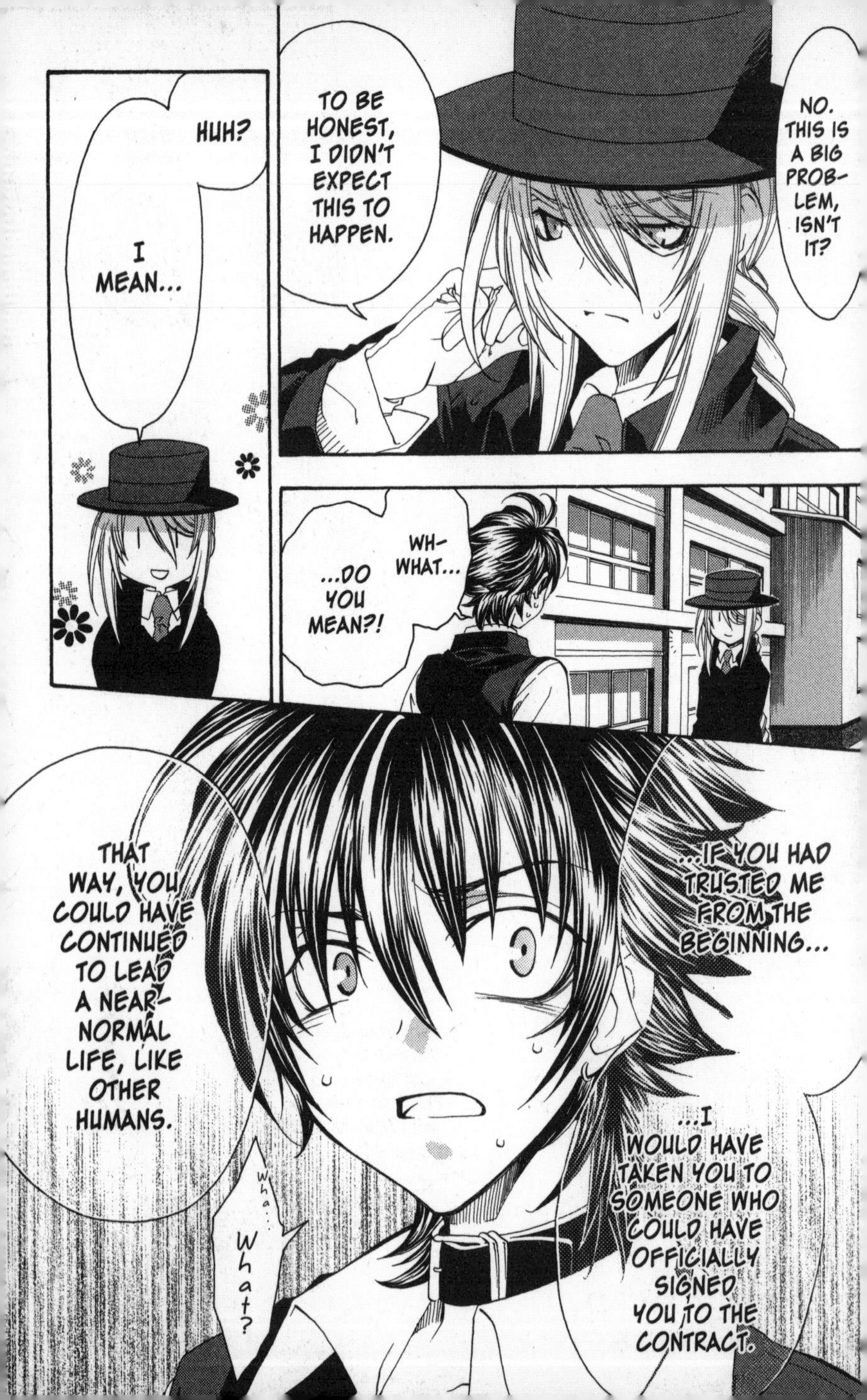
NO. THIS IS A BIG PROB-LEM, ISN'T IT?
TO BE HONEST, I DIDN'T EXPECT THIS TO HAPPEN.
WH-WHAT...
...DO YOU MEAN?!
HUH?
I MEAN...
...IF YOU HAD TRUSTED ME FROM THE BEGINNING...
...I WOULD HAVE TAKEN YOU TO SOMEONE WHO COULD HAVE OFFICIALLY SIGNED YOU TO THE CONTRACT.
Wha... What?
THAT WAY, YOU COULD HAVE CONTINUED TO LEAD A NEAR-NORMAL LIFE, LIKE OTHER HUMANS.

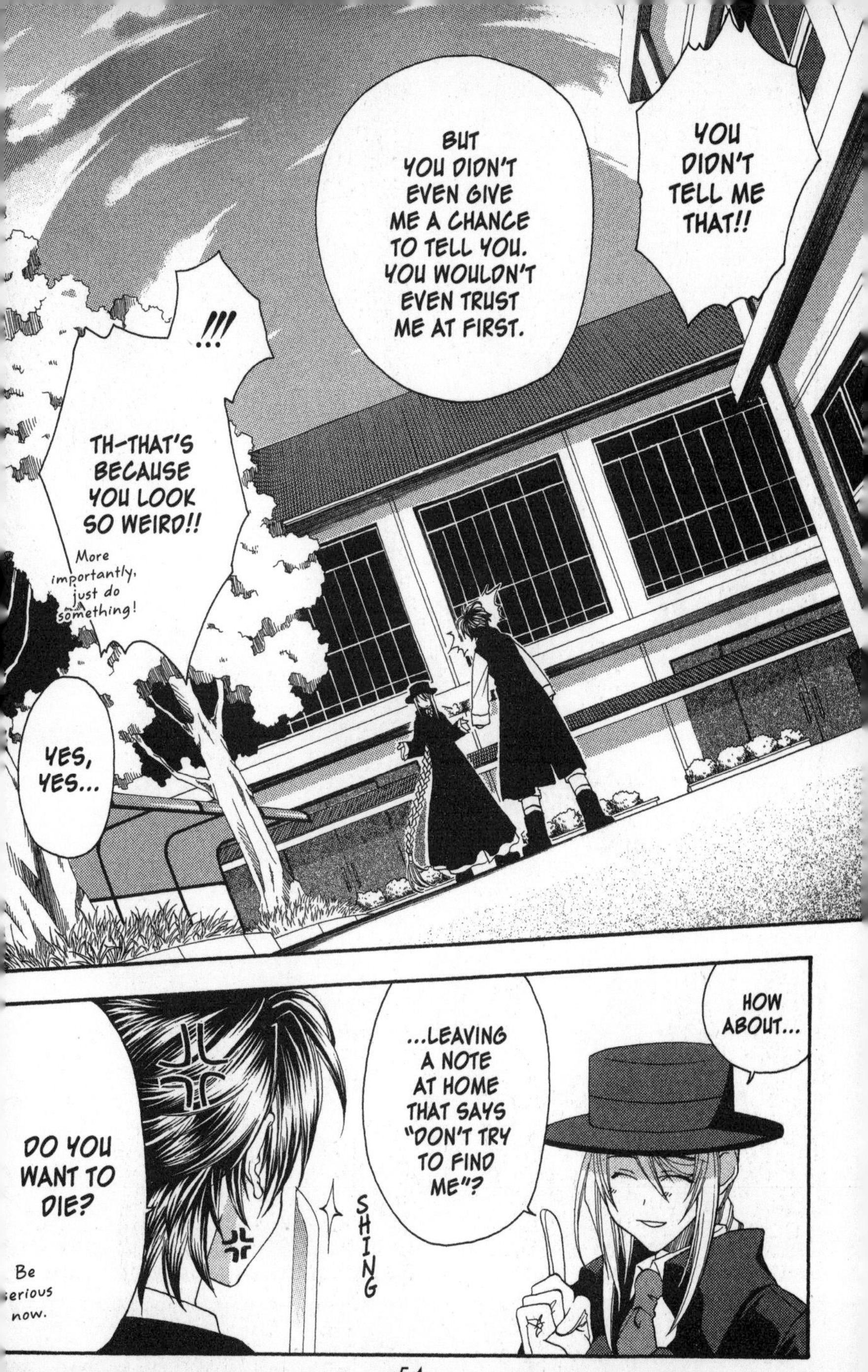
YOU DIDN'T TELL ME THAT!!
BUT YOU DIDN'T EVEN GIVE ME A CHANCE TO TELL YOU. YOU WOULDN'T EVEN TRUST ME AT FIRST.
!!!
TH-THAT'S BECAUSE YOU LOOK SO WEIRD!!
More importantly, just do something!
YES, YES...
HOW ABOUT...
...LEAVING A NOTE AT HOME THAT SAYS "DON'T TRY TO FIND ME"?
SHING
DO YOU WANT TO DIE?
Be serious now.

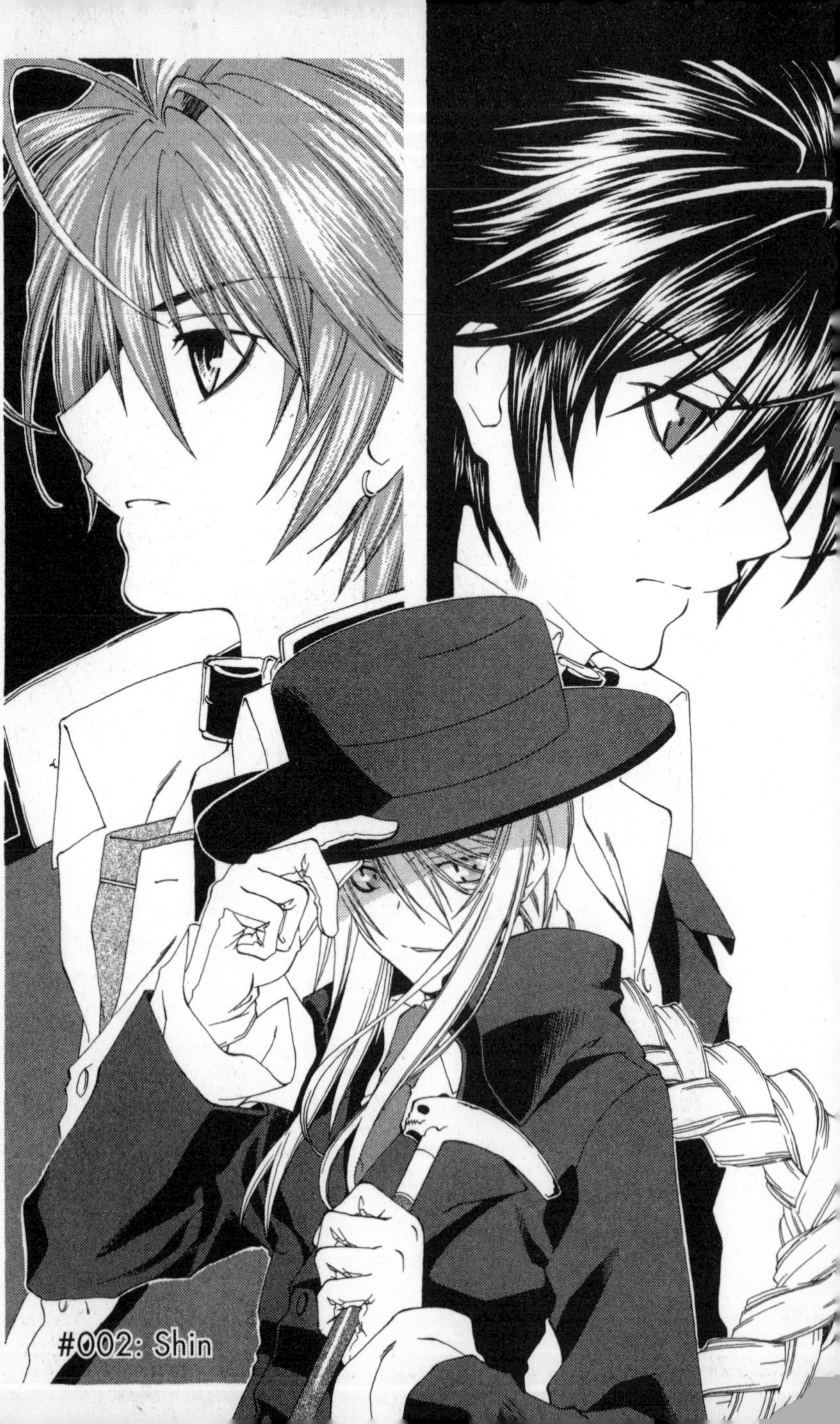
#002: Shin

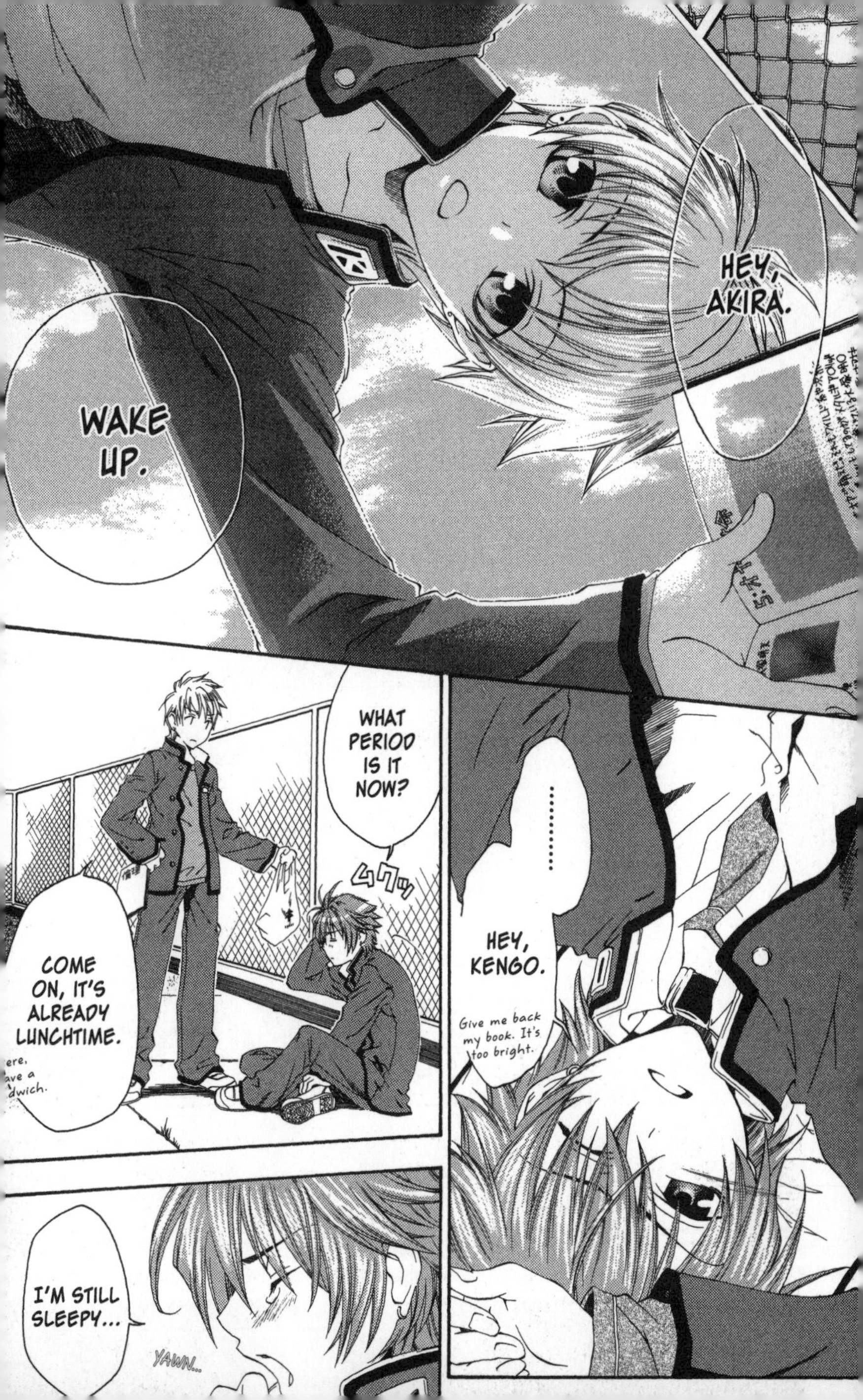
HEY, AKIRA.
WAKE UP.
......
HEY, KENGO.
Give me back my book. It's too bright.
WHAT PERIOD IS IT NOW?
ムクッ
COME ON, IT'S ALREADY LUNCHTIME.
I'M STILL SLEEPY...
YAWN...

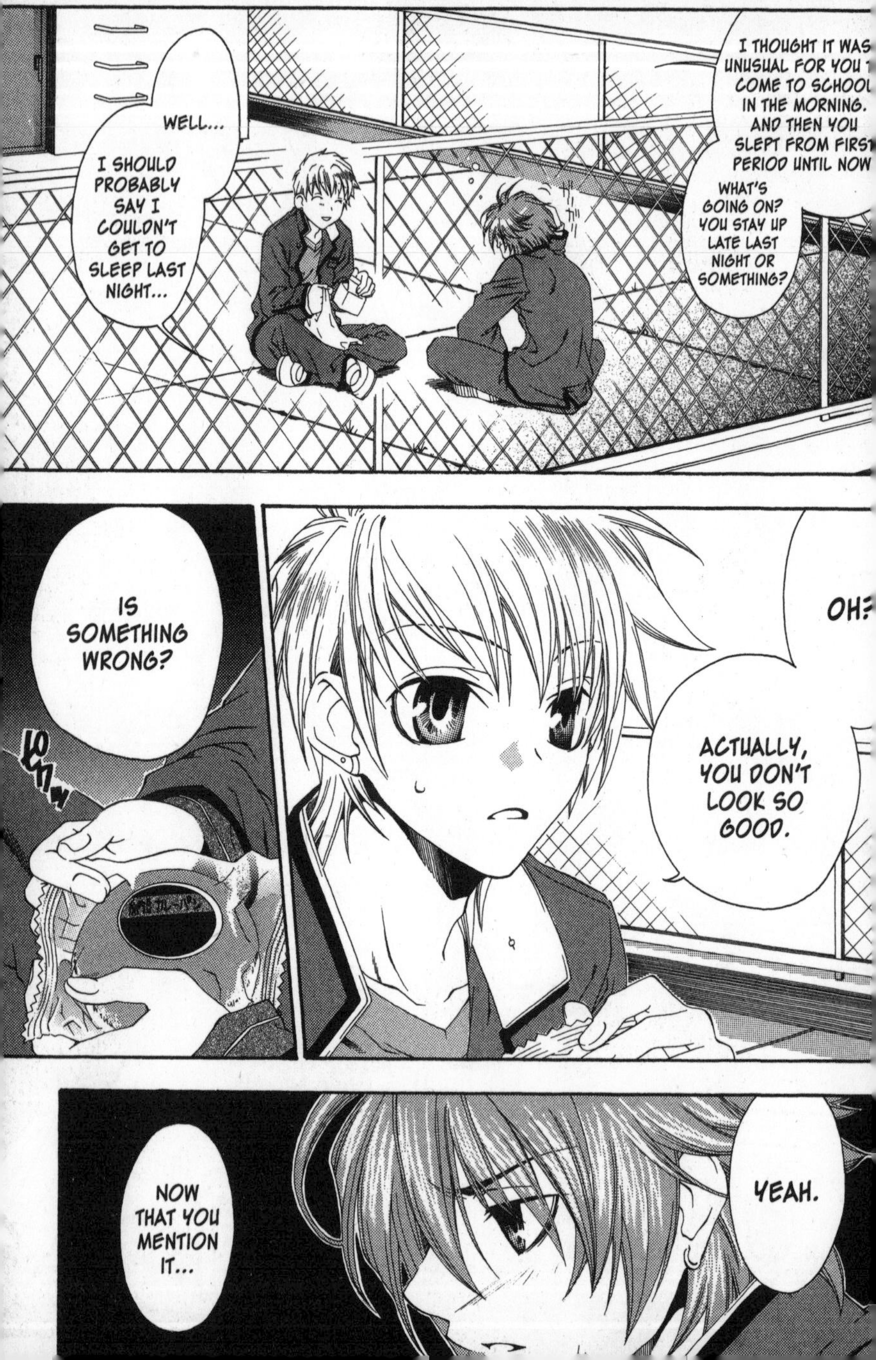
I THOUGHT IT WAS UNUSUAL FOR YOU T COME TO SCHOOL IN THE MORNING. AND THEN YOU SLEPT FROM FIRST PERIOD UNTIL NOW
WHAT'S GOING ON? YOU STAY UP LATE LAST NIGHT OR SOMETHING?
WELL...
I SHOULD PROBABLY SAY I COULDN'T GET TO SLEEP LAST NIGHT...
OH?
ACTUALLY, YOU DON'T LOOK SO GOOD.
IS SOMETHING WRONG?
YEAH.
NOW THAT YOU MENTION IT...

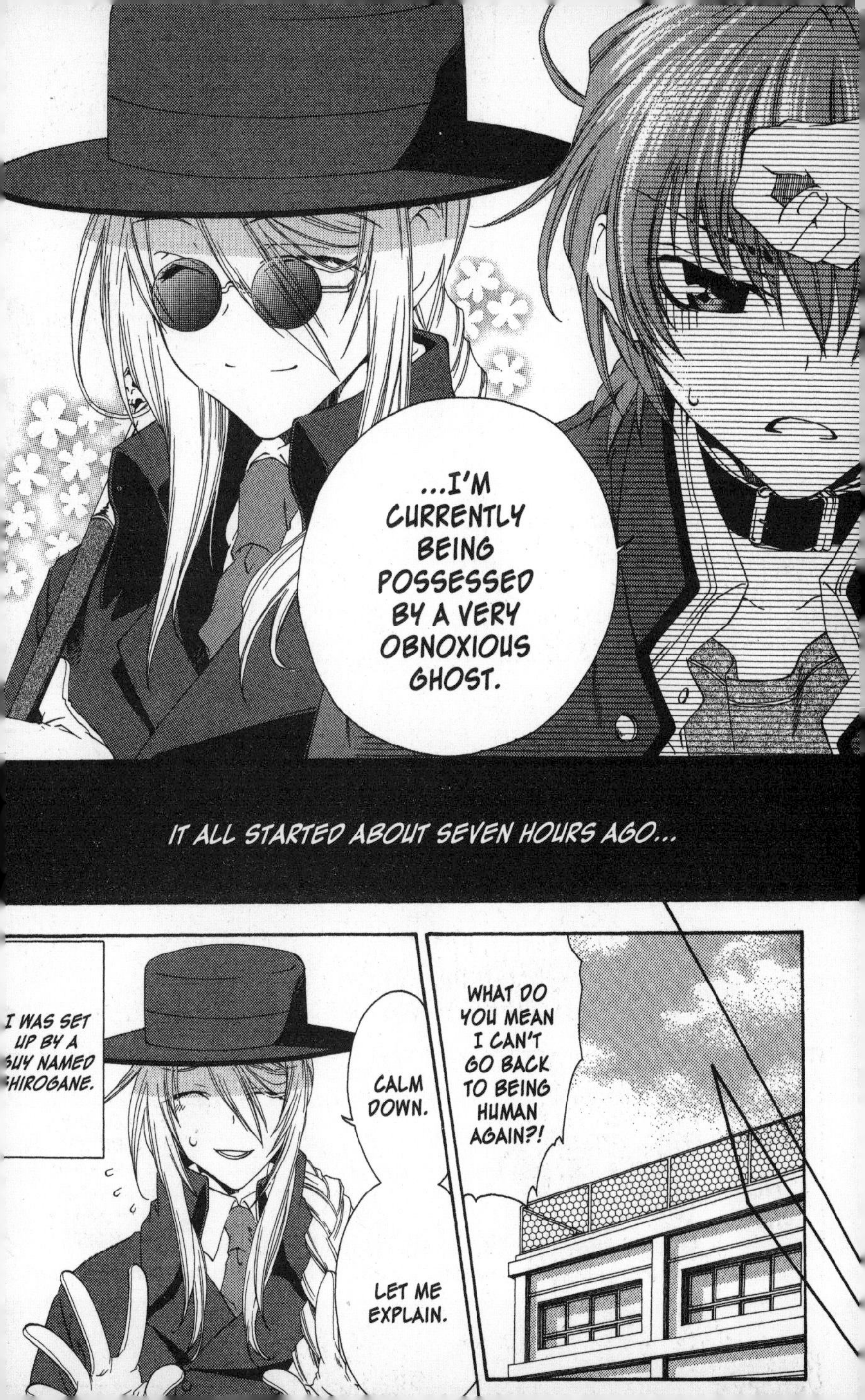
...I'M CURRENTLY BEING POSSESSED BY A VERY OBNOXIOUS GHOST.
IT ALL STARTED ABOUT SEVEN HOURS AGO...
WHAT DO YOU MEAN I CAN'T GO BACK TO BEING HUMAN AGAIN?!
I WAS SET UP BY A GUY NAMED SHIROGANE.
CALM DOWN.
LET ME EXPLAIN.

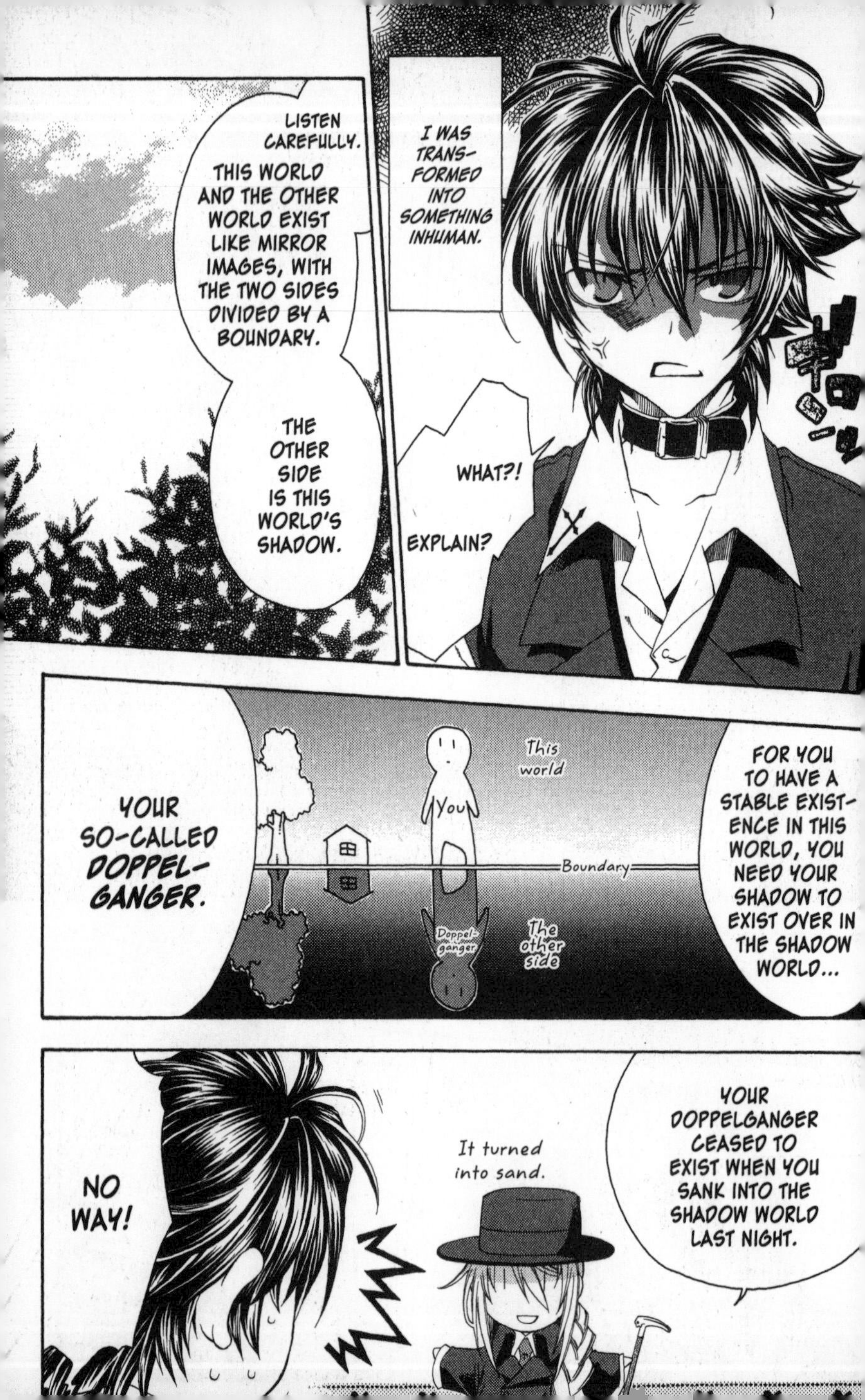
I WAS TRANSFORMED INTO SOMETHING INHUMAN.
WHAT?!
EXPLAIN?
LISTEN CAREFULLY.
THIS WORLD AND THE OTHER WORLD EXIST LIKE MIRROR IMAGES, WITH THE TWO SIDES DIVIDED BY A BOUNDARY.
THE OTHER SIDE IS THIS WORLD'S SHADOW.
FOR YOU TO HAVE A STABLE EXISTENCE IN THIS WORLD, YOU NEED YOUR SHADOW TO EXIST OVER IN THE SHADOW WORLD...
This world
You
Boundary
Doppelganger
The other side
YOUR SO-CALLED DOPPELGANGER.
YOUR DOPPELGANGER CEASED TO EXIST WHEN YOU SANK INTO THE SHADOW WORLD LAST NIGHT.
It turned into sand.
NO WAY!

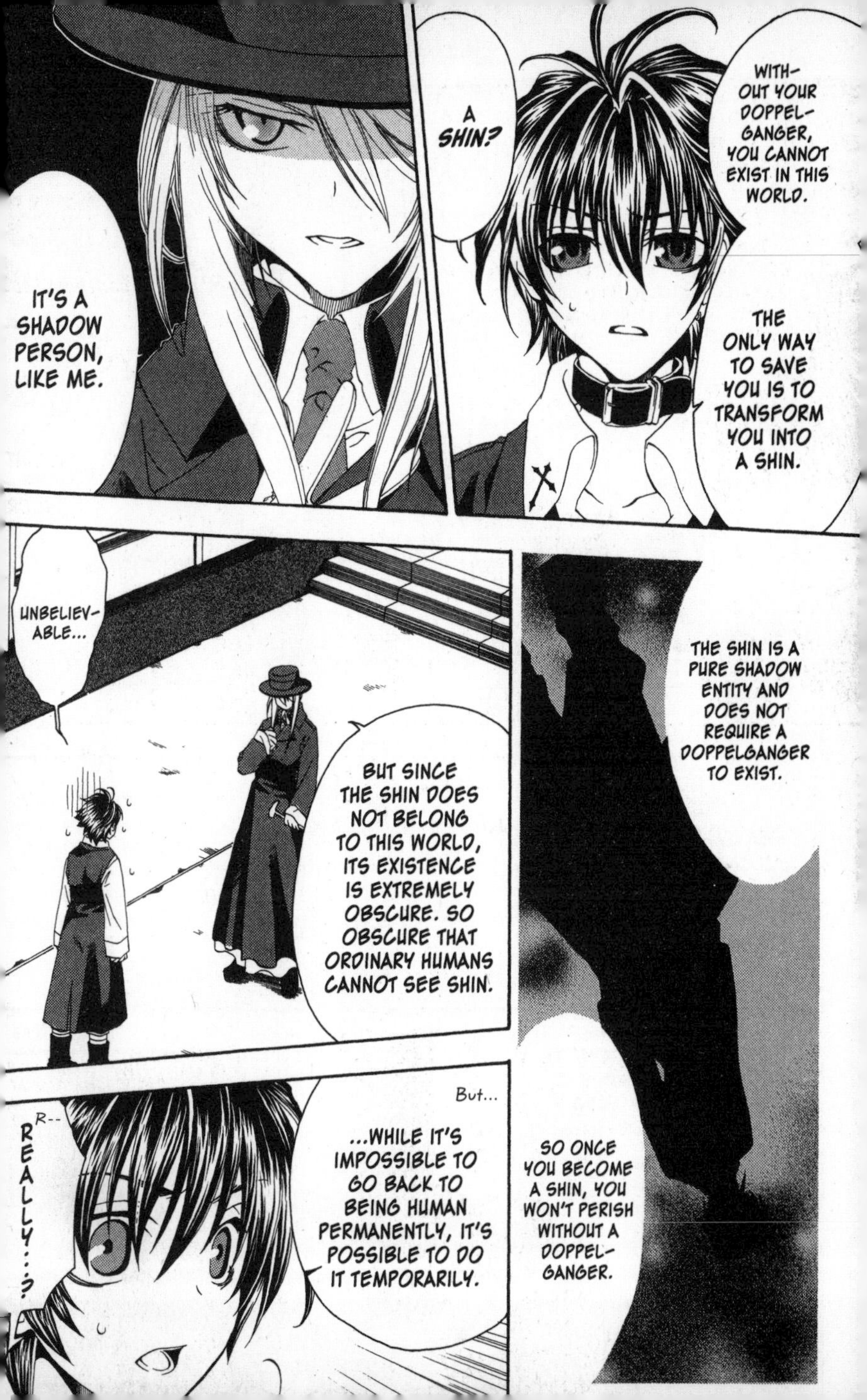
WITH-OUT YOUR DOPPEL-GANGER, YOU CANNOT EXIST IN THIS WORLD.
THE ONLY WAY TO SAVE YOU IS TO TRANSFORM YOU INTO A SHIN.
A SHIN?
IT'S A SHADOW PERSON, LIKE ME.
THE SHIN IS A PURE SHADOW ENTITY AND DOES NOT REQUIRE A DOPPELGANGER TO EXIST.
SO ONCE YOU BECOME A SHIN, YOU WON'T PERISH WITHOUT A DOPPEL-GANGER.
BUT SINCE THE SHIN DOES NOT BELONG TO THIS WORLD, ITS EXISTENCE IS EXTREMELY OBSCURE. SO OBSCURE THAT ORDINARY HUMANS CANNOT SEE SHIN.
UNBELIEV-ABLE...
But...
...WHILE IT'S IMPOSSIBLE TO GO BACK TO BEING HUMAN PERMANENTLY, IT'S POSSIBLE TO DO IT TEMPORARILY.
R-- REALLY...?

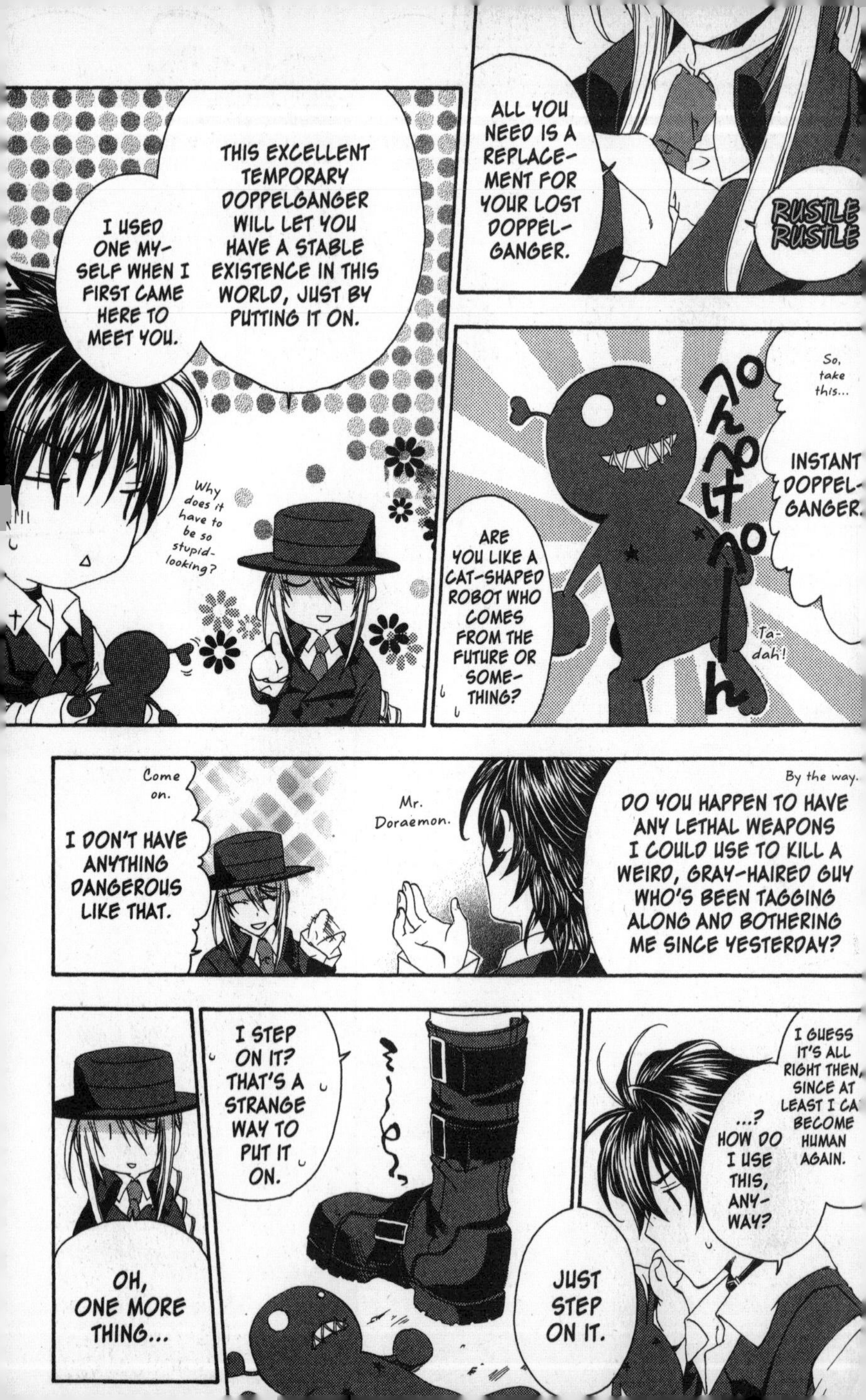
RUSTLE RUSTLE
ALL YOU NEED IS A REPLACEMENT FOR YOUR LOST DOPPELGANGER.
So, take this...
INSTANT DOPPELGANGER.
Ta-dah!
ARE YOU LIKE A CAT-SHAPED ROBOT WHO COMES FROM THE FUTURE OR SOMETHING?
THIS EXCELLENT TEMPORARY DOPPELGANGER WILL LET YOU HAVE A STABLE EXISTENCE IN THIS WORLD, JUST BY PUTTING IT ON.
I USED ONE MYSELF WHEN I FIRST CAME HERE TO MEET YOU.
Why does it have to be so stupid-looking?
By the way.
DO YOU HAPPEN TO HAVE ANY LETHAL WEAPONS I COULD USE TO KILL A WEIRD, GRAY-HAIRED GUY WHO'S BEEN TAGGING ALONG AND BOTHERING ME SINCE YESTERDAY?
Mr. Doraemon.
Come on.
I DON'T HAVE ANYTHING DANGEROUS LIKE THAT.
I GUESS IT'S ALL RIGHT THEN, SINCE AT LEAST I CA BECOME HUMAN AGAIN.
...? HOW DO I USE THIS, ANYWAY?
JUST STEP ON IT.
I STEP ON IT? THAT'S A STRANGE WAY TO PUT IT ON.
OH, ONE MORE THING...

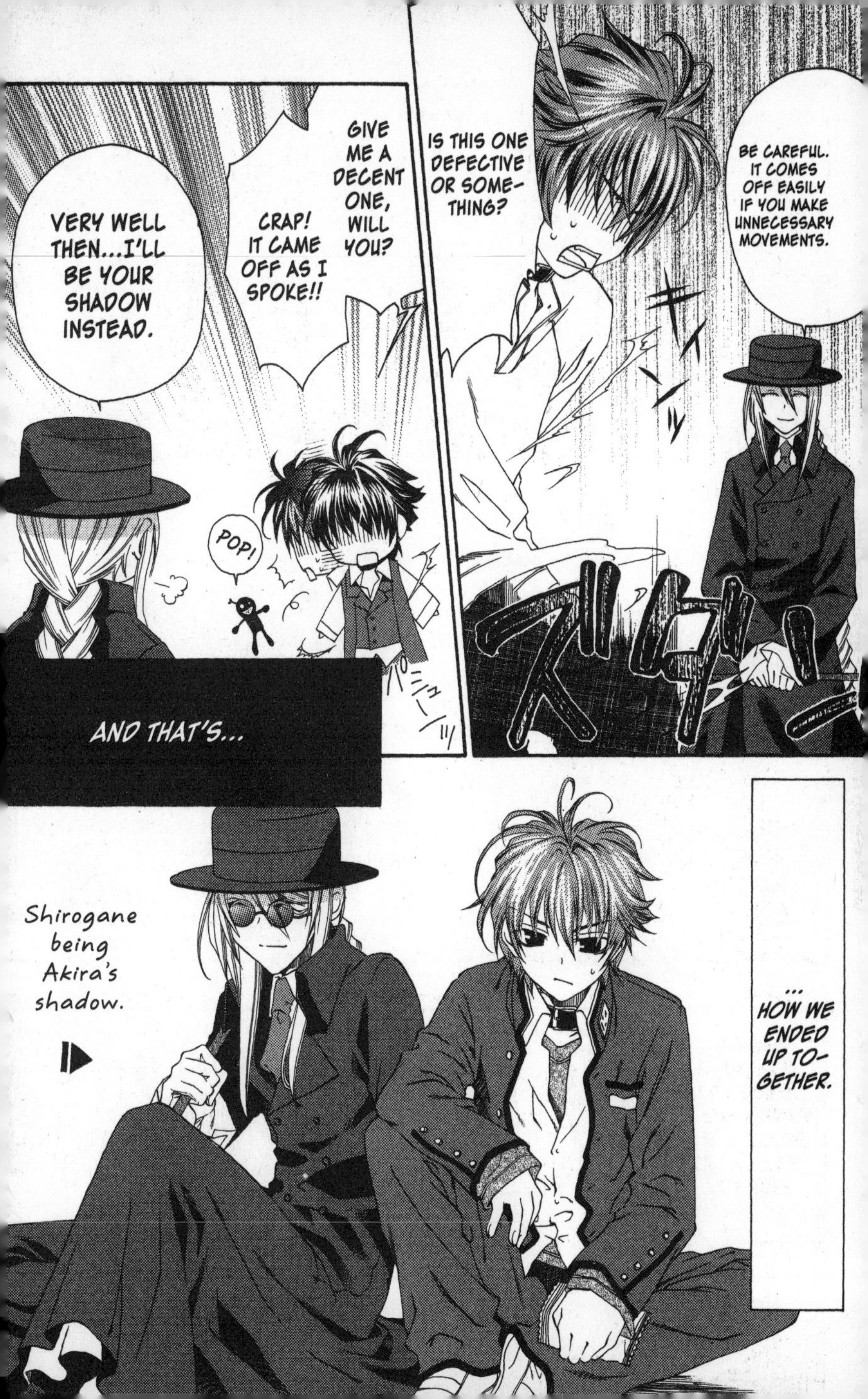
BE CAREFUL. IT COMES OFF EASILY IF YOU MAKE UNNECESSARY MOVEMENTS.
IS THIS ONE DEFECTIVE OR SOME-THING?
GIVE ME A DECENT ONE, WILL YOU?
CRAP! IT CAME OFF AS I SPOKE!!
POP!
VERY WELL THEN...I'LL BE YOUR SHADOW INSTEAD.
AND THAT'S...
...HOW WE ENDED UP TO-GETHER.
Shirogane being Akira's shadow.

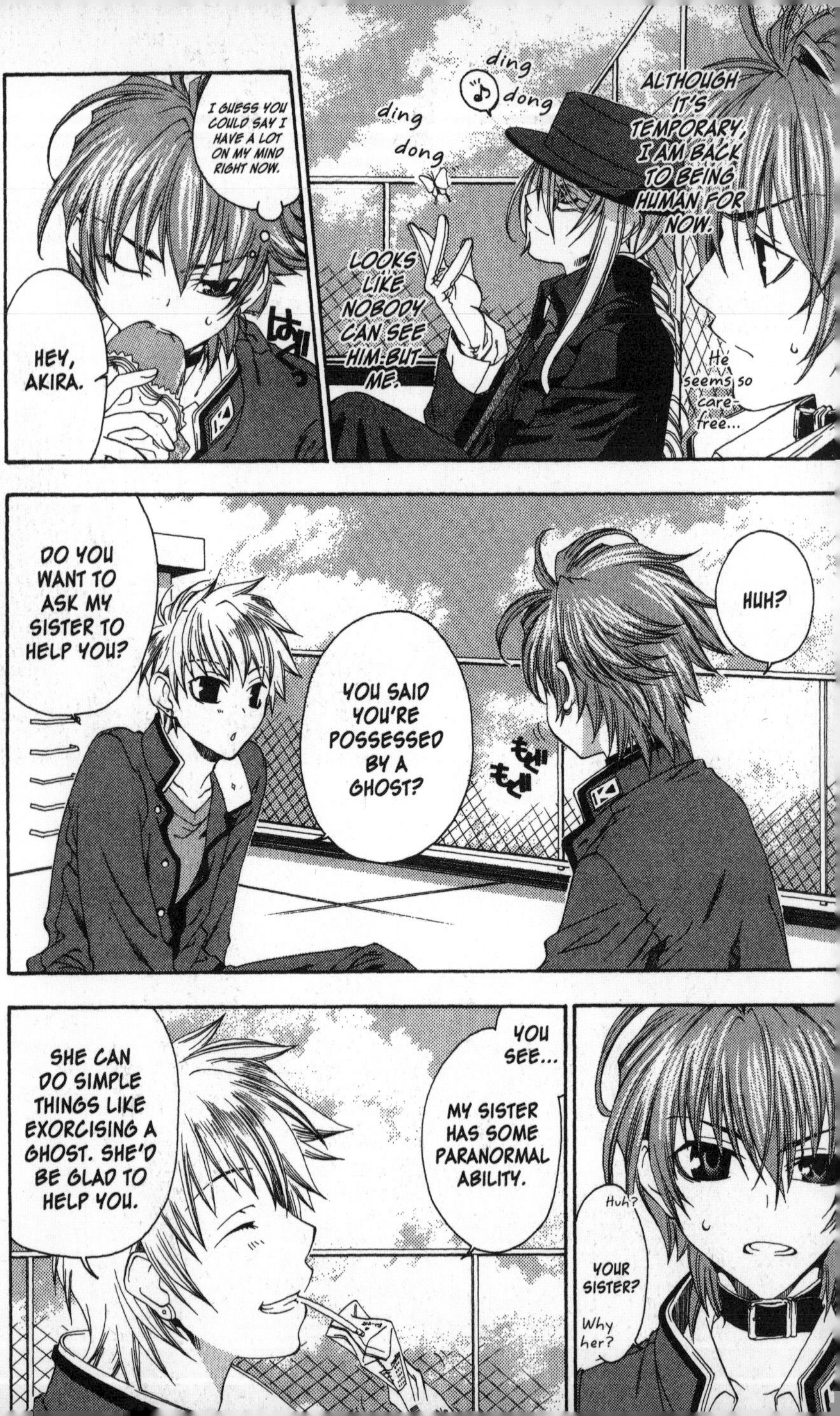
ALTHOUGH IT'S TEMPORARY, I AM BACK TO BEING HUMAN FOR NOW.
He seems so carefree...
ding dong
ding dong
LOOKS LIKE NOBODY CAN SEE HIM BUT ME.
I GUESS YOU COULD SAY I HAVE A LOT ON MY MIND RIGHT NOW.
はぐっ
HEY, AKIRA.
HUH?
もぐもぐ
YOU SAID YOU'RE POSSESSED BY A GHOST?
DO YOU WANT TO ASK MY SISTER TO HELP YOU?
Huh?
YOUR SISTER?
Why her?
YOU SEE...
MY SISTER HAS SOME PARANORMAL ABILITY.
SHE CAN DO SIMPLE THINGS LIKE EXORCISING A GHOST. SHE'D BE GLAD TO HELP YOU.

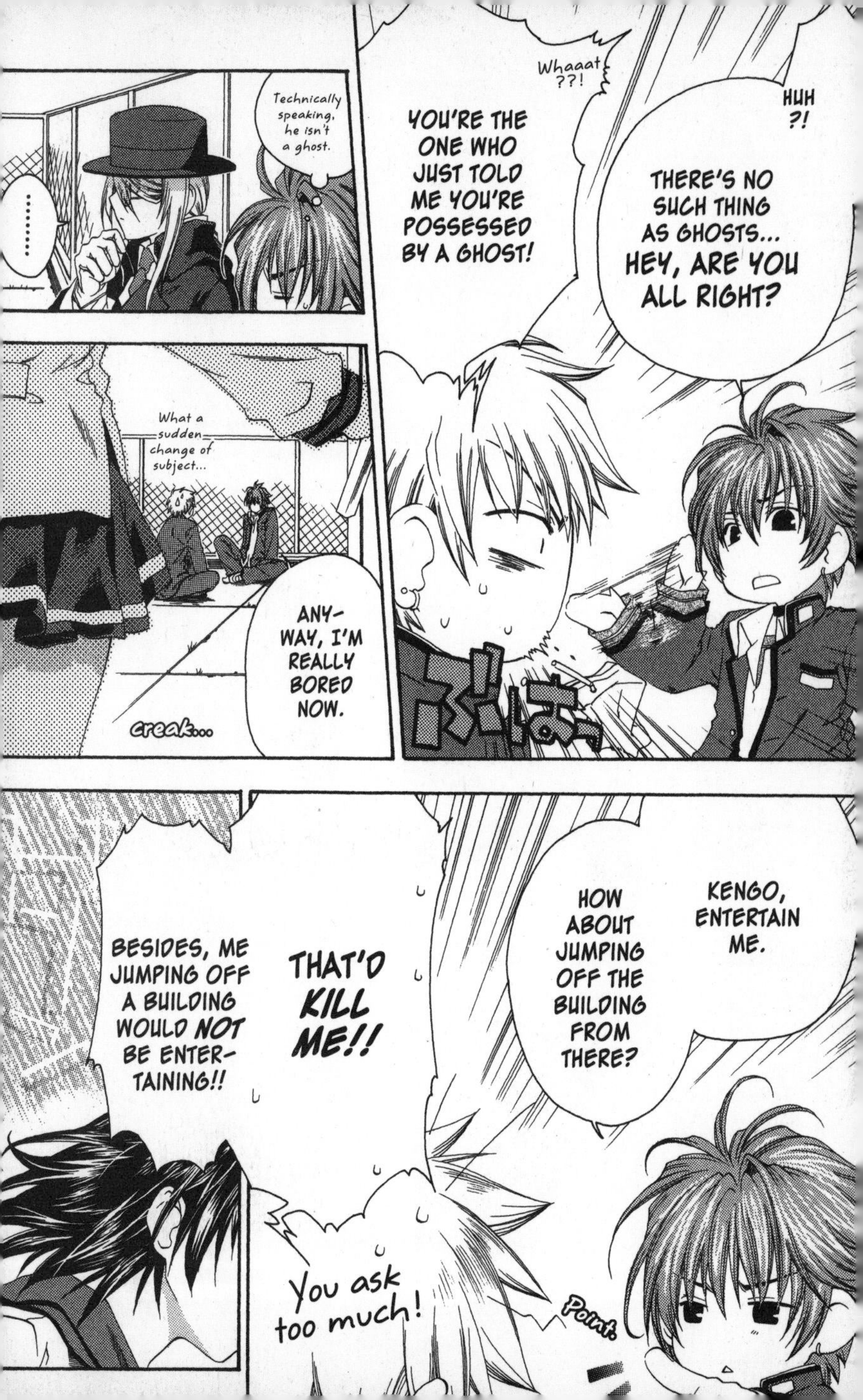
HUH ?!
Whaaat ??!
THERE'S NO SUCH THING AS GHOSTS... HEY, ARE YOU ALL RIGHT?
YOU'RE THE ONE WHO JUST TOLD ME YOU'RE POSSESSED BY A GHOST!
Technically speaking, he isn't a ghost.
......
ANY-WAY, I'M REALLY BORED NOW.
What a sudden change of subject...
creak...
KENGO, ENTERTAIN ME.
HOW ABOUT JUMPING OFF THE BUILDING FROM THERE?
THAT'D KILL ME!!
BESIDES, ME JUMPING OFF A BUILDING WOULD NOT BE ENTER-TAINING!!
Point.
You ask too much!

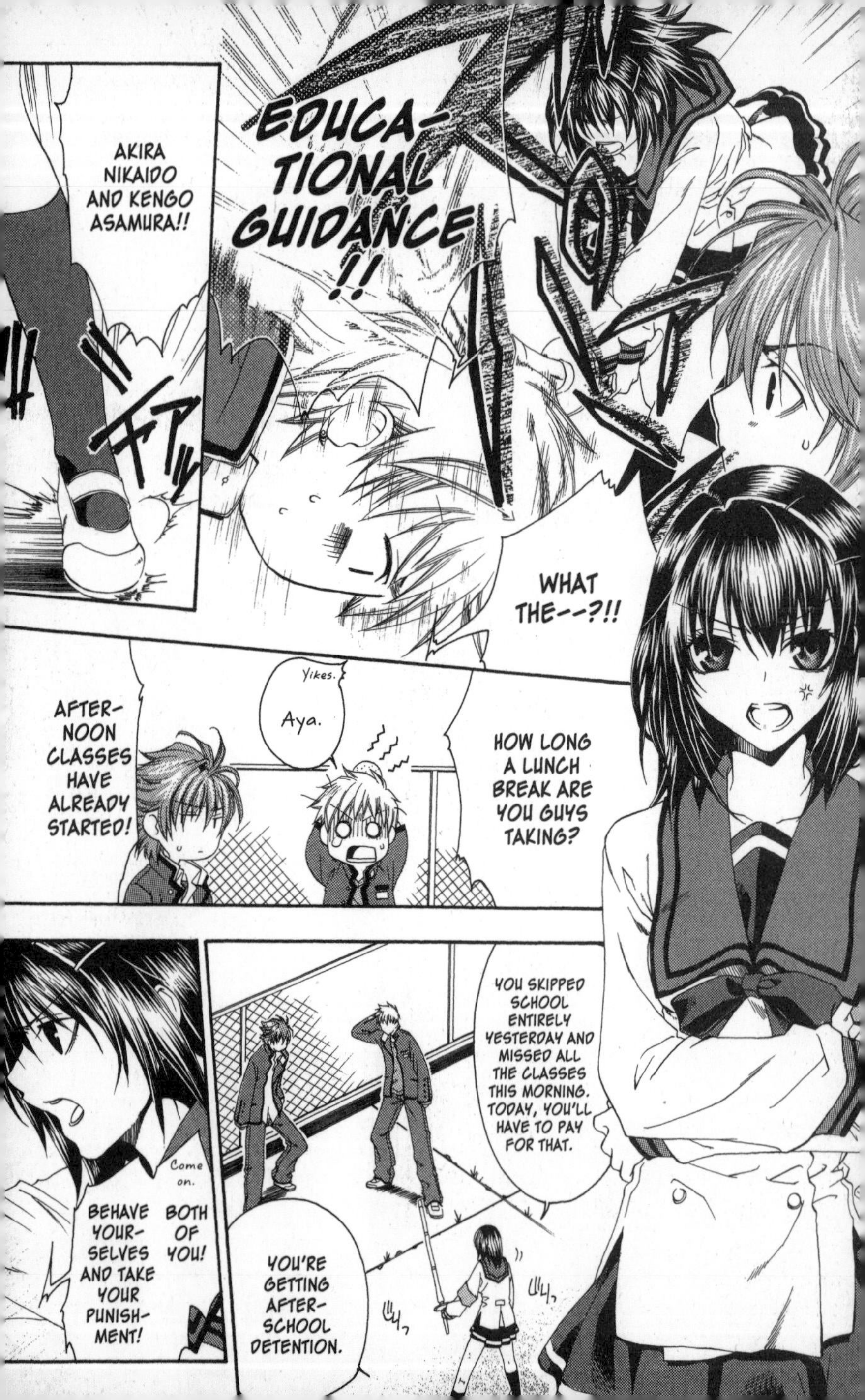
EDUCATIONAL GUIDANCE!!
WHAT THE--?!!
AKIRA NIKAIDO AND KENGO ASAMURA!!
HOW LONG A LUNCH BREAK ARE YOU GUYS TAKING?
YOU SKIPPED SCHOOL ENTIRELY YESTERDAY AND MISSED ALL THE CLASSES THIS MORNING. TODAY, YOU'LL HAVE TO PAY FOR THAT.
Yikes.
Aya.
AFTERNOON CLASSES HAVE ALREADY STARTED!
YOU'RE GETTING AFTER-SCHOOL DETENTION.
Come on.
BOTH OF YOU!
BEHAVE YOURSELVES AND TAKE YOUR PUNISHMENT!

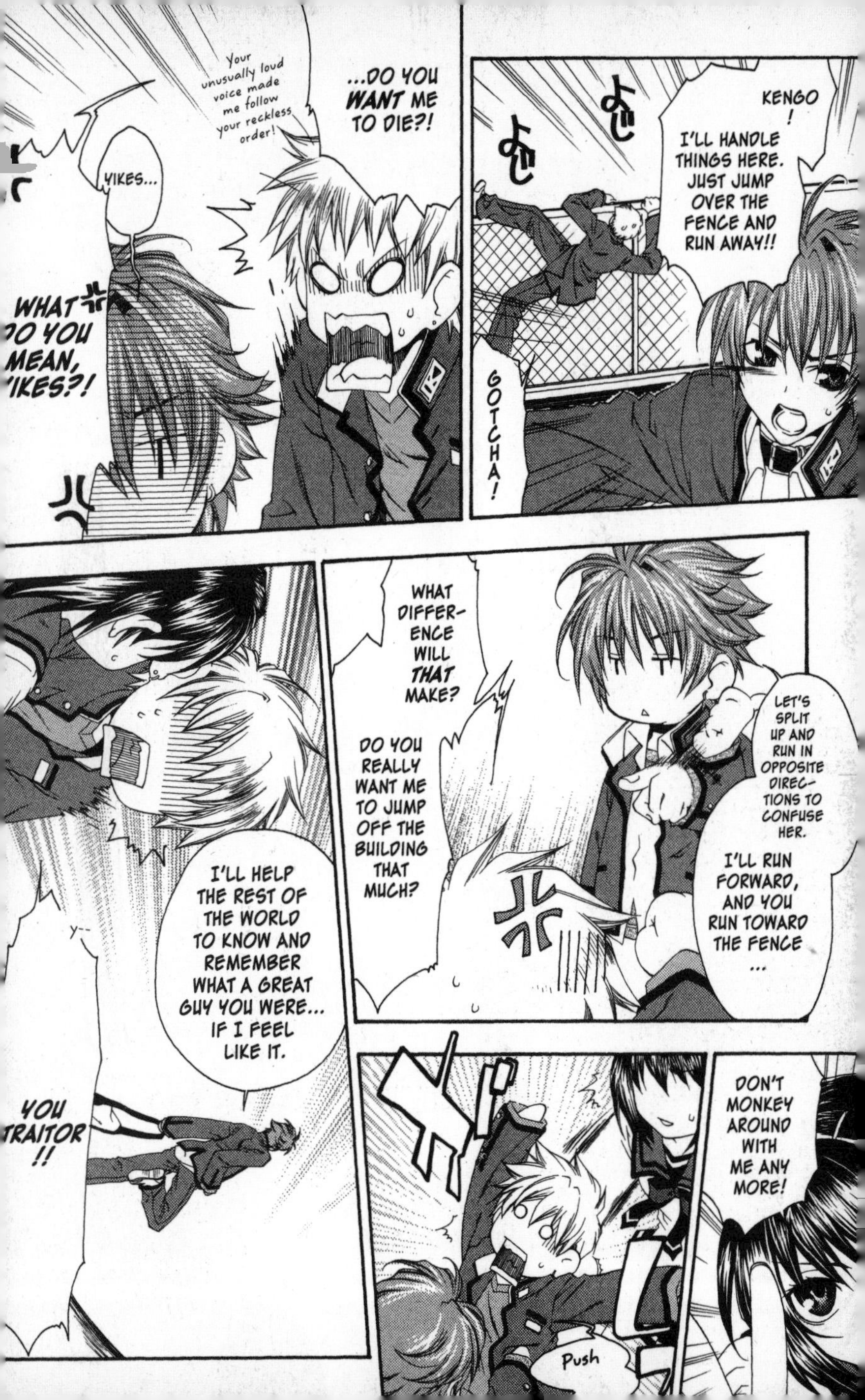
よじ よじ
KENGO!
I'LL HANDLE THINGS HERE. JUST JUMP OVER THE FENCE AND RUN AWAY!!
GOTCHA!
...DO YOU *WANT* ME TO DIE?!
Your unusually loud voice made me follow your reckless order!
YIKES...
WHAT DO YOU MEAN, YIKES?!
LET'S SPLIT UP AND RUN IN OPPOSITE DIRECTIONS TO CONFUSE HER.
I'LL RUN FORWARD, AND YOU RUN TOWARD THE FENCE...
WHAT DIFFERENCE WILL *THAT* MAKE?
DO YOU REALLY WANT ME TO JUMP OFF THE BUILDING THAT MUCH?
DON'T MONKEY AROUND WITH ME ANY MORE!
Push
I'LL HELP THE REST OF THE WORLD TO KNOW AND REMEMBER WHAT A GREAT GUY YOU WERE... IF I FEEL LIKE IT.
Y--
YOU TRAITOR!!

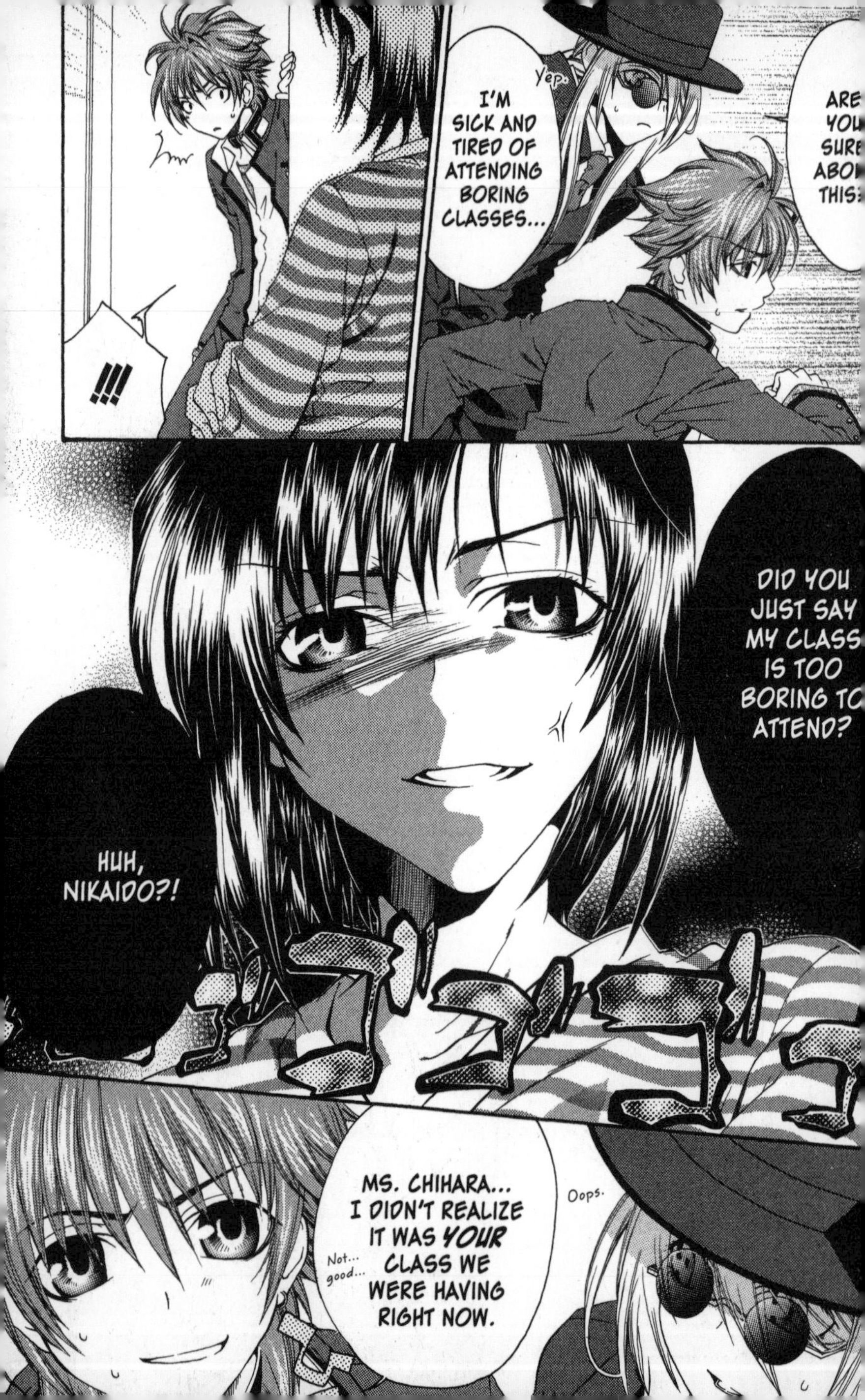
ARE YOU SURE ABO THIS
Yep.
I'M SICK AND TIRED OF ATTENDING BORING CLASSES...
!!!
DID YOU JUST SAY MY CLASS IS TOO BORING TO ATTEND?
HUH, NIKAIDO?!
Oops.
MS. CHIHARA... I DIDN'T REALIZE IT WAS *YOUR* CLASS WE WERE HAVING RIGHT NOW.
Not... good...

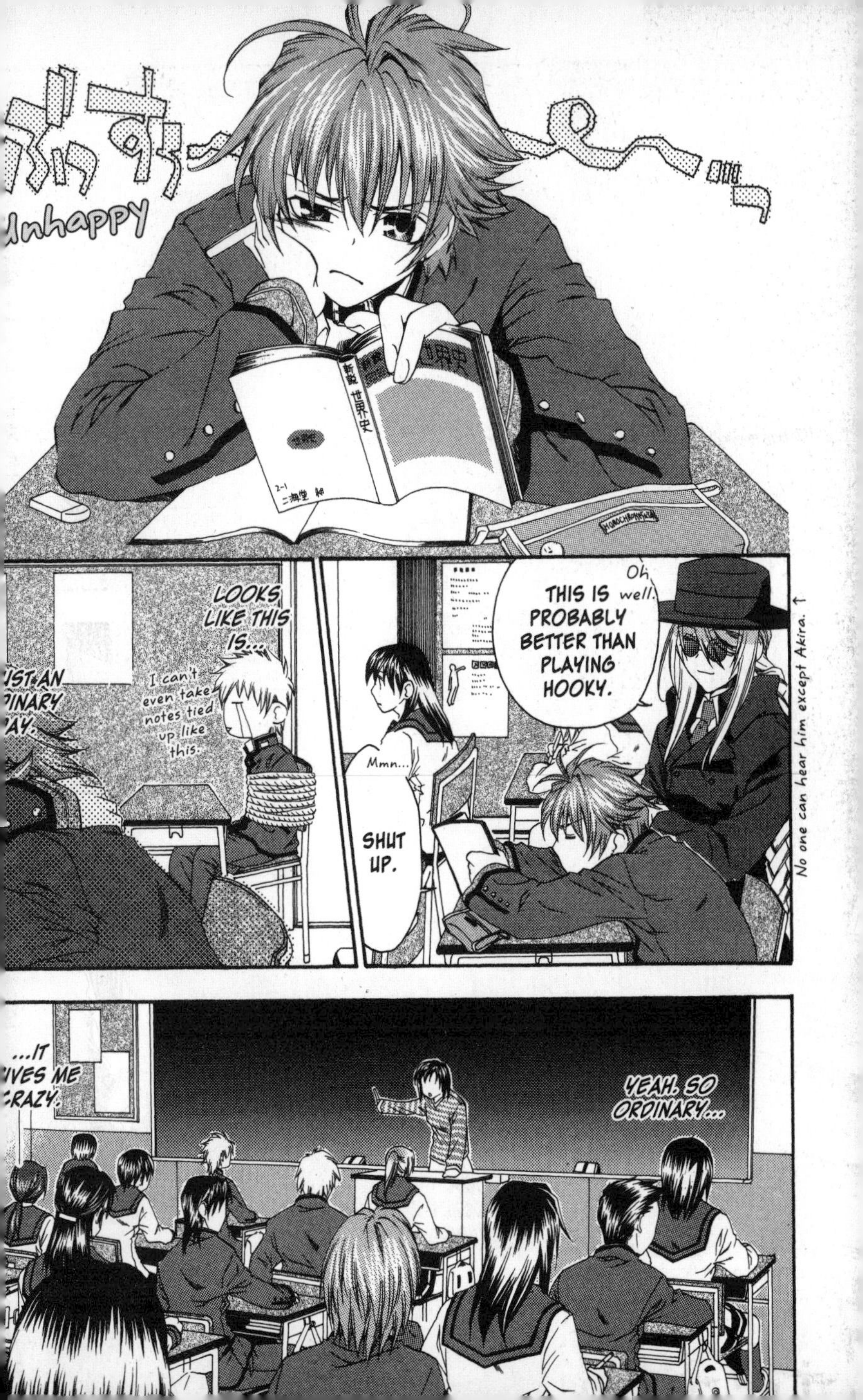
ぶっすぅ～～～っ
Unhappy
Oh well.
THIS IS PROBABLY BETTER THAN PLAYING HOOKY.
No one can hear him except Akira. ↑
Mmn...
SHUT UP.
LOOKS LIKE THIS IS...
UST AN DINARY AY.
I can't even take notes tied up like this.
YEAH. SO ORDINARY...
...IT RIVES ME RAZY.

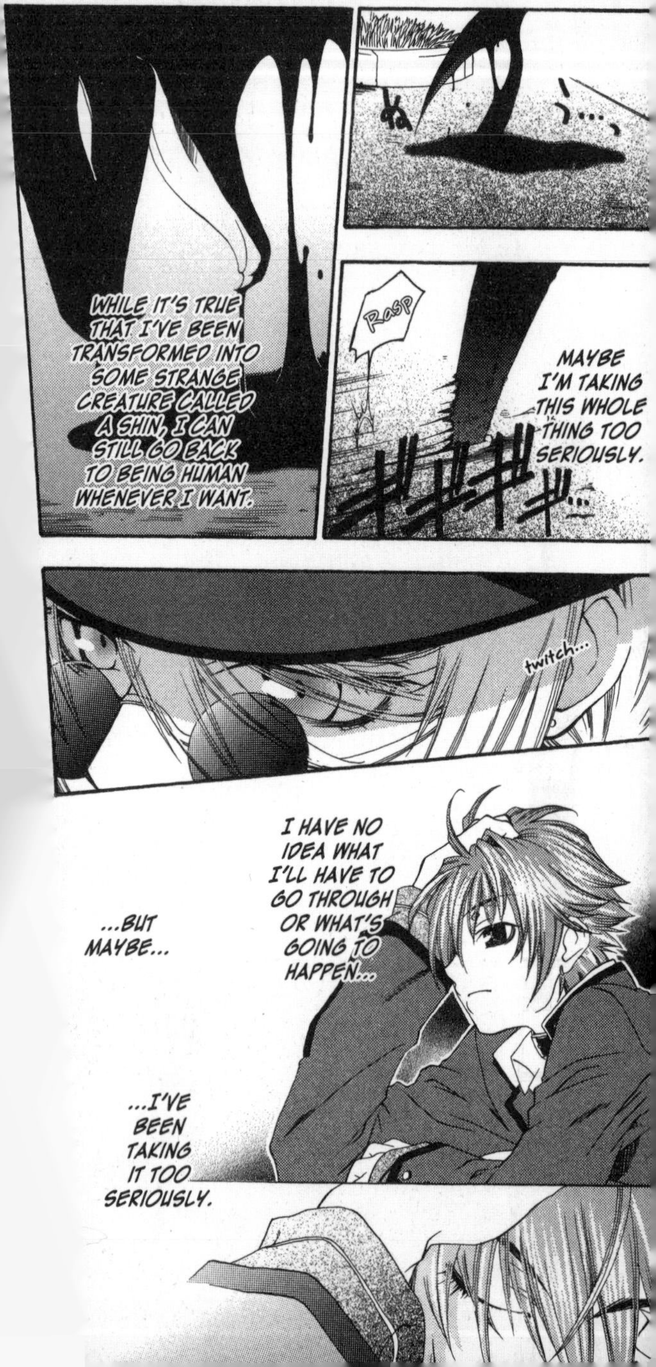
Rasp
MAYBE I'M TAKING THIS WHOLE THING TOO SERIOUSLY.
WHILE IT'S TRUE THAT I'VE BEEN TRANSFORMED INTO SOME STRANGE CREATURE CALLED A SHIN, I CAN STILL GO BACK TO BEING HUMAN WHENEVER I WANT.
twitch...
I HAVE NO IDEA WHAT I'LL HAVE TO GO THROUGH OR WHAT'S GOING TO HAPPEN...
...BUT MAYBE...
...I'VE BEEN TAKING IT TOO SERIOUSLY.

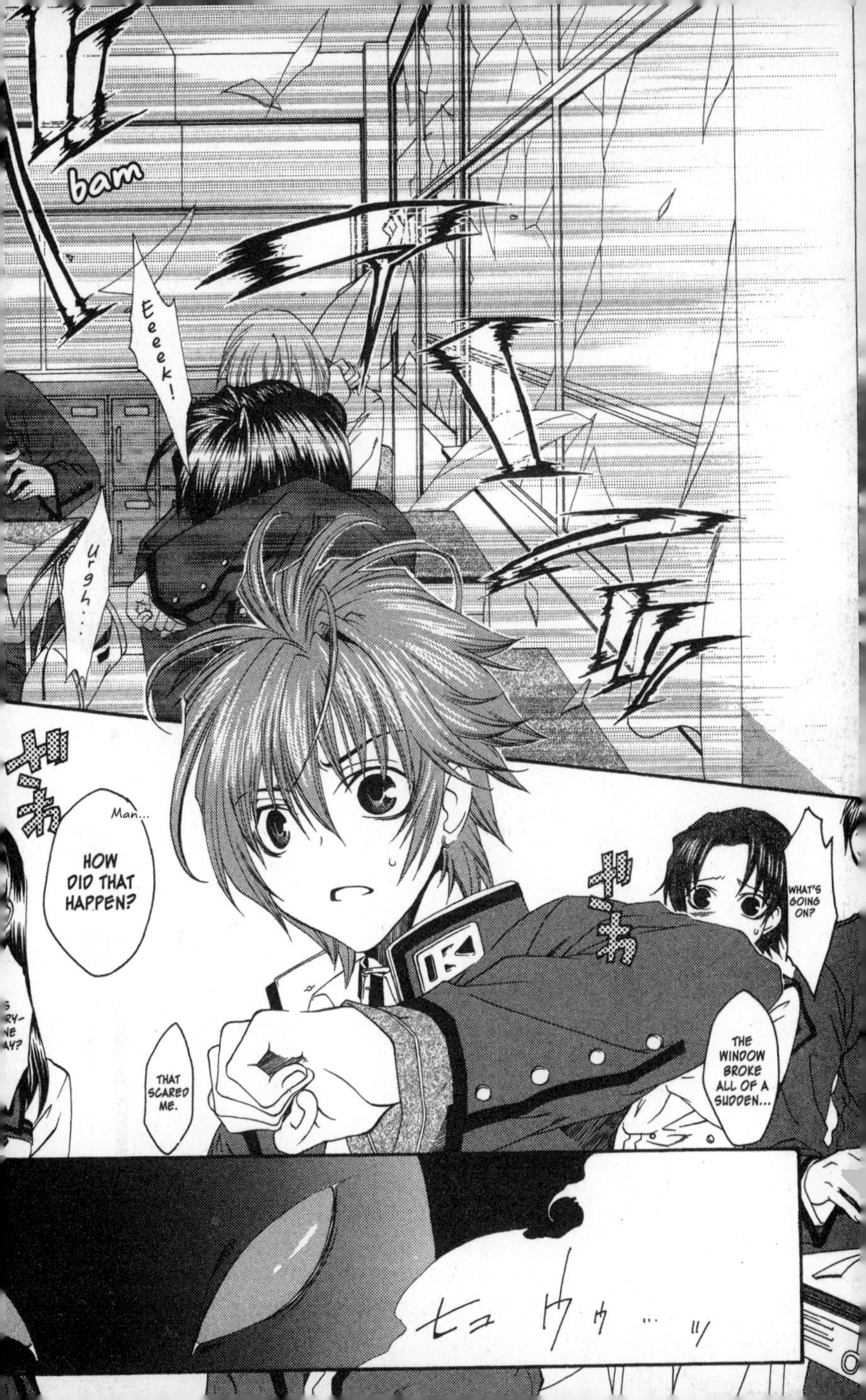
bam
Eeeek!
Urgh...
WHAT'S GOING ON?
THE WINDOW BROKE ALL OF A SUDDEN...
THAT SCARED ME.
Man...
HOW DID THAT HAPPEN?
ヒュウゥ…ッ

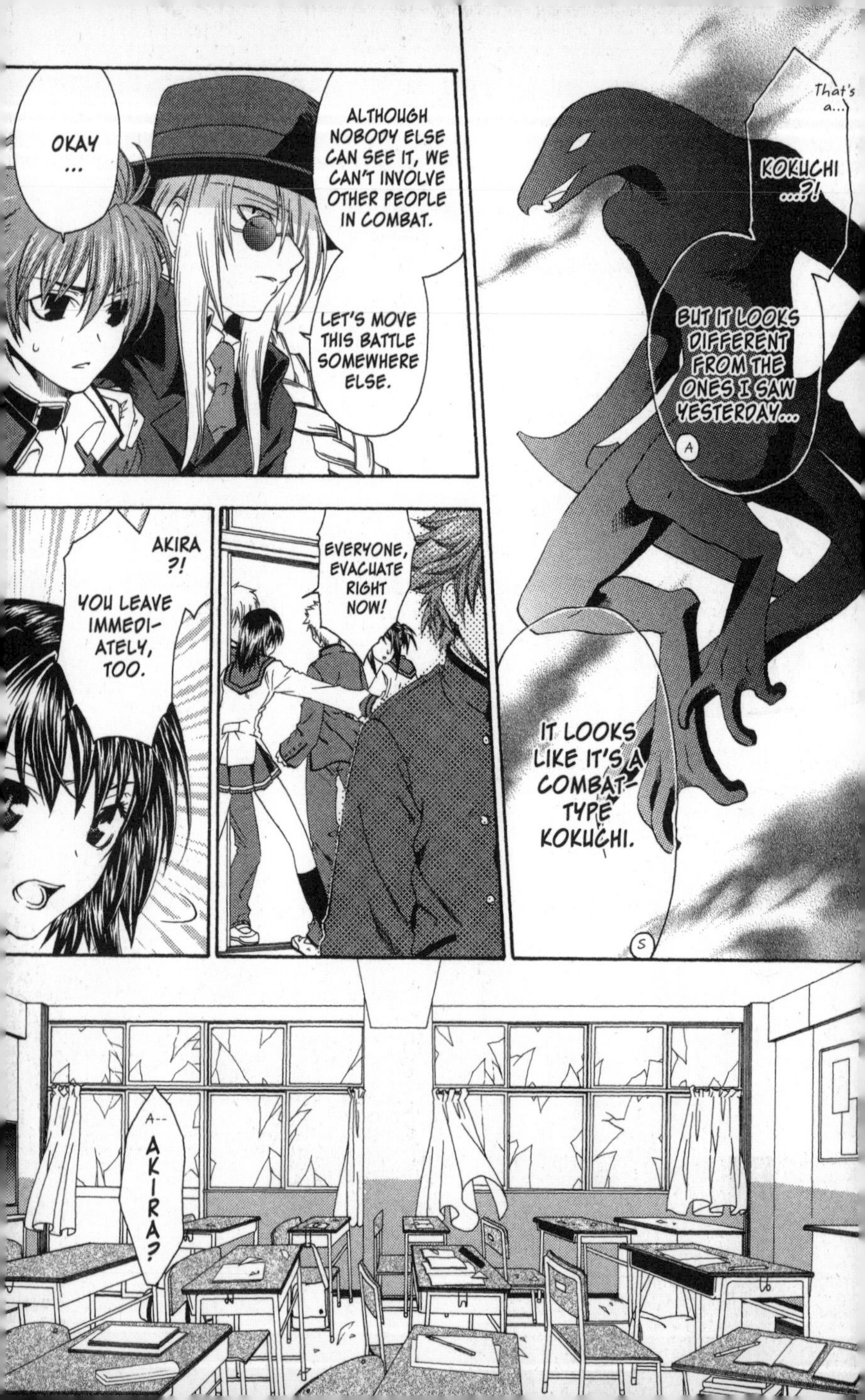

That's a...
KOKUCHI ...?!
BUT IT LOOKS DIFFERENT FROM THE ONES I SAW YESTERDAY...
IT LOOKS LIKE IT'S A COMBAT-TYPE KOKUCHI.
ALTHOUGH NOBODY ELSE CAN SEE IT, WE CAN'T INVOLVE OTHER PEOPLE IN COMBAT.
LET'S MOVE THIS BATTLE SOMEWHERE ELSE.
OKAY ...
EVERYONE, EVACUATE RIGHT NOW!
AKIRA ?!
YOU LEAVE IMMEDIATELY, TOO.
A-- AKIRA?

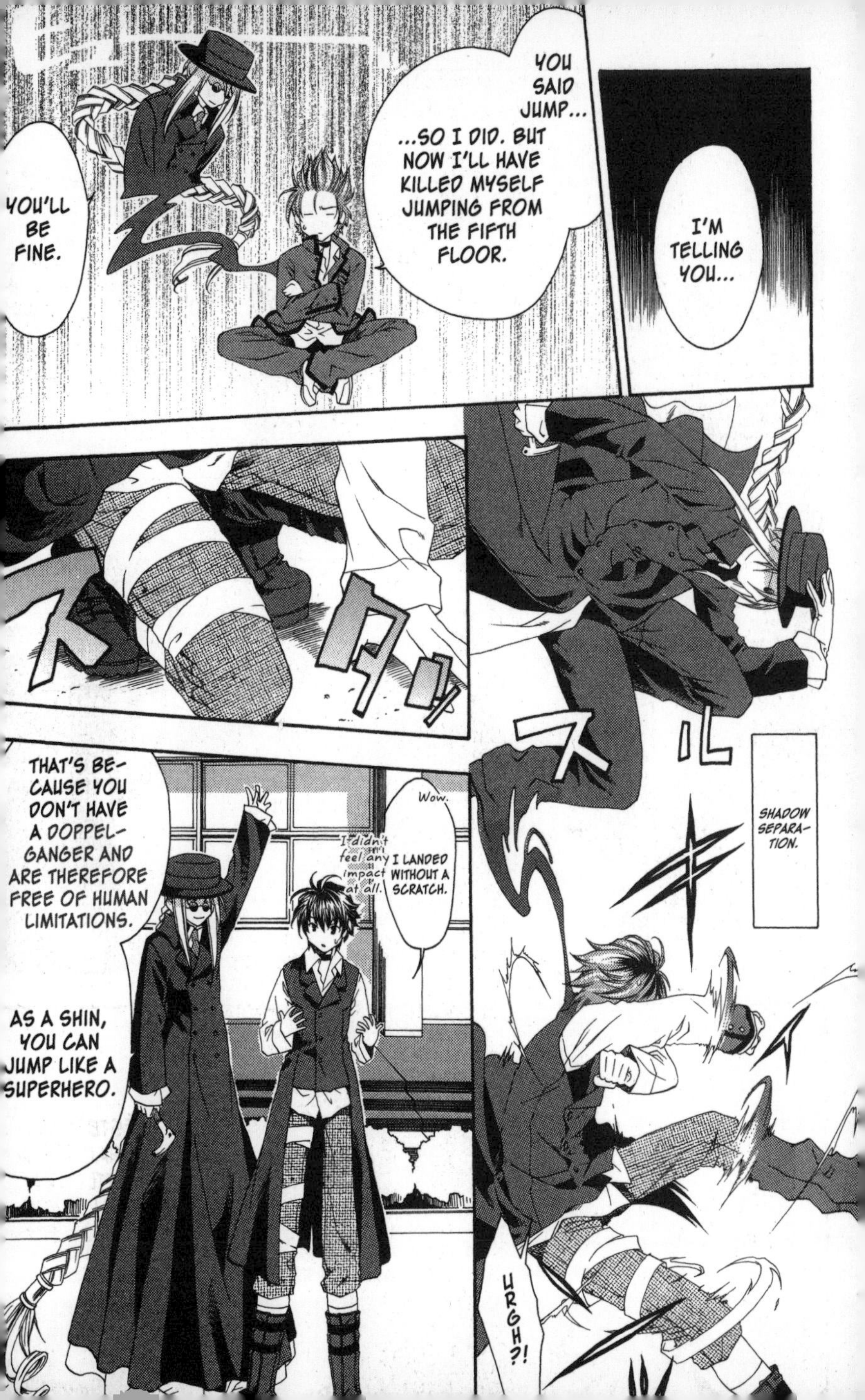
I'M TELLING YOU...
YOU SAID JUMP...
...SO I DID. BUT NOW I'LL HAVE KILLED MYSELF JUMPING FROM THE FIFTH FLOOR.
YOU'LL BE FINE.
SHADOW SEPARATION.
URGH?!
Wow.
I LANDED WITHOUT A SCRATCH.
I didn't feel any impact at all.
THAT'S BECAUSE YOU DON'T HAVE A DOPPELGANGER AND ARE THEREFORE FREE OF HUMAN LIMITATIONS.
AS A SHIN, YOU CAN JUMP LIKE A SUPERHERO.

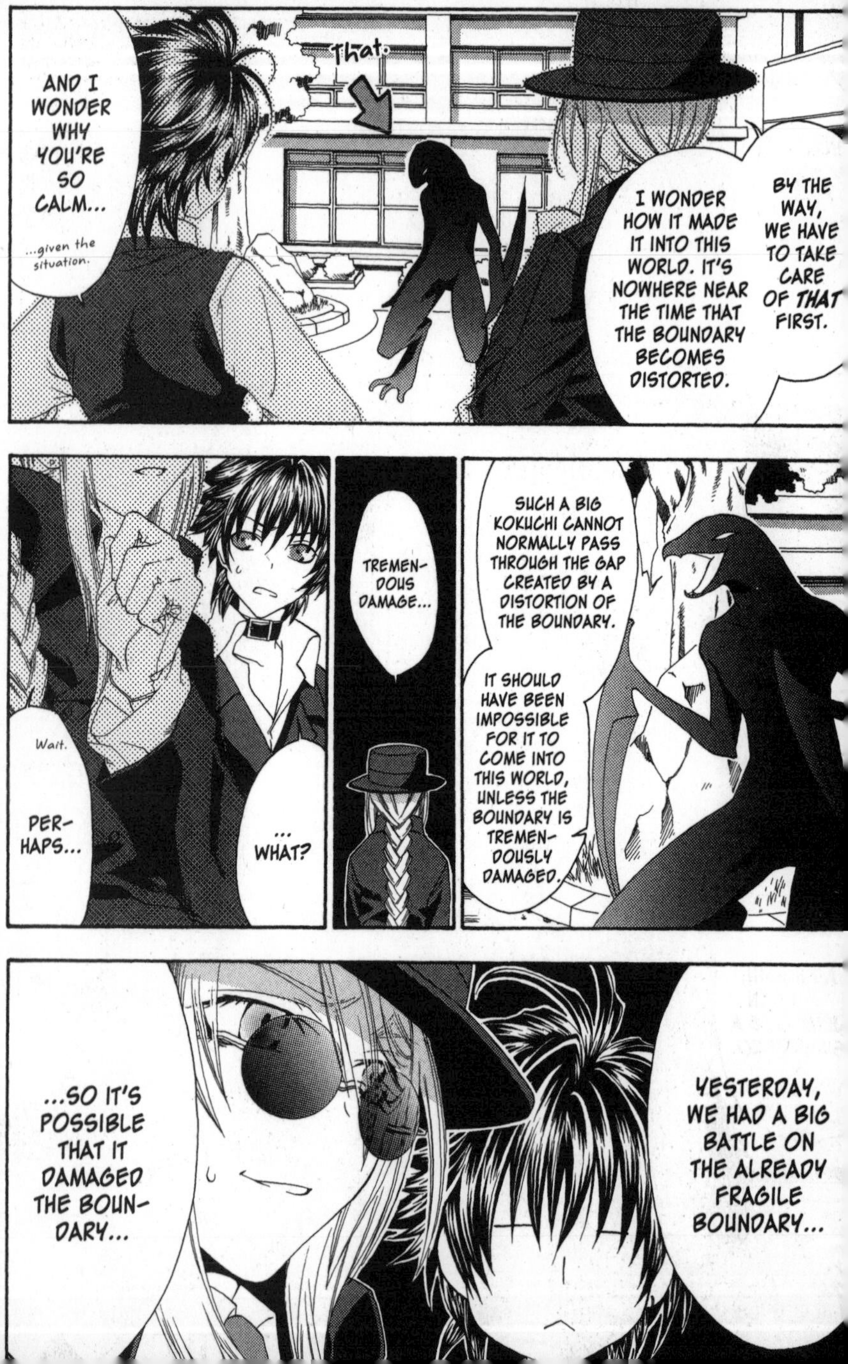
BY THE WAY, WE HAVE TO TAKE CARE OF *THAT* FIRST.
I WONDER HOW IT MADE IT INTO THIS WORLD. IT'S NOWHERE NEAR THE TIME THAT THE BOUNDARY BECOMES DISTORTED.
That.
AND I WONDER WHY YOU'RE SO CALM...
...given the situation.
SUCH A BIG KOKUCHI CANNOT NORMALLY PASS THROUGH THE GAP CREATED BY A DISTORTION OF THE BOUNDARY.
IT SHOULD HAVE BEEN IMPOSSIBLE FOR IT TO COME INTO THIS WORLD, UNLESS THE BOUNDARY IS TREMEN-DOUSLY DAMAGED.
TREMEN-DOUS DAMAGE...
... WHAT?
Wait.
PER-HAPS...
YESTERDAY, WE HAD A BIG BATTLE ON THE ALREADY FRAGILE BOUNDARY...
...SO IT'S POSSIBLE THAT IT DAMAGED THE BOUN-DARY...

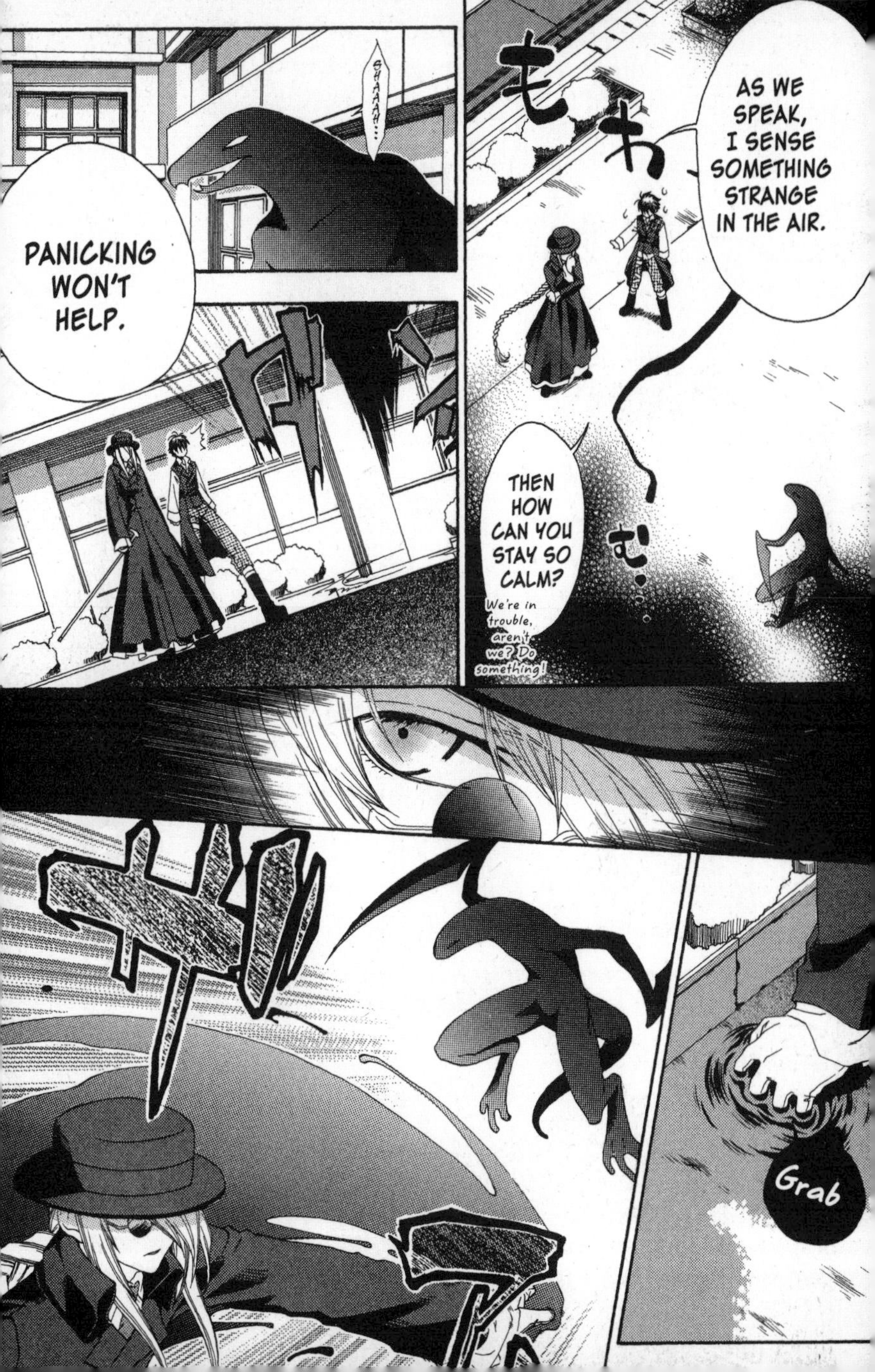
AS WE SPEAK, I SENSE SOMETHING STRANGE IN THE AIR.
THEN HOW CAN YOU STAY SO CALM?
We're in trouble, aren't we? Do something!
SHAAAH...
PANICKING WON'T HELP.
Grab

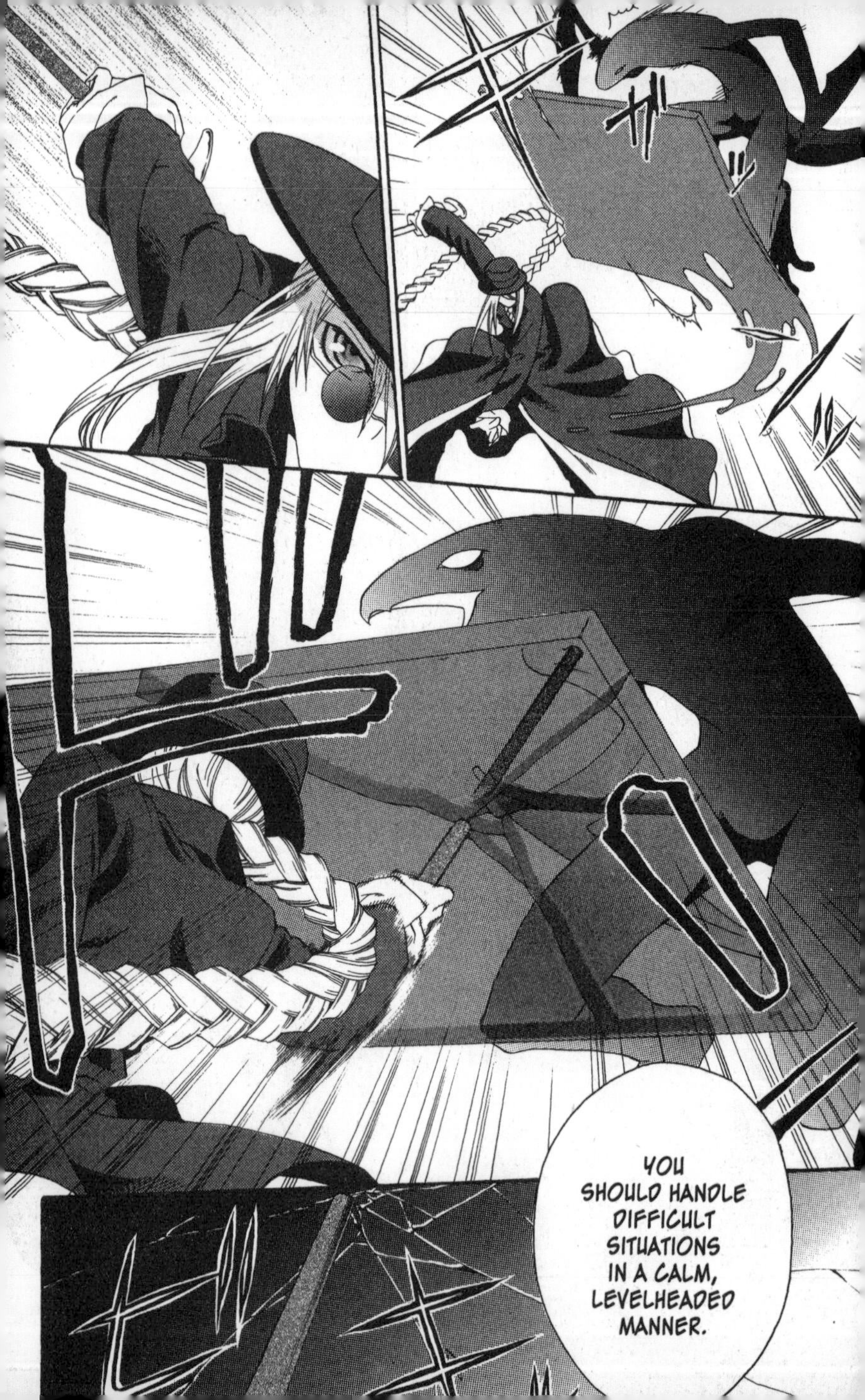
YOU SHOULD HANDLE DIFFICULT SITUATIONS IN A CALM, LEVELHEADED MANNER.

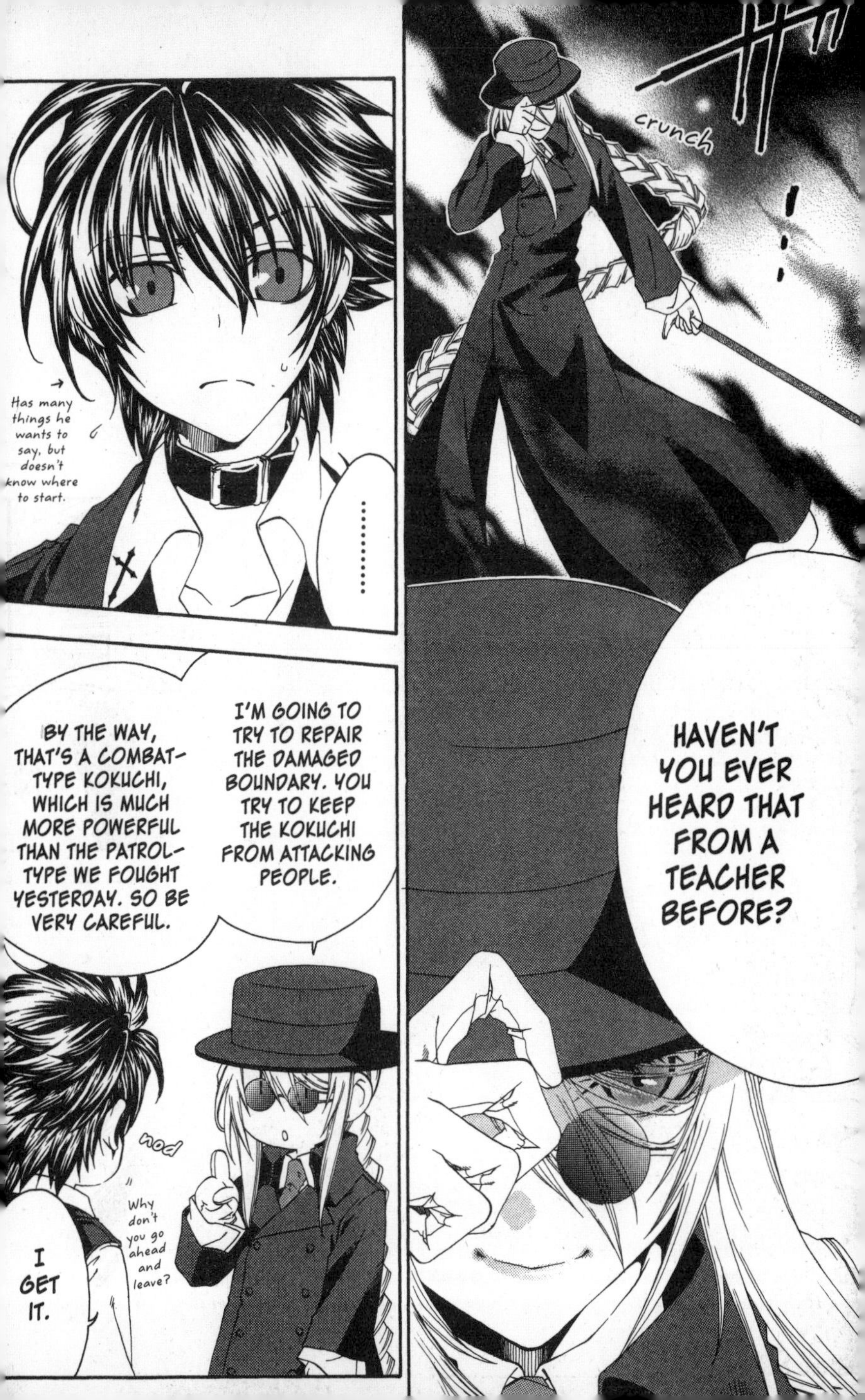
crunch
!
......
Has many things he wants to say, but doesn't know where to start.
HAVEN'T YOU EVER HEARD THAT FROM A TEACHER BEFORE?
I'M GOING TO TRY TO REPAIR THE DAMAGED BOUNDARY. YOU TRY TO KEEP THE KOKUCHI FROM ATTACKING PEOPLE.
BY THE WAY, THAT'S A COMBAT-TYPE KOKUCHI, WHICH IS MUCH MORE POWERFUL THAN THE PATROL-TYPE WE FOUGHT YESTERDAY. SO BE VERY CAREFUL.
nod
Why don't you go ahead and leave?
I GET IT.

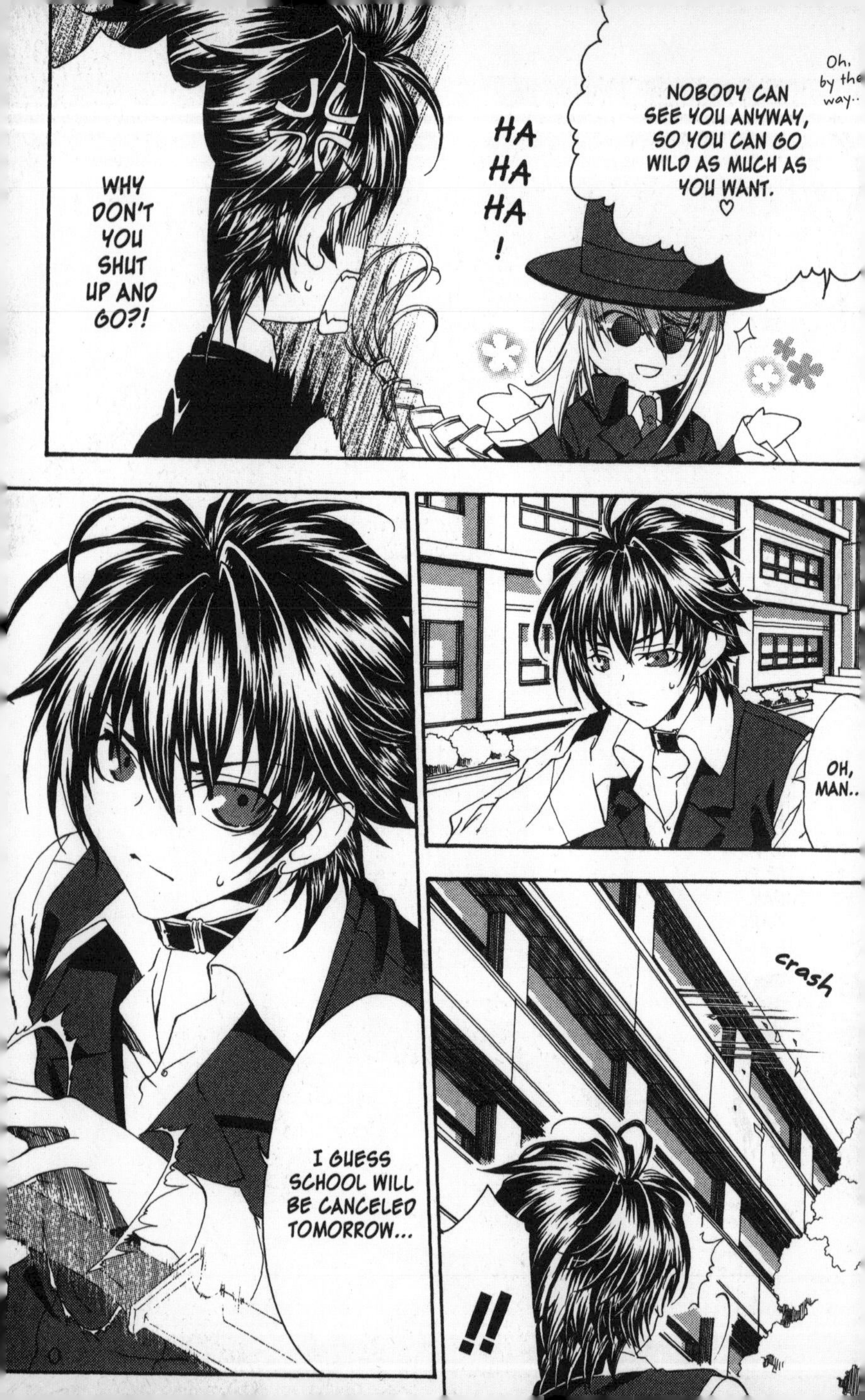

Oh, by the way..
NOBODY CAN SEE YOU ANYWAY, SO YOU CAN GO WILD AS MUCH AS YOU WANT. ♡
HA HA HA!
WHY DON'T YOU SHUT UP AND GO?!
OH, MAN..
crash
!!
I GUESS SCHOOL WILL BE CANCELED TOMORROW...

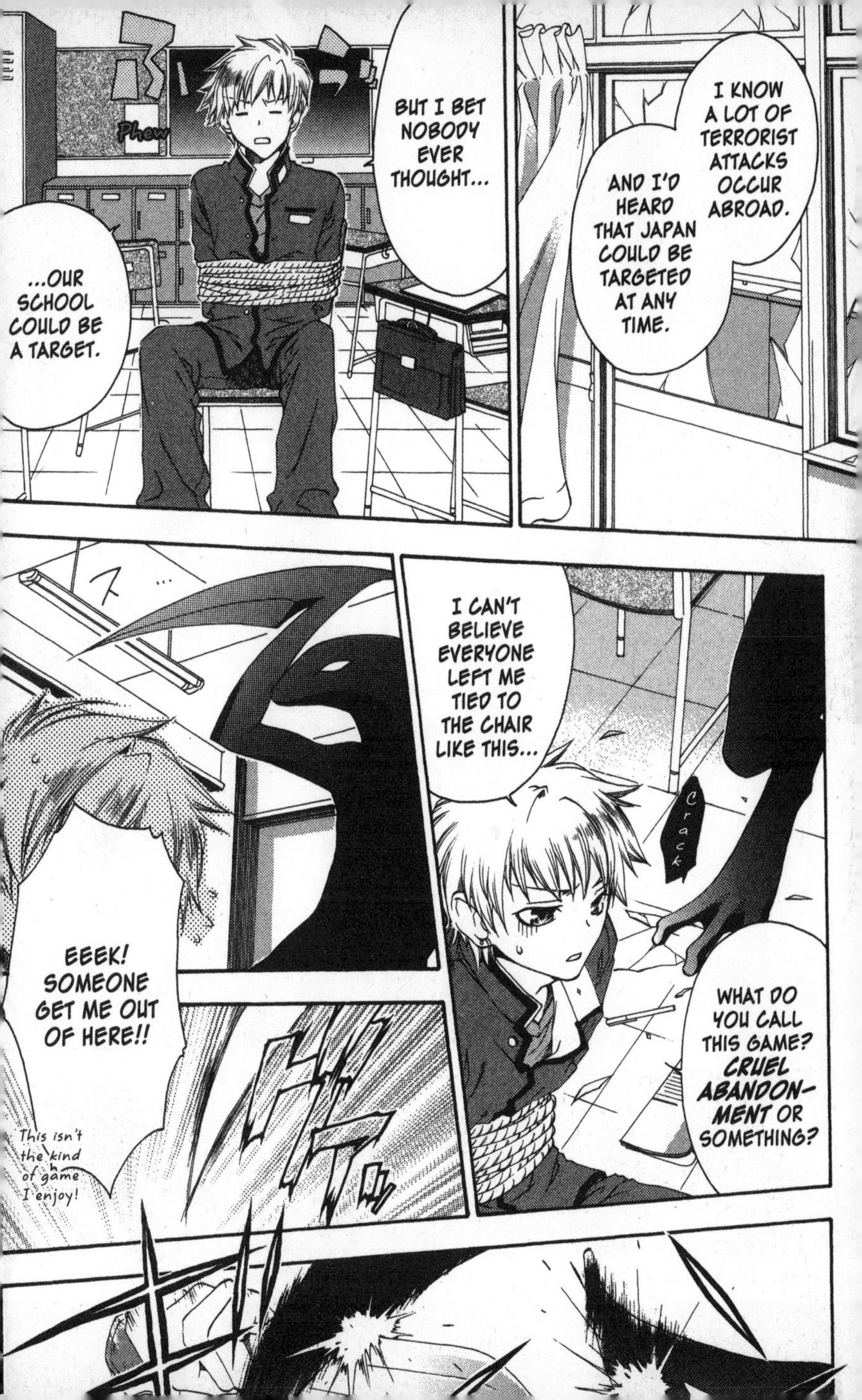
I KNOW A LOT OF TERRORIST ATTACKS OCCUR ABROAD.
AND I'D HEARD THAT JAPAN COULD BE TARGETED AT ANY TIME.
BUT I BET NOBODY EVER THOUGHT...
Phew
...OUR SCHOOL COULD BE A TARGET.
I CAN'T BELIEVE EVERYONE LEFT ME TIED TO THE CHAIR LIKE THIS...
Crack
WHAT DO YOU CALL THIS GAME? **CRUEL ABANDONMENT** OR SOMETHING?
EEEK! SOMEONE GET ME OUT OF HERE!!
This isn't the kind of game I enjoy!

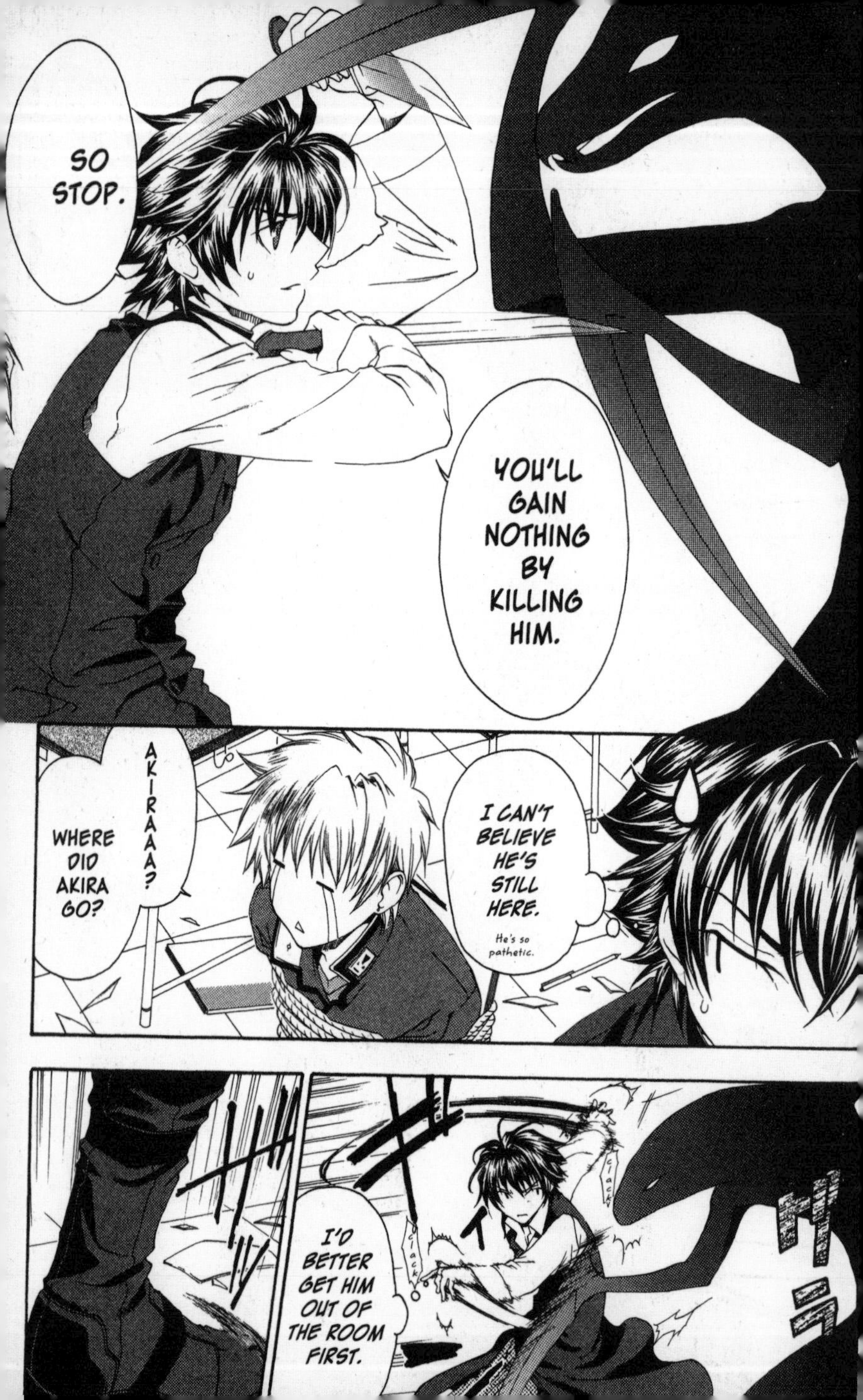
YOU'LL GAIN NOTHING BY KILLING HIM.
SO STOP.
I CAN'T BELIEVE HE'S STILL HERE.
He's so pathetic.
AKIRAAAA?
WHERE DID AKIRA GO?
clack
clack
I'D BETTER GET HIM OUT OF THE ROOM FIRST.

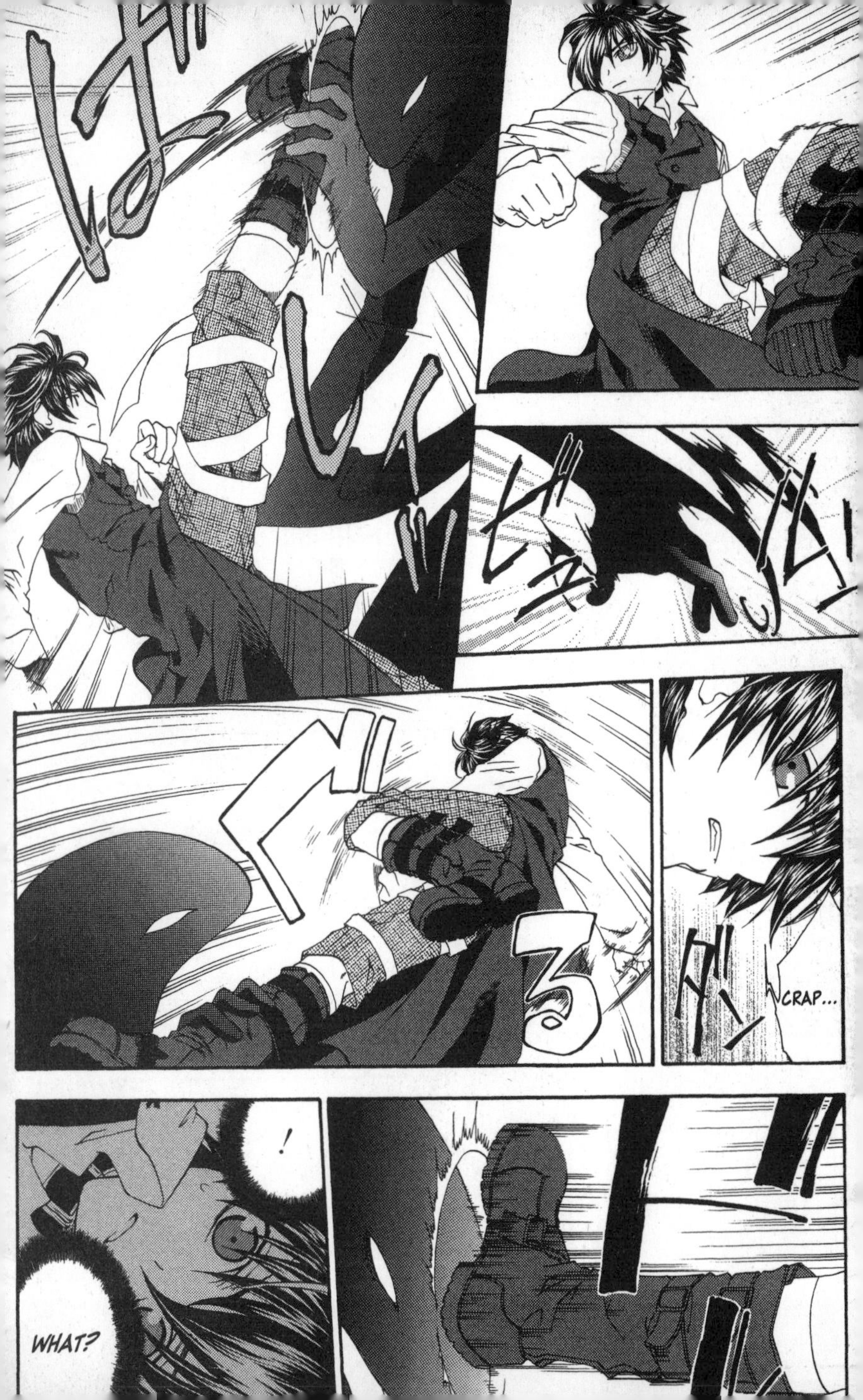
CRAP...
!
WHAT?

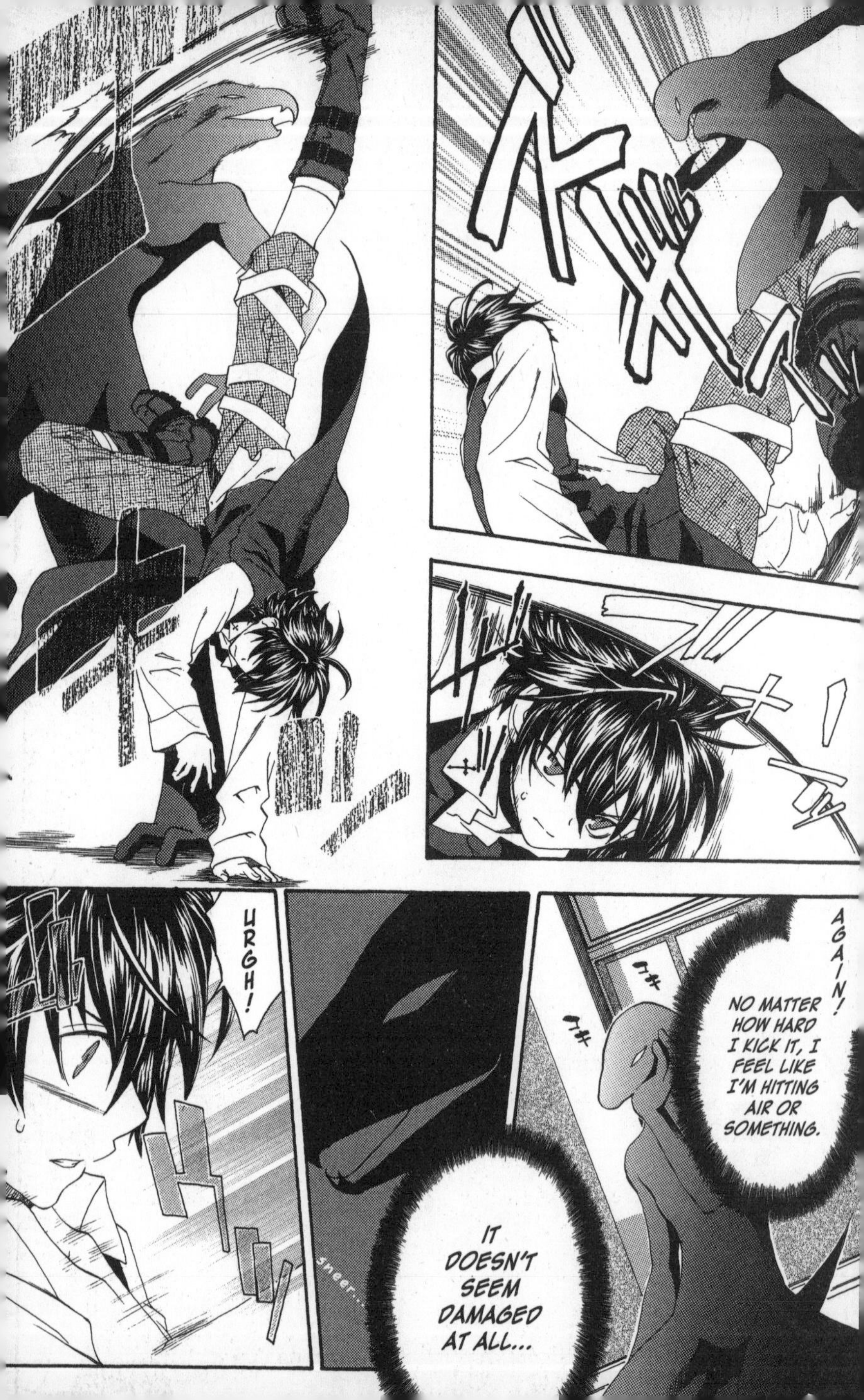
AGAIN!
NO MATTER HOW HARD I KICK IT, I FEEL LIKE I'M HITTING AIR OR SOMETHING.
IT DOESN'T SEEM DAMAGED AT ALL...
sneer...
URGH!

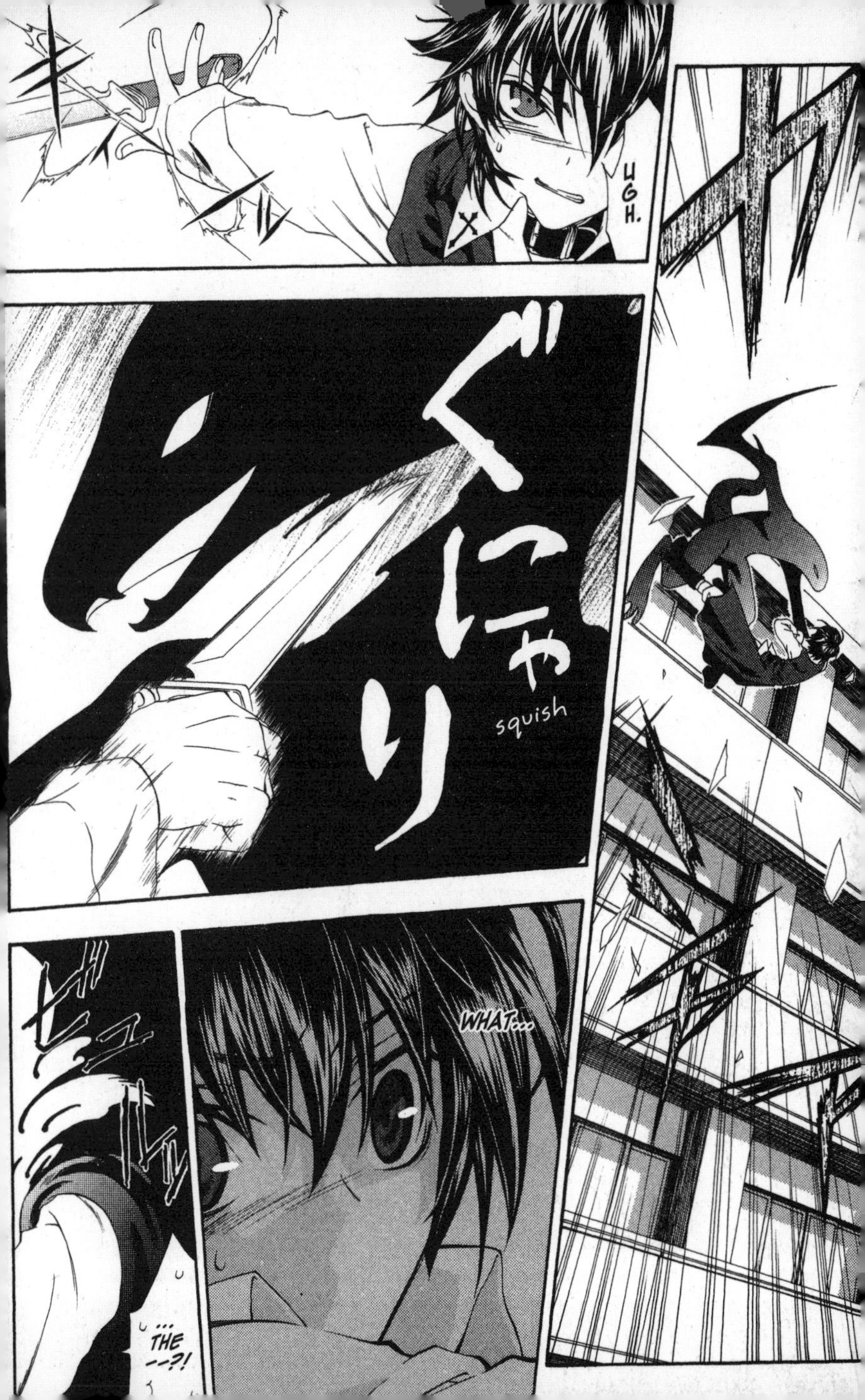

UGH.
ぐにゃり
squish
WHAT...
...THE--?!

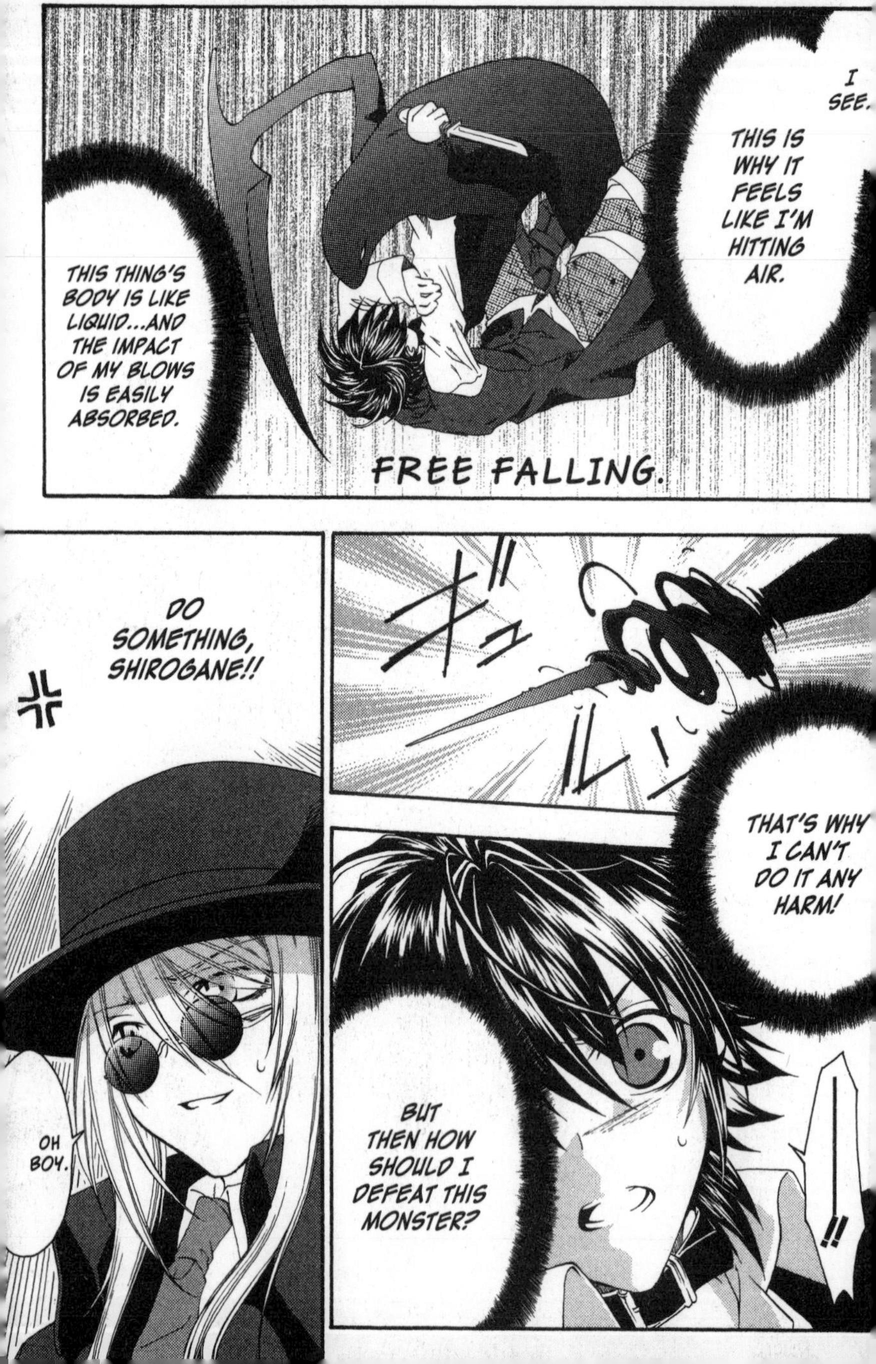
I SEE.
THIS IS WHY IT FEELS LIKE I'M HITTING AIR.
THIS THING'S BODY IS LIKE LIQUID...AND THE IMPACT OF MY BLOWS IS EASILY ABSORBED.
FREE FALLING.
THAT'S WHY I CAN'T DO IT ANY HARM!
!!
BUT THEN HOW SHOULD I DEFEAT THIS MONSTER?
DO SOMETHING, SHIROGANE!!
OH BOY.

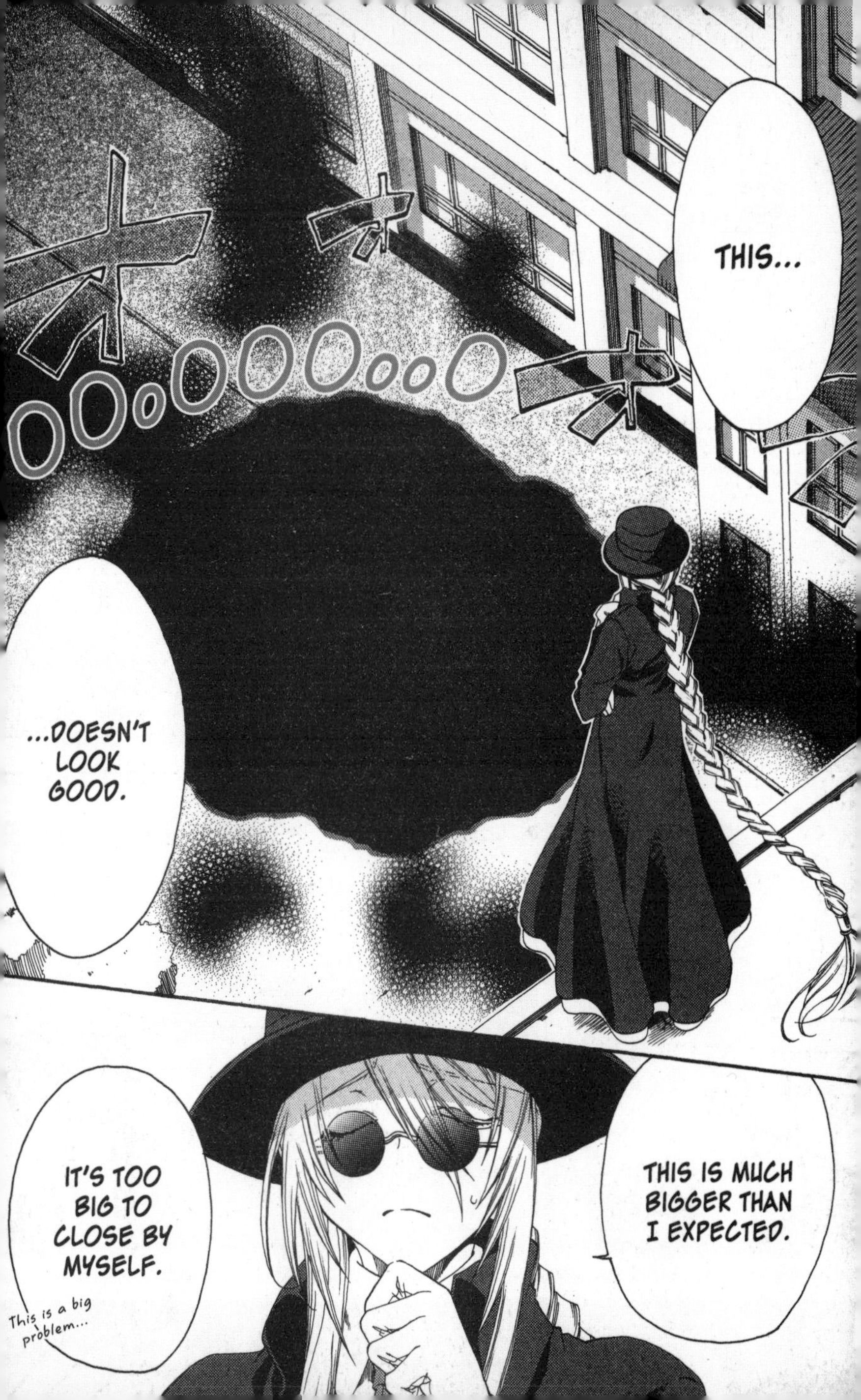
THIS...
OOoOOOOOooO
...DOESN'T LOOK GOOD.
THIS IS MUCH BIGGER THAN I EXPECTED.
IT'S TOO BIG TO CLOSE BY MYSELF.
This is a big problem...

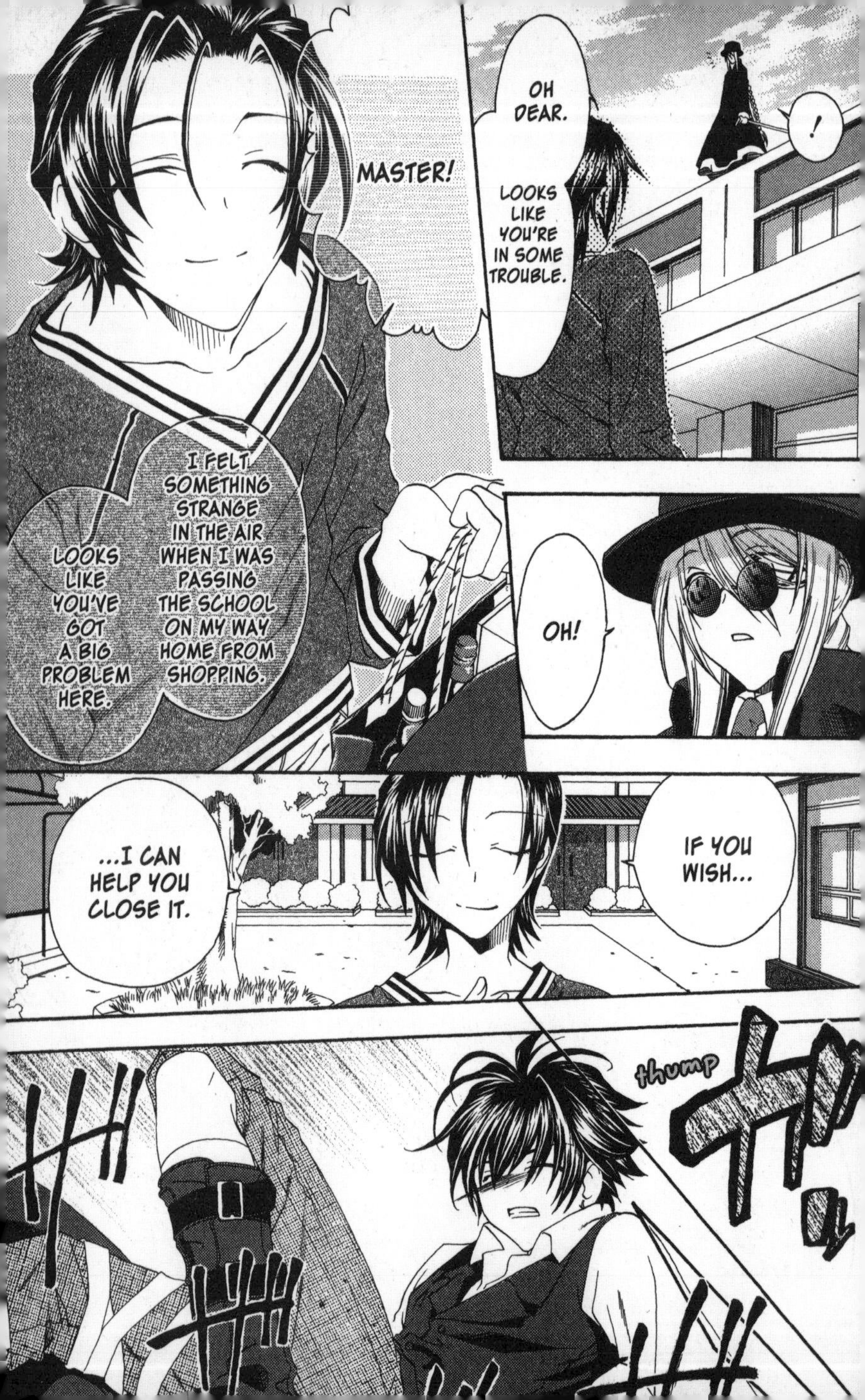
OH DEAR.
LOOKS LIKE YOU'RE IN SOME TROUBLE.
!
OH!
MASTER!
I FELT SOMETHING STRANGE IN THE AIR WHEN I WAS PASSING THE SCHOOL ON MY WAY HOME FROM SHOPPING.
LOOKS LIKE YOU'VE GOT A BIG PROBLEM HERE.
IF YOU WISH...
...I CAN HELP YOU CLOSE IT.
thump

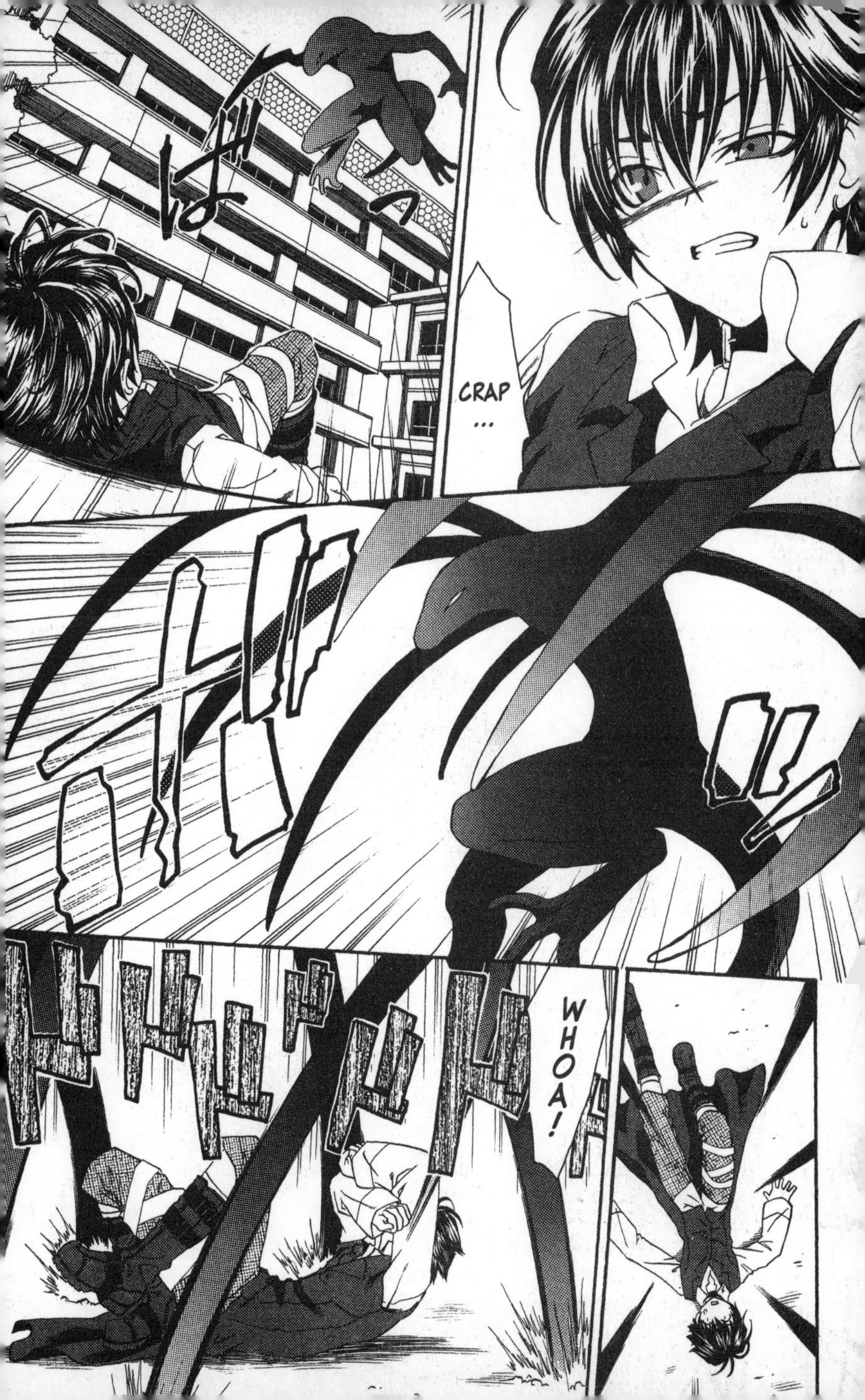
CRAP ...
ばっ
WHOA!

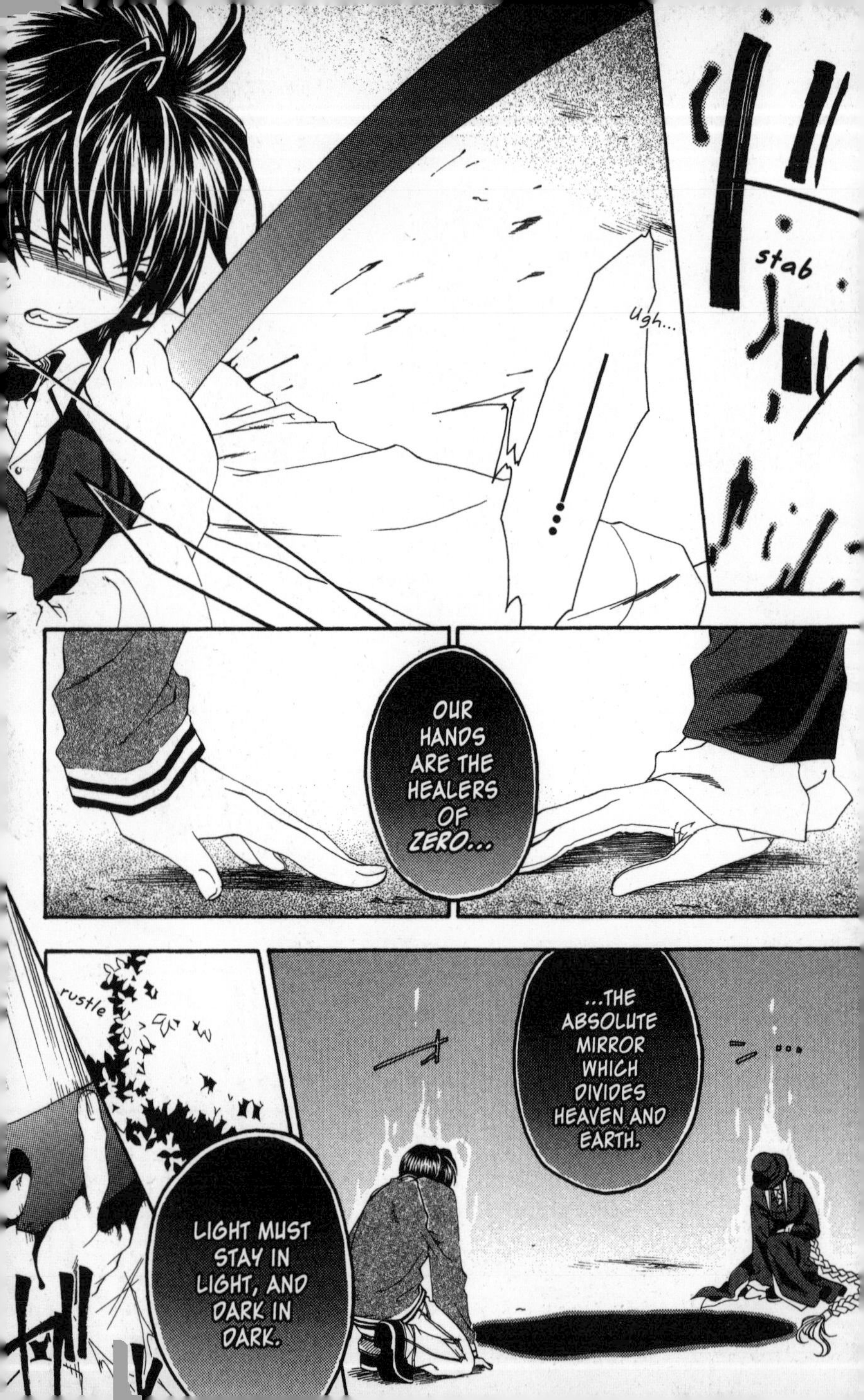
stab
Ugh...
OUR HANDS ARE THE HEALERS OF ZERO...
...THE ABSOLUTE MIRROR WHICH DIVIDES HEAVEN AND EARTH.
rustle
LIGHT MUST STAY IN LIGHT, AND DARK IN DARK.

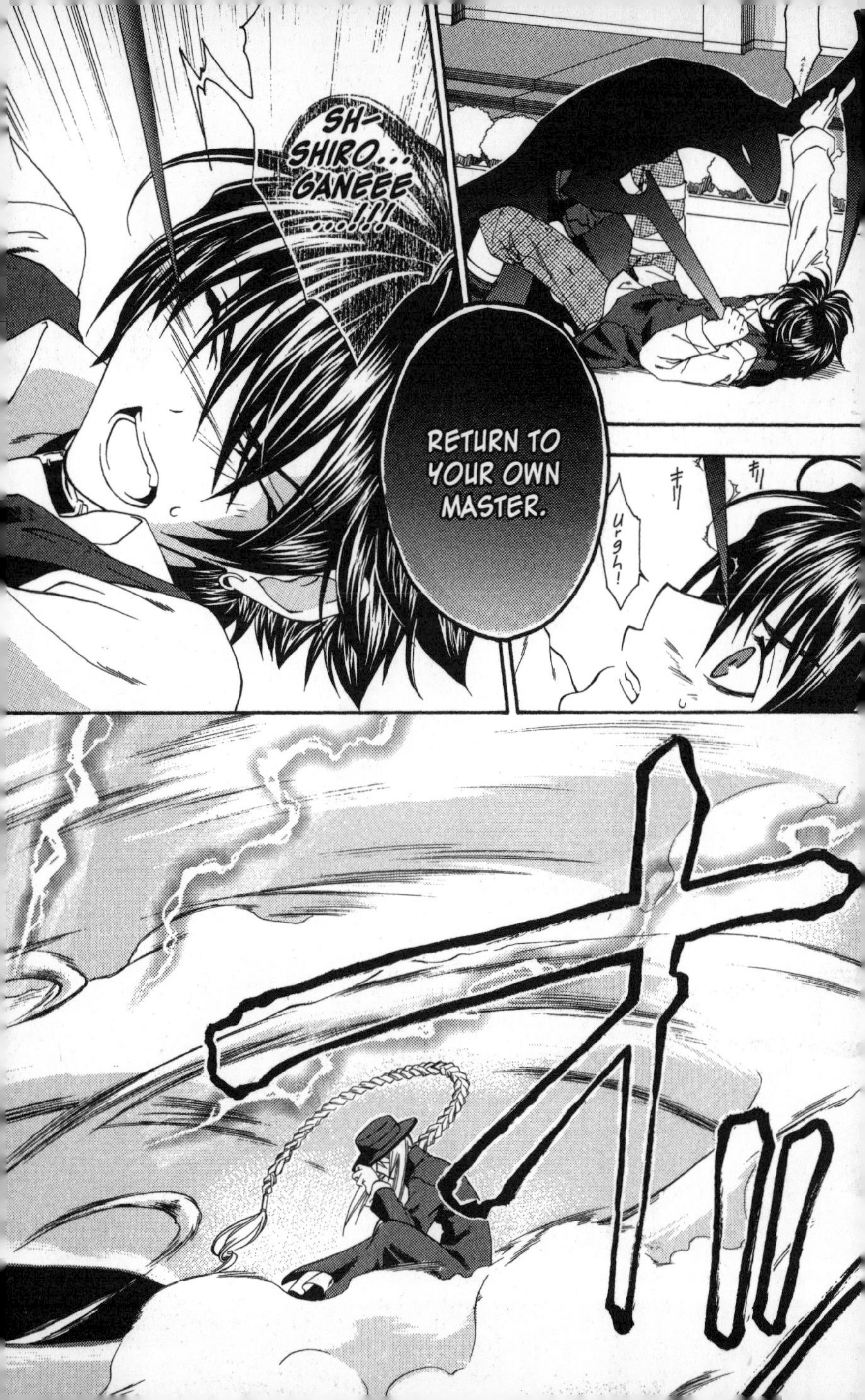
SH-SHIRO... GANEEE ...!!!
RETURN TO YOUR OWN MASTER.
Urgh!

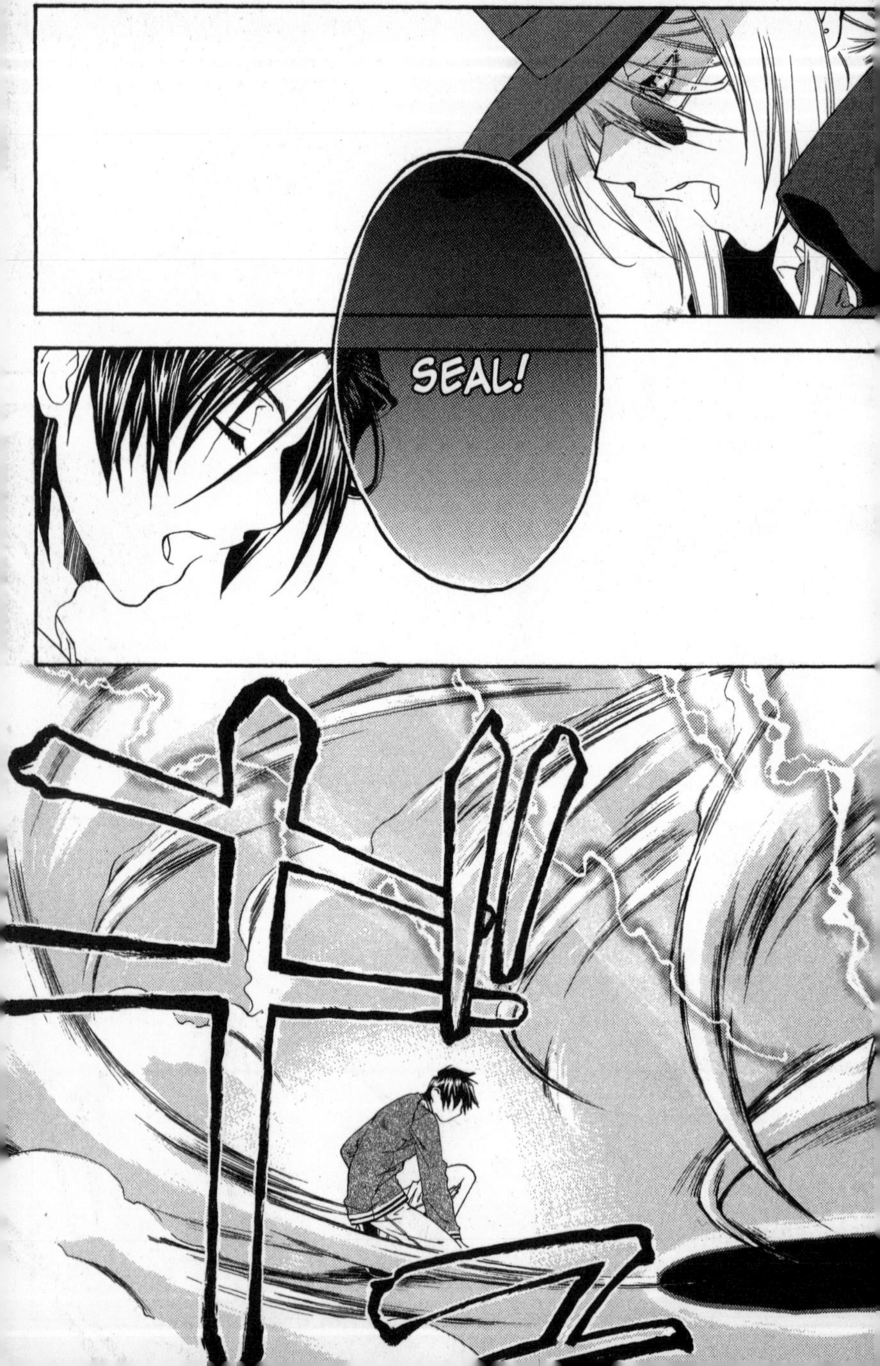
SEAL!

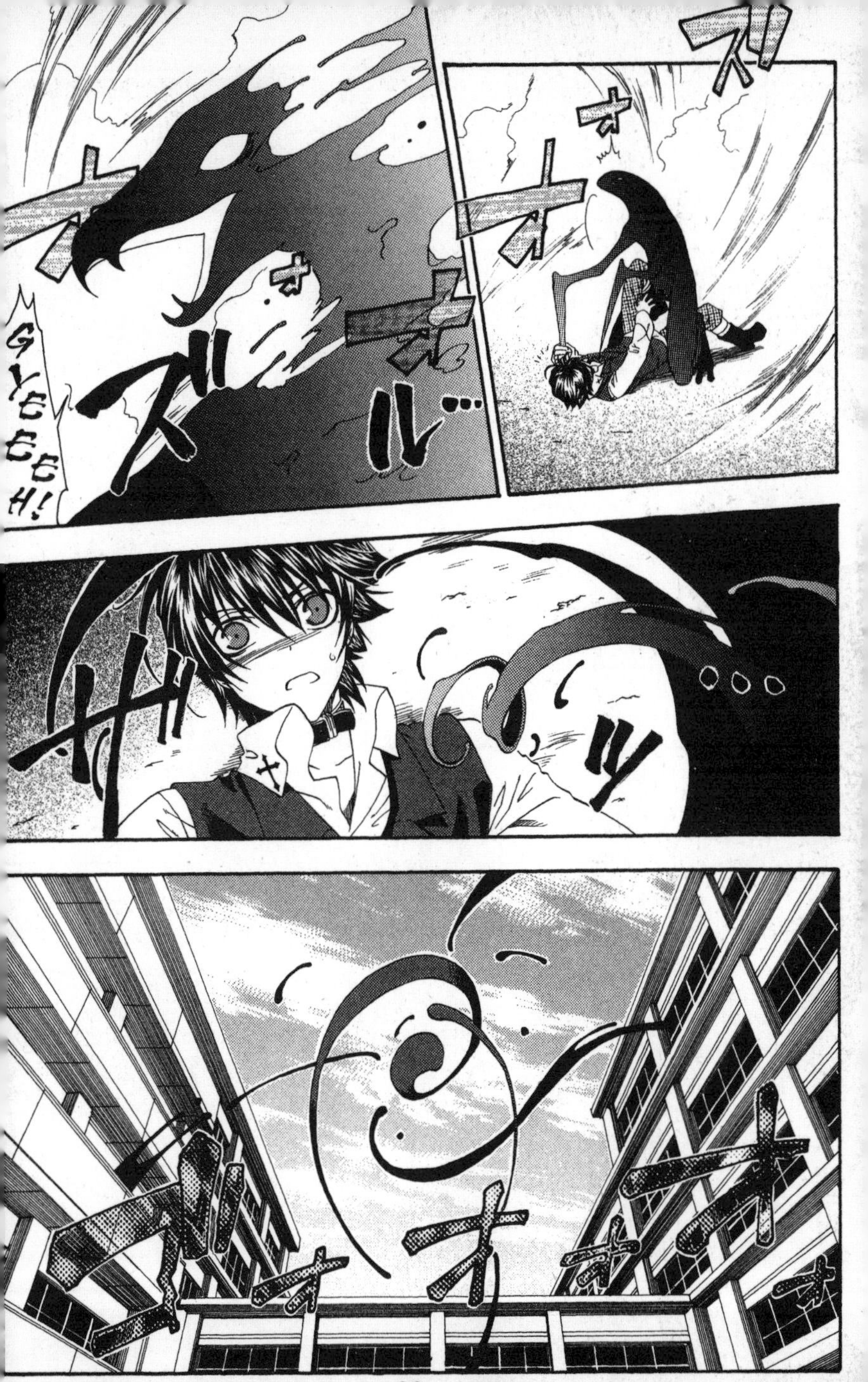
GYEEEH!

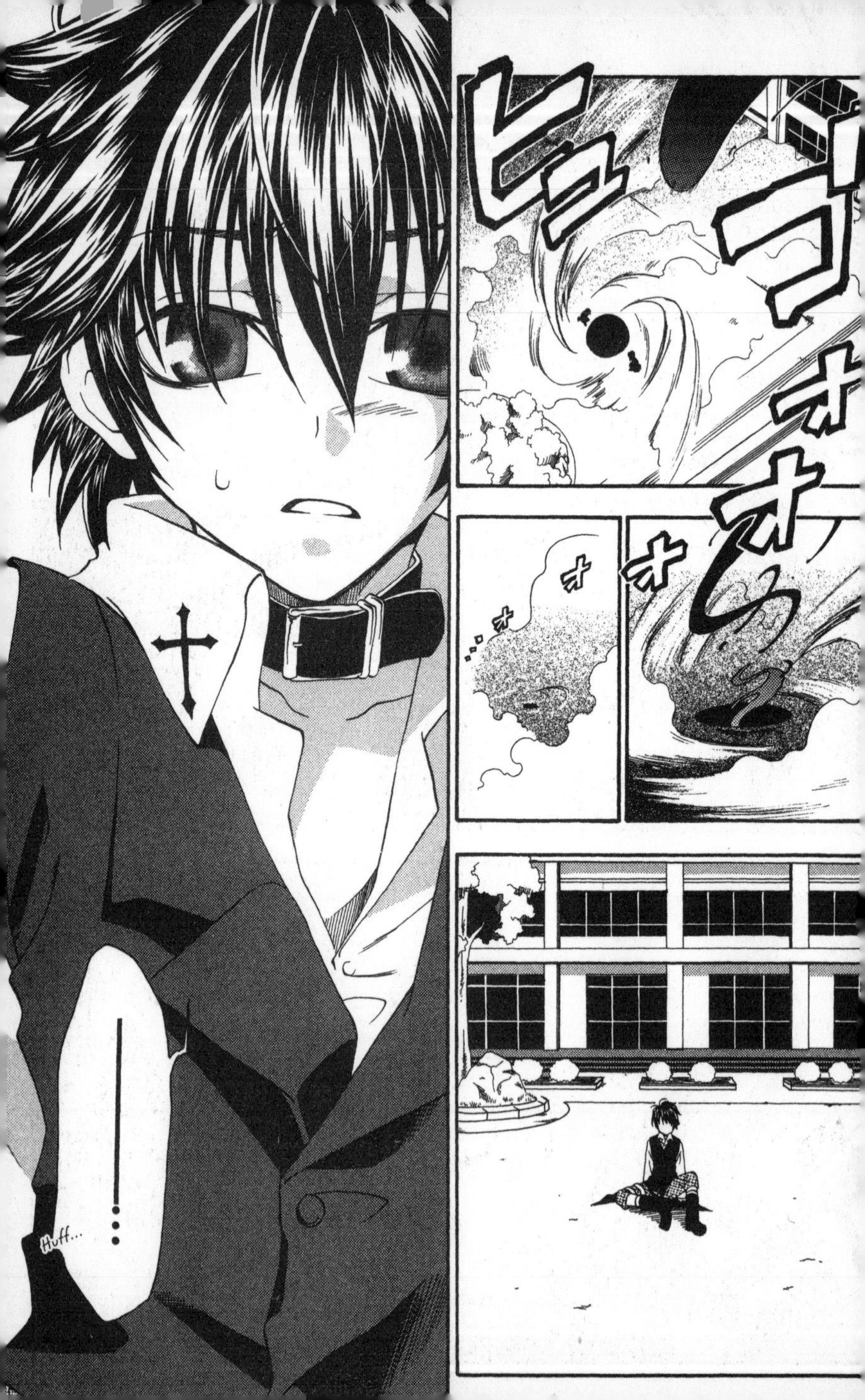

ヒュゴオオ
オ
オ
オ
――――…
Huff...

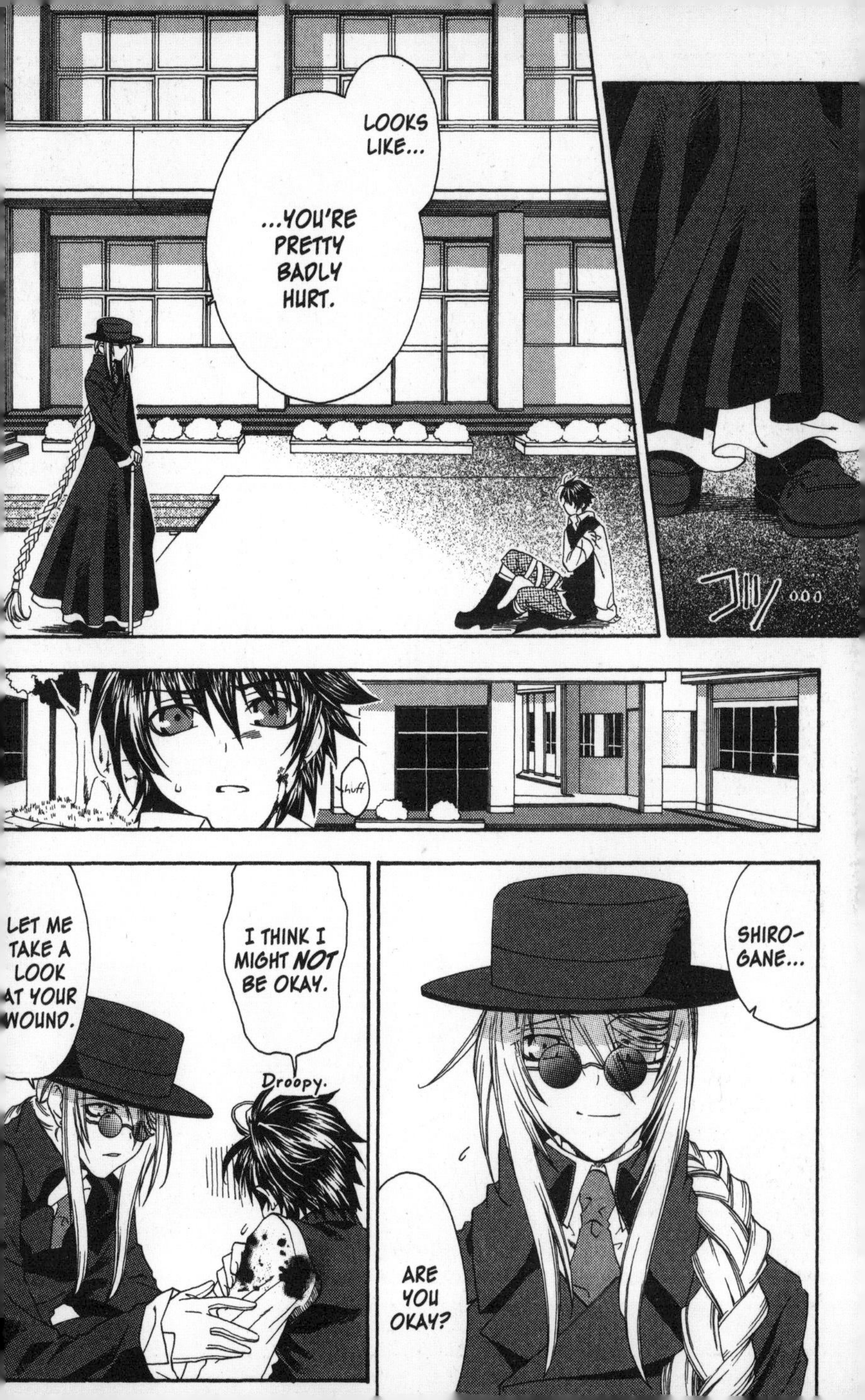
コツ…
LOOKS LIKE...
...YOU'RE PRETTY BADLY HURT.
huff
SHIRO-GANE...
ARE YOU OKAY?
I THINK I MIGHT NOT BE OKAY.
Droopy.
LET ME TAKE A LOOK AT YOUR WOUND.

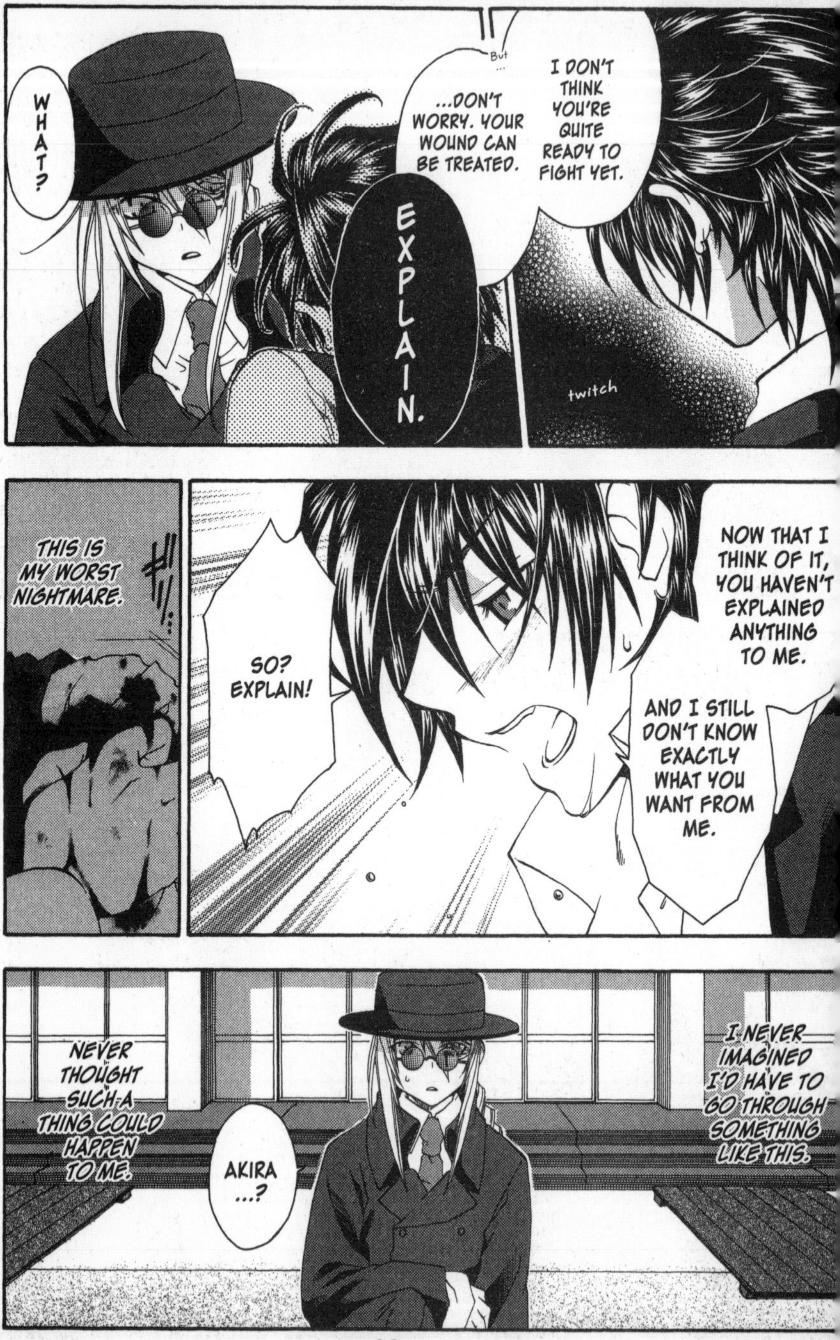
I DON'T THINK YOU'RE QUITE READY TO FIGHT YET.
But ...
...DON'T WORRY. YOUR WOUND CAN BE TREATED.
EXPLAIN.
twitch
WHAT?
NOW THAT I THINK OF IT, YOU HAVEN'T EXPLAINED ANYTHING TO ME.
AND I STILL DON'T KNOW EXACTLY WHAT YOU WANT FROM ME.
SO? EXPLAIN!
THIS IS MY WORST NIGHTMARE.
I NEVER IMAGINED I'D HAVE TO GO THROUGH SOMETHING LIKE THIS.
NEVER THOUGHT SUCH A THING COULD HAPPEN TO ME.
AKIRA ...?

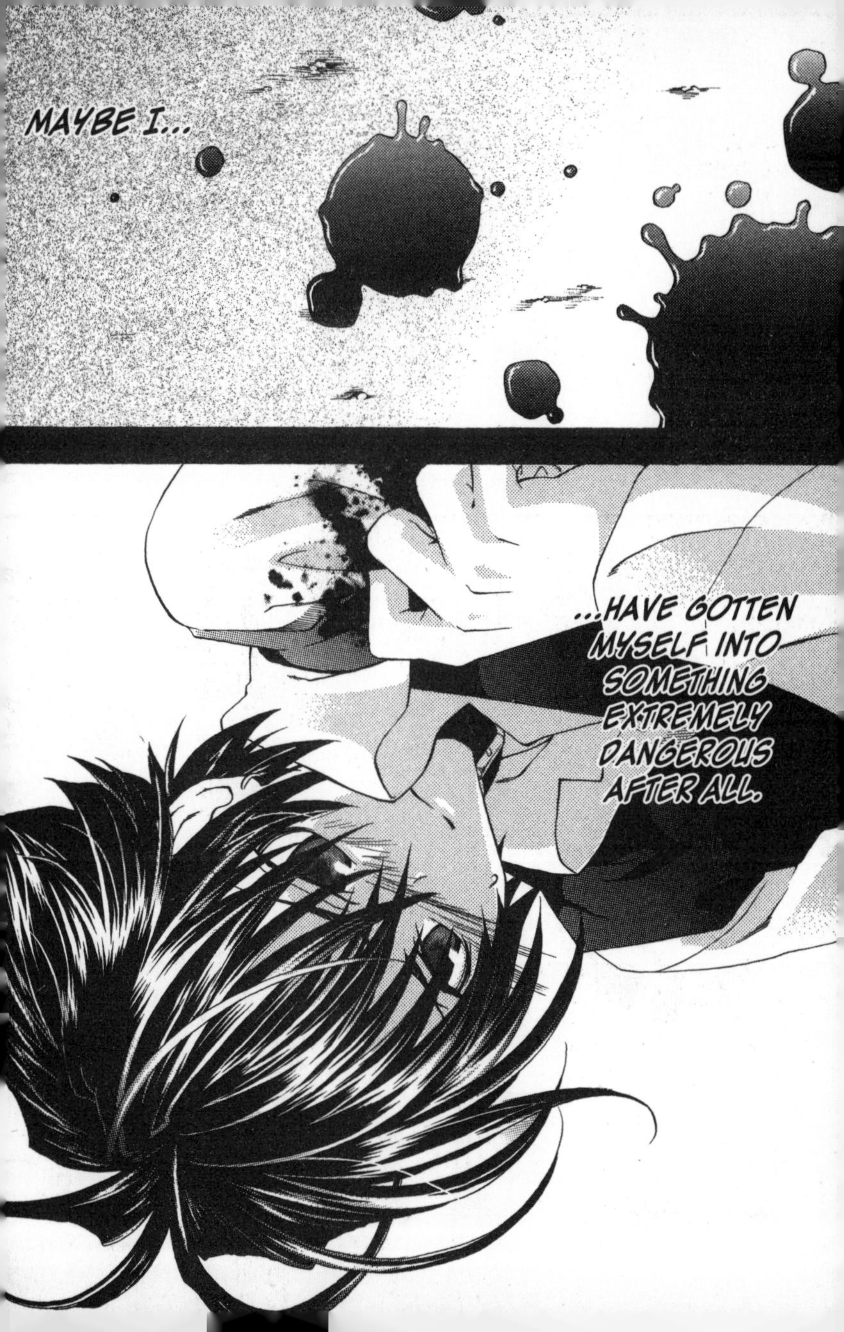
MAYBE I...
...HAVE GOTTEN MYSELF INTO SOMETHING EXTREMELY DANGEROUS AFTER ALL.

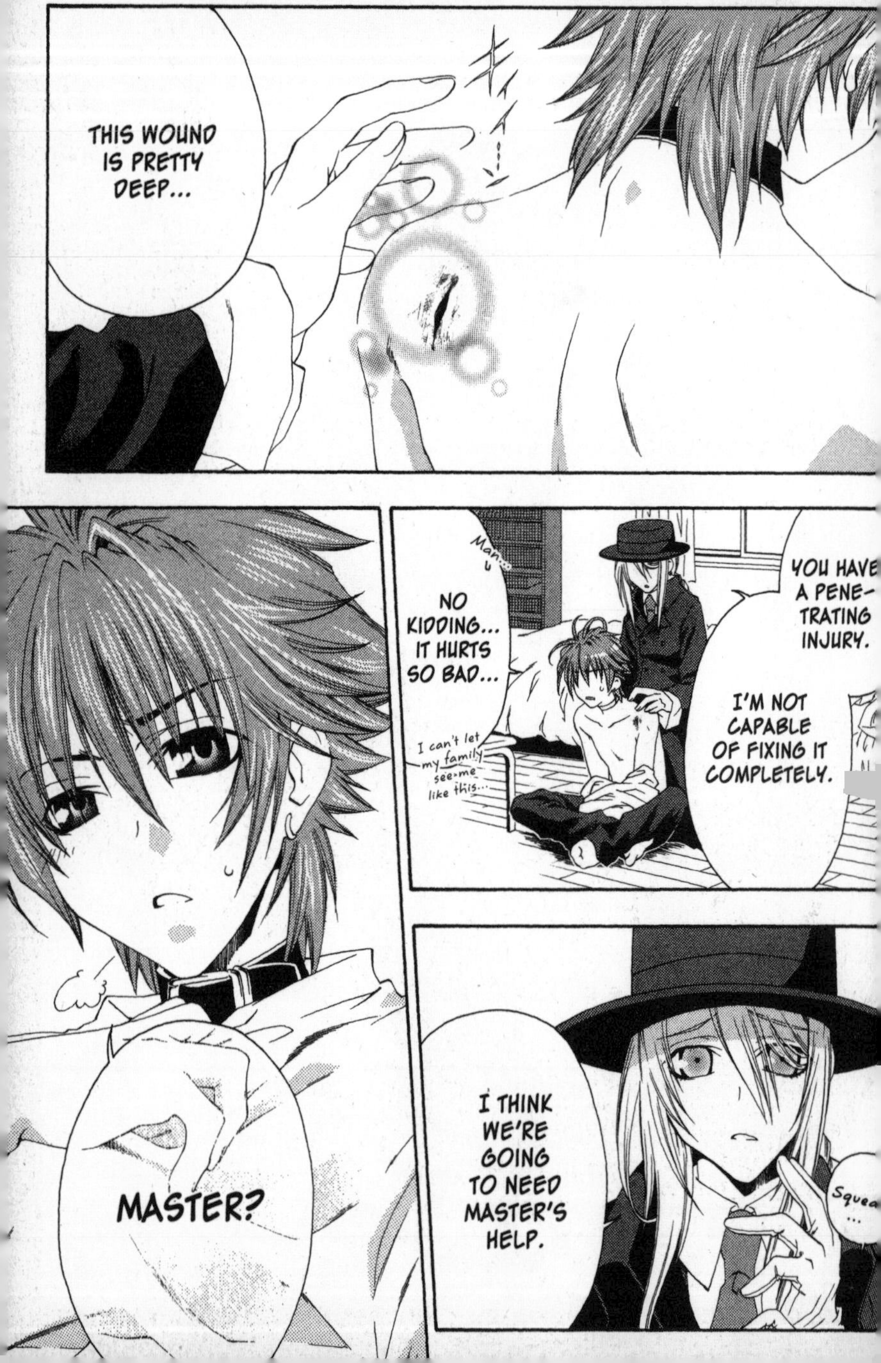
THIS WOUND IS PRETTY DEEP...
YOU HAVE A PENE-TRATING INJURY.
I'M NOT CAPABLE OF FIXING IT COMPLETELY.
Man...
NO KIDDING... IT HURTS SO BAD...
I can't let my family see me like this...
I THINK WE'RE GOING TO NEED MASTER'S HELP.
Squea ...
MASTER?

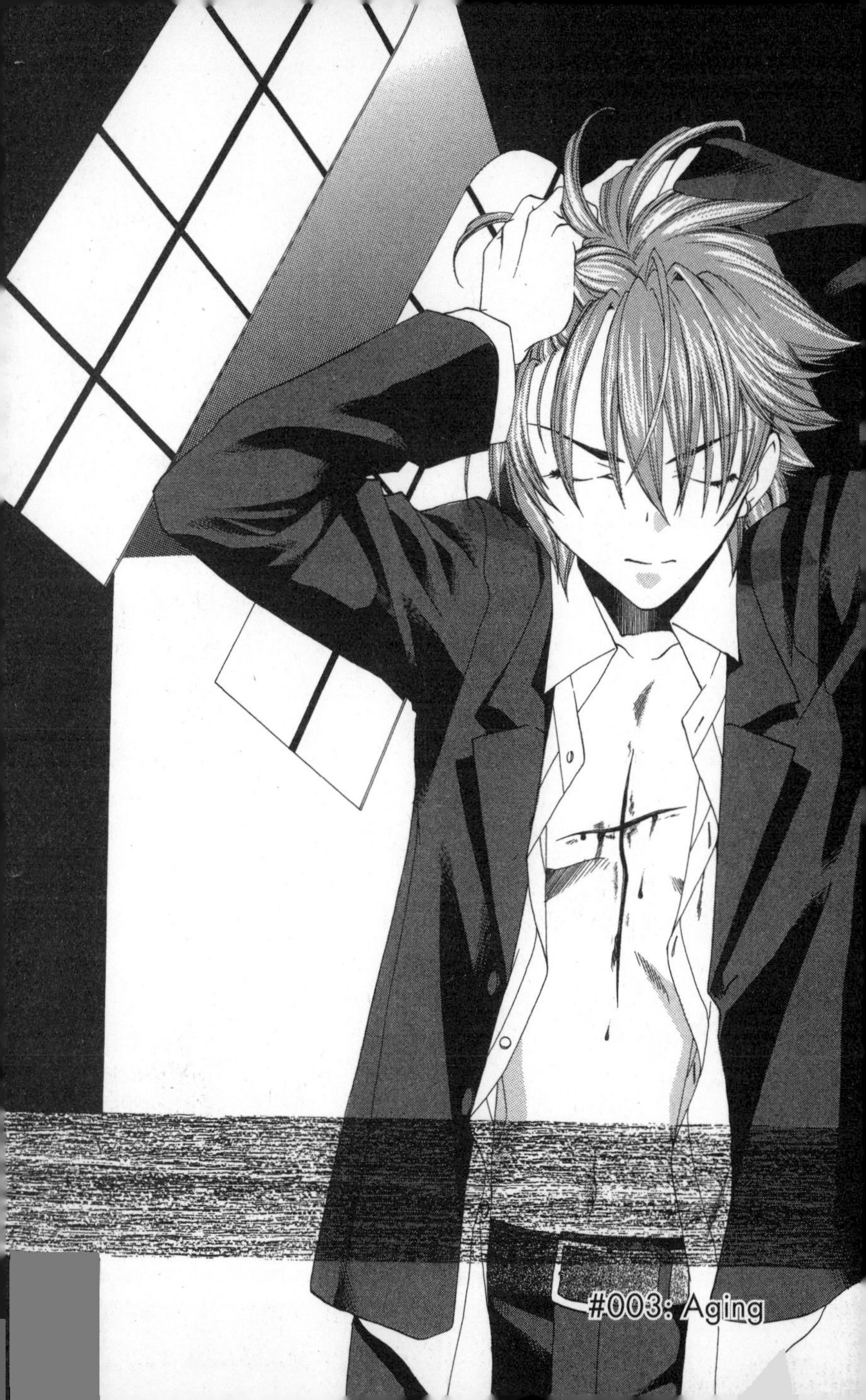
#003: Aging

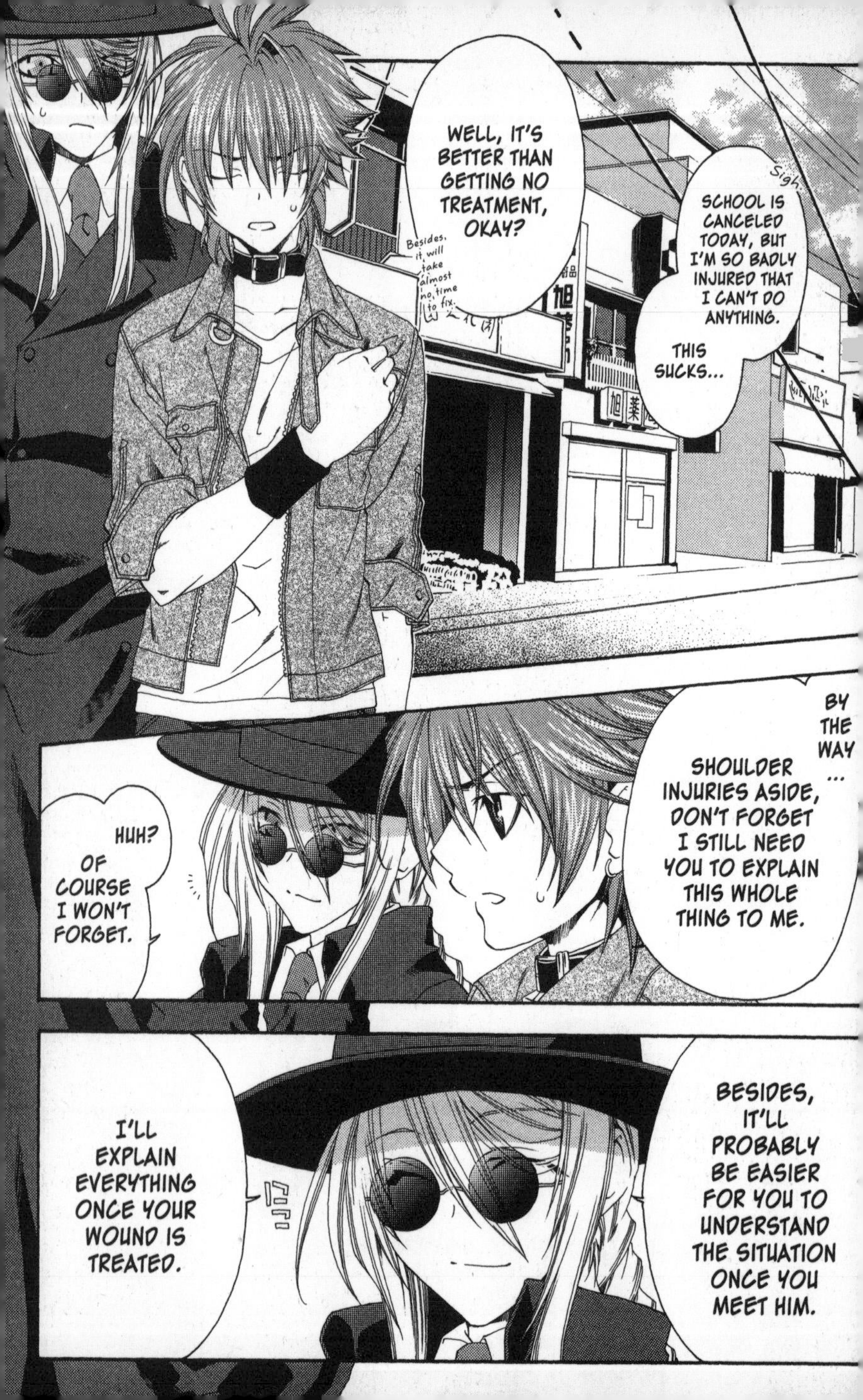
Sigh.
SCHOOL IS CANCELED TODAY, BUT I'M SO BADLY INJURED THAT I CAN'T DO ANYTHING.
THIS SUCKS...
WELL, IT'S BETTER THAN GETTING NO TREATMENT, OKAY?
Besides, it will take almost no time to fix.
BY THE WAY ...
SHOULDER INJURIES ASIDE, DON'T FORGET I STILL NEED YOU TO EXPLAIN THIS WHOLE THING TO ME.
HUH? OF COURSE I WON'T FORGET.
BESIDES, IT'LL PROBABLY BE EASIER FOR YOU TO UNDERSTAND THE SITUATION ONCE YOU MEET HIM.
I'LL EXPLAIN EVERYTHING ONCE YOUR WOUND IS TREATED.

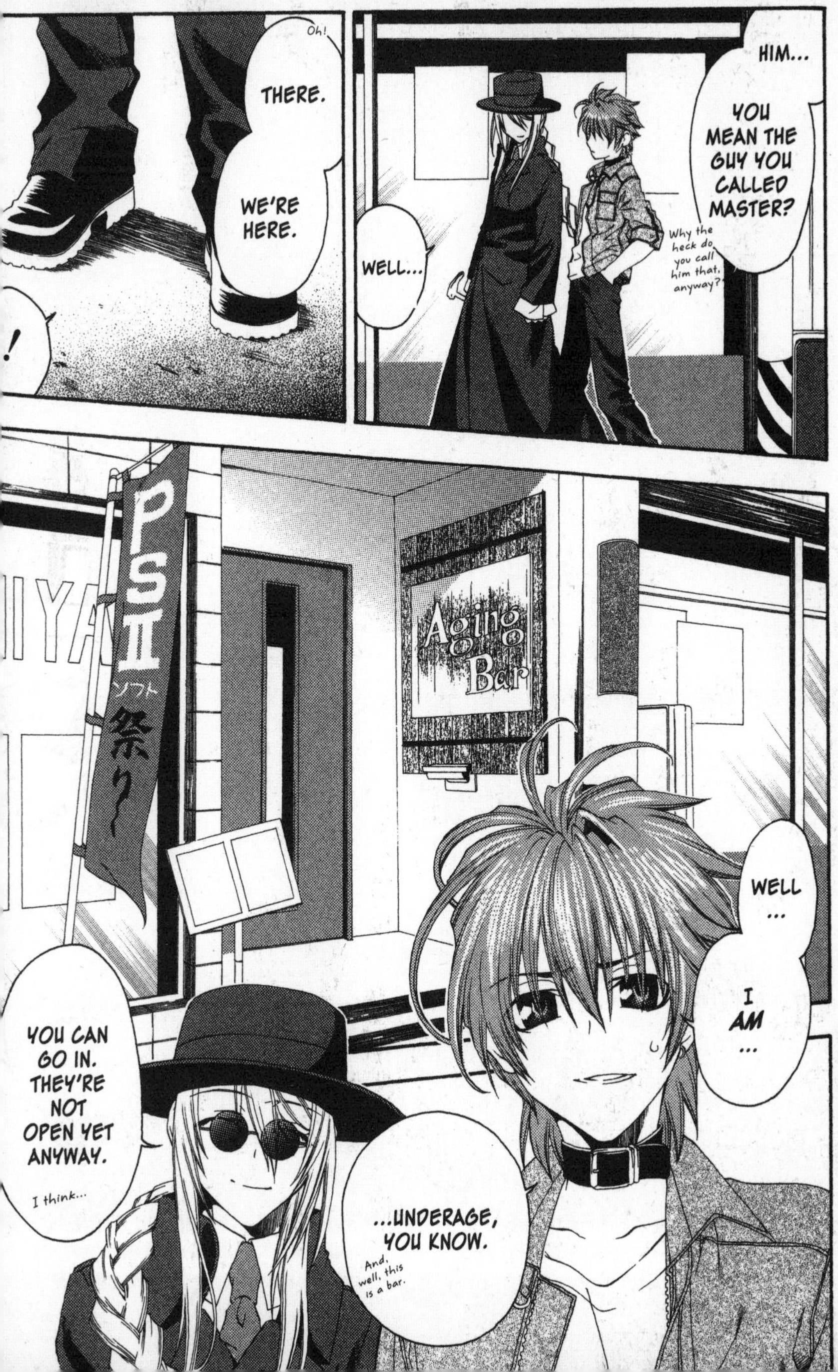
HIM...
YOU MEAN THE GUY YOU CALLED MASTER?
Why the heck do you call him that, anyway?
WELL...
Oh!
THERE.
WE'RE HERE.
!
PS II
ソフト
祭り~
Aging Bar
WELL ...
I AM ...
...UNDERAGE, YOU KNOW.
And, well, this is a bar.
YOU CAN GO IN. THEY'RE NOT OPEN YET ANYWAY.
I think...

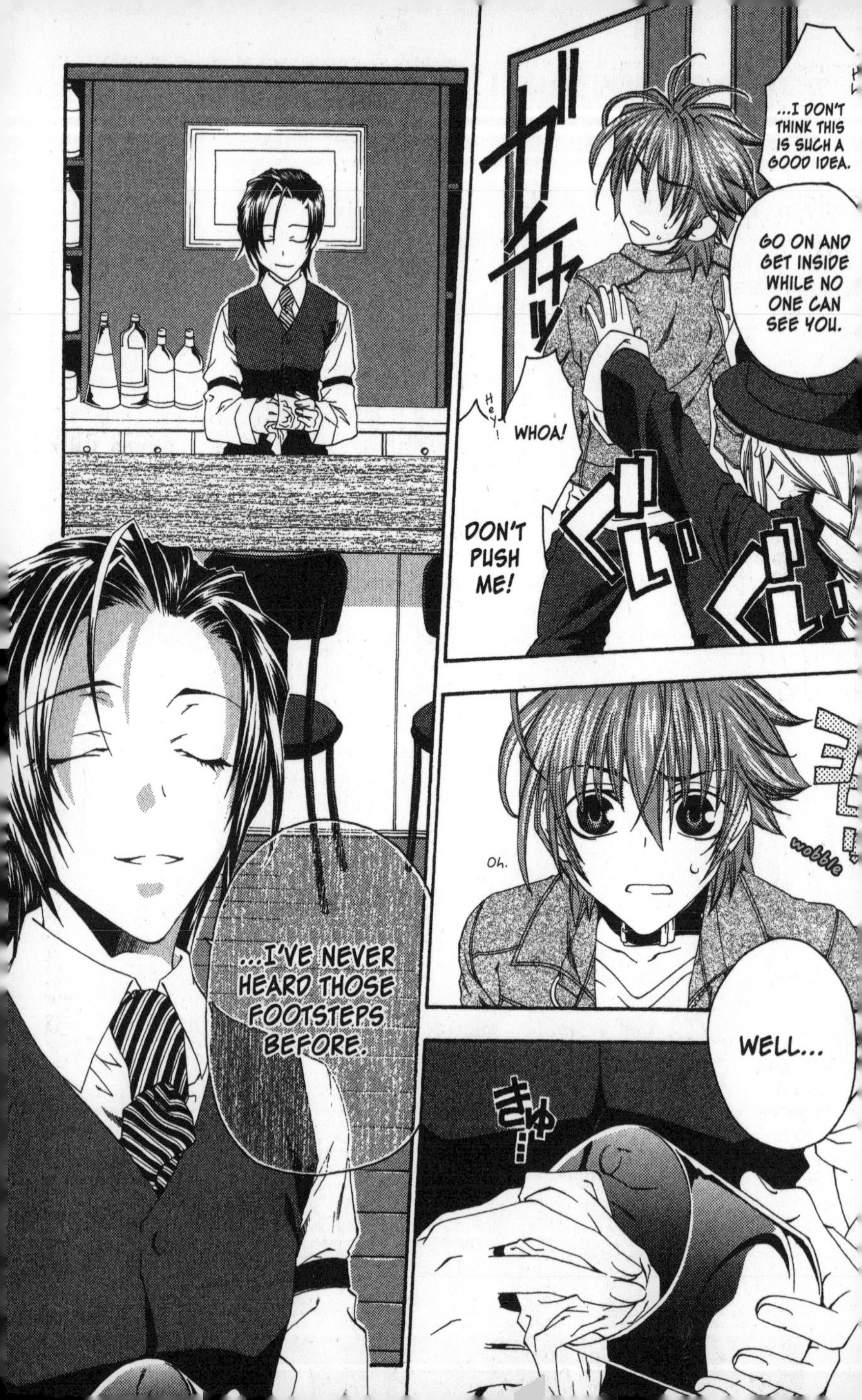
...I DON'T THINK THIS IS SUCH A GOOD IDEA.
GO ON AND GET INSIDE WHILE NO ONE CAN SEE YOU.
Hey!
WHOA!
DON'T PUSH ME!
wobble
Oh.
WELL...
...I'VE NEVER HEARD THOSE FOOTSTEPS BEFORE.

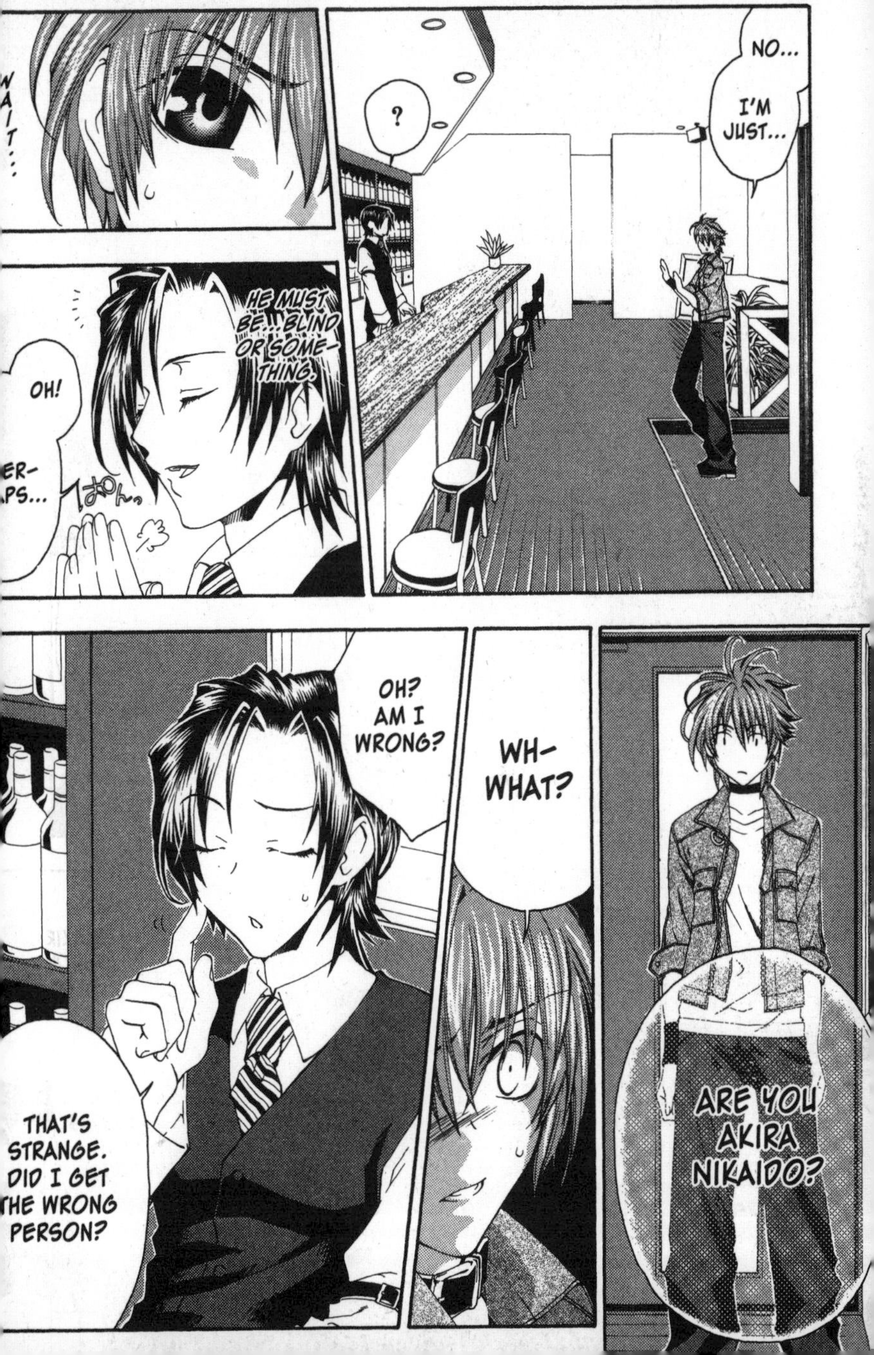
NO... I'M JUST...
?
WAIT...
HE MUST BE... BLIND OR SOME-THING.
OH!
ER-PS...
ぽんっ
ARE YOU AKIRA NIKAIDO?
WH-WHAT?
OH? AM I WRONG?
THAT'S STRANGE. DID I GET THE WRONG PERSON?

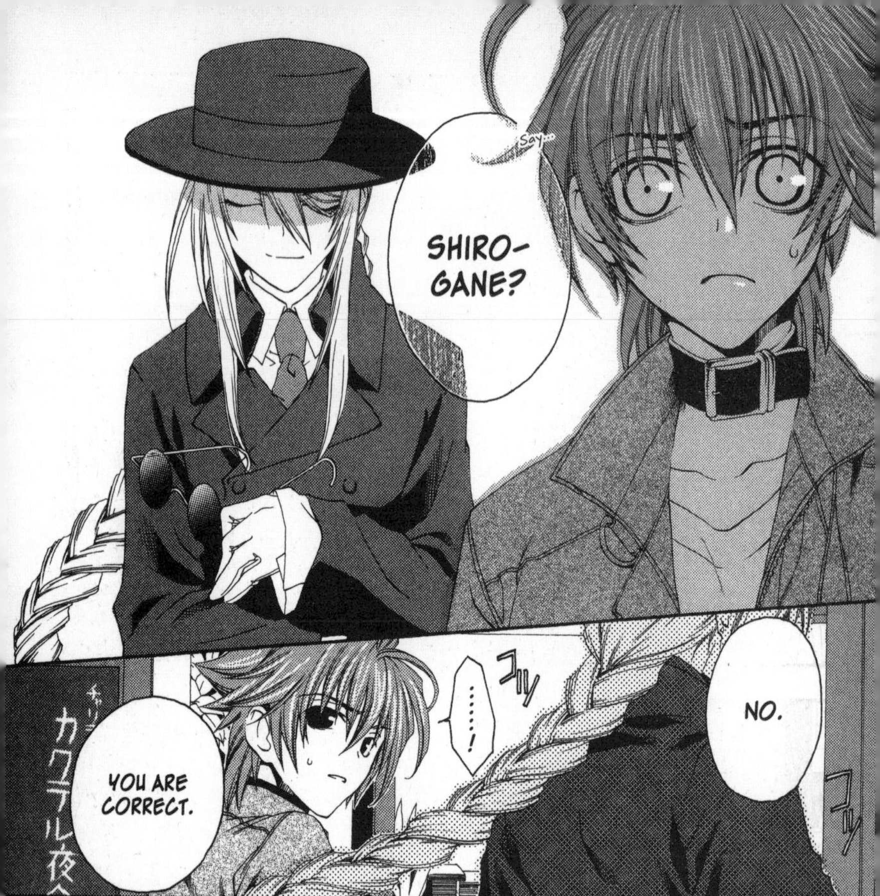
Say...
SHIRO-GANE?
NO.
……!
YOU ARE CORRECT.

*Note: In Japan, the owner of a bar is often referred to as its master.

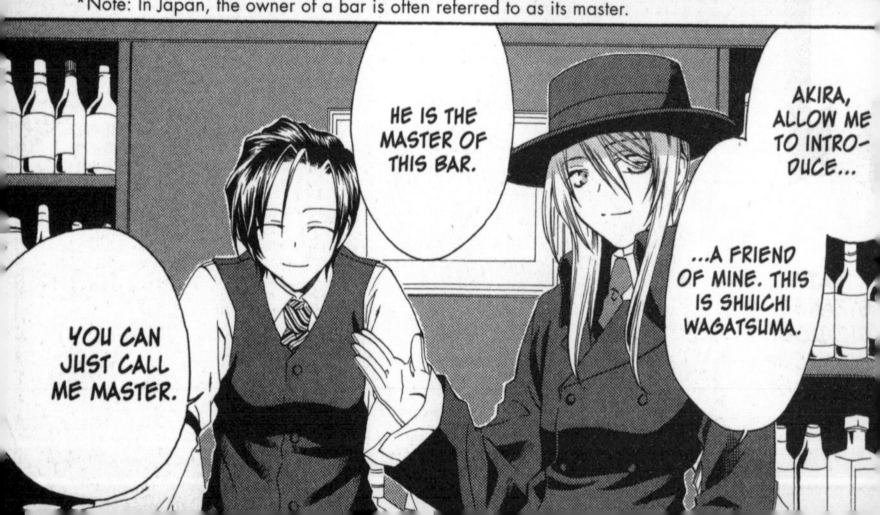
AKIRA, ALLOW ME TO INTRO-DUCE...
HE IS THE MASTER OF THIS BAR.
...A FRIEND OF MINE. THIS IS SHUICHI WAGATSUMA.
YOU CAN JUST CALL ME MASTER.

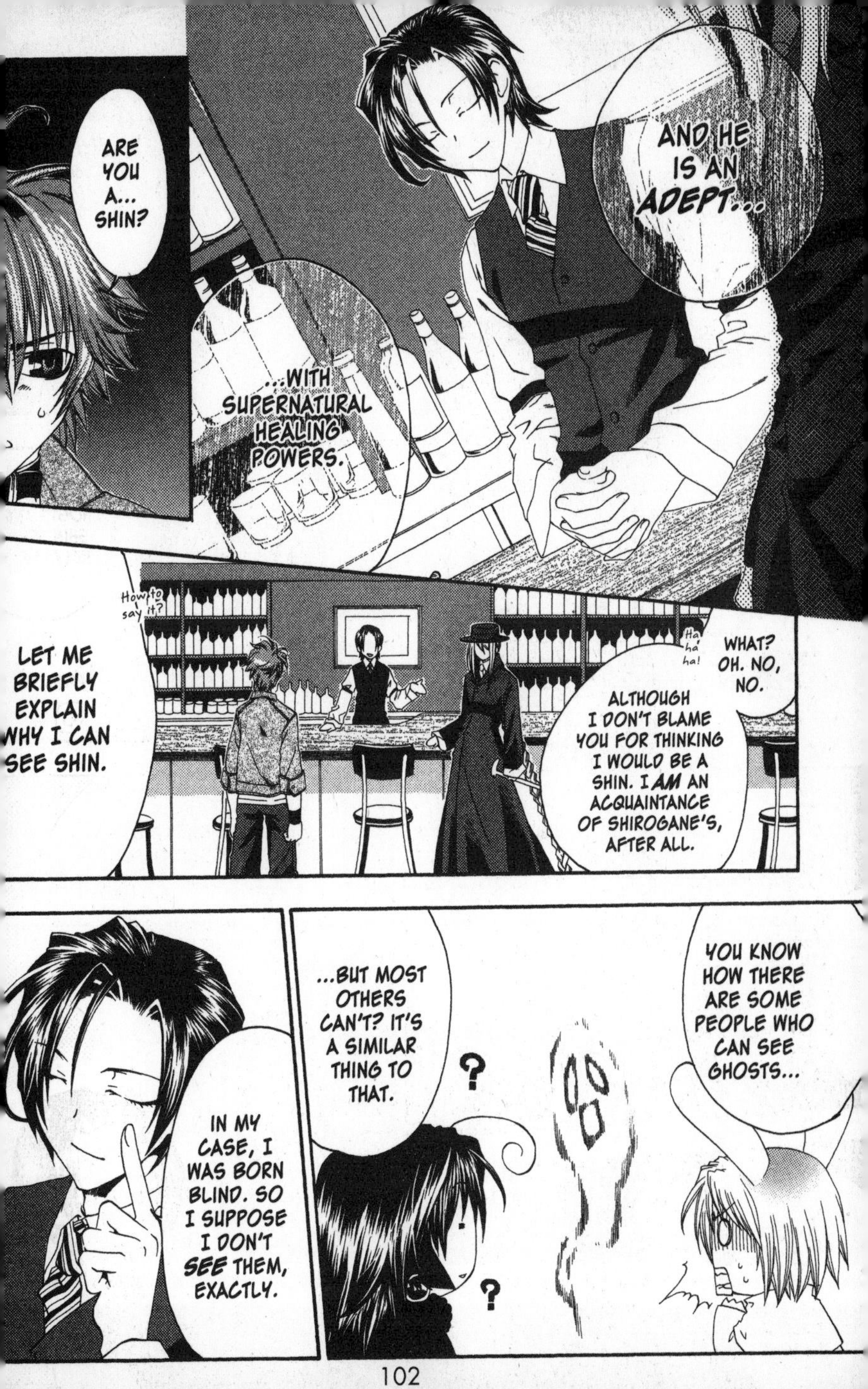
AND HE IS AN ADEPT...
...WITH SUPERNATURAL HEALING POWERS.
ARE YOU A... SHIN?
WHAT? OH. NO, NO.
Ha ha ha!
ALTHOUGH I DON'T BLAME YOU FOR THINKING I WOULD BE A SHIN. I AM AN ACQUAINTANCE OF SHIROGANE'S, AFTER ALL.
How to say it?
LET ME BRIEFLY EXPLAIN WHY I CAN SEE SHIN.
YOU KNOW HOW THERE ARE SOME PEOPLE WHO CAN SEE GHOSTS...
...BUT MOST OTHERS CAN'T? IT'S A SIMILAR THING TO THAT.
?
?
IN MY CASE, I WAS BORN BLIND. SO I SUPPOSE I DON'T SEE THEM, EXACTLY.

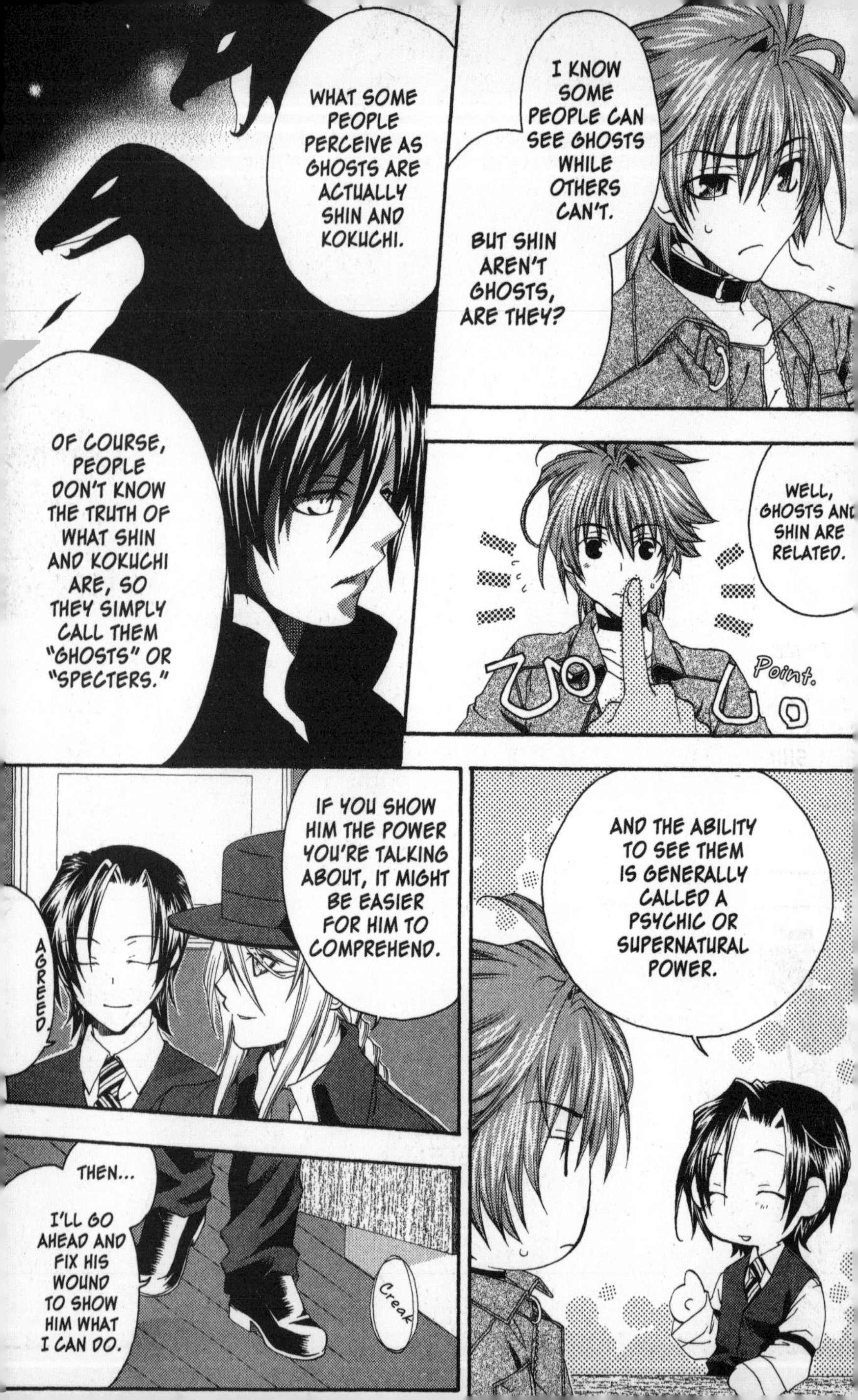
I KNOW SOME PEOPLE CAN SEE GHOSTS WHILE OTHERS CAN'T.
BUT SHIN AREN'T GHOSTS, ARE THEY?
WHAT SOME PEOPLE PERCEIVE AS GHOSTS ARE ACTUALLY SHIN AND KOKUCHI.
OF COURSE, PEOPLE DON'T KNOW THE TRUTH OF WHAT SHIN AND KOKUCHI ARE, SO THEY SIMPLY CALL THEM "GHOSTS" OR "SPECTERS."
WELL, GHOSTS AND SHIN ARE RELATED.
Point.
AND THE ABILITY TO SEE THEM IS GENERALLY CALLED A PSYCHIC OR SUPERNATURAL POWER.
IF YOU SHOW HIM THE POWER YOU'RE TALKING ABOUT, IT MIGHT BE EASIER FOR HIM TO COMPREHEND.
AGREED.
THEN...
I'LL GO AHEAD AND FIX HIS WOUND TO SHOW HIM WHAT I CAN DO.
Creak

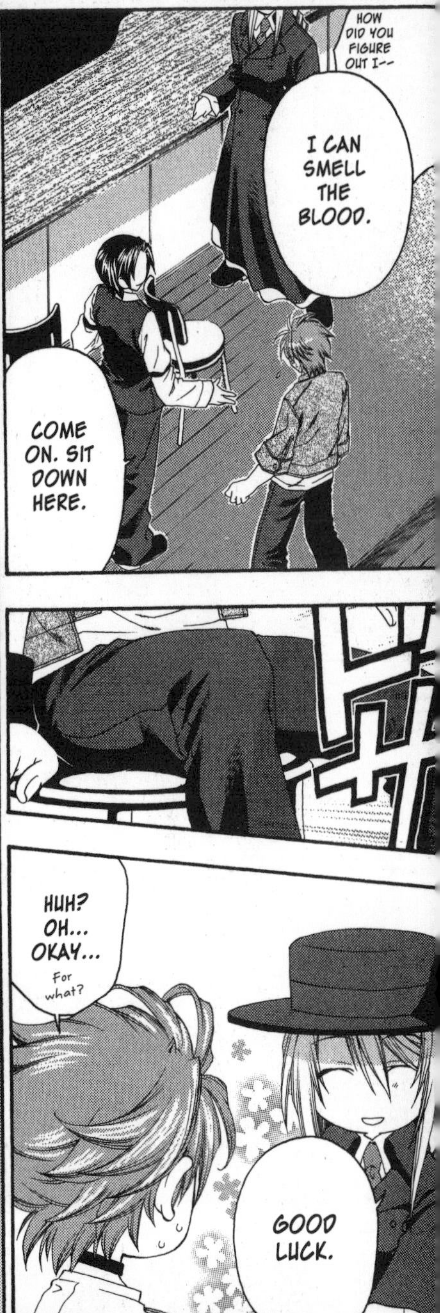
HOW DID YOU FIGURE OUT I--
I CAN SMELL THE BLOOD.
COME ON. SIT DOWN HERE.
HUH? OH... OKAY...
For what?
GOOD LUCK.

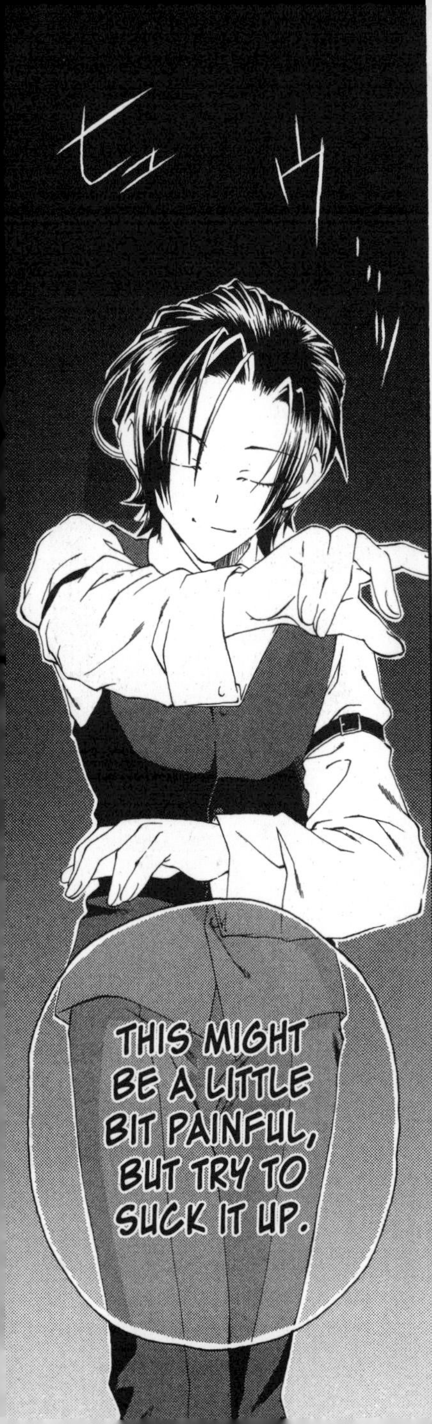
THIS MIGHT BE A LITTLE BIT PAINFUL, BUT TRY TO SUCK IT UP.

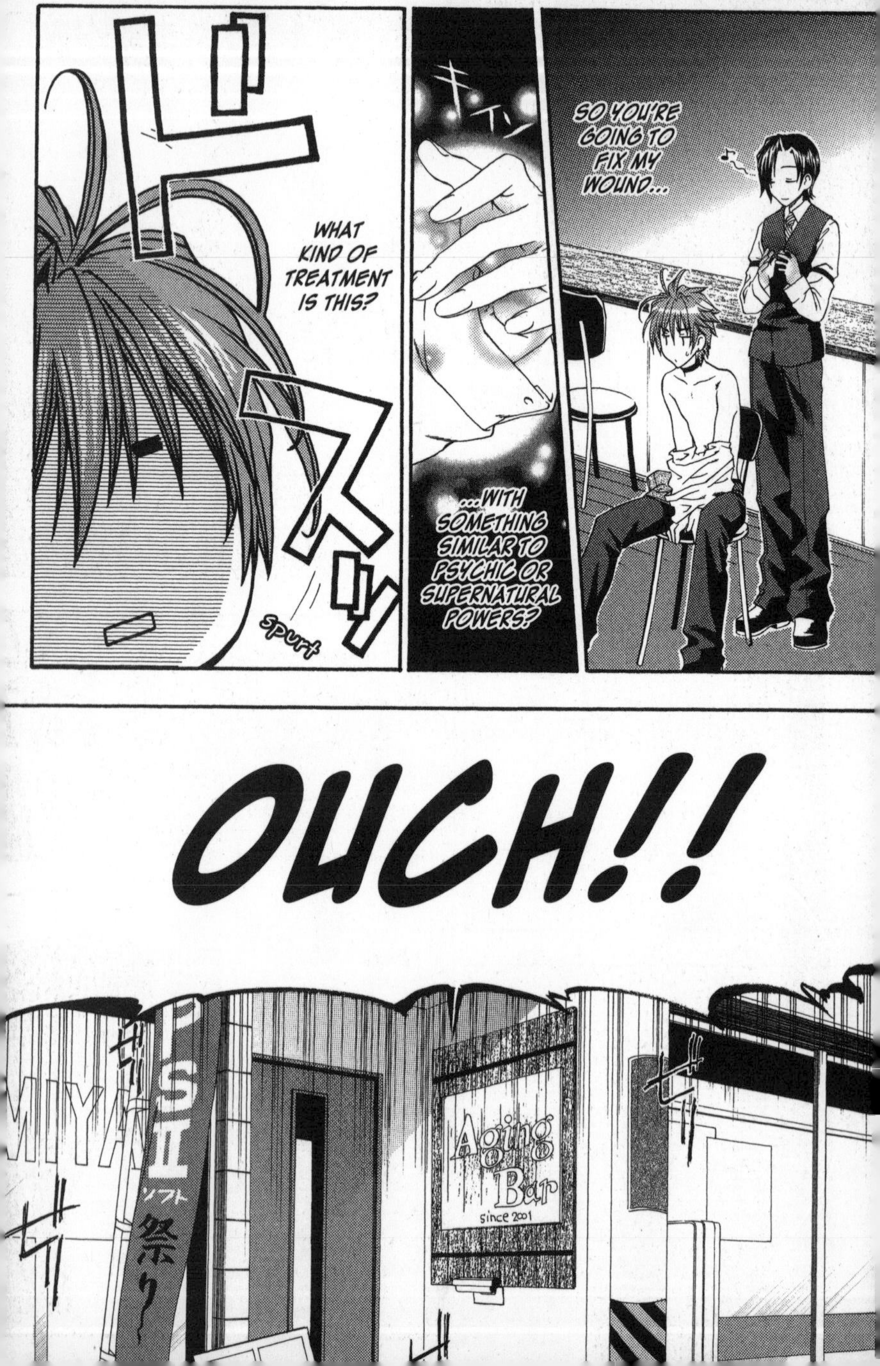
SO YOU'RE GOING TO FIX MY WOUND...
...WITH SOMETHING SIMILAR TO PSYCHIC OR SUPERNATURAL POWERS?
WHAT KIND OF TREATMENT IS THIS?
Spurt
OUCH!!
Aging Bar
since 2001
PS II
ソフト
祭り～
MIYA

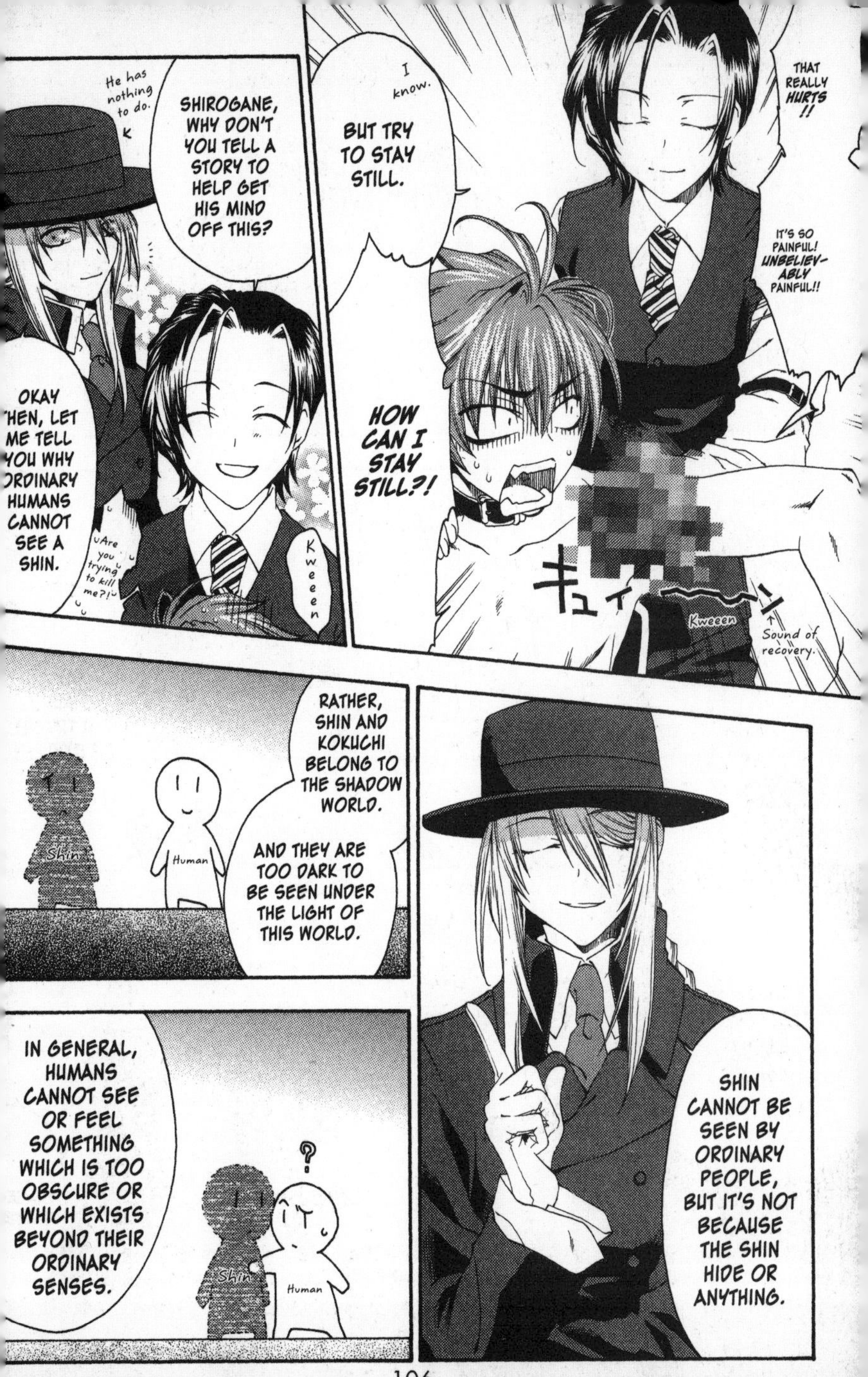
I know.
BUT TRY TO STAY STILL.
THAT REALLY HURTS!!
IT'S SO PAINFUL! UNBELIEVABLY PAINFUL!!
HOW CAN I STAY STILL?!
キュイーーン
Kweeen
Sound of recovery.
He has nothing to do.
SHIROGANE, WHY DON'T YOU TELL A STORY TO HELP GET HIS MIND OFF THIS?
Kweeen
Are you trying to kill me?!
OKAY THEN, LET ME TELL YOU WHY ORDINARY HUMANS CANNOT SEE A SHIN.
SHIN CANNOT BE SEEN BY ORDINARY PEOPLE, BUT IT'S NOT BECAUSE THE SHIN HIDE OR ANYTHING.
RATHER, SHIN AND KOKUCHI BELONG TO THE SHADOW WORLD.
Shin
Human
AND THEY ARE TOO DARK TO BE SEEN UNDER THE LIGHT OF THIS WORLD.
IN GENERAL, HUMANS CANNOT SEE OR FEEL SOMETHING WHICH IS TOO OBSCURE OR WHICH EXISTS BEYOND THEIR ORDINARY SENSES.
?
Shin
Human

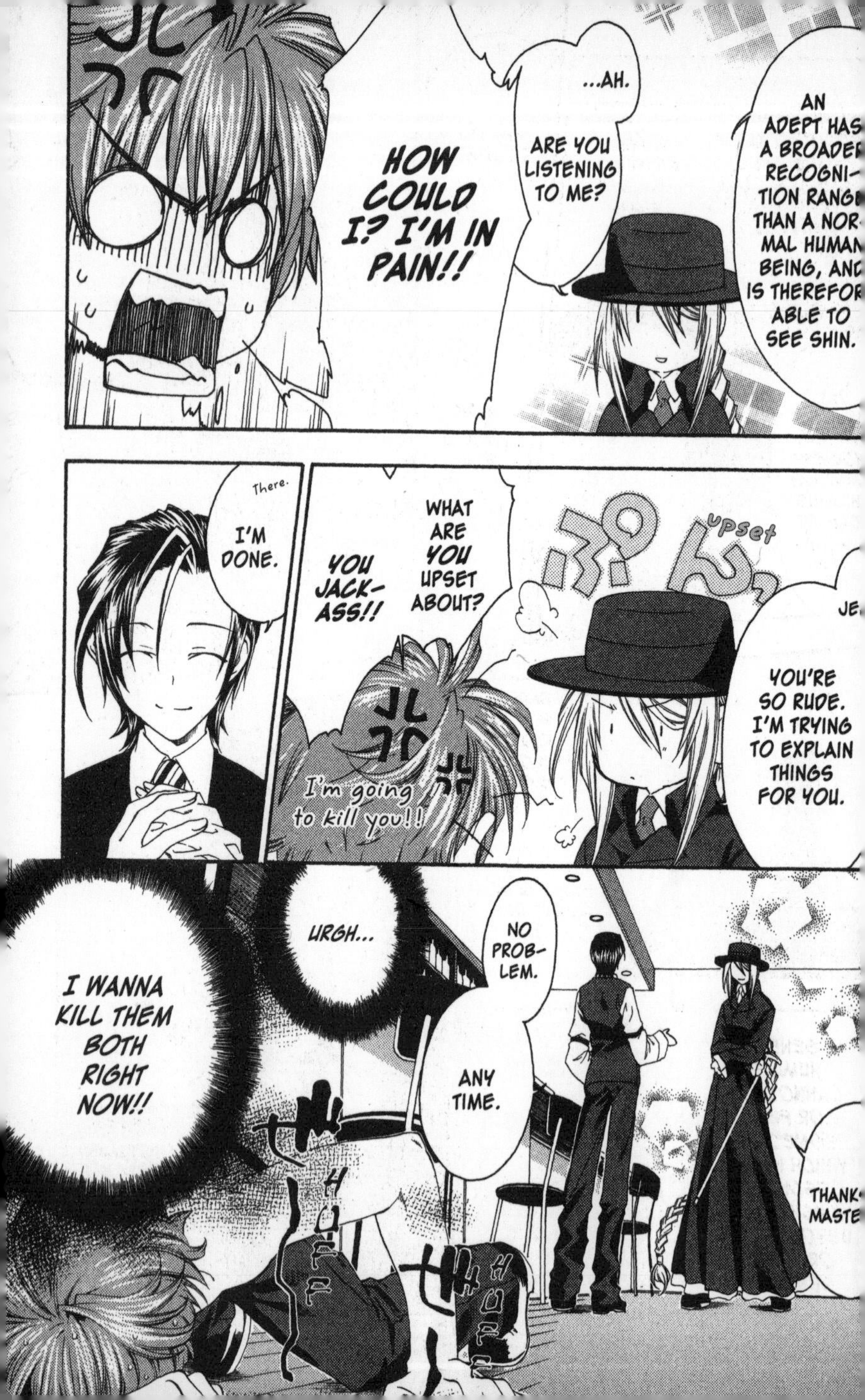
AN ADEPT HAS A BROADER RECOGNITION RANGE THAN A NORMAL HUMAN BEING, AND IS THEREFORE ABLE TO SEE SHIN.
...AH.
ARE YOU LISTENING TO ME?
HOW COULD I? I'M IN PAIN!!
JE
YOU'RE SO RUDE. I'M TRYING TO EXPLAIN THINGS FOR YOU.
upset
WHAT ARE YOU UPSET ABOUT?
YOU JACKASS!!
I'm going to kill you!!
There.
I'M DONE.
THANK-
MASTE
NO PROBLEM.
ANY TIME.
URGH...
I WANNA KILL THEM BOTH RIGHT NOW!!

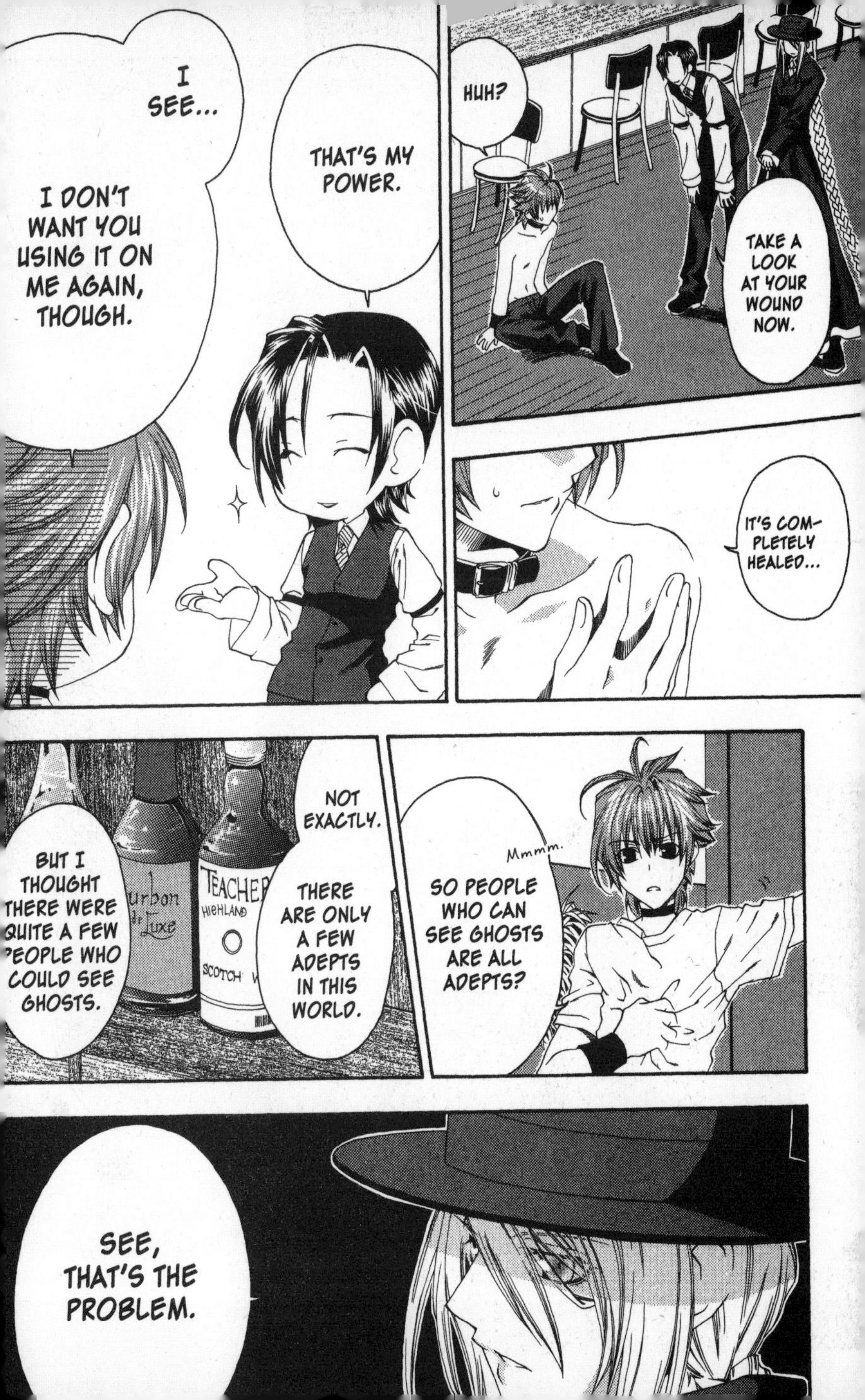
HUH?
TAKE A LOOK AT YOUR WOUND NOW.
IT'S COM-PLETELY HEALED...
THAT'S MY POWER.
I SEE...
I DON'T WANT YOU USING IT ON ME AGAIN, THOUGH.
Mmmm.
SO PEOPLE WHO CAN SEE GHOSTS ARE ALL ADEPTS?
NOT EXACTLY.
THERE ARE ONLY A FEW ADEPTS IN THIS WORLD.
urbon de Luxe
TEACHER
HIGHLAND
SCOTCH
BUT I THOUGHT THERE WERE QUITE A FEW PEOPLE WHO COULD SEE GHOSTS.
SEE, THAT'S THE PROBLEM.

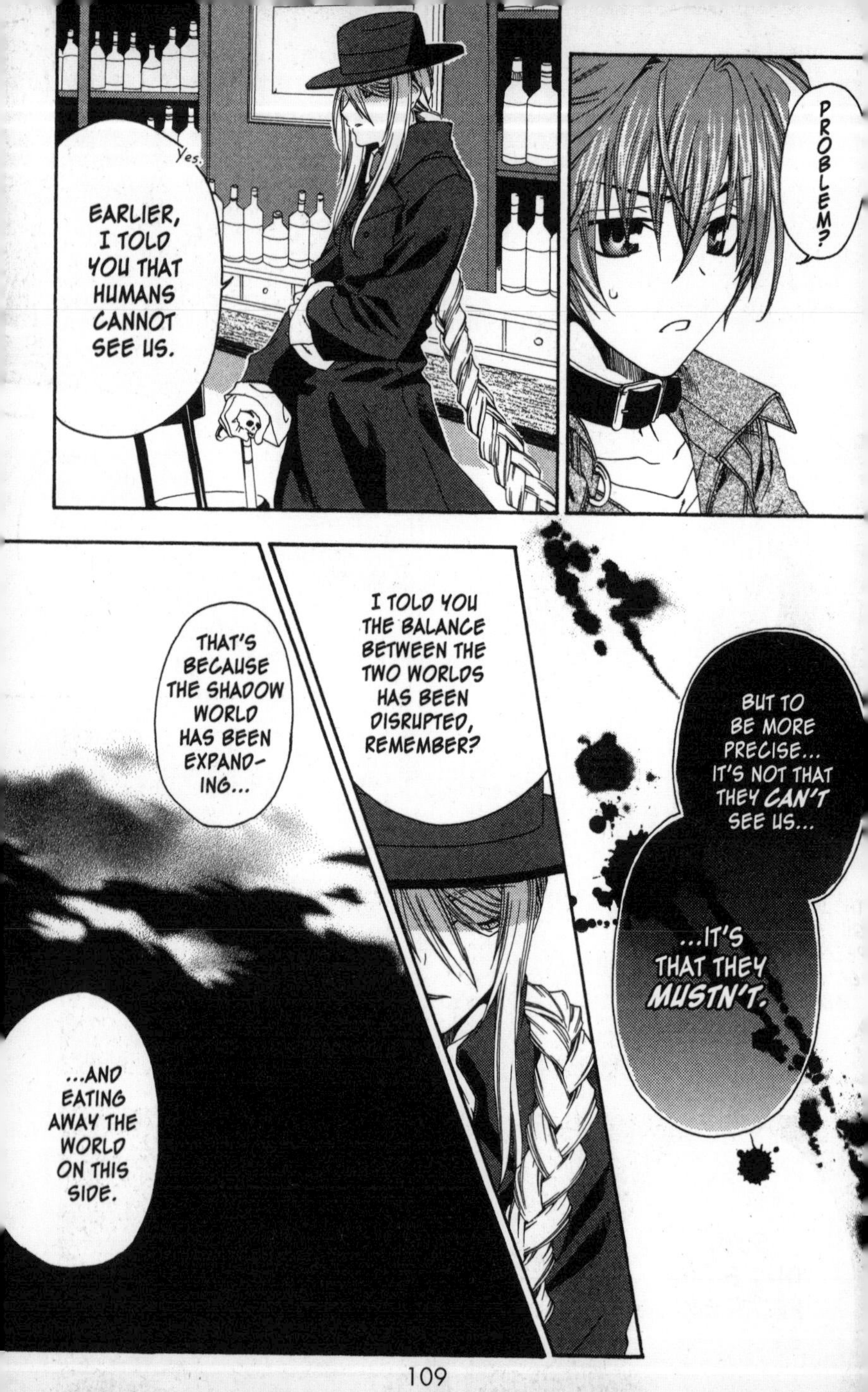
PROBLEM?
Yes.
EARLIER, I TOLD YOU THAT HUMANS CANNOT SEE US.
BUT TO BE MORE PRECISE... IT'S NOT THAT THEY CAN'T SEE US...
...IT'S THAT THEY MUSTN'T.
I TOLD YOU THE BALANCE BETWEEN THE TWO WORLDS HAS BEEN DISRUPTED, REMEMBER?
THAT'S BECAUSE THE SHADOW WORLD HAS BEEN EXPAND-ING...
...AND EATING AWAY THE WORLD ON THIS SIDE.

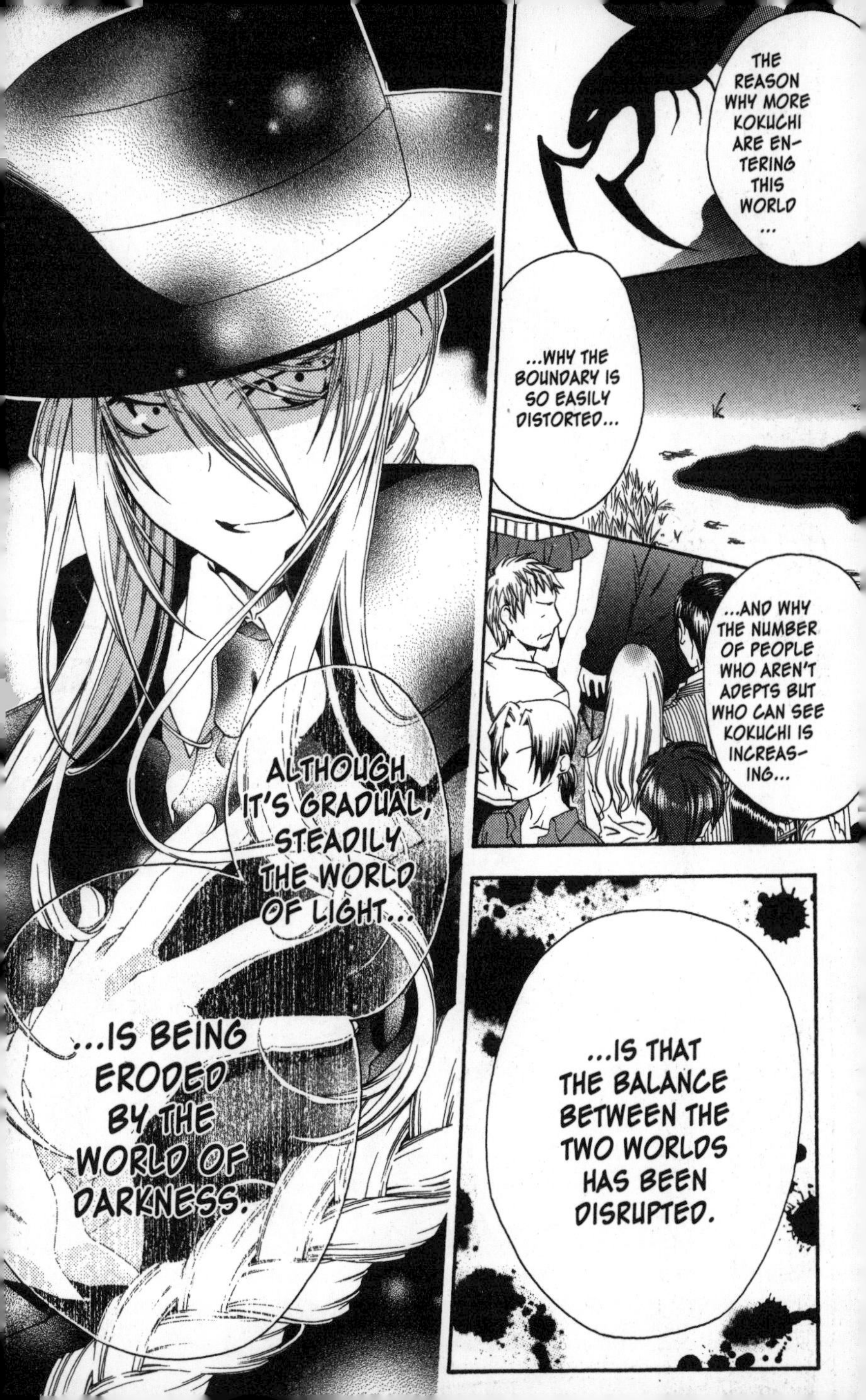
THE REASON WHY MORE KOKUCHI ARE ENTERING THIS WORLD...
...WHY THE BOUNDARY IS SO EASILY DISTORTED...
...AND WHY THE NUMBER OF PEOPLE WHO AREN'T ADEPTS BUT WHO CAN SEE KOKUCHI IS INCREASING...
...IS THAT THE BALANCE BETWEEN THE TWO WORLDS HAS BEEN DISRUPTED.
ALTHOUGH IT'S GRADUAL, STEADILY THE WORLD OF LIGHT...
...IS BEING ERODED BY THE WORLD OF DARKNESS.

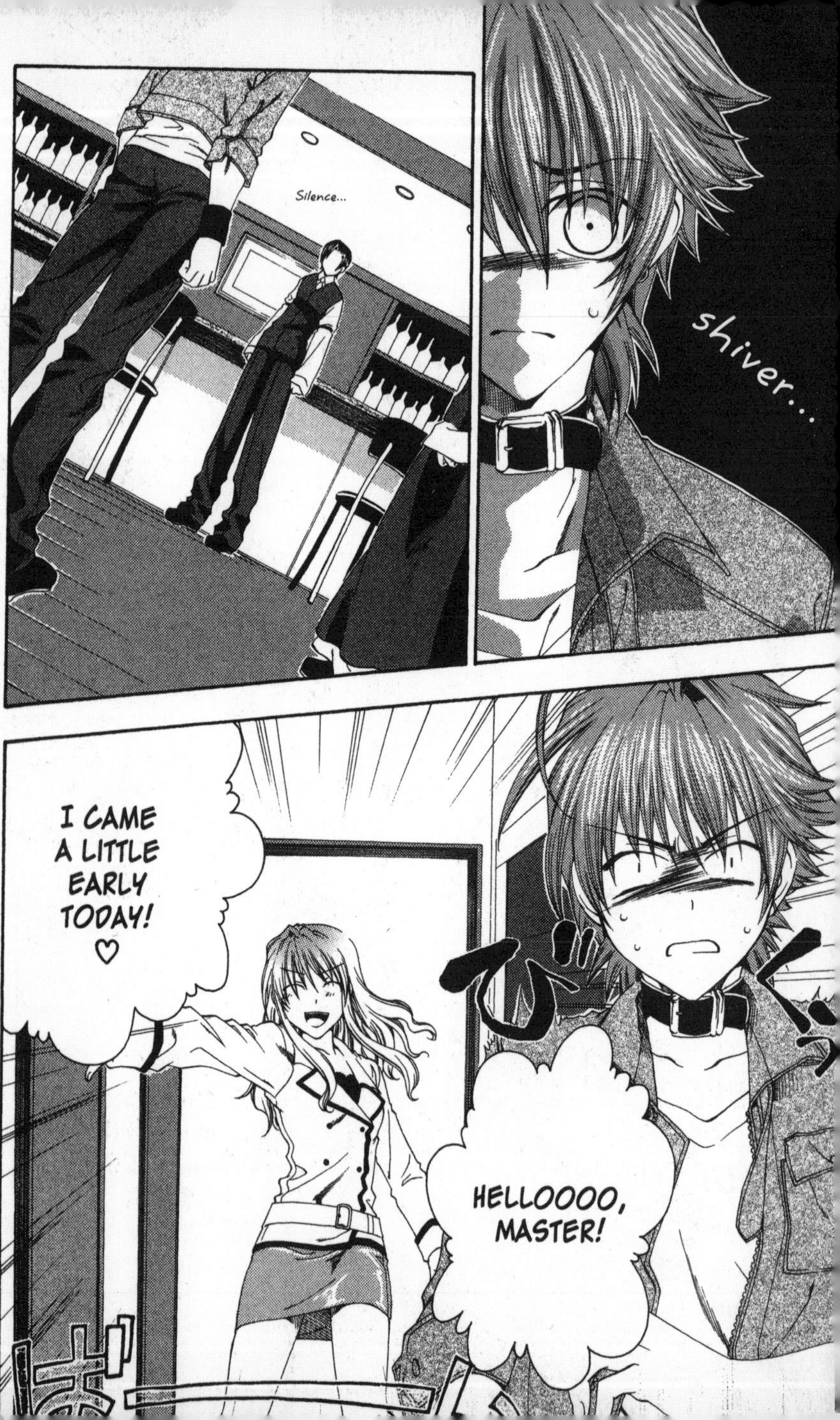
shiver...
Silence...
HELLOOOO, MASTER!
I CAME A LITTLE EARLY TODAY! ♡

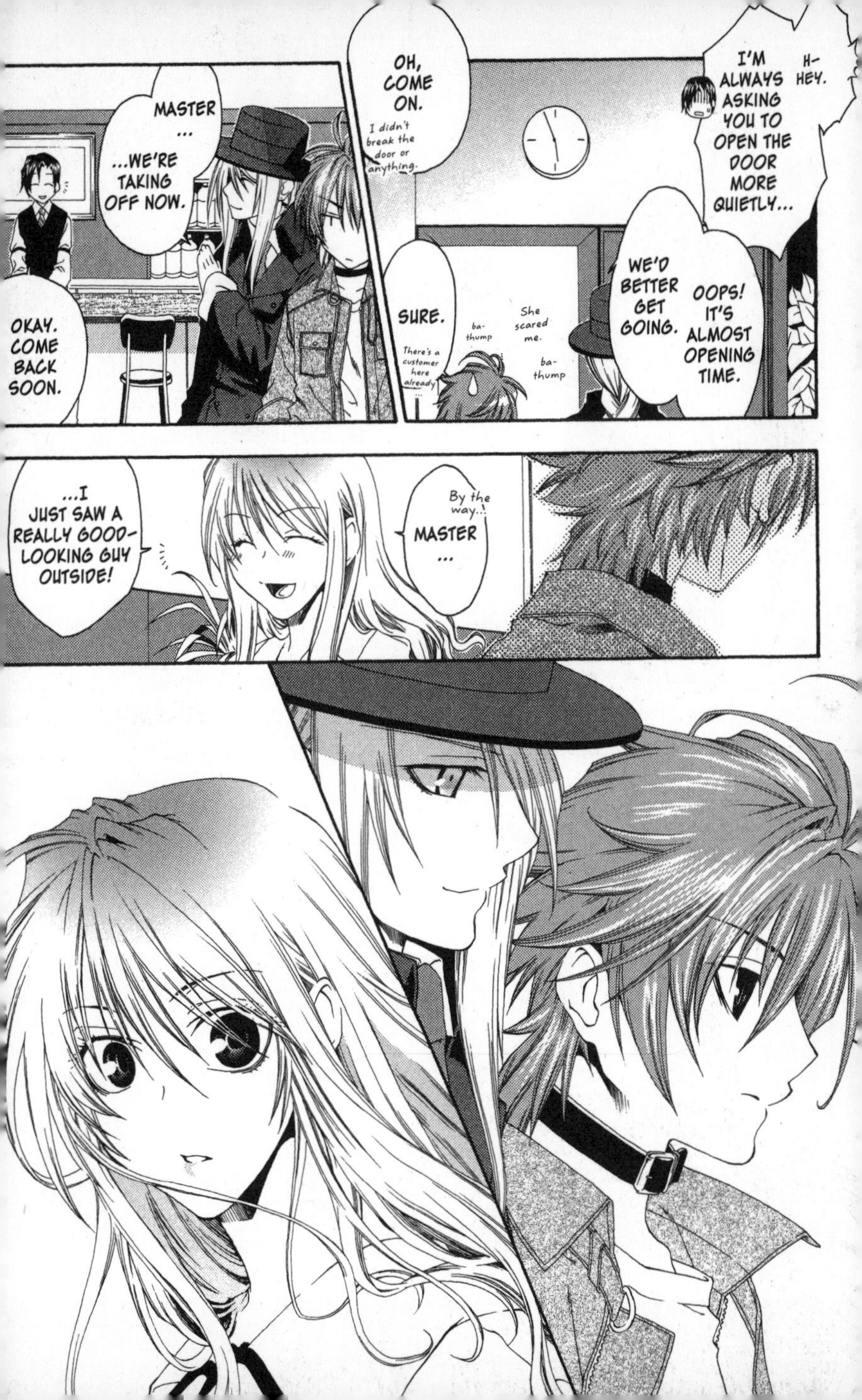
H-HEY.
I'M ALWAYS ASKING YOU TO OPEN THE DOOR MORE QUIETLY...
OH, COME ON.
I didn't break the door or anything.
OOPS! IT'S ALMOST OPENING TIME.
WE'D BETTER GET GOING.
She scared me.
ba-thump
ba-thump
There's a customer here already...
SURE.
MASTER ...
...WE'RE TAKING OFF NOW.
OKAY. COME BACK SOON.
MASTER ...
By the way..!
...I JUST SAW A REALLY GOOD-LOOKING GUY OUTSIDE!

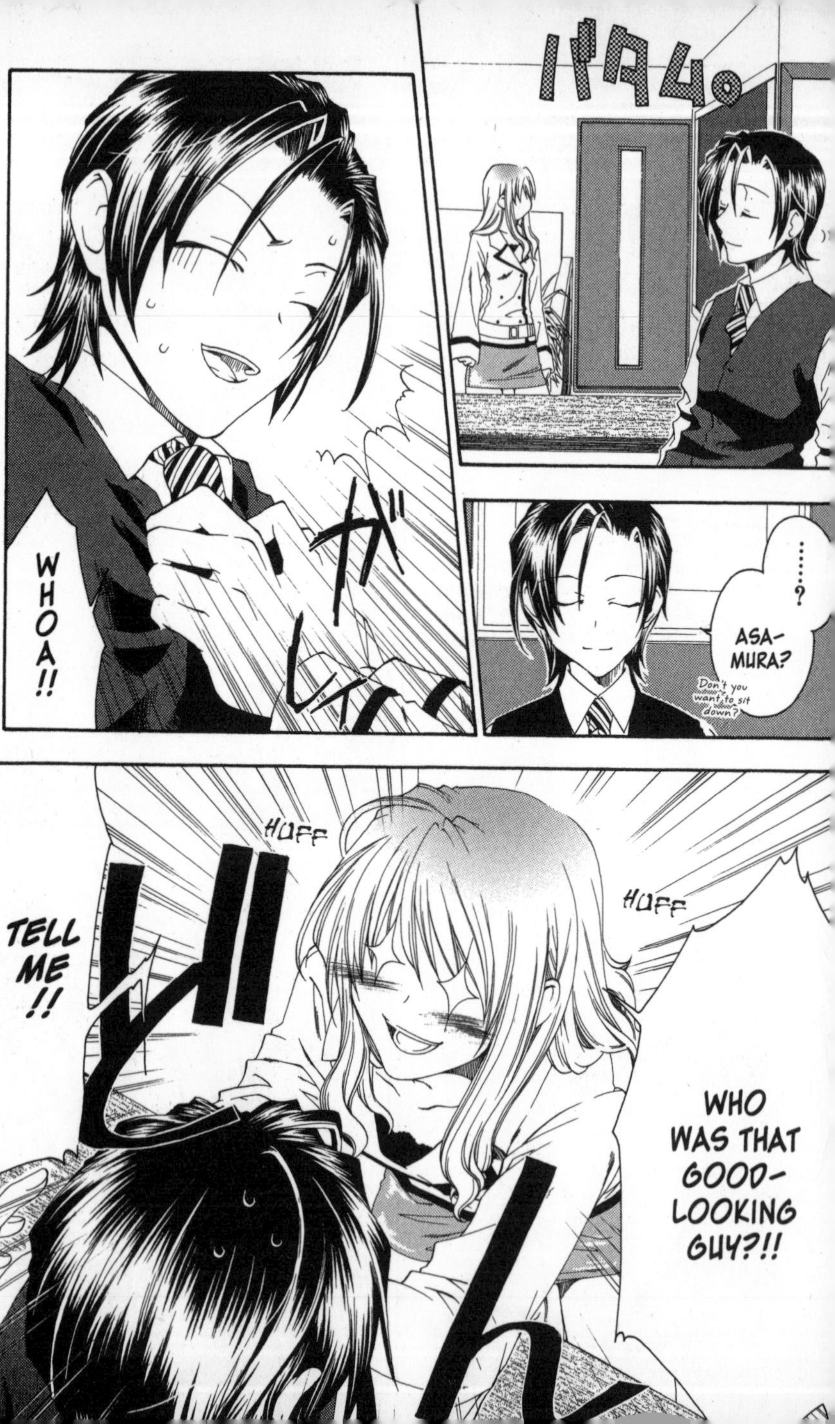

パタム。
......?
ASA-MURA?
Don't you want to sit down?
WHOA!!
HUFF
HUFF
WHO WAS THAT GOOD-LOOKING GUY?!!
TELL ME!!

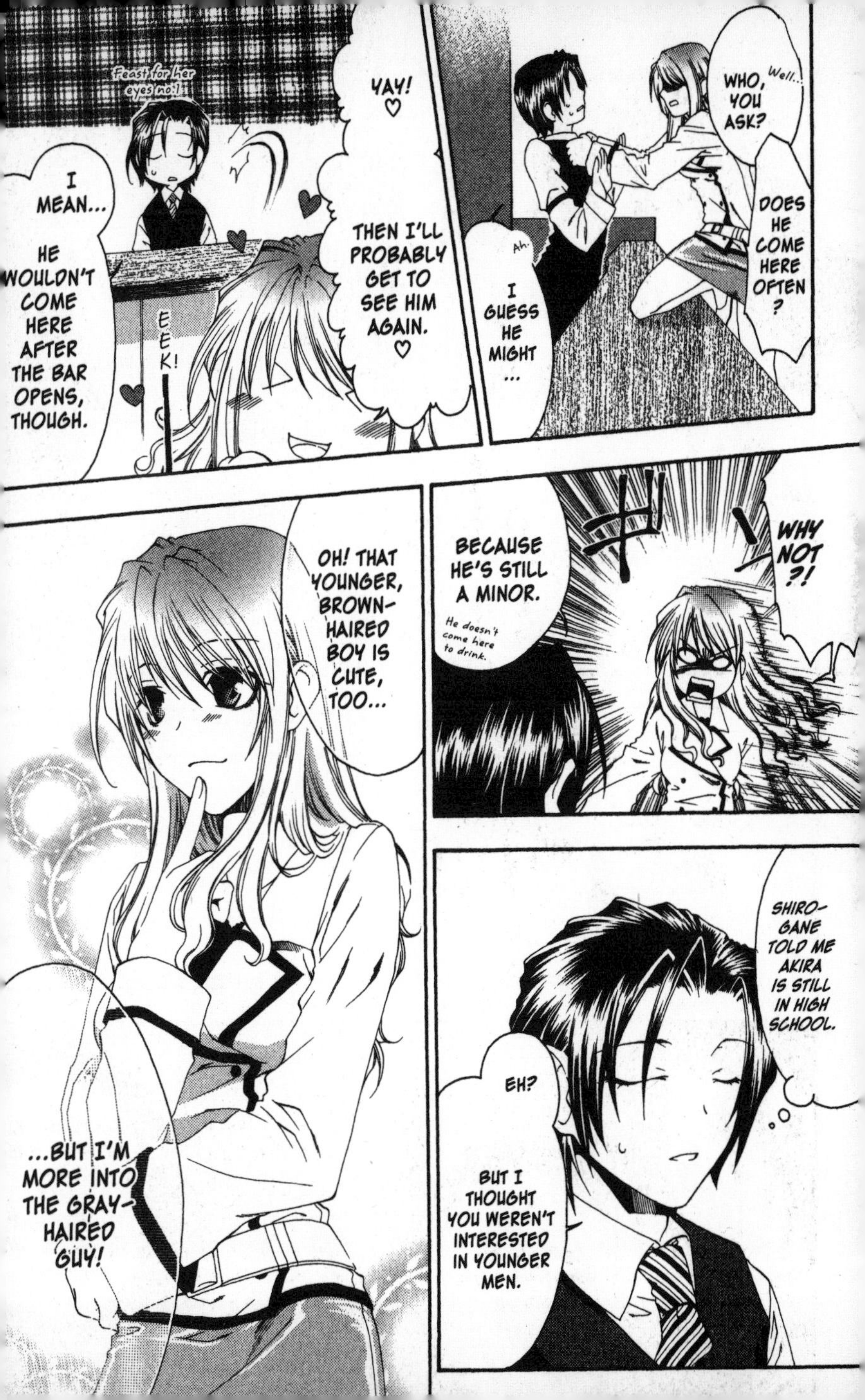
Well...
WHO, YOU ASK?
DOES HE COME HERE OFTEN?
Ah.
I GUESS HE MIGHT...
YAY! ♡
Feast for her eyes no. 1
THEN I'LL PROBABLY GET TO SEE HIM AGAIN. ♡
I MEAN...
HE WOULDN'T COME HERE AFTER THE BAR OPENS, THOUGH.
EEK!
WHY NOT?!
BECAUSE HE'S STILL A MINOR.
He doesn't come here to drink.
SHIRO-GANE TOLD ME AKIRA IS STILL IN HIGH SCHOOL.
EH?
BUT I THOUGHT YOU WEREN'T INTERESTED IN YOUNGER MEN.
OH! THAT YOUNGER, BROWN-HAIRED BOY IS CUTE, TOO...
...BUT I'M MORE INTO THE GRAY-HAIRED GUY!

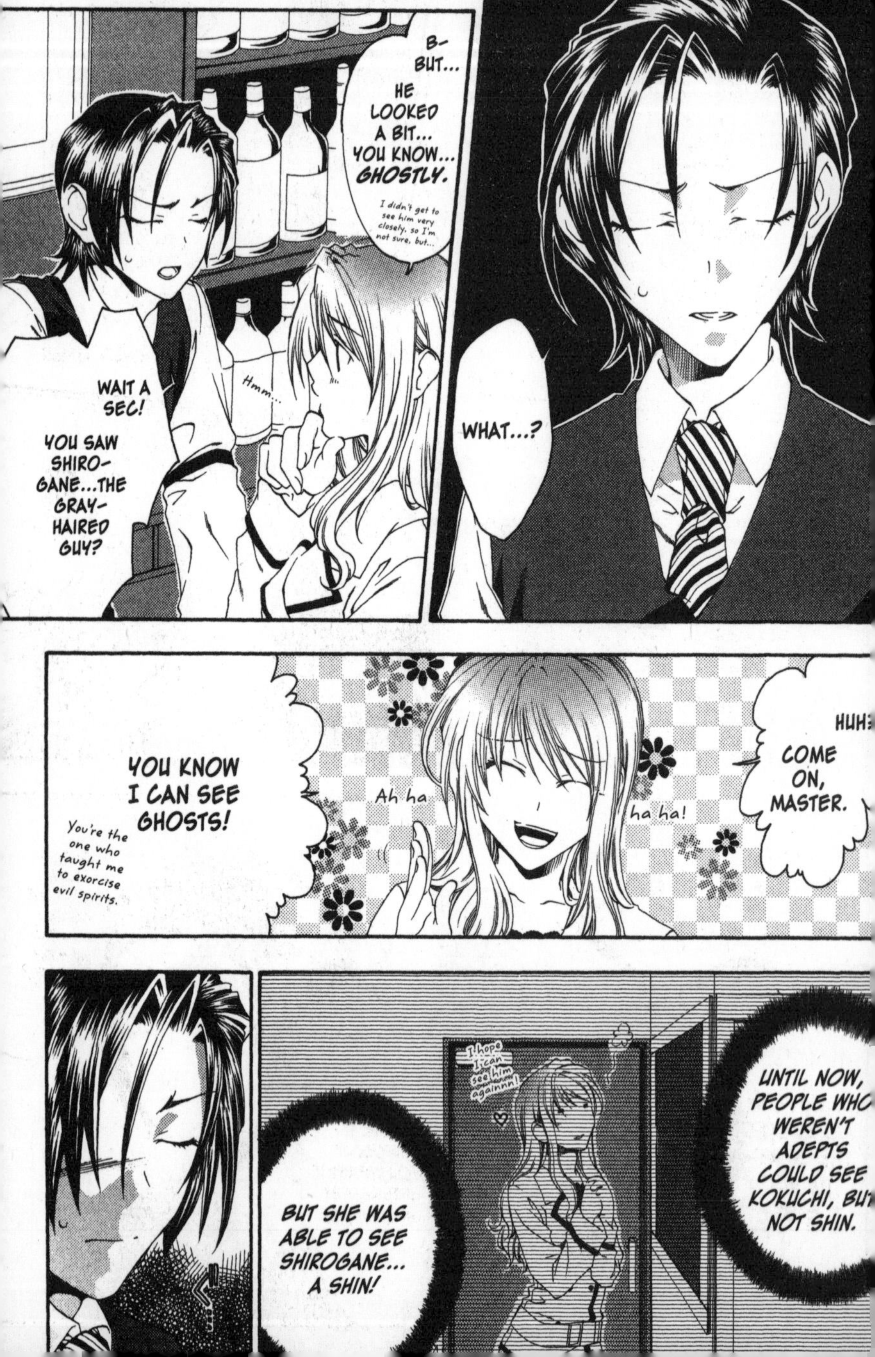
WHAT...?
B-BUT... HE LOOKED A BIT... YOU KNOW... GHOSTLY.
I didn't get to see him very closely, so I'm not sure, but...
Hmm...
WAIT A SEC!
YOU SAW SHIRO-GANE...THE GRAY-HAIRED GUY?
HUH?
COME ON, MASTER.
Ah ha ha ha!
YOU KNOW I CAN SEE GHOSTS!
You're the one who taught me to exorcise evil spirits.
UNTIL NOW, PEOPLE WHO WEREN'T ADEPTS COULD SEE KOKUCHI, BUT NOT SHIN.
I hope I can see him againnn!
BUT SHE WAS ABLE TO SEE SHIROGANE... A SHIN!

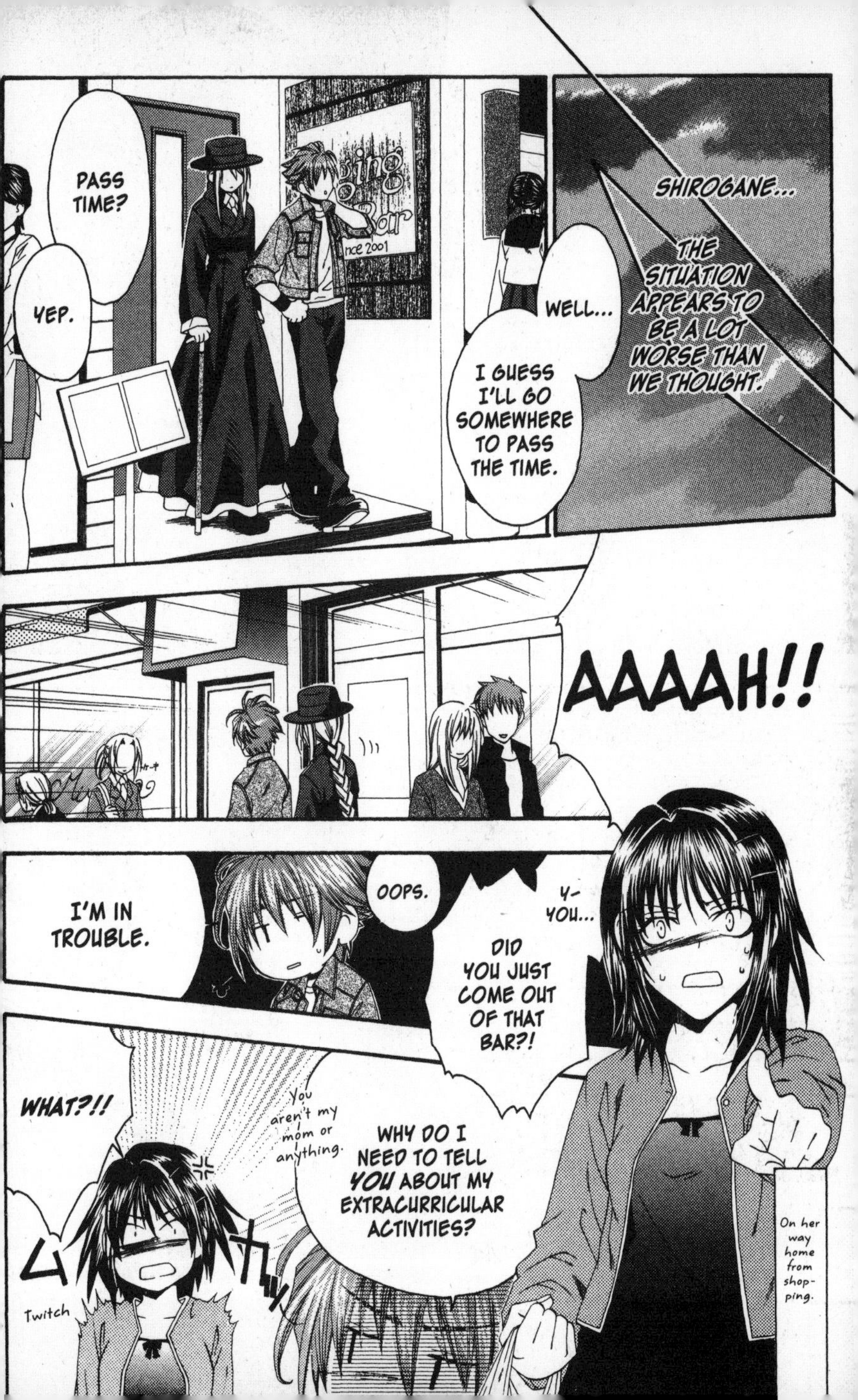
SHIROGANE...
THE SITUATION APPEARS TO BE A LOT WORSE THAN WE THOUGHT.
WELL...
I GUESS I'LL GO SOMEWHERE TO PASS THE TIME.
PASS TIME?
YEP.
AAAAH!!
Y-YOU...
DID YOU JUST COME OUT OF THAT BAR?!
OOPS.
I'M IN TROUBLE.
On her way home from shop-ping.
WHY DO I NEED TO TELL YOU ABOUT MY EXTRACURRICULAR ACTIVITIES?
You aren't my mom or anything.
WHAT?!!
Twitch

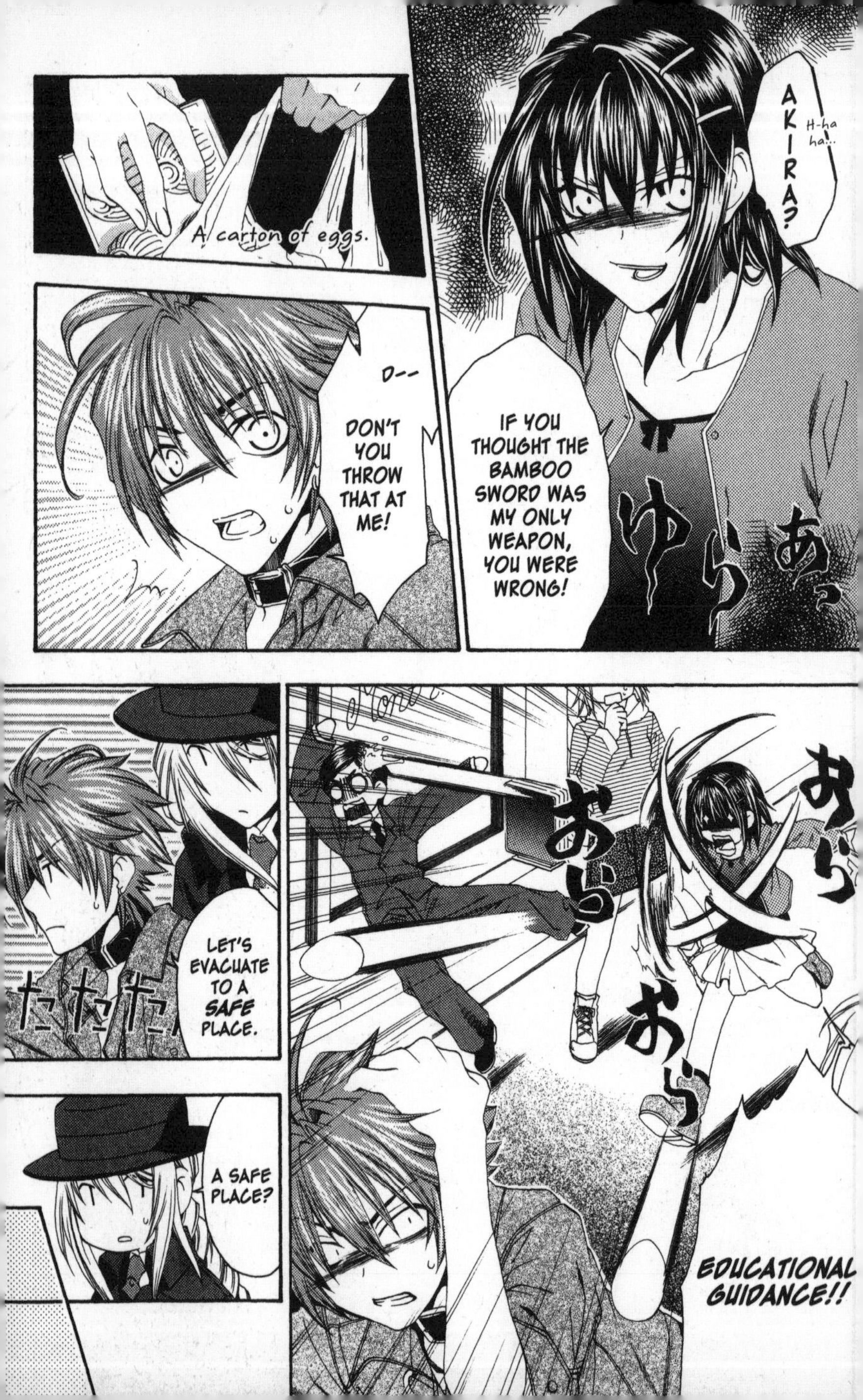
AKIRA?
H-ha ha...
IF YOU THOUGHT THE BAMBOO SWORD WAS MY ONLY WEAPON, YOU WERE WRONG!
ゆらあっ
A carton of eggs.
D--
DON'T YOU THROW THAT AT ME!
おら
おら
おら
EDUCATIONAL GUIDANCE!!
LET'S EVACUATE TO A SAFE PLACE.
A SAFE PLACE?

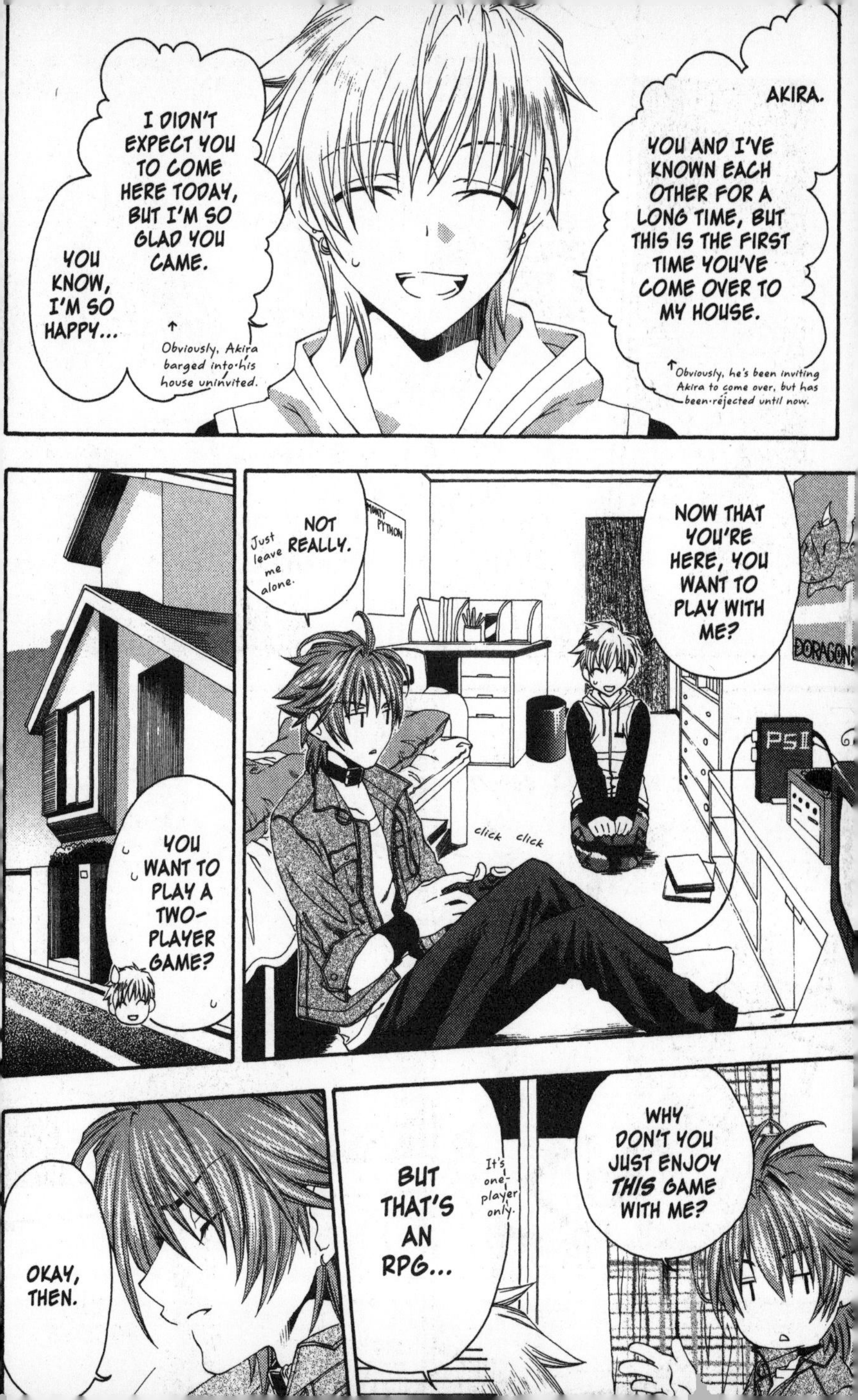
AKIRA.
YOU AND I'VE KNOWN EACH OTHER FOR A LONG TIME, BUT THIS IS THE FIRST TIME YOU'VE COME OVER TO MY HOUSE.
Obviously, he's been inviting Akira to come over, but has been rejected until now.
I DIDN'T EXPECT YOU TO COME HERE TODAY, BUT I'M SO GLAD YOU CAME.
YOU KNOW, I'M SO HAPPY...
Obviously, Akira barged into his house uninvited.
NOW THAT YOU'RE HERE, YOU WANT TO PLAY WITH ME?
DORAGONS
PS II
MONTY PYTHON
NOT REALLY.
Just leave me alone.
click click
YOU WANT TO PLAY A TWO-PLAYER GAME?
WHY DON'T YOU JUST ENJOY THIS GAME WITH ME?
BUT THAT'S AN RPG...
It's one-player only.
OKAY, THEN.

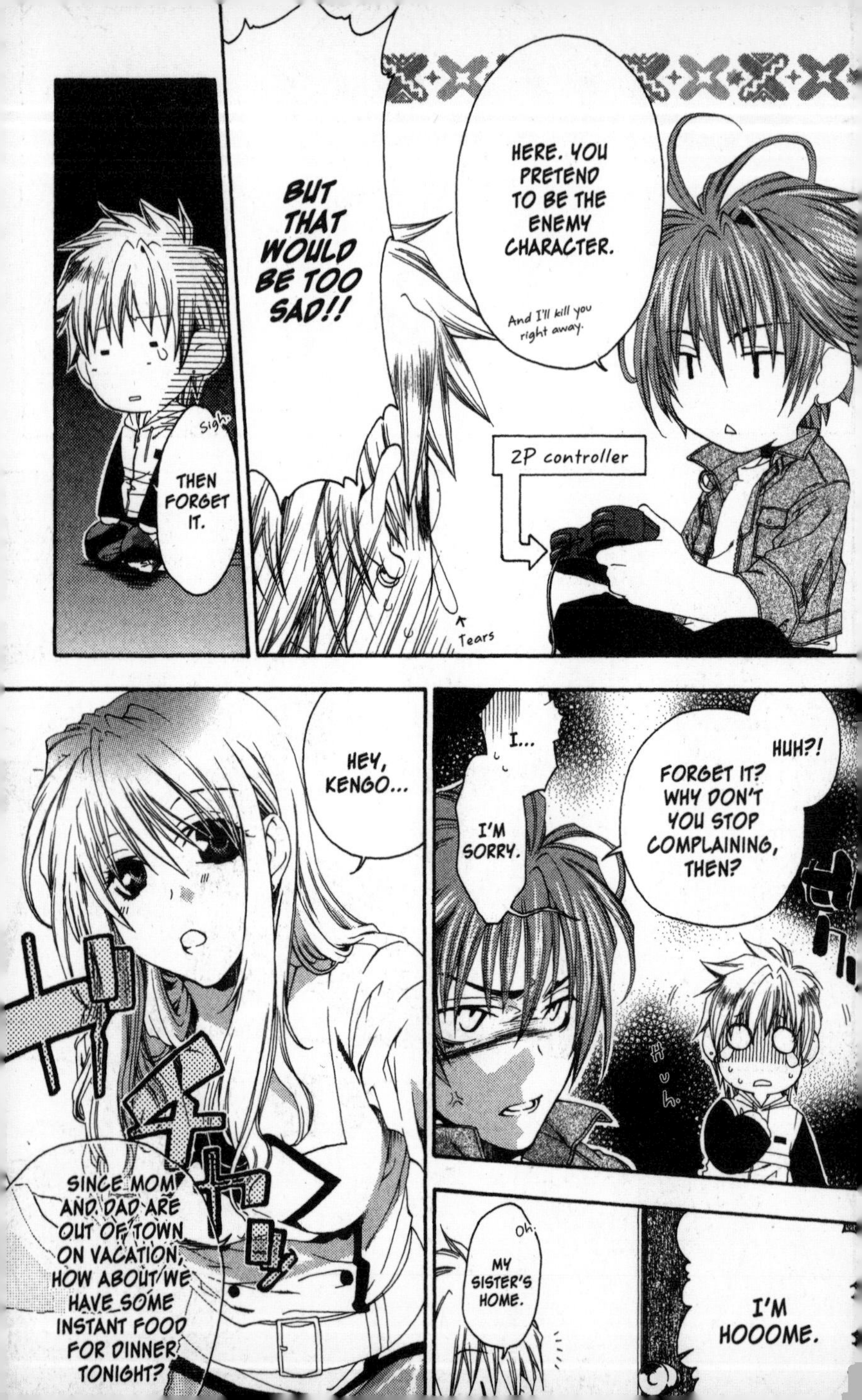

HERE. YOU PRETEND TO BE THE ENEMY CHARACTER.
And I'll kill you right away.
2P controller
BUT THAT WOULD BE TOO SAD!!
Tears
Sigh.
THEN FORGET IT.
HUH?!
FORGET IT? WHY DON'T YOU STOP COMPLAINING, THEN?
I...
I'M SORRY.
Huh.
I'M HOOOME.
Oh.
MY SISTER'S HOME.
HEY, KENGO...
SINCE MOM AND DAD ARE OUT OF TOWN ON VACATION, HOW ABOUT WE HAVE SOME INSTANT FOOD FOR DINNER TONIGHT?

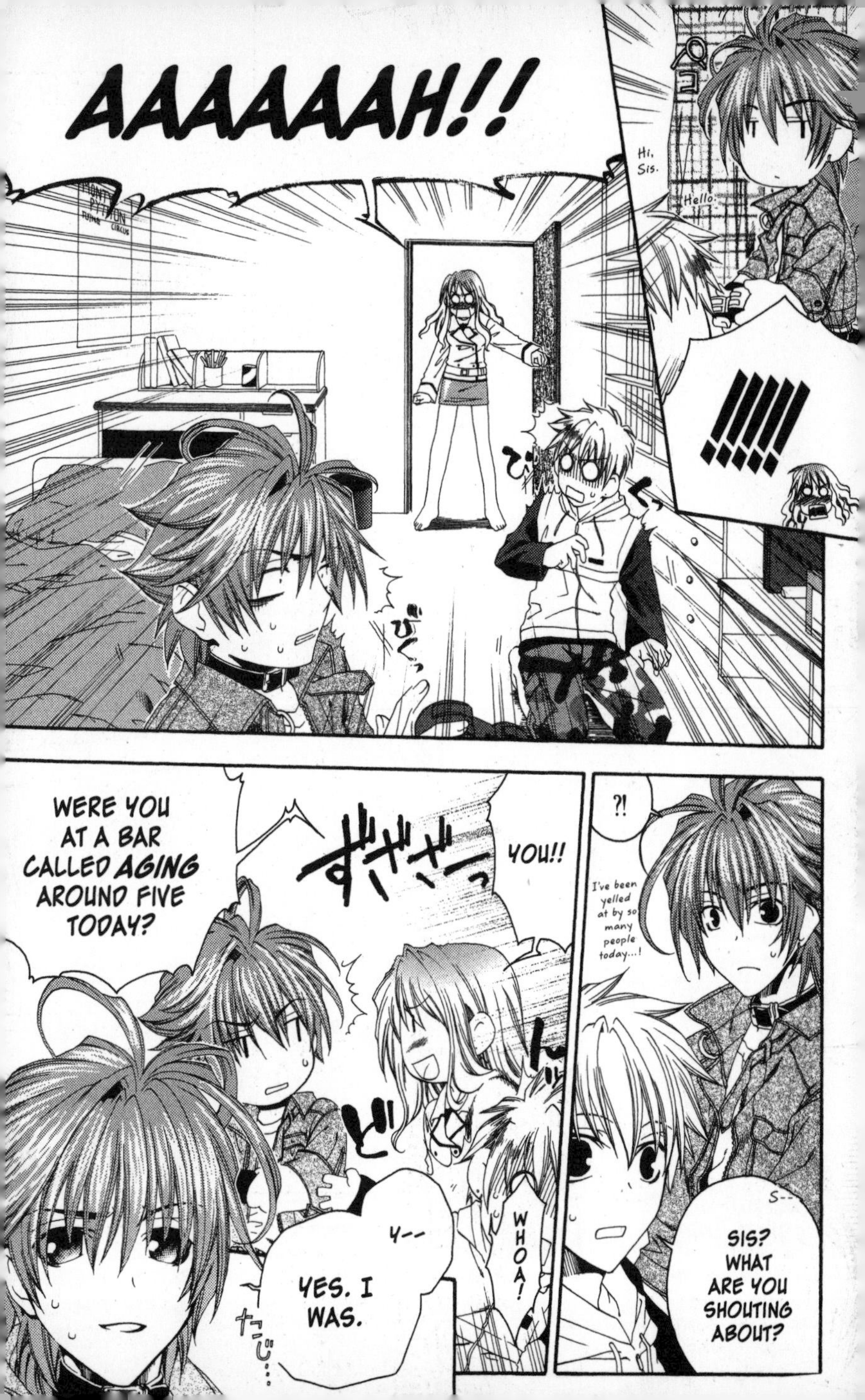
Hi, Sis.
Hello.
!!!!!!
AAAAAAH!!
?!
I've been yelled at by so many people today...!
S--
SIS? WHAT ARE YOU SHOUTING ABOUT?
YOU!!
WERE YOU AT A BAR CALLED AGING AROUND FIVE TODAY?
WHOA!
Y--
YES. I WAS.

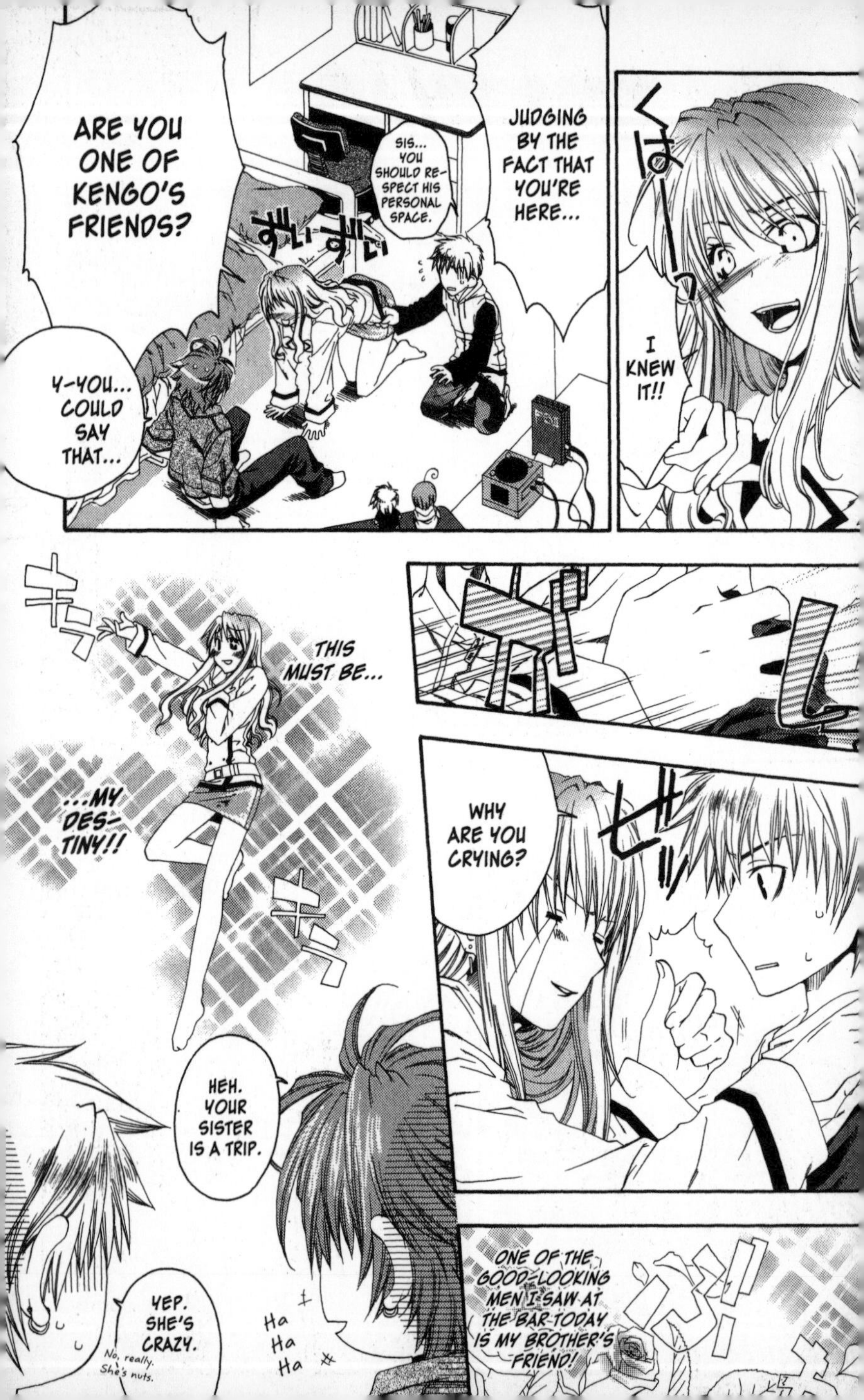
くはーっ
I KNEW IT!!
JUDGING BY THE FACT THAT YOU'RE HERE...
ARE YOU ONE OF KENGO'S FRIENDS?
SIS... YOU SHOULD RE- SPECT HIS PERSONAL SPACE.
ずいずい
Y-YOU... COULD SAY THAT...
WHY ARE YOU CRYING?
ONE OF THE GOOD-LOOKING MEN I SAW AT THE BAR TODAY IS MY BROTHER'S FRIEND!
キラ
THIS MUST BE...
...MY DES- TINY!!
キラ
HEH. YOUR SISTER IS A TRIP.
YEP. SHE'S CRAZY.
No, really. She's nuts.
Ha Ha Ha

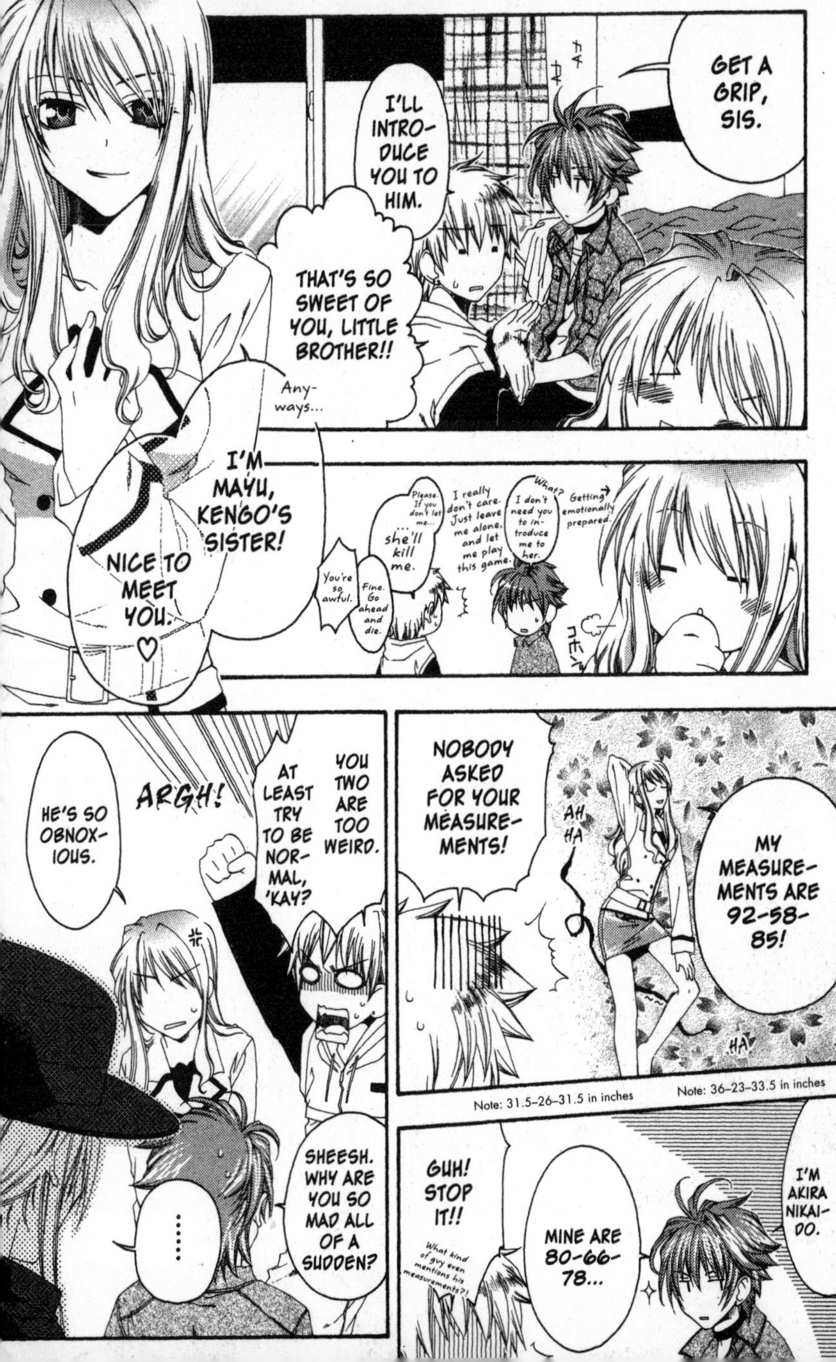
GET A GRIP, SIS.
I'LL INTRO-DUCE YOU TO HIM.
THAT'S SO SWEET OF YOU, LITTLE BROTHER!!
Getting emotionally prepared.
What?
I don't need you to in-troduce me to her.
I really don't care. Just leave me alone, and let me play this game.
Please. If you don't let me... ...she'll kill me.
Fine. Go ahead and die.
You're so awful.
Any-ways...
I'M MAYU, KENGO'S SISTER!
NICE TO MEET YOU. ♡
MY MEASURE-MENTS ARE 92-58-85!
AH HA
HA
NOBODY ASKED FOR YOUR MEASURE-MENTS!
Note: 36-23-33.5 in inches
Note: 31.5-26-31.5 in inches
I'M AKIRA NIKAI-DO.
MINE ARE 80-66-78...
GUH! STOP IT!!
What kind of guy even mentions his measurements?!
YOU TWO ARE TOO WEIRD.
AT LEAST TRY TO BE NOR-MAL, 'KAY?
ARGH!
HE'S SO OBNOX-IOUS.
SHEESH. WHY ARE YOU SO MAD ALL OF A SUDDEN?
......

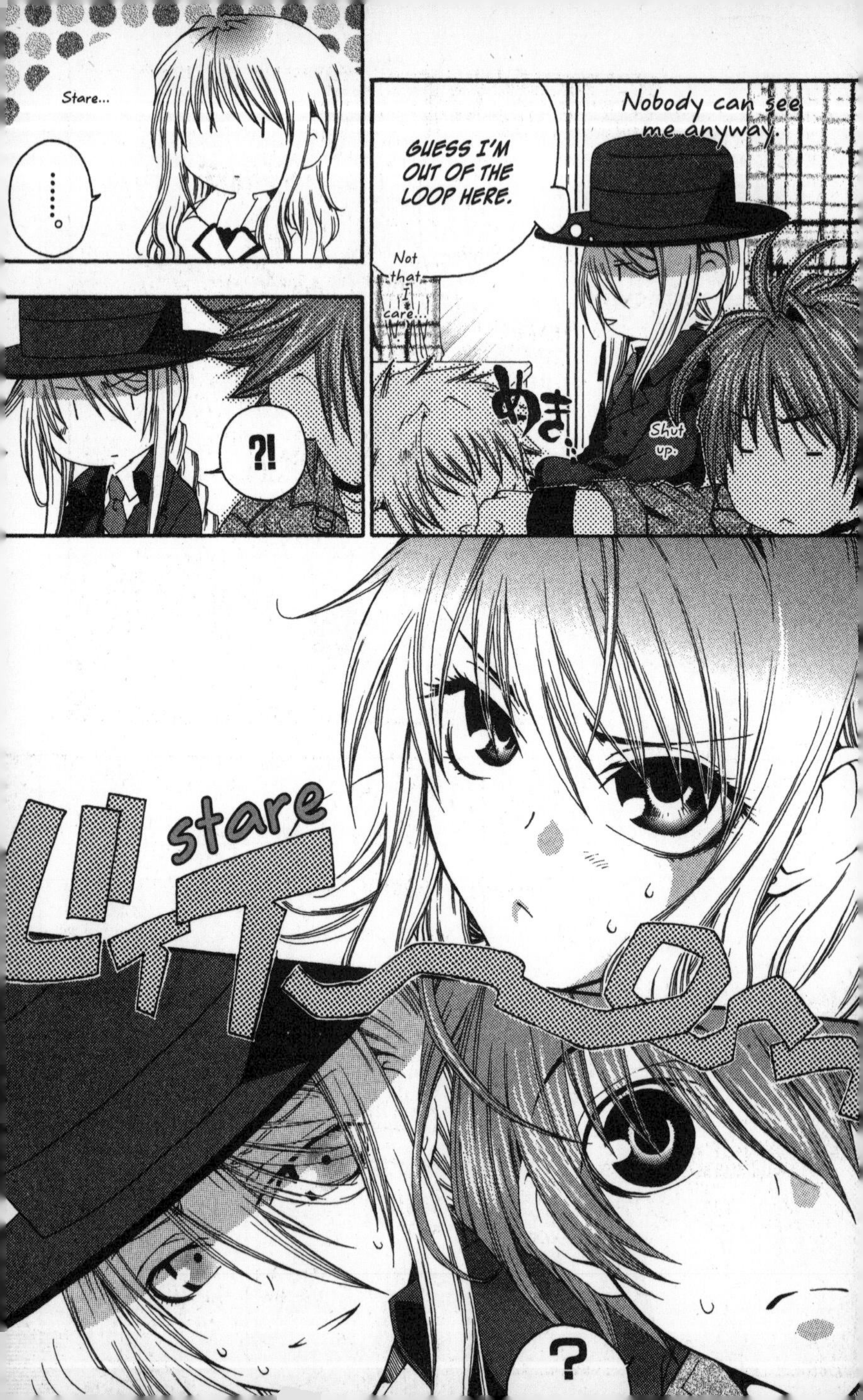
Nobody can see me anyway.
GUESS I'M OUT OF THE LOOP HERE.
Not that I care...
めき
Shut up.
Stare...
......。
?!
stare
?

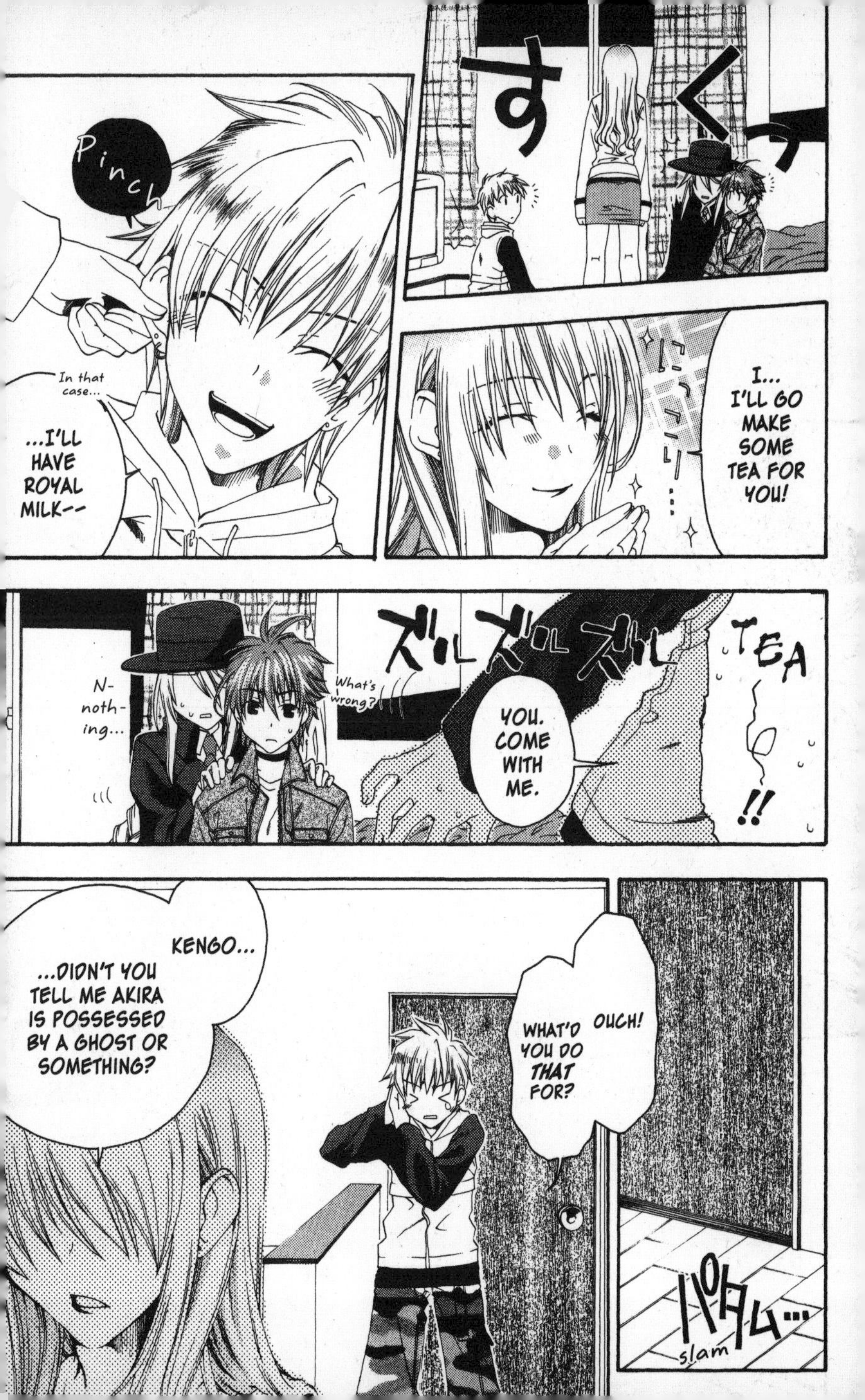

すくっ
にっこり…
I... I'LL GO MAKE SOME TEA FOR YOU!
Pinch
In that case...
...I'LL HAVE ROYAL MILK--
TEA !!
ズルズルズル
YOU. COME WITH ME.
What's wrong?
N-nothing...
パタム…
slam
OUCH!
WHAT'D YOU DO THAT FOR?
KENGO...
...DIDN'T YOU TELL ME AKIRA IS POSSESSED BY A GHOST OR SOMETHING?

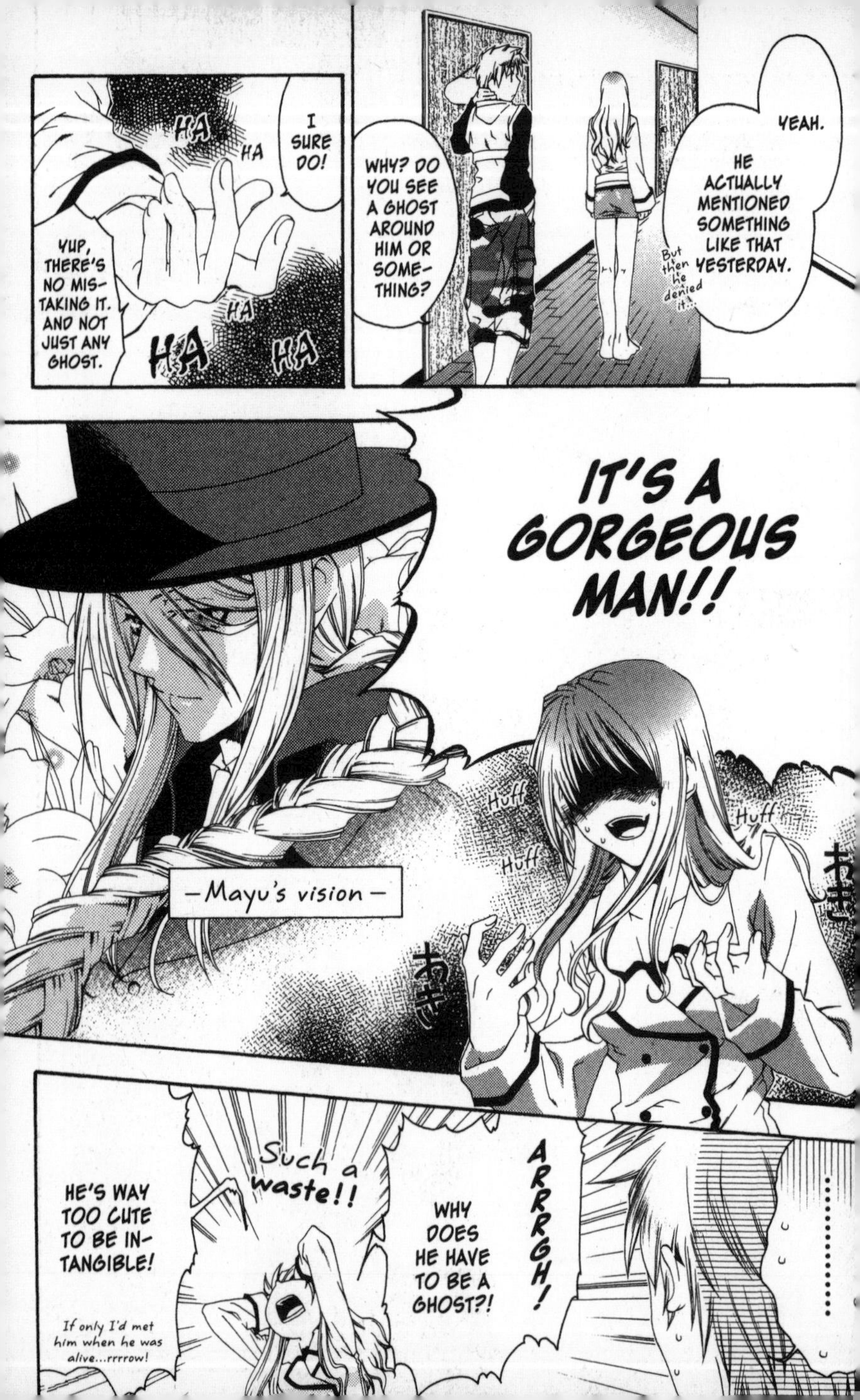
YEAH.
HE ACTUALLY MENTIONED SOMETHING LIKE THAT YESTERDAY.
But then he denied it.
WHY? DO YOU SEE A GHOST AROUND HIM OR SOME-THING?
I SURE DO!
HA
HA
YUP, THERE'S NO MIS-TAKING IT. AND NOT JUST ANY GHOST.
HA
HA
HA
IT'S A GORGEOUS MAN!!
Huff
Huff
Huff
—Mayu's vision—
......
ARRRGH!
WHY DOES HE HAVE TO BE A GHOST?!
Such a waste!!
HE'S WAY TOO CUTE TO BE IN-TANGIBLE!
If only I'd met him when he was alive...rrrrow!

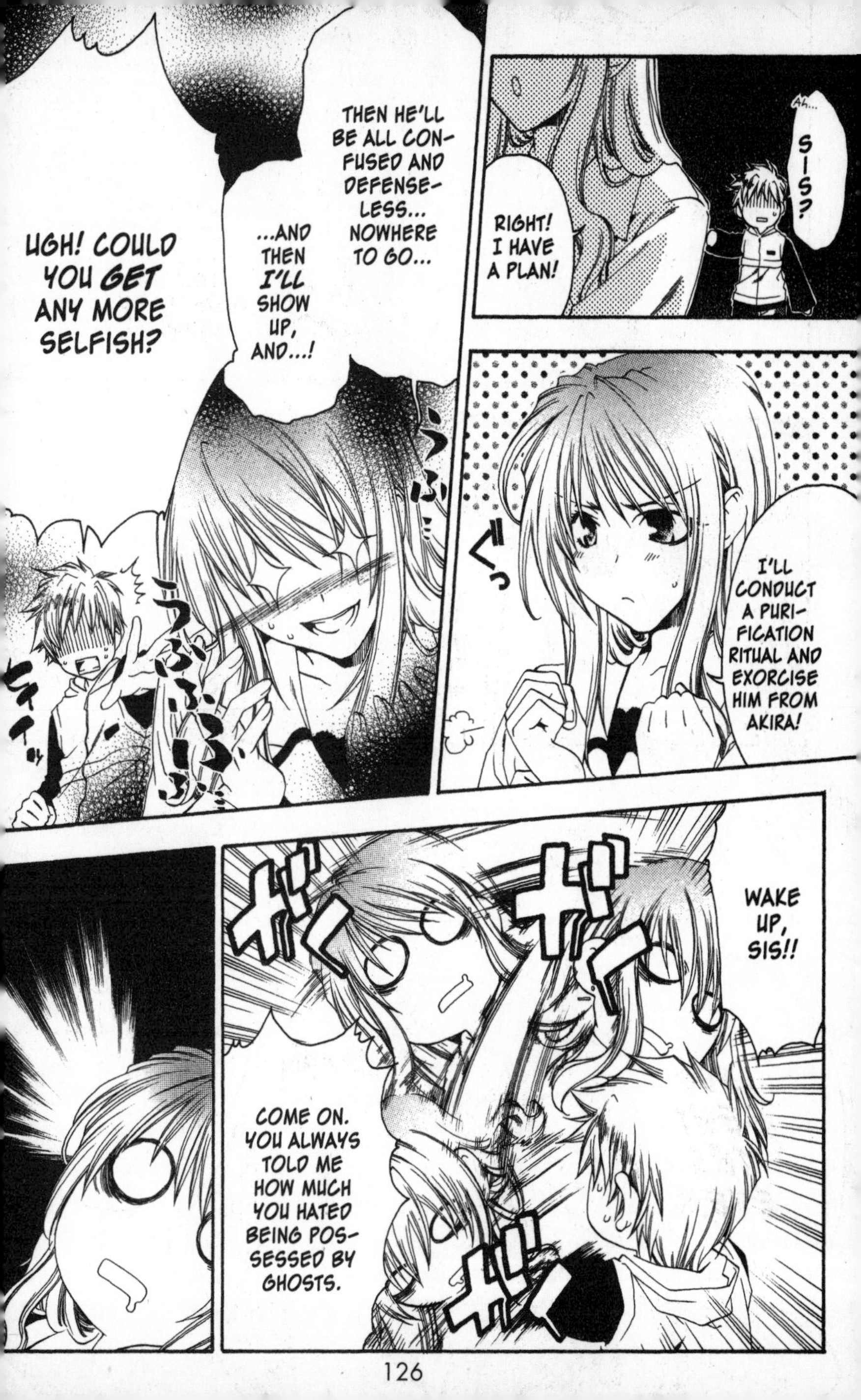

Ah...
SIS?
RIGHT! I HAVE A PLAN!
I'LL CONDUCT A PURIFICATION RITUAL AND EXORCISE HIM FROM AKIRA!
THEN HE'LL BE ALL CONFUSED AND DEFENSELESS... NOWHERE TO GO...
...AND THEN *I'LL* SHOW UP, AND...!
UGH! COULD YOU ***GET*** ANY MORE SELFISH?
WAKE UP, SIS!!
COME ON. YOU ALWAYS TOLD ME HOW MUCH YOU HATED BEING POSSESSED BY GHOSTS.

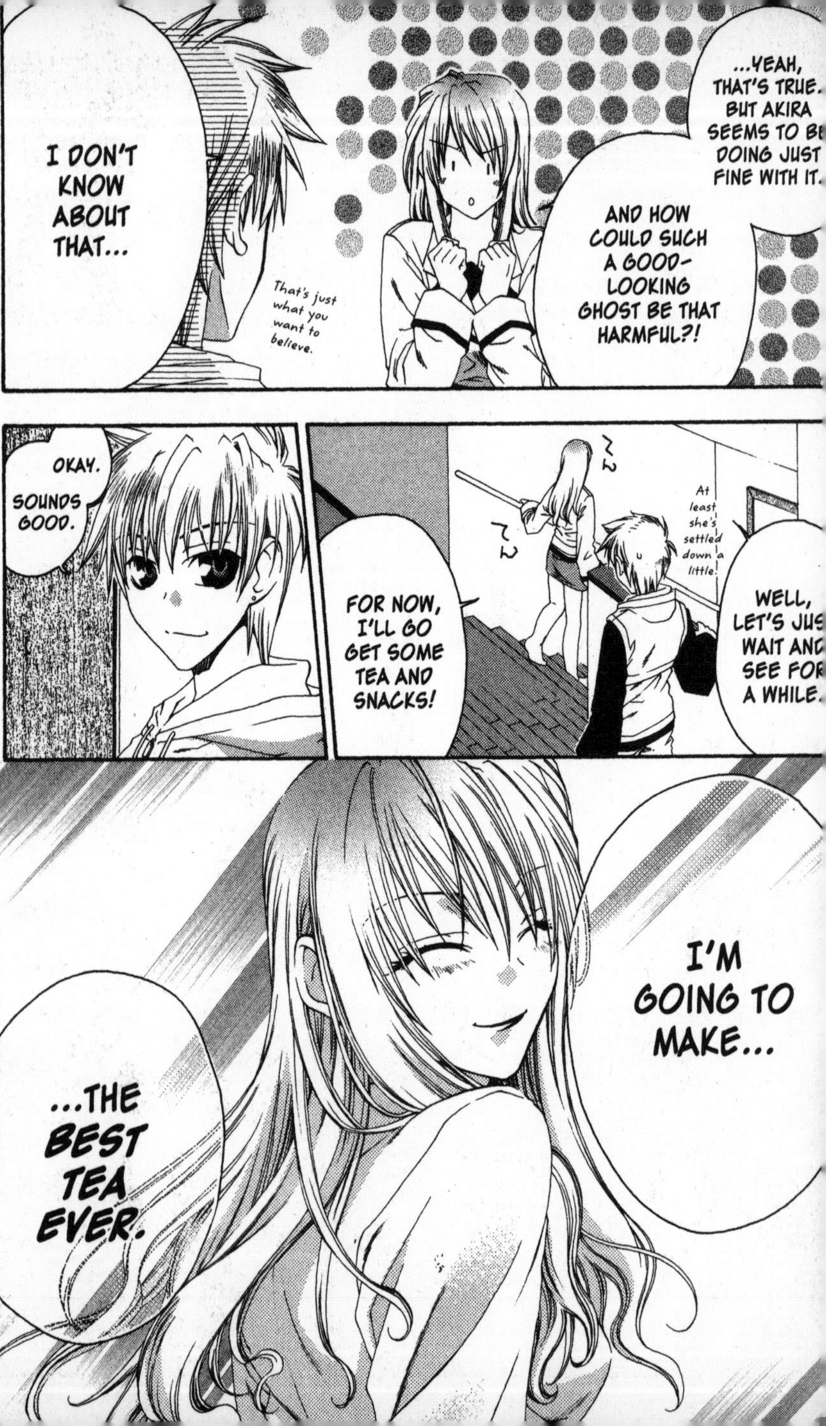
...YEAH, THAT'S TRUE. BUT AKIRA SEEMS TO BE DOING JUST FINE WITH IT.
AND HOW COULD SUCH A GOOD-LOOKING GHOST BE THAT HARMFUL?!
That's just what you want to believe.
I DON'T KNOW ABOUT THAT...
WELL, LET'S JUST WAIT AND SEE FOR A WHILE.
At least she's settled down a little.
FOR NOW, I'LL GO GET SOME TEA AND SNACKS!
OKAY.
SOUNDS GOOD.
I'M GOING TO MAKE...
...THE BEST TEA EVER.

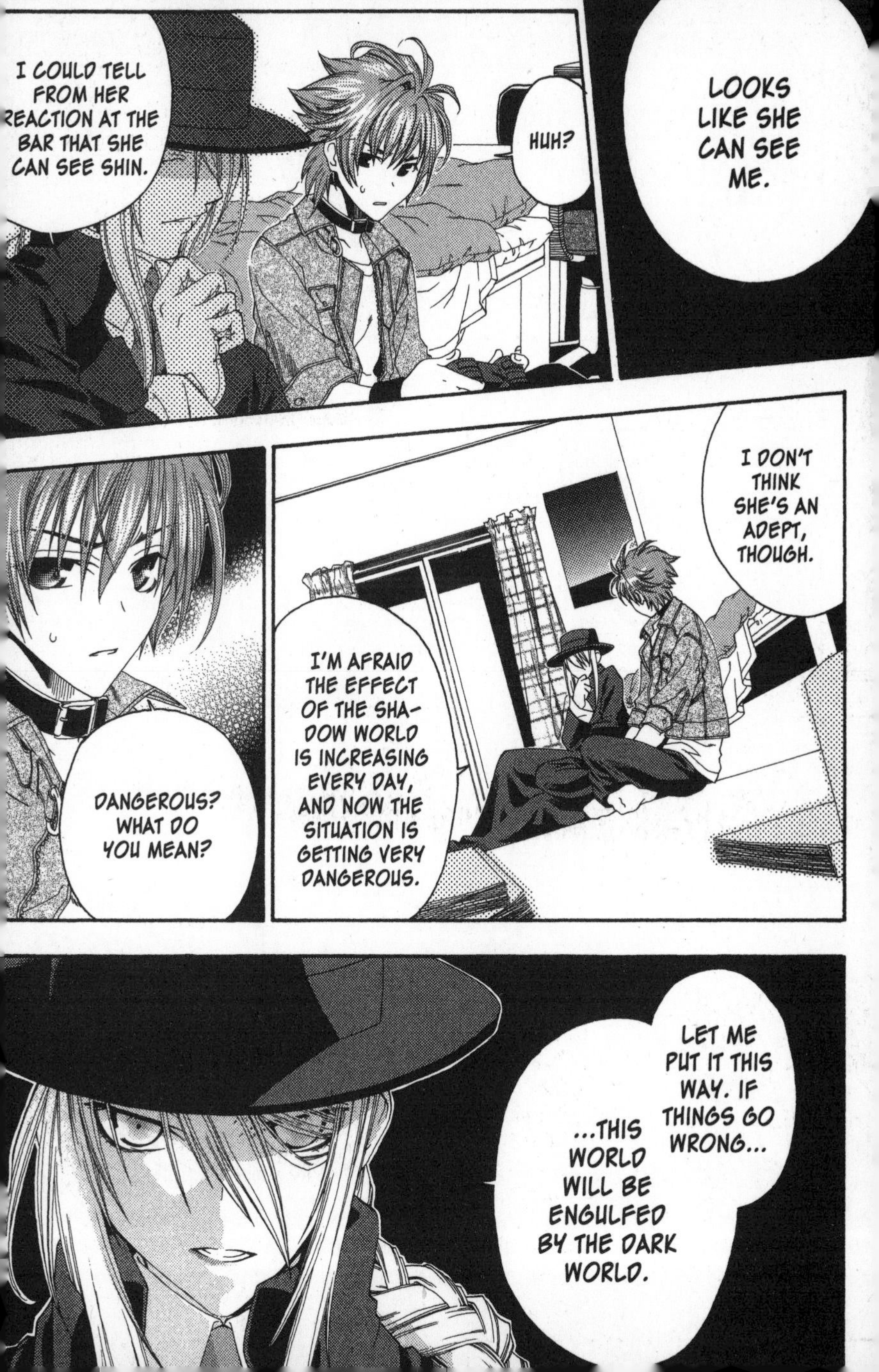
LOOKS LIKE SHE CAN SEE ME.
HUH?
I COULD TELL FROM HER REACTION AT THE BAR THAT SHE CAN SEE SHIN.
I DON'T THINK SHE'S AN ADEPT, THOUGH.
I'M AFRAID THE EFFECT OF THE SHA-DOW WORLD IS INCREASING EVERY DAY, AND NOW THE SITUATION IS GETTING VERY DANGEROUS.
DANGEROUS? WHAT DO YOU MEAN?
LET ME PUT IT THIS WAY. IF THINGS GO WRONG...
...THIS WORLD WILL BE ENGULFED BY THE DARK WORLD.

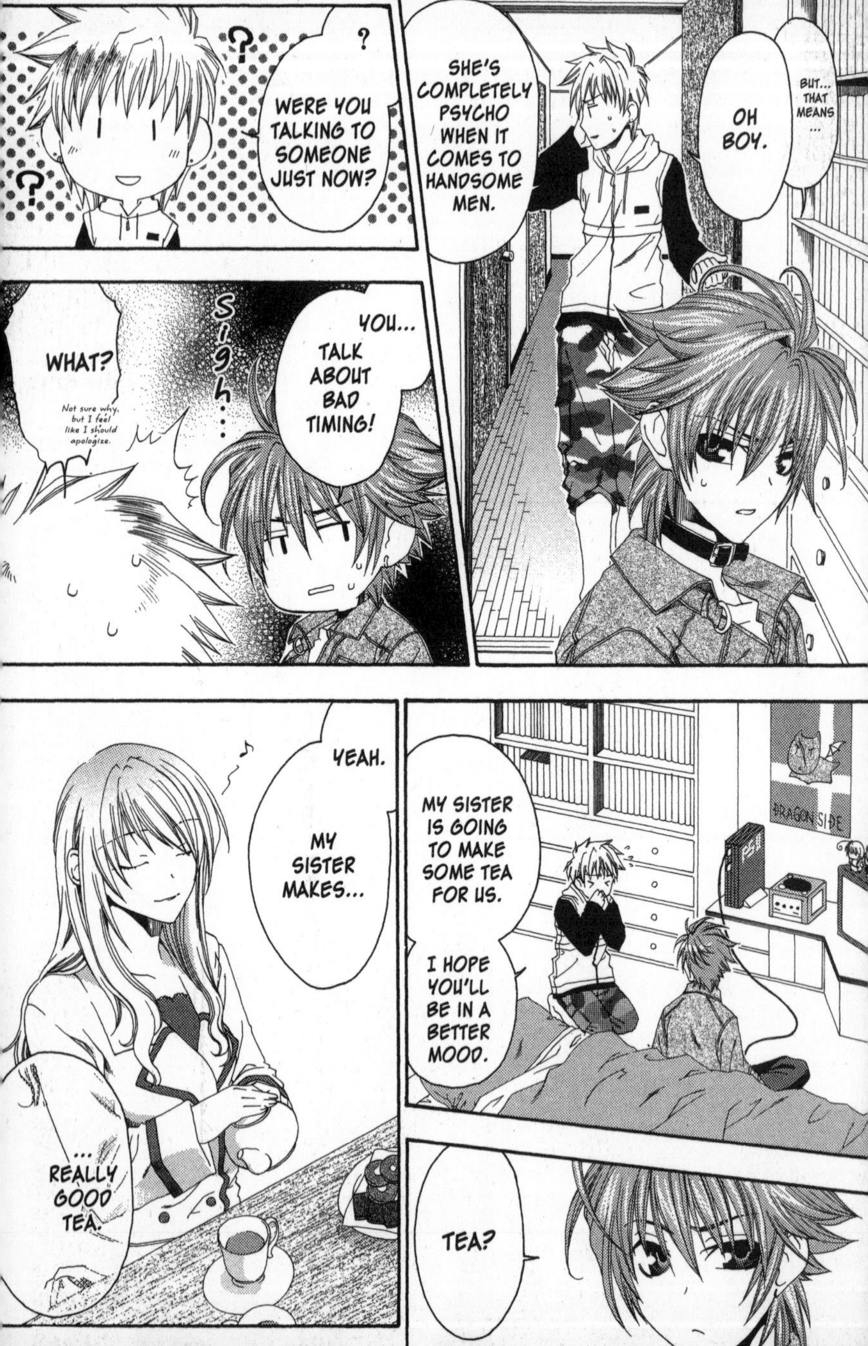

OH BOY.
BUT... THAT MEANS...
SHE'S COMPLETELY PSYCHO WHEN IT COMES TO HANDSOME MEN.
?
WERE YOU TALKING TO SOMEONE JUST NOW?
YOU... TALK ABOUT BAD TIMING!
Sigh...
WHAT?
Not sure why, but I feel like I should apologize.
MY SISTER IS GOING TO MAKE SOME TEA FOR US.
I HOPE YOU'LL BE IN A BETTER MOOD.
DRAGON SIDE
TEA?
YEAH.
MY SISTER MAKES...
...REALLY GOOD TEA.

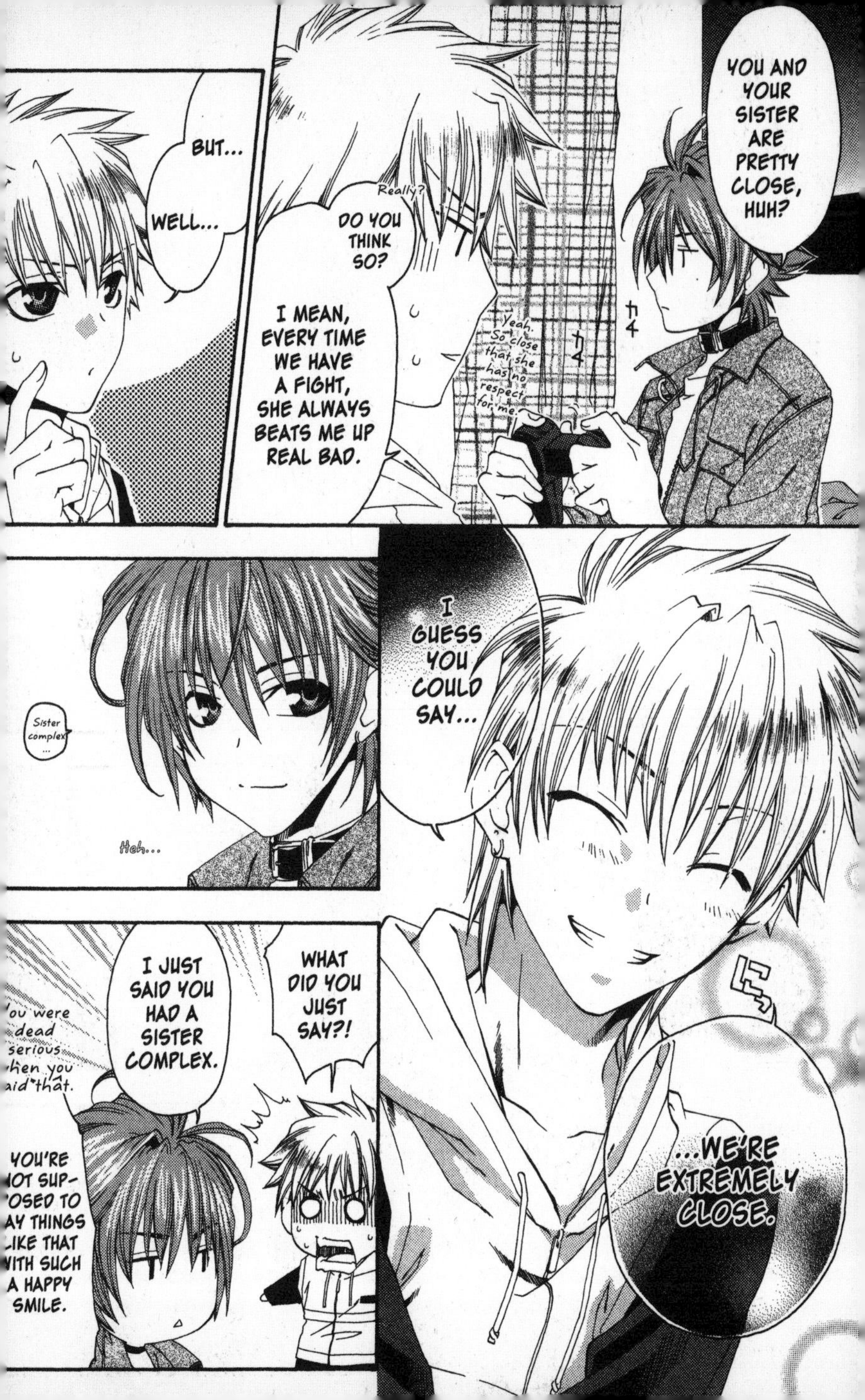
YOU AND YOUR SISTER ARE PRETTY CLOSE, HUH?
Yeah. So close that she has no respect for me.
Really?
DO YOU THINK SO?
I MEAN, EVERY TIME WE HAVE A FIGHT, SHE ALWAYS BEATS ME UP REAL BAD.
BUT...
WELL...
I GUESS YOU COULD SAY...
...WE'RE EXTREMELY CLOSE.
Sister complex...
Heh...
WHAT DID YOU JUST SAY?!
I JUST SAID YOU HAD A SISTER COMPLEX.
ou were dead serious hen you aid that.
YOU'RE OT SUP- OSED TO AY THINGS LIKE THAT VITH SUCH A HAPPY SMILE.

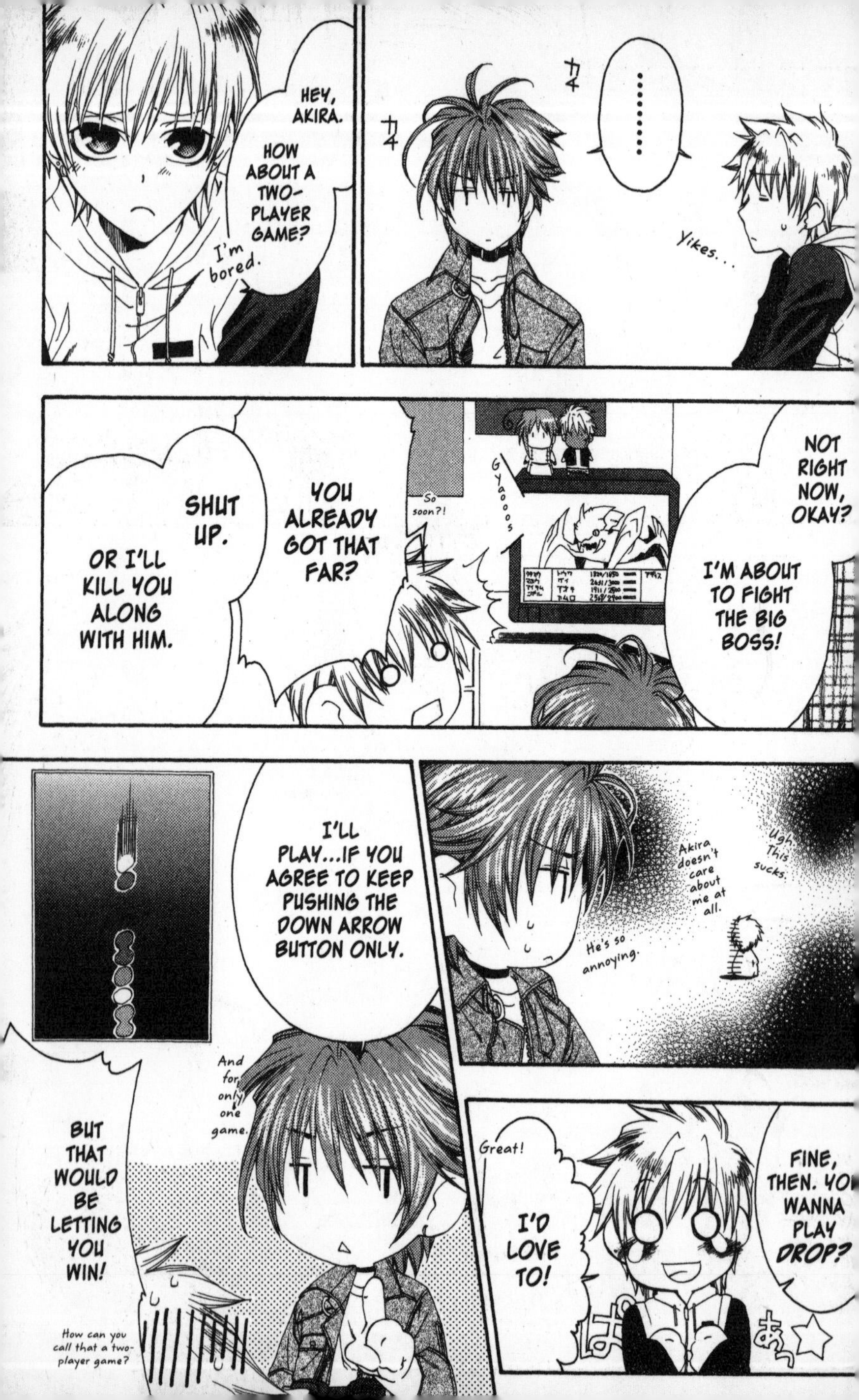

......
Yikes...
HEY, AKIRA.
HOW ABOUT A TWO-PLAYER GAME?
I'm bored.
NOT RIGHT NOW, OKAY?
I'M ABOUT TO FIGHT THE BIG BOSS!
Gyaooos
So soon?!
YOU ALREADY GOT THAT FAR?
SHUT UP.
OR I'LL KILL YOU ALONG WITH HIM.
Ugh. This sucks.
Akira doesn't care about me at all.
He's so annoying.
FINE, THEN. YOU WANNA PLAY DROP?
Great!
I'D LOVE TO!
I'LL PLAY...IF YOU AGREE TO KEEP PUSHING THE DOWN ARROW BUTTON ONLY.
And for only one game.
BUT THAT WOULD BE LETTING YOU WIN!
How can you call that a two-player game?

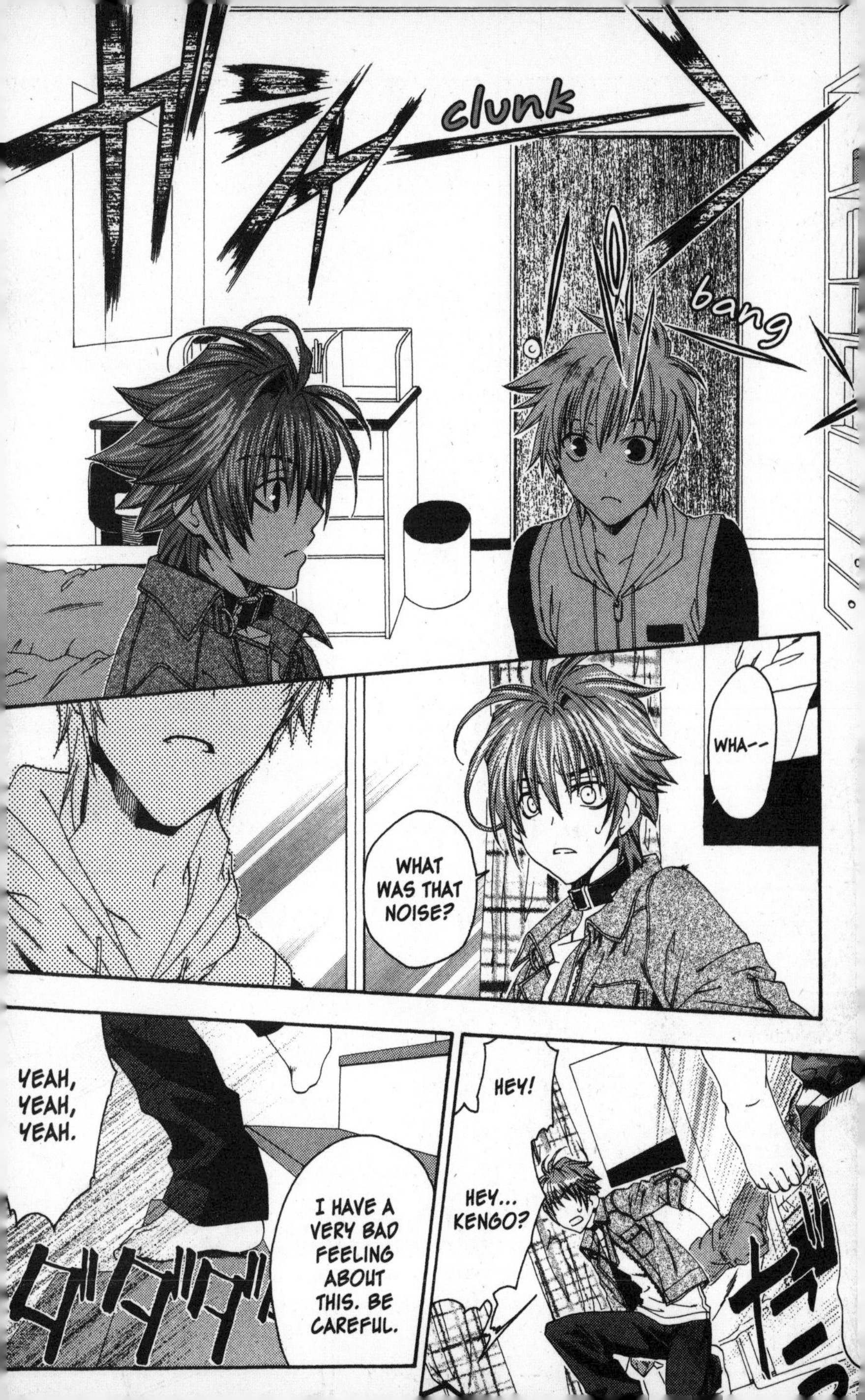
clunk
bang
WHA--
WHAT WAS THAT NOISE?
HEY!
HEY... KENGO?
YEAH, YEAH, YEAH.
I HAVE A VERY BAD FEELING ABOUT THIS. BE CAREFUL.

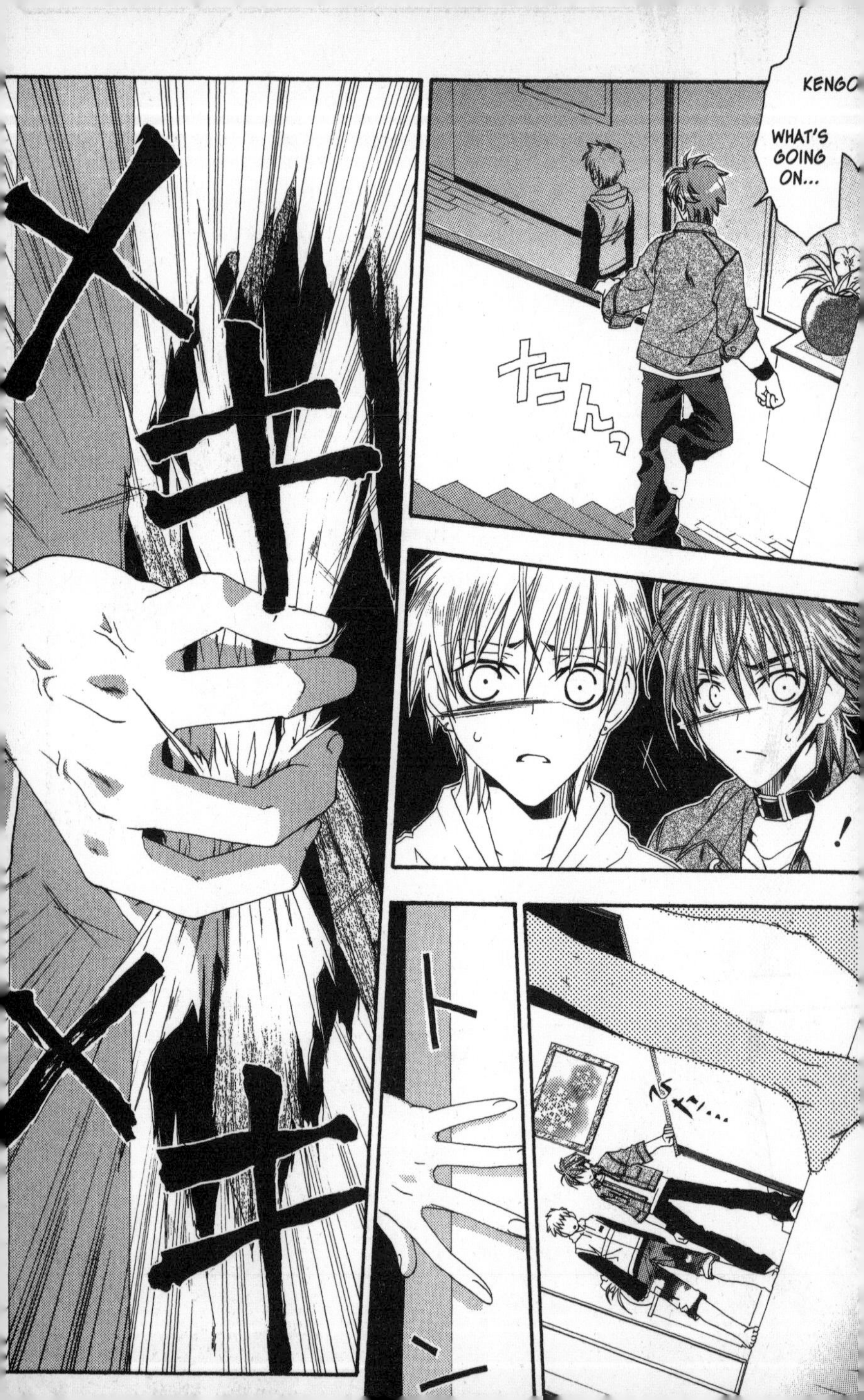
KENGO
WHAT'S GOING ON...
たんっ
メキ
メキ

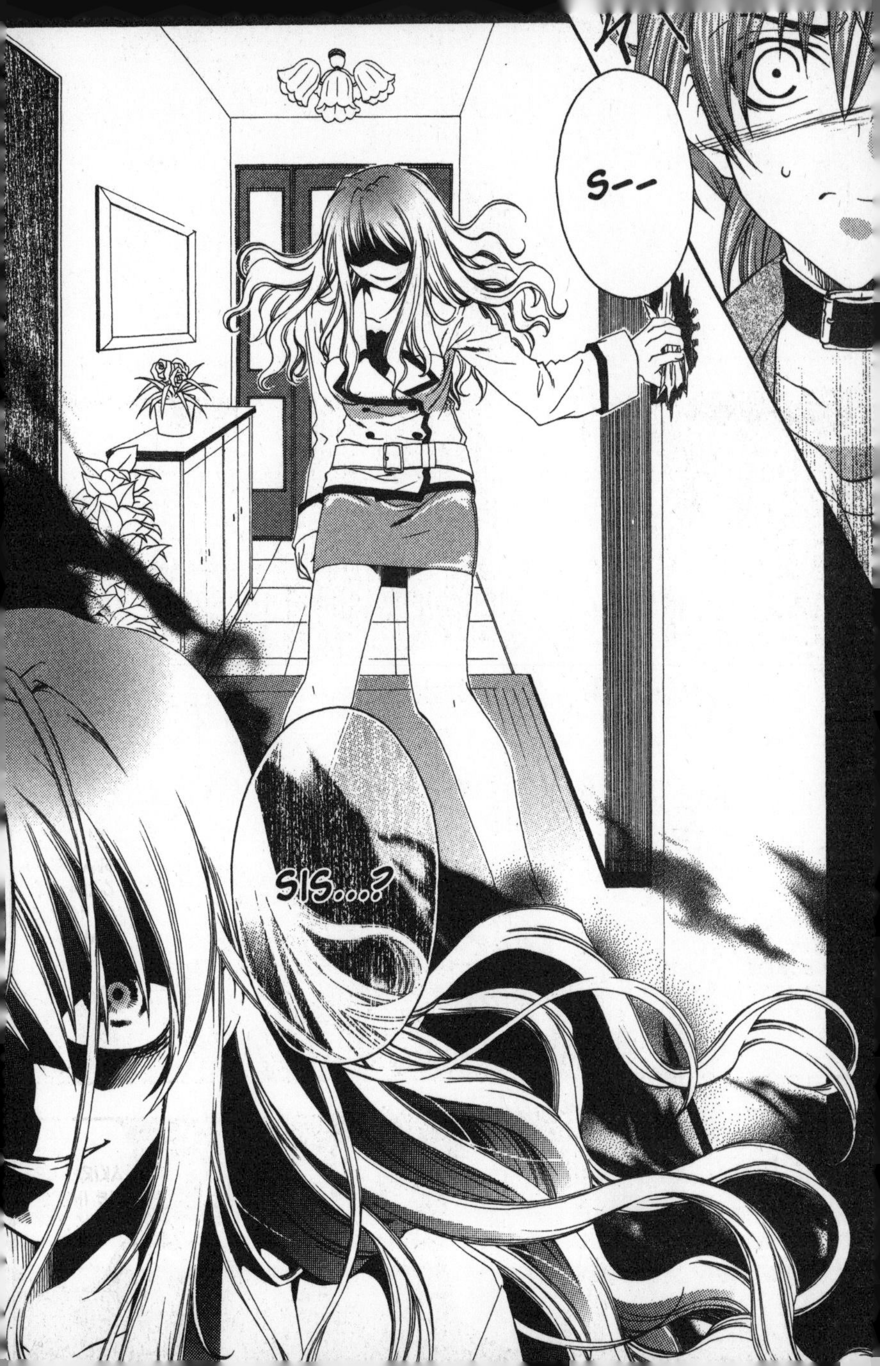
S--
SIS...?

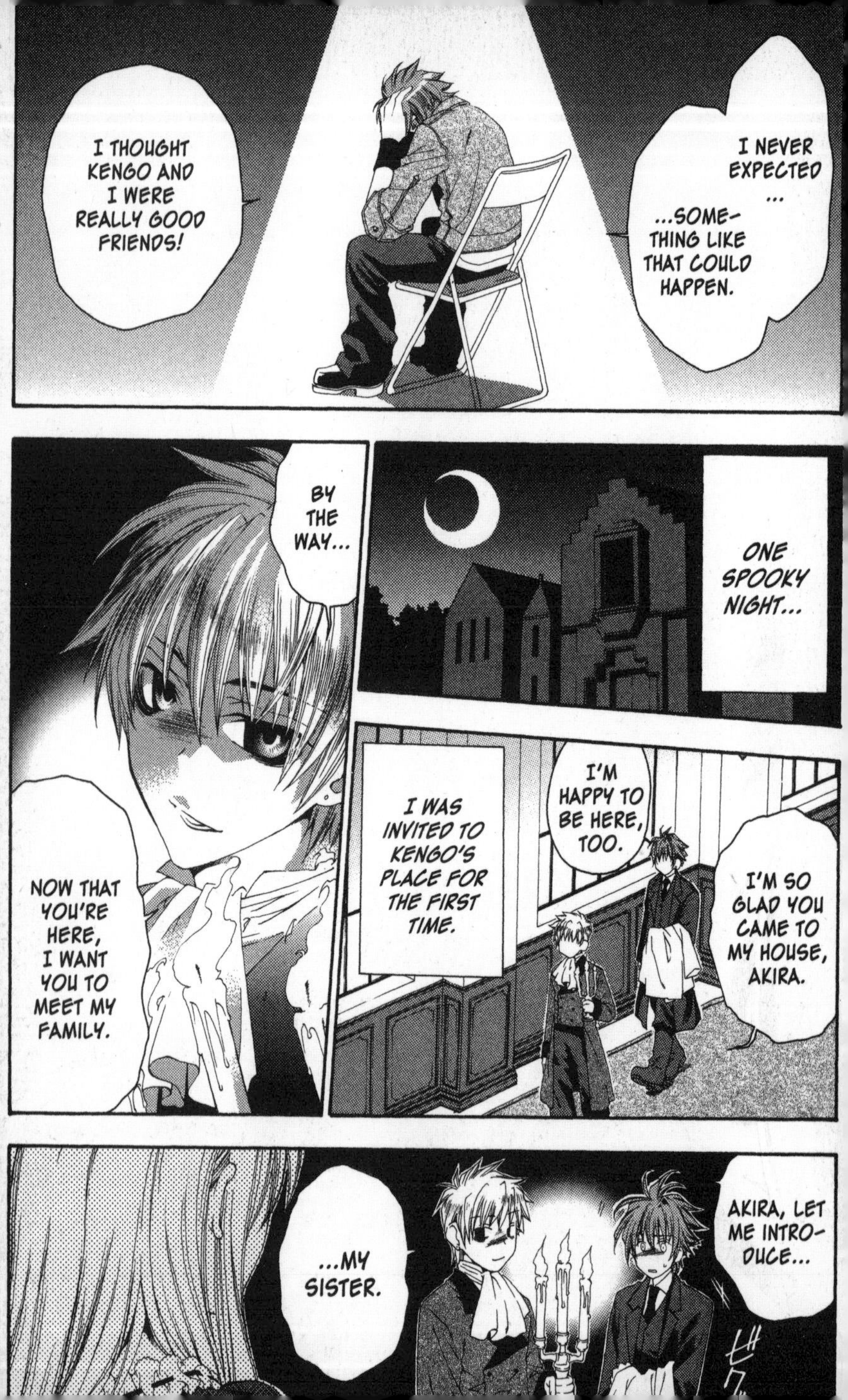
I NEVER EXPECTED ...
...SOME-THING LIKE THAT COULD HAPPEN.
I THOUGHT KENGO AND I WERE REALLY GOOD FRIENDS!
ONE SPOOKY NIGHT...
I'M SO GLAD YOU CAME TO MY HOUSE, AKIRA.
I'M HAPPY TO BE HERE, TOO.
I WAS INVITED TO KENGO'S PLACE FOR THE FIRST TIME.
BY THE WAY...
NOW THAT YOU'RE HERE, I WANT YOU TO MEET MY FAMILY.
AKIRA, LET ME INTRO-DUCE...
...MY SISTER.

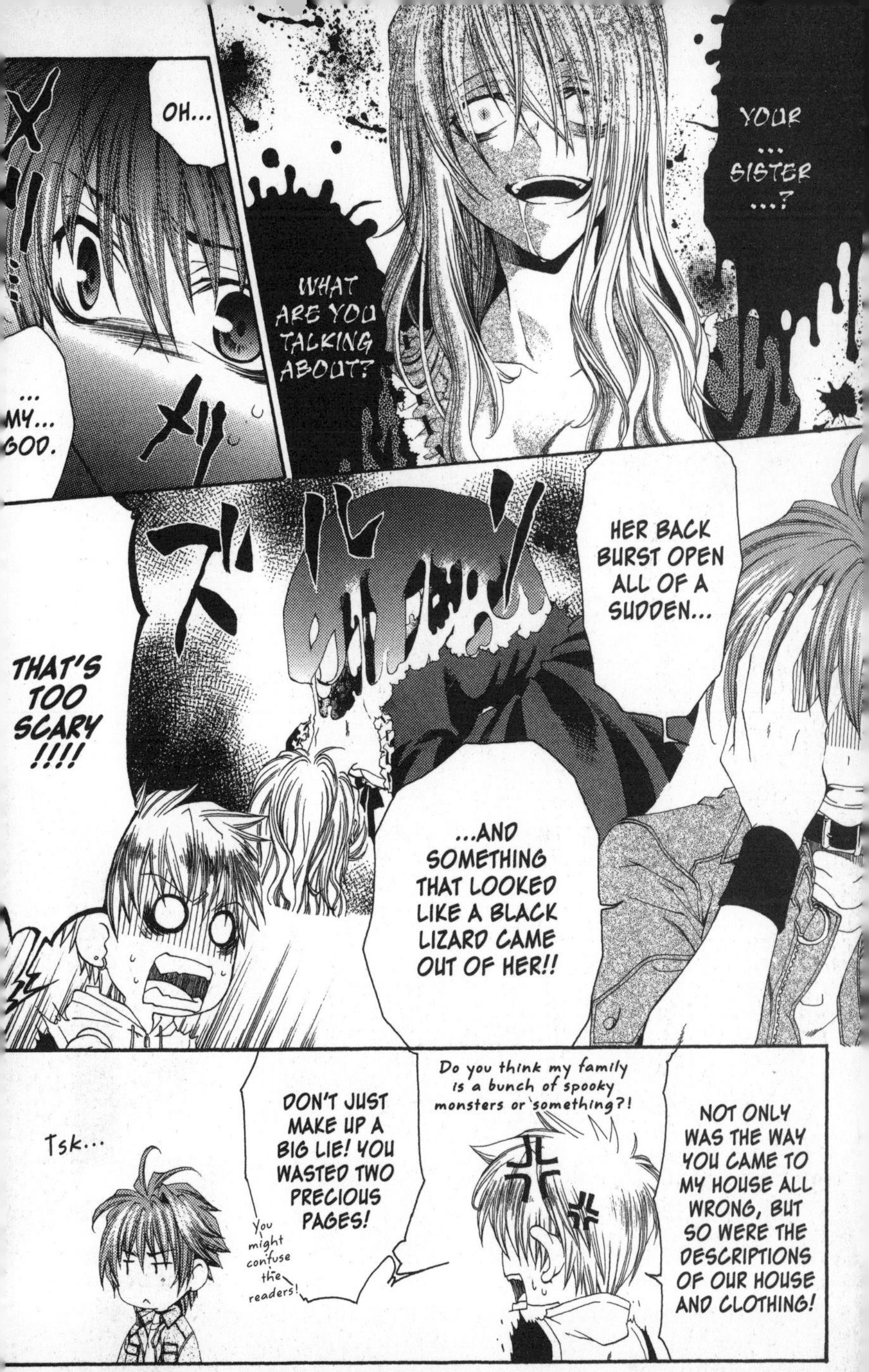
YOUR ... SISTER ...?
WHAT ARE YOU TALKING ABOUT?
OH...
... MY... GOD.
HER BACK BURST OPEN ALL OF A SUDDEN...
...AND SOMETHING THAT LOOKED LIKE A BLACK LIZARD CAME OUT OF HER!!
THAT'S TOO SCARY!!!!
NOT ONLY WAS THE WAY YOU CAME TO MY HOUSE ALL WRONG, BUT SO WERE THE DESCRIPTIONS OF OUR HOUSE AND CLOTHING!
Do you think my family is a bunch of spooky monsters or something?!
DON'T JUST MAKE UP A BIG LIE! YOU WASTED TWO PRECIOUS PAGES!
You might confuse the readers!
Tsk...

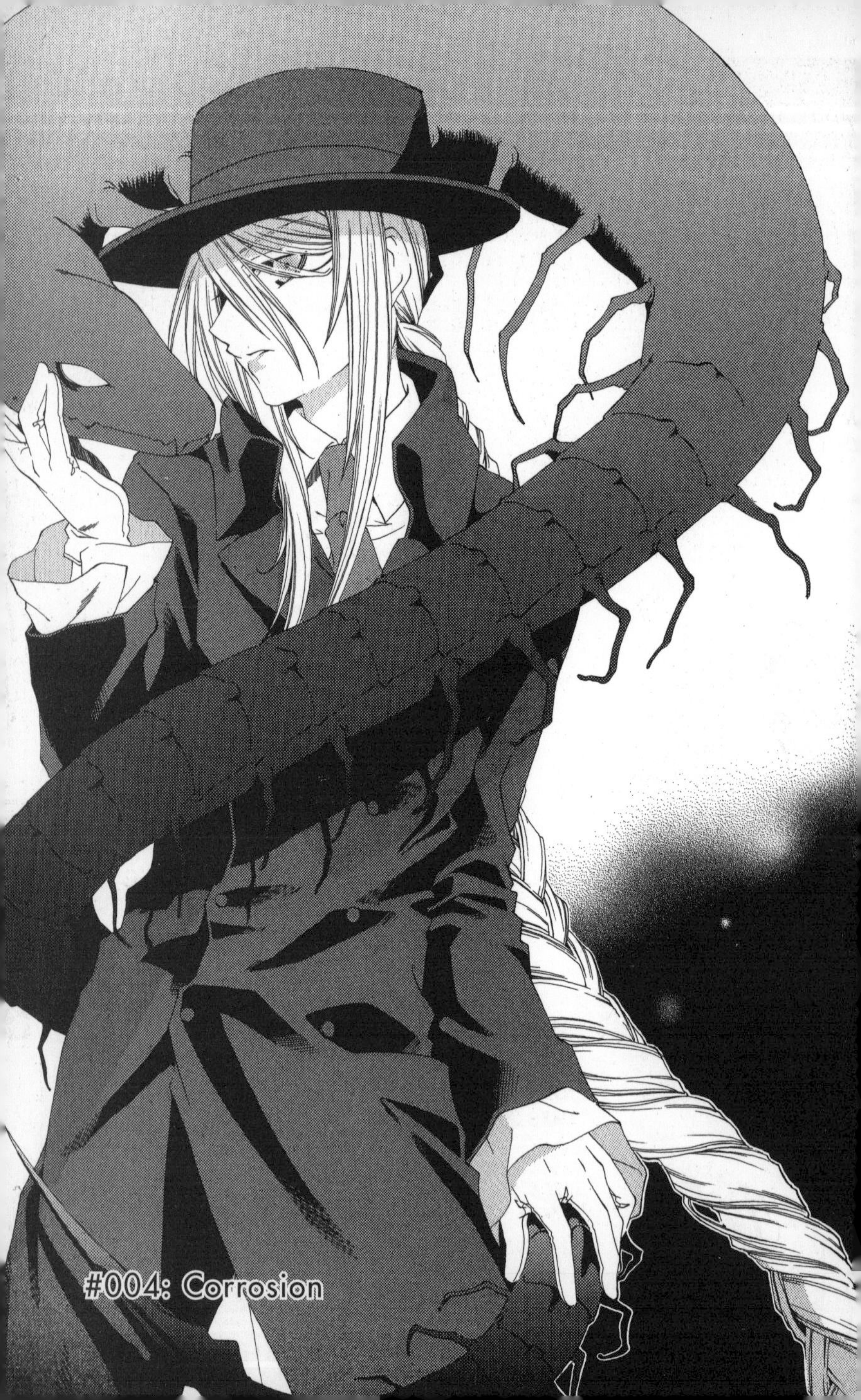
#004: Corrosion

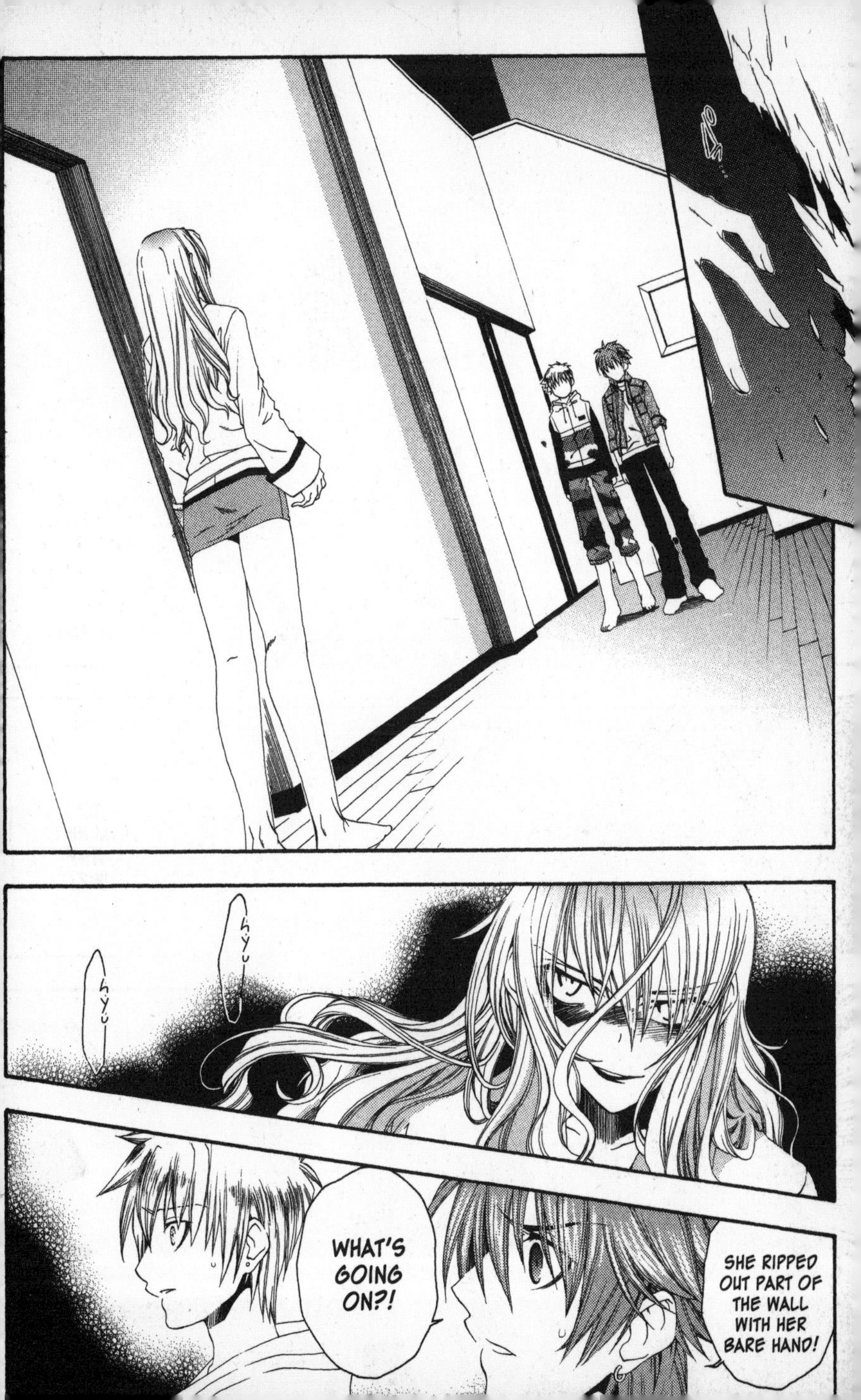
SHE RIPPED OUT PART OF THE WALL WITH HER BARE HAND!
WHAT'S GOING ON?!

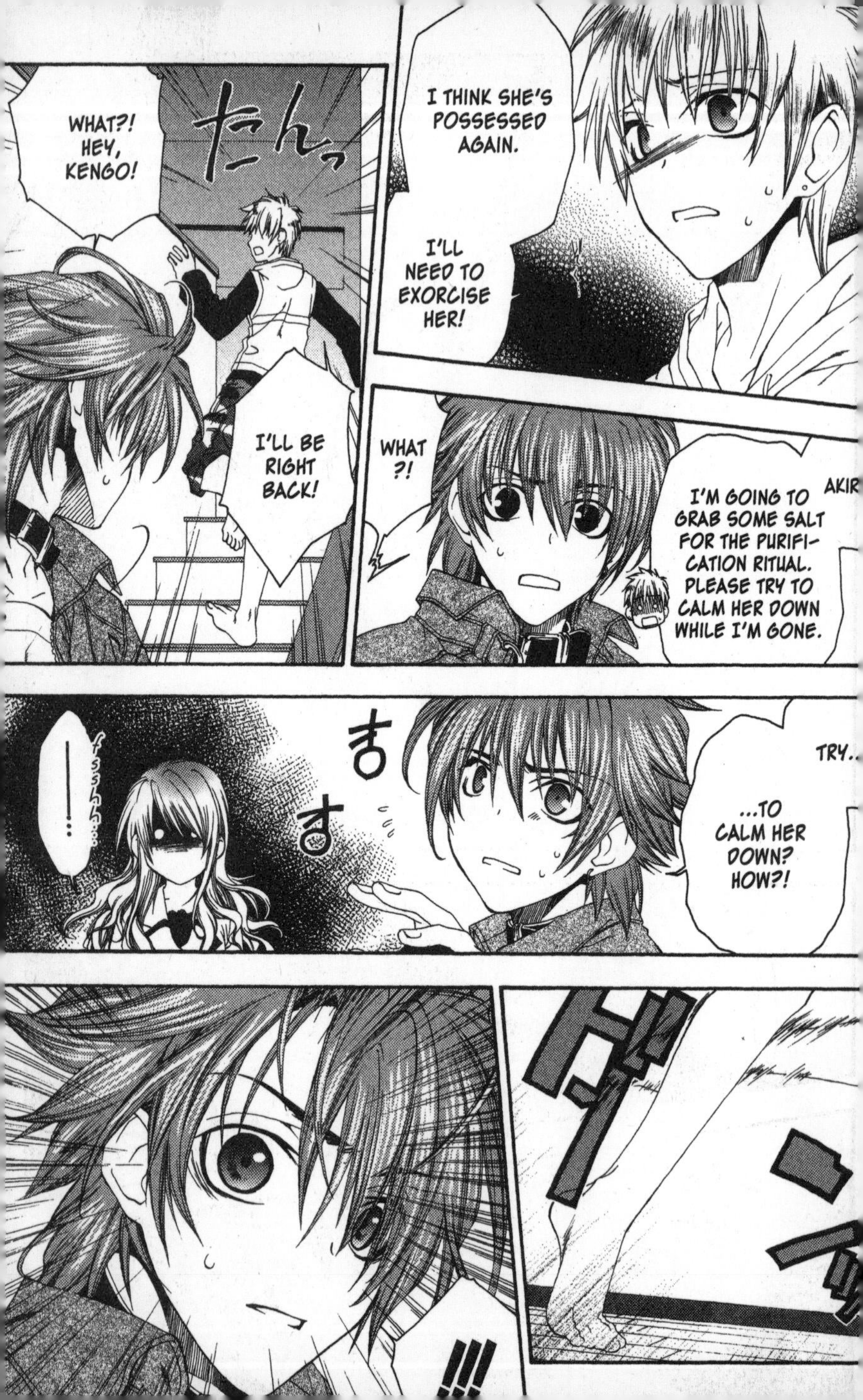

I THINK SHE'S POSSESSED AGAIN.
I'LL NEED TO EXORCISE HER!
AKIR
I'M GOING TO GRAB SOME SALT FOR THE PURIFICATION RITUAL. PLEASE TRY TO CALM HER DOWN WHILE I'M GONE.
WHAT ?!
WHAT?! HEY, KENGO!
たんっ
I'LL BE RIGHT BACK!
TRY...
...TO CALM HER DOWN? HOW?!
ま
す
!!!

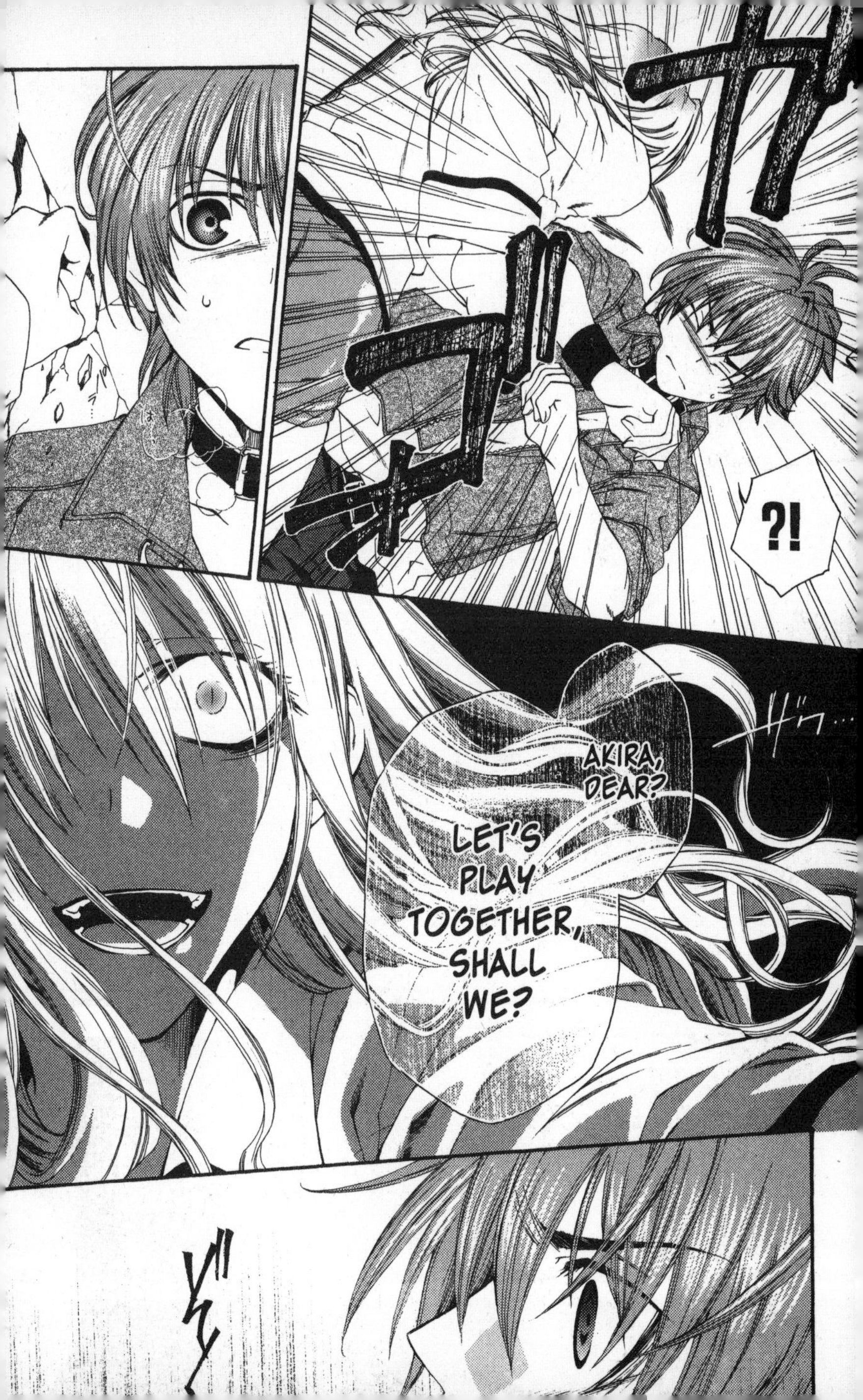
?!
AKIRA, DEAR?
LET'S PLAY TOGETHER, SHALL WE?

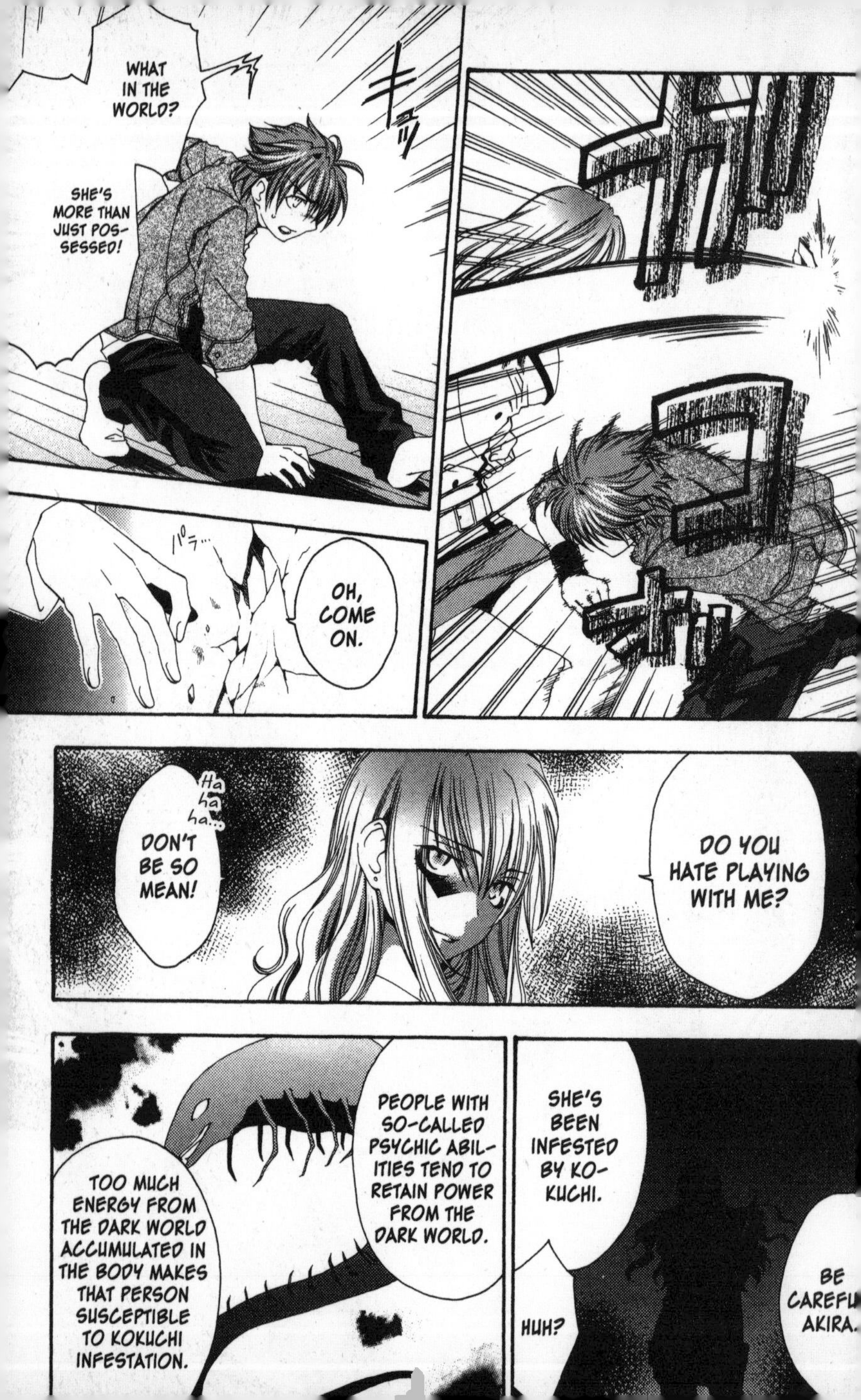
WHAT IN THE WORLD?
SHE'S MORE THAN JUST POS-SESSED!
パラ…
OH, COME ON.
DO YOU HATE PLAYING WITH ME?
Ha ha ha...
DON'T BE SO MEAN!
SHE'S BEEN INFESTED BY KO-KUCHI.
BE CAREFU AKIRA.
HUH?
PEOPLE WITH SO-CALLED PSYCHIC ABIL-ITIES TEND TO RETAIN POWER FROM THE DARK WORLD.
TOO MUCH ENERGY FROM THE DARK WORLD ACCUMULATED IN THE BODY MAKES THAT PERSON SUSCEPTIBLE TO KOKUCHI INFESTATION.

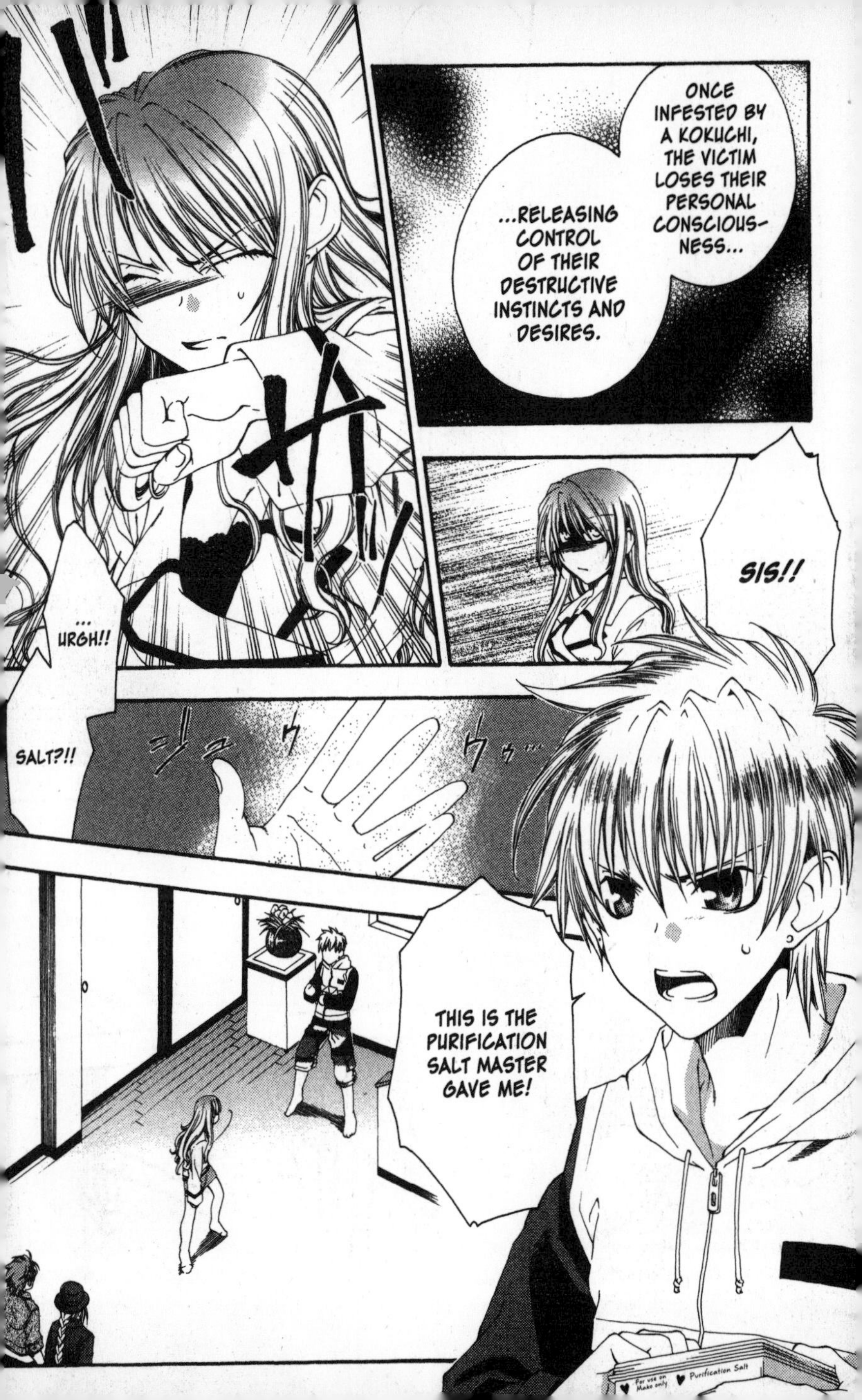
ONCE INFESTED BY A KOKUCHI, THE VICTIM LOSES THEIR PERSONAL CONSCIOUS-NESS...
...RELEASING CONTROL OF THEIR DESTRUCTIVE INSTINCTS AND DESIRES.
SIS!!
...URGH!!
SALT?!!
THIS IS THE PURIFICATION SALT MASTER GAVE ME!
Purification Salt

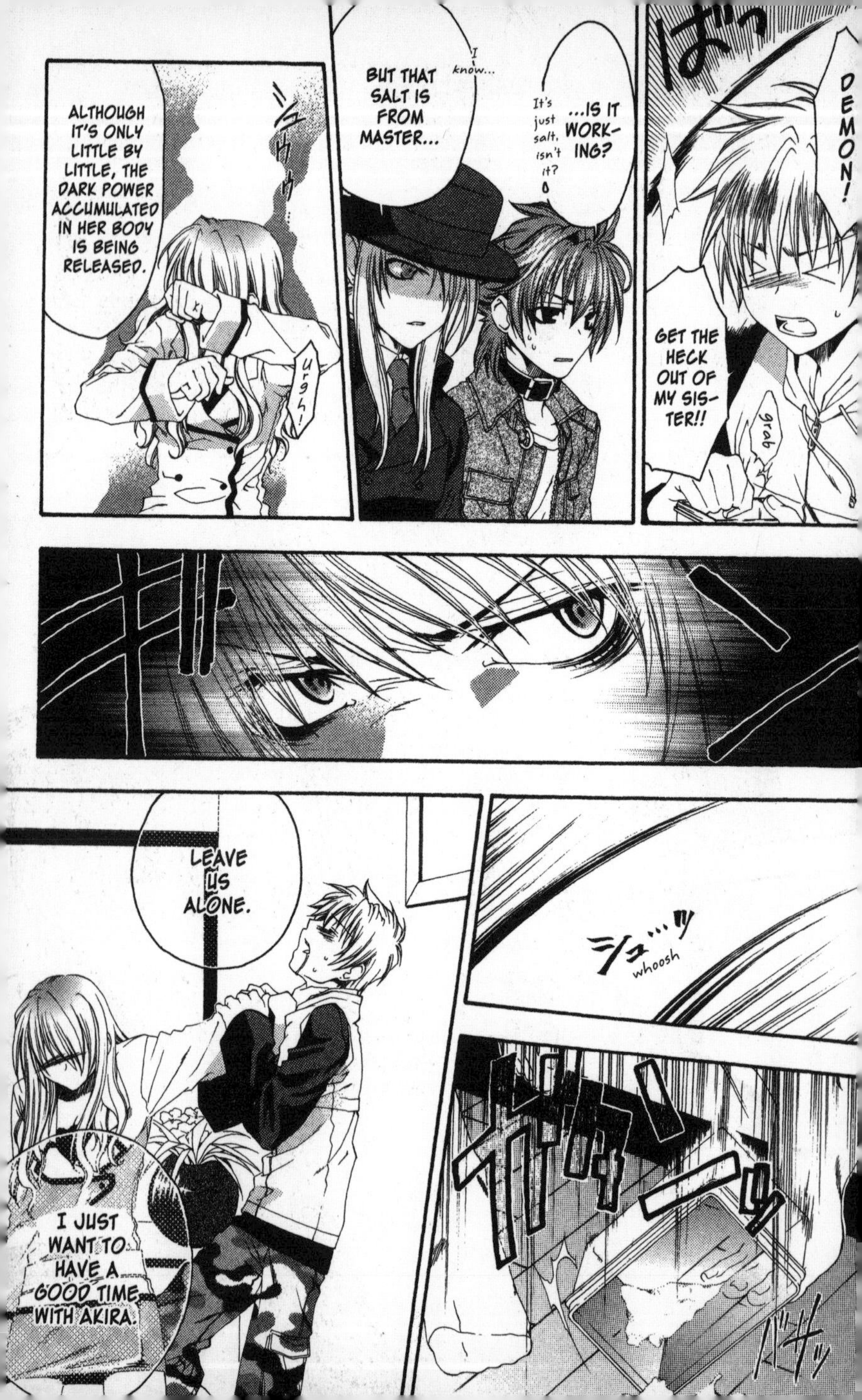
ばっ
DEMON!
GET THE HECK OUT OF MY SISTER!!
grab
...IS IT WORKING?
It's just salt, isn't it?
BUT THAT SALT IS FROM MASTER...
I know...
ALTHOUGH IT'S ONLY LITTLE BY LITTLE, THE DARK POWER ACCUMULATED IN HER BODY IS BEING RELEASED.
Urgh!
whoosh
LEAVE US ALONE.
I JUST WANT TO HAVE A GOOD TIME WITH AKIRA.

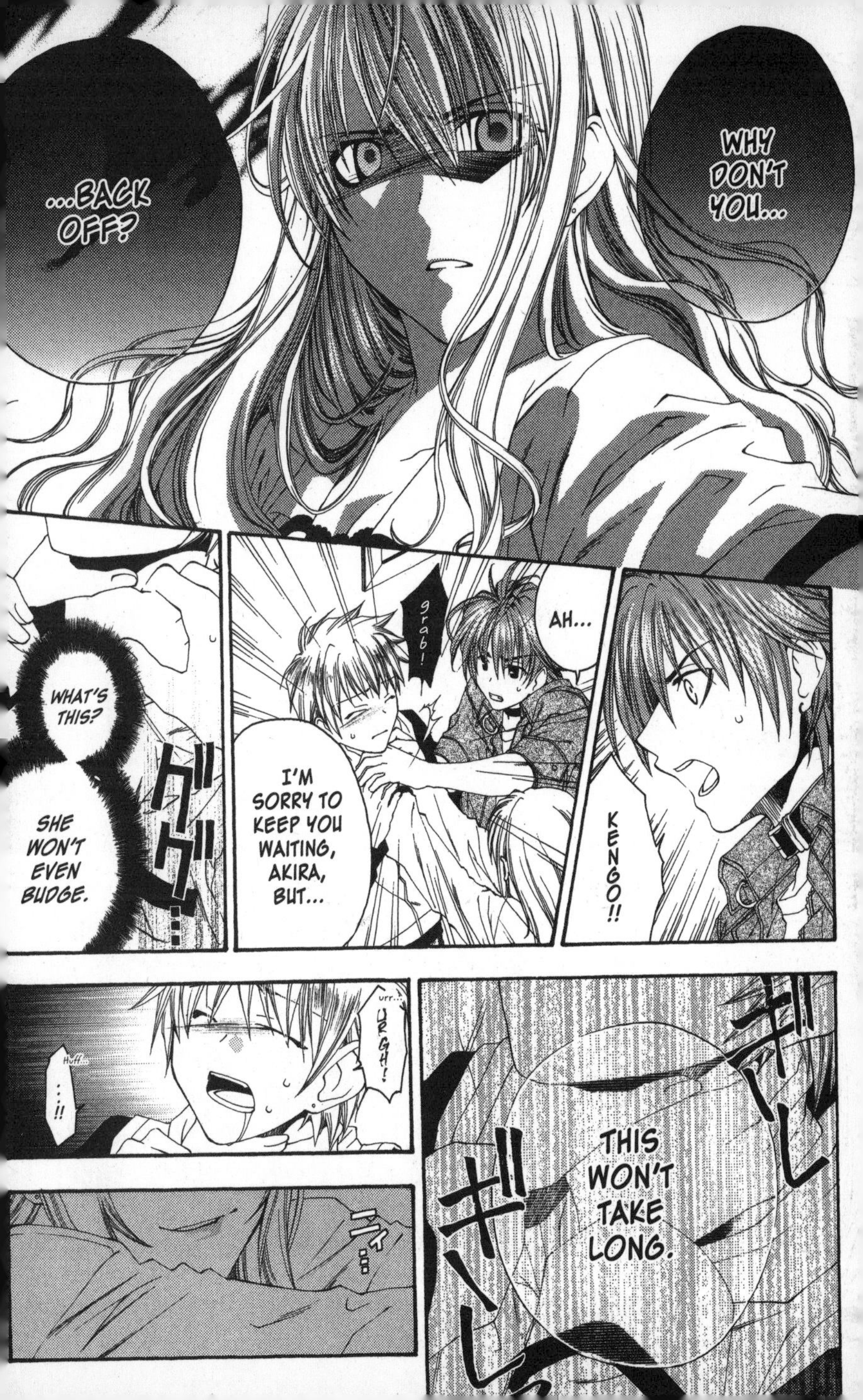
WHY DON'T YOU...
...BACK OFF?
KENGO!!
AH...
grab!
I'M SORRY TO KEEP YOU WAITING, AKIRA, BUT...
WHAT'S THIS?
SHE WON'T EVEN BUDGE.
THIS WON'T TAKE LONG.
urr... URGH!
Huff...
...!!

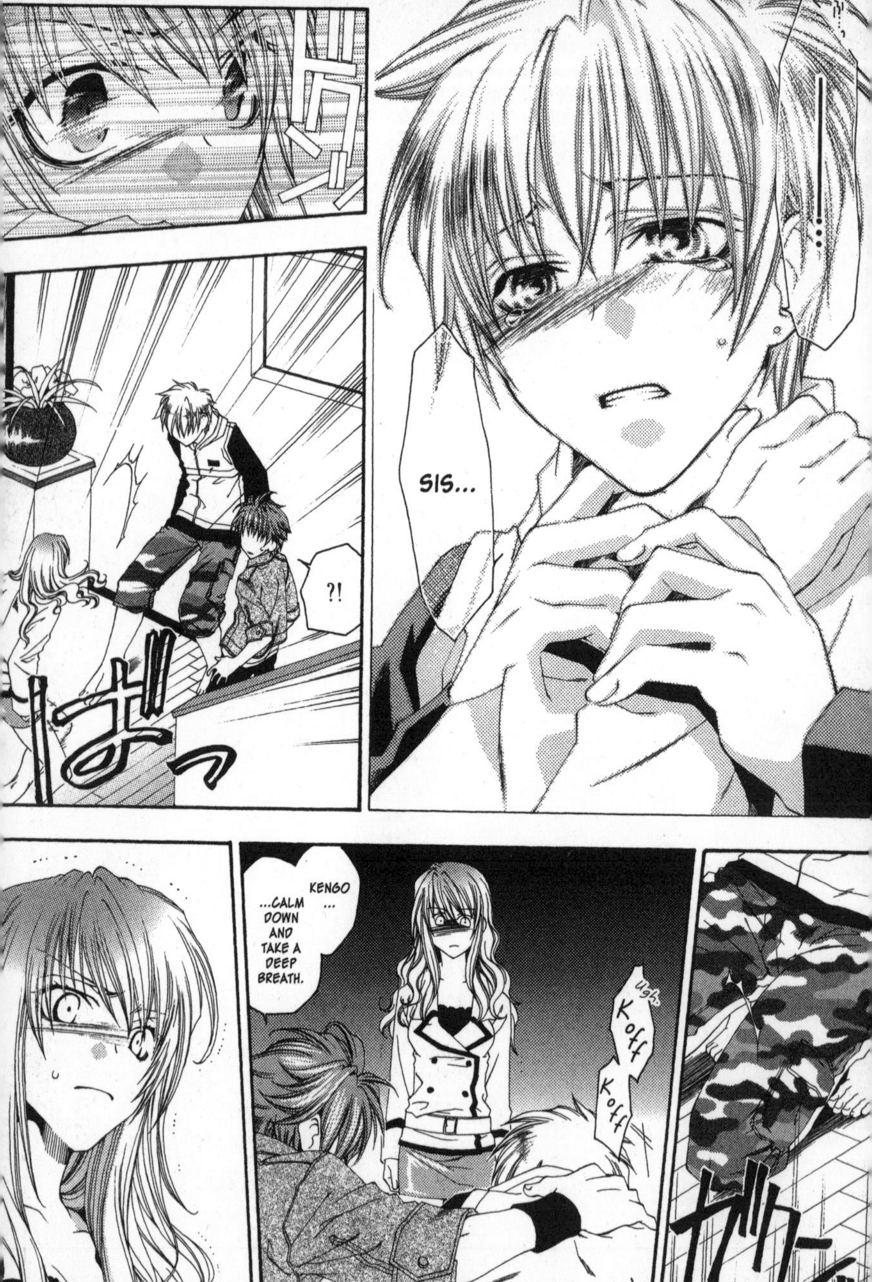
SIS...
?!
KENGO ... ...CALM DOWN AND TAKE A DEEP BREATH.
Ugh. Koff Koff

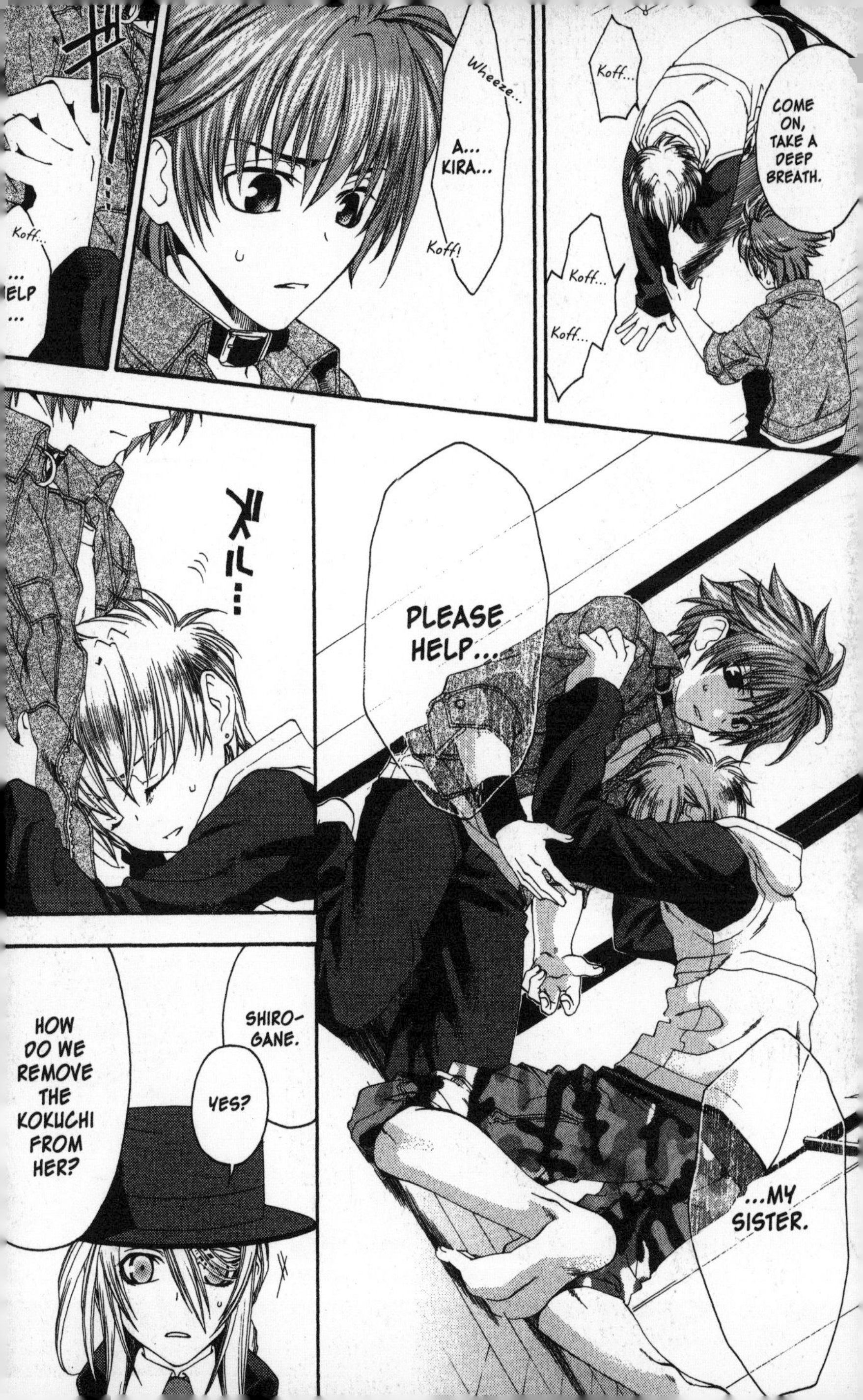
Koff...
COME ON, TAKE A DEEP BREATH.
Koff...
Koff...
Wheeze...
A... KIRA...
Koff!
Koff...
... ELP ...
PLEASE HELP...
...MY SISTER.
ズル…
SHIRO-GANE.
YES?
HOW DO WE REMOVE THE KOKUCHI FROM HER?

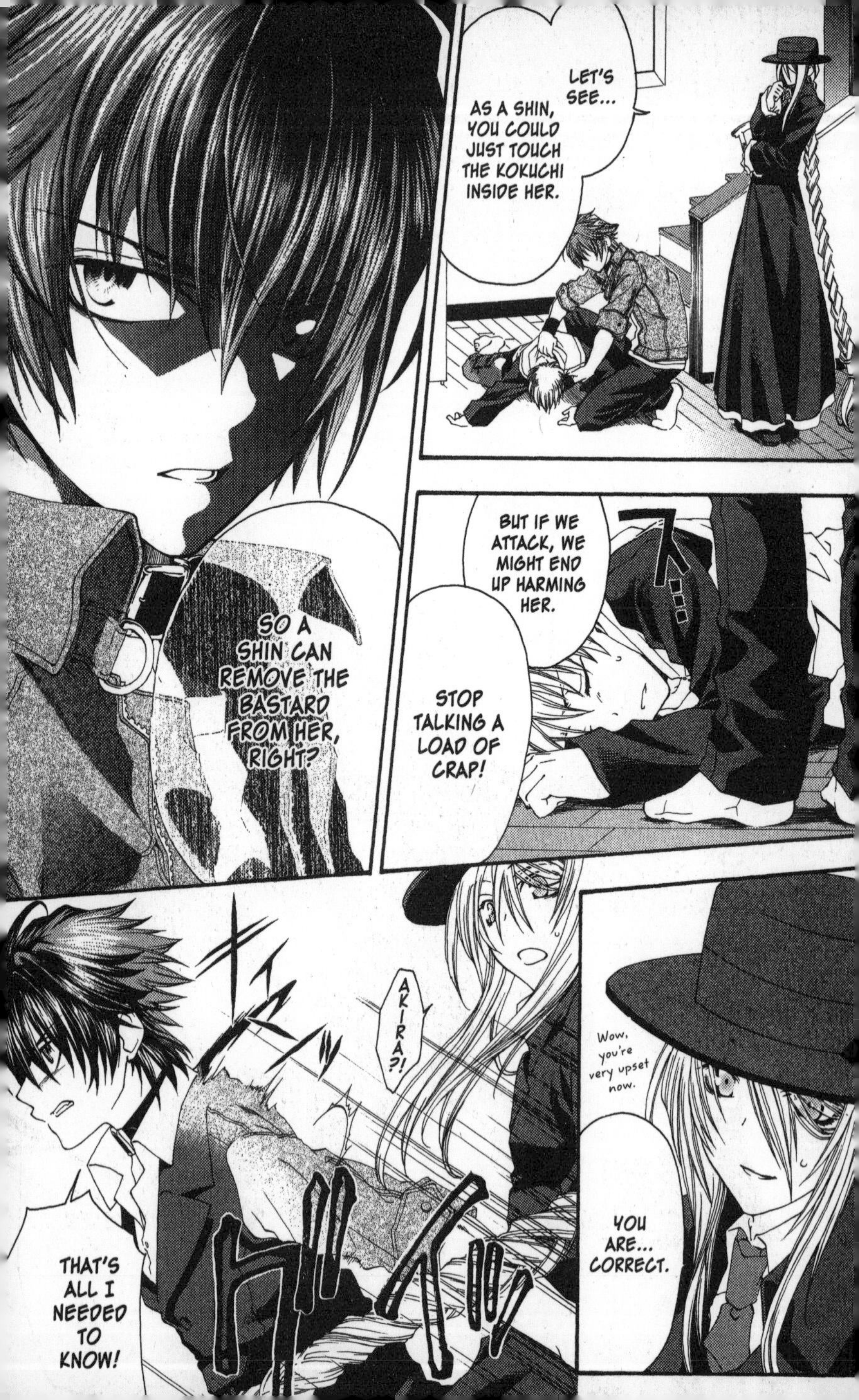
LET'S SEE...
AS A SHIN, YOU COULD JUST TOUCH THE KOKUCHI INSIDE HER.
BUT IF WE ATTACK, WE MIGHT END UP HARMING HER.
STOP TALKING A LOAD OF CRAP!
SO A SHIN CAN REMOVE THE BASTARD FROM HER, RIGHT?
Wow, you're very upset now.
YOU ARE... CORRECT.
AKIRA?!
THAT'S ALL I NEEDED TO KNOW!

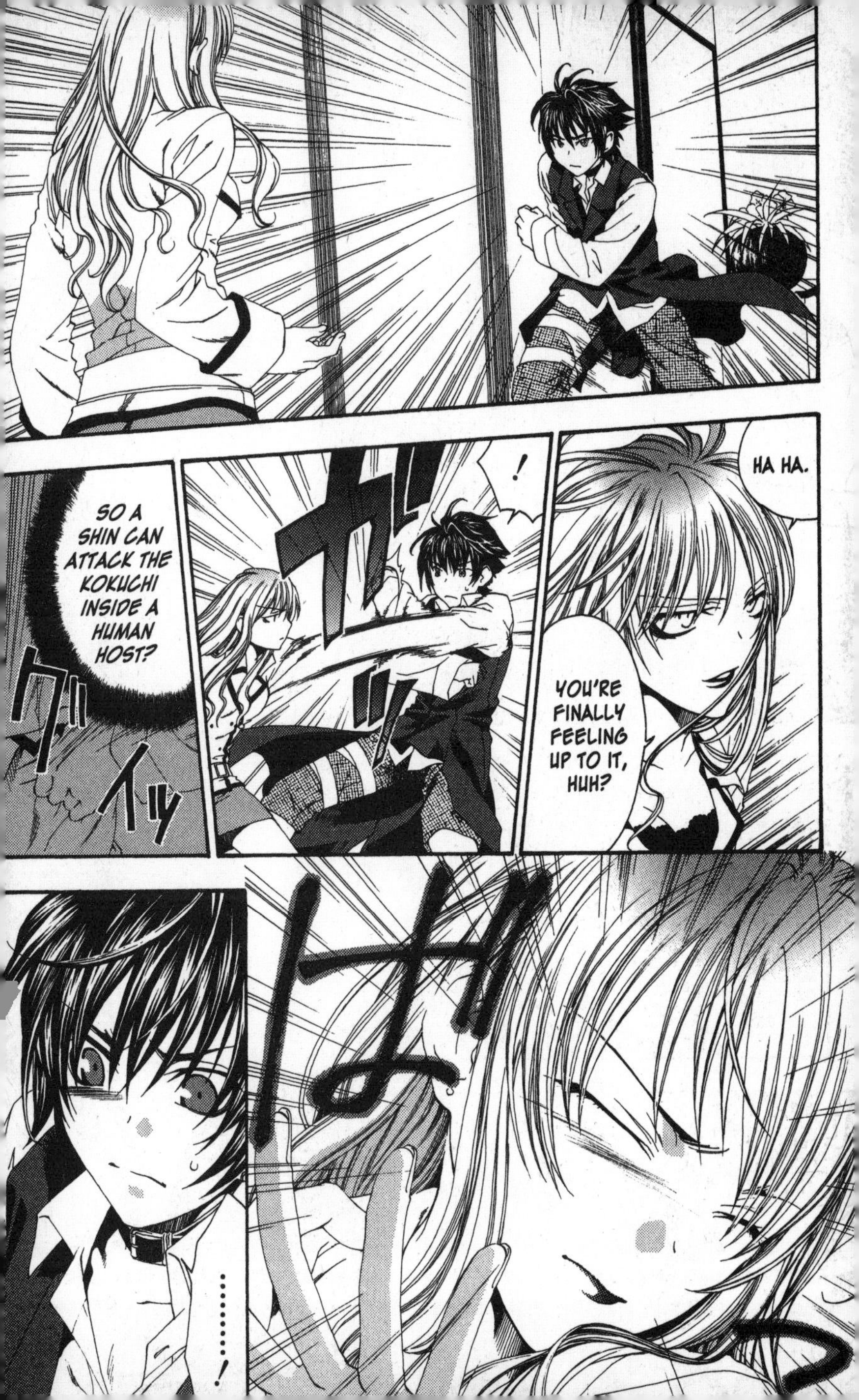
HA HA.
YOU'RE FINALLY FEELING UP TO IT, HUH?
!
SO A SHIN CAN ATTACK THE KOKUCHI INSIDE A HUMAN HOST?
........!

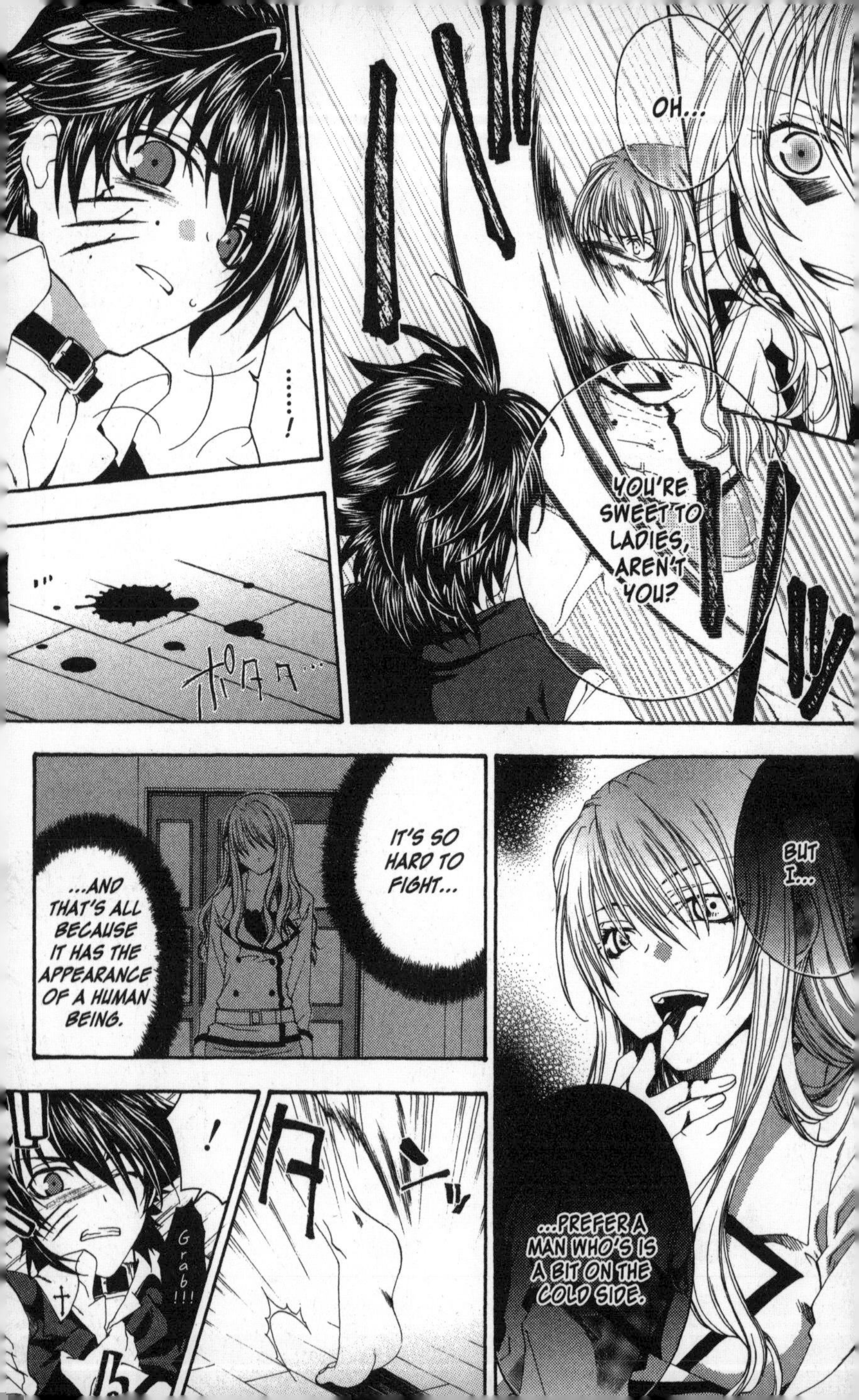
OH...
YOU'RE SWEET TO LADIES, AREN'T YOU?
......!
BUT I...
...PREFER A MAN WHO'S IS A BIT ON THE COLD SIDE.
IT'S SO HARD TO FIGHT...
...AND THAT'S ALL BECAUSE IT HAS THE APPEARANCE OF A HUMAN BEING.
!
Grab!!!

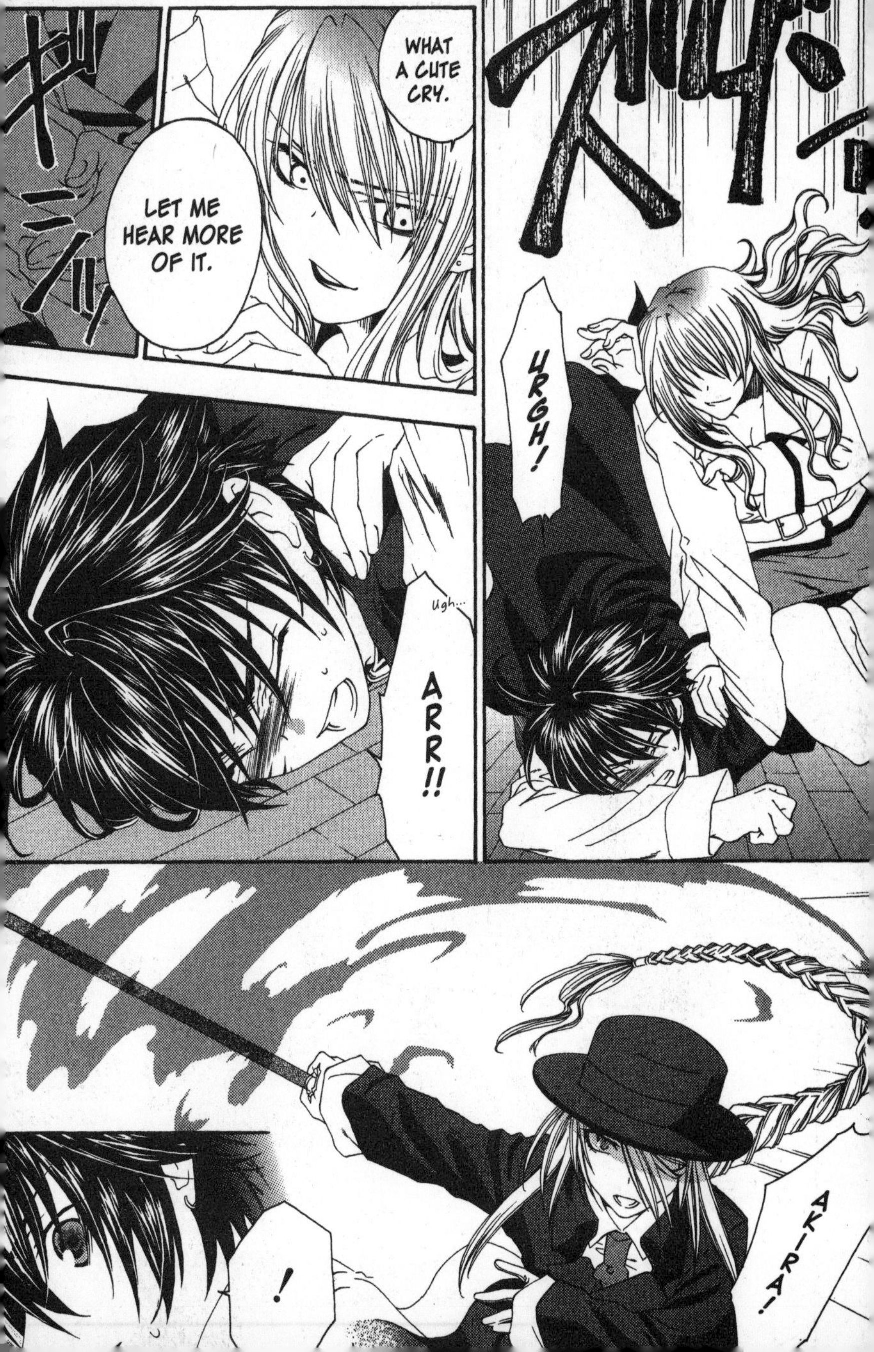
URGH!
WHAT A CUTE CRY.
LET ME HEAR MORE OF IT.
Ugh...
ARRR!!
AKIRA!
!

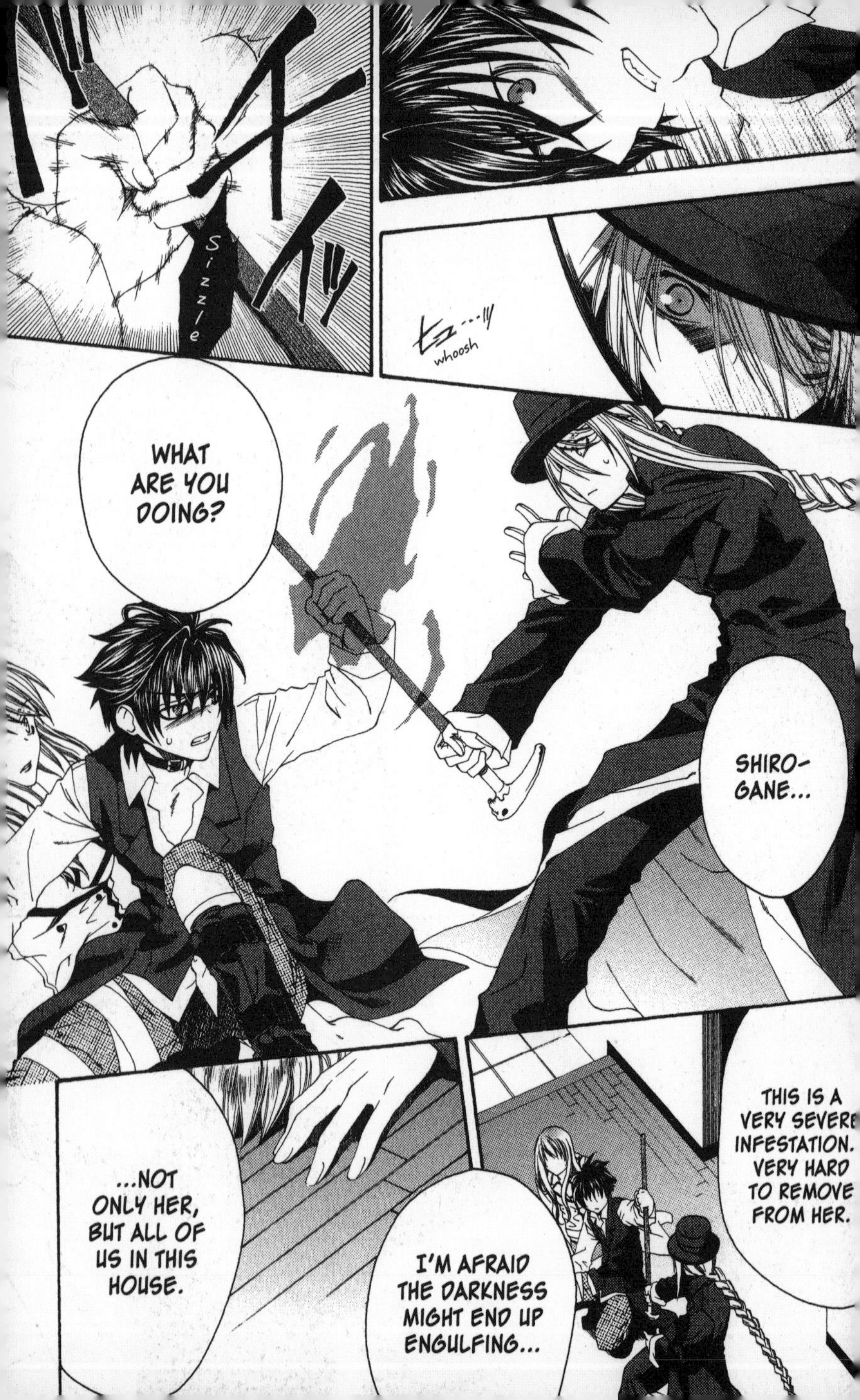
whoosh
Sizzle
SHIRO-GANE...
WHAT ARE YOU DOING?
THIS IS A VERY SEVERE INFESTATION. VERY HARD TO REMOVE FROM HER.
I'M AFRAID THE DARKNESS MIGHT END UP ENGULFING...
...NOT ONLY HER, BUT ALL OF US IN THIS HOUSE.

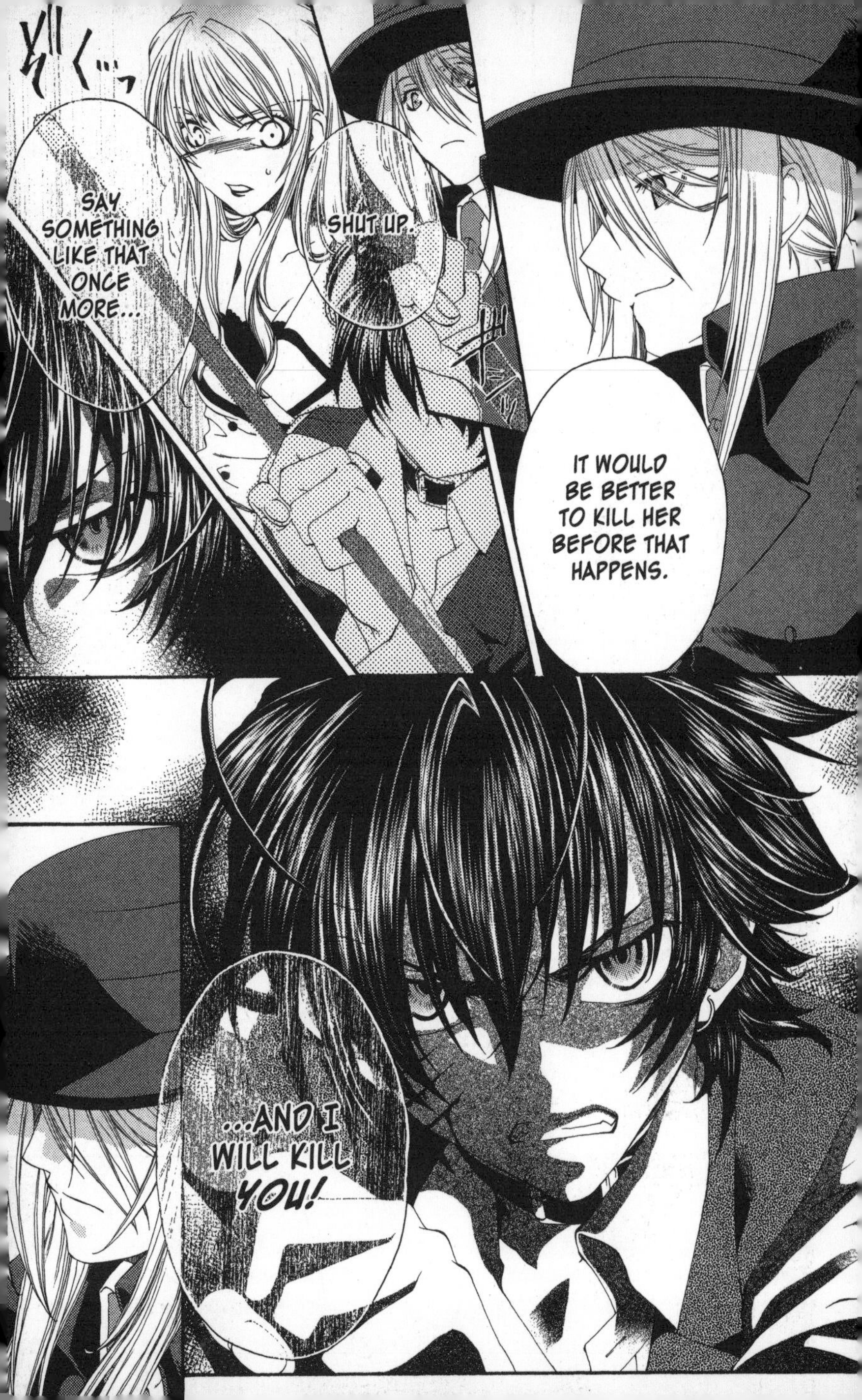
IT WOULD BE BETTER TO KILL HER BEFORE THAT HAPPENS.
SHUT UP.
SAY SOMETHING LIKE THAT ONCE MORE...
...AND I WILL KILL YOU!

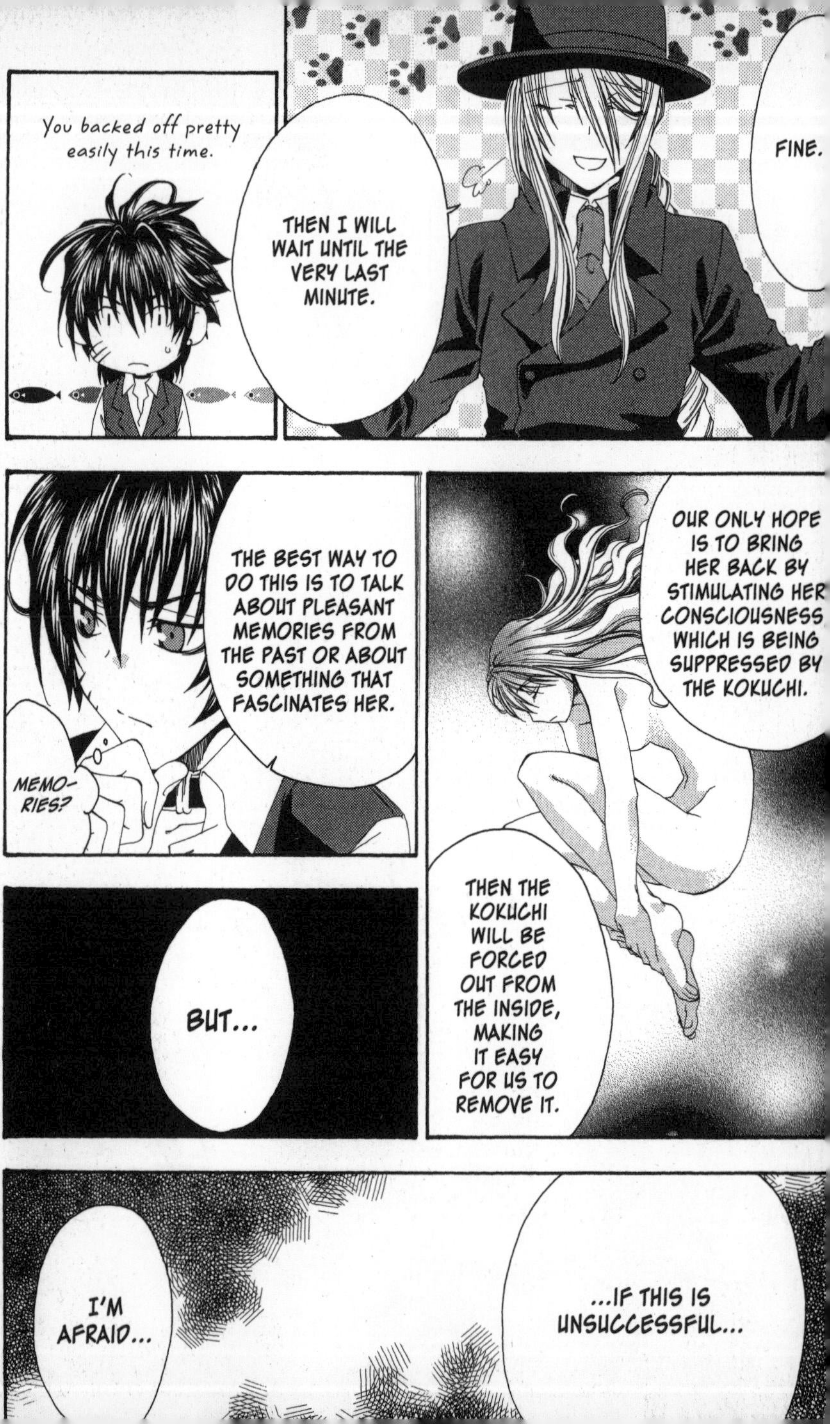
FINE.
THEN I WILL WAIT UNTIL THE VERY LAST MINUTE.
You backed off pretty easily this time.
OUR ONLY HOPE IS TO BRING HER BACK BY STIMULATING HER CONSCIOUSNESS WHICH IS BEING SUPPRESSED BY THE KOKUCHI.
THEN THE KOKUCHI WILL BE FORCED OUT FROM THE INSIDE, MAKING IT EASY FOR US TO REMOVE IT.
THE BEST WAY TO DO THIS IS TO TALK ABOUT PLEASANT MEMORIES FROM THE PAST OR ABOUT SOMETHING THAT FASCINATES HER.
MEMO- RIES?
BUT...
...IF THIS IS UNSUCCESSFUL...
I'M AFRAID...

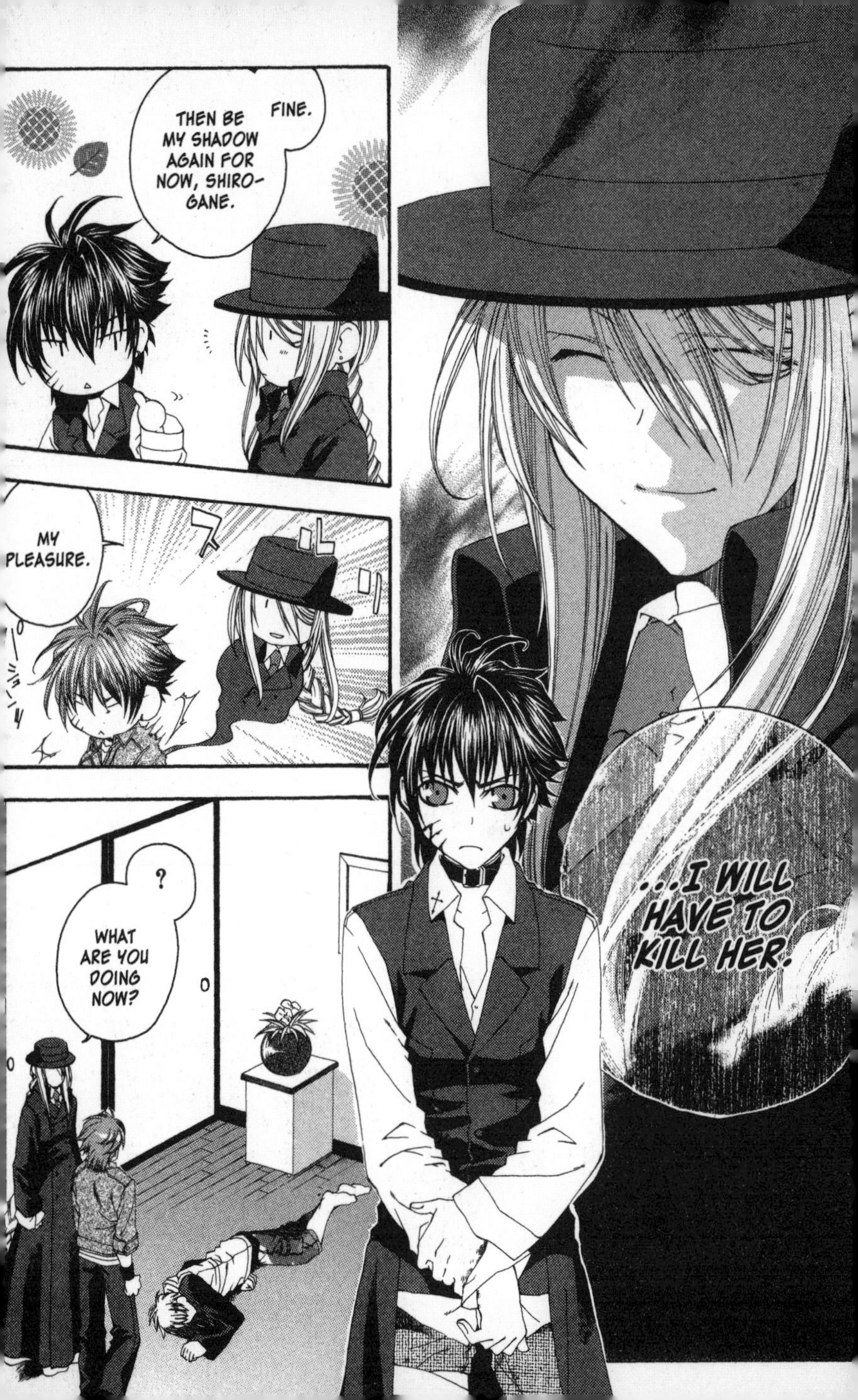
...I WILL HAVE TO KILL HER.
FINE.
THEN BE MY SHADOW AGAIN FOR NOW, SHIRO-GANE.
MY PLEASURE.
?
WHAT ARE YOU DOING NOW?

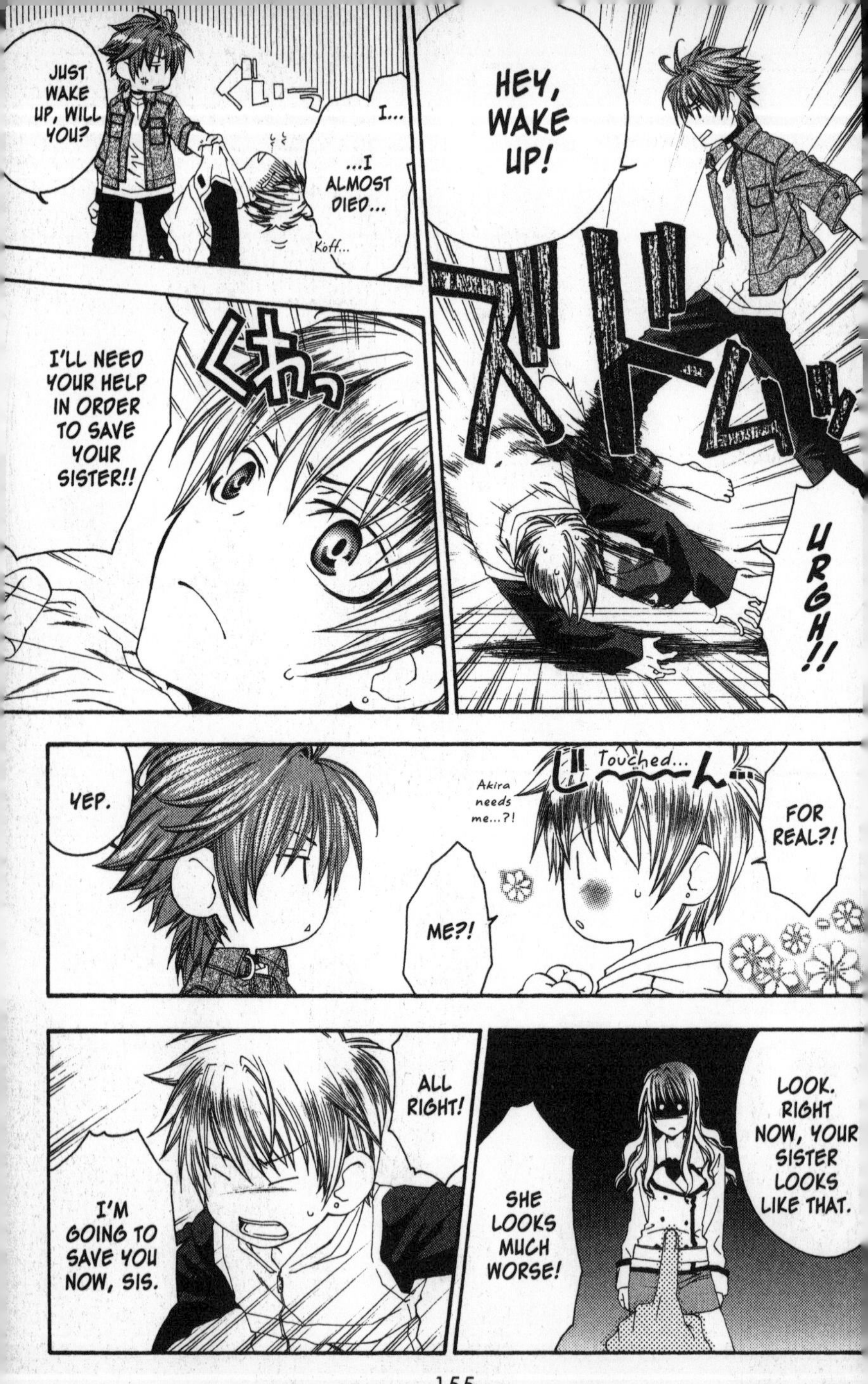
HEY, WAKE UP!
URGH!!
I...
...I ALMOST DIED...
Koff...
JUST WAKE UP, WILL YOU?
I'LL NEED YOUR HELP IN ORDER TO SAVE YOUR SISTER!!
Touched...
FOR REAL?!
Akira needs me...?!
ME?!
YEP.
LOOK. RIGHT NOW, YOUR SISTER LOOKS LIKE THAT.
SHE LOOKS MUCH WORSE!
ALL RIGHT!
I'M GOING TO SAVE YOU NOW, SIS.

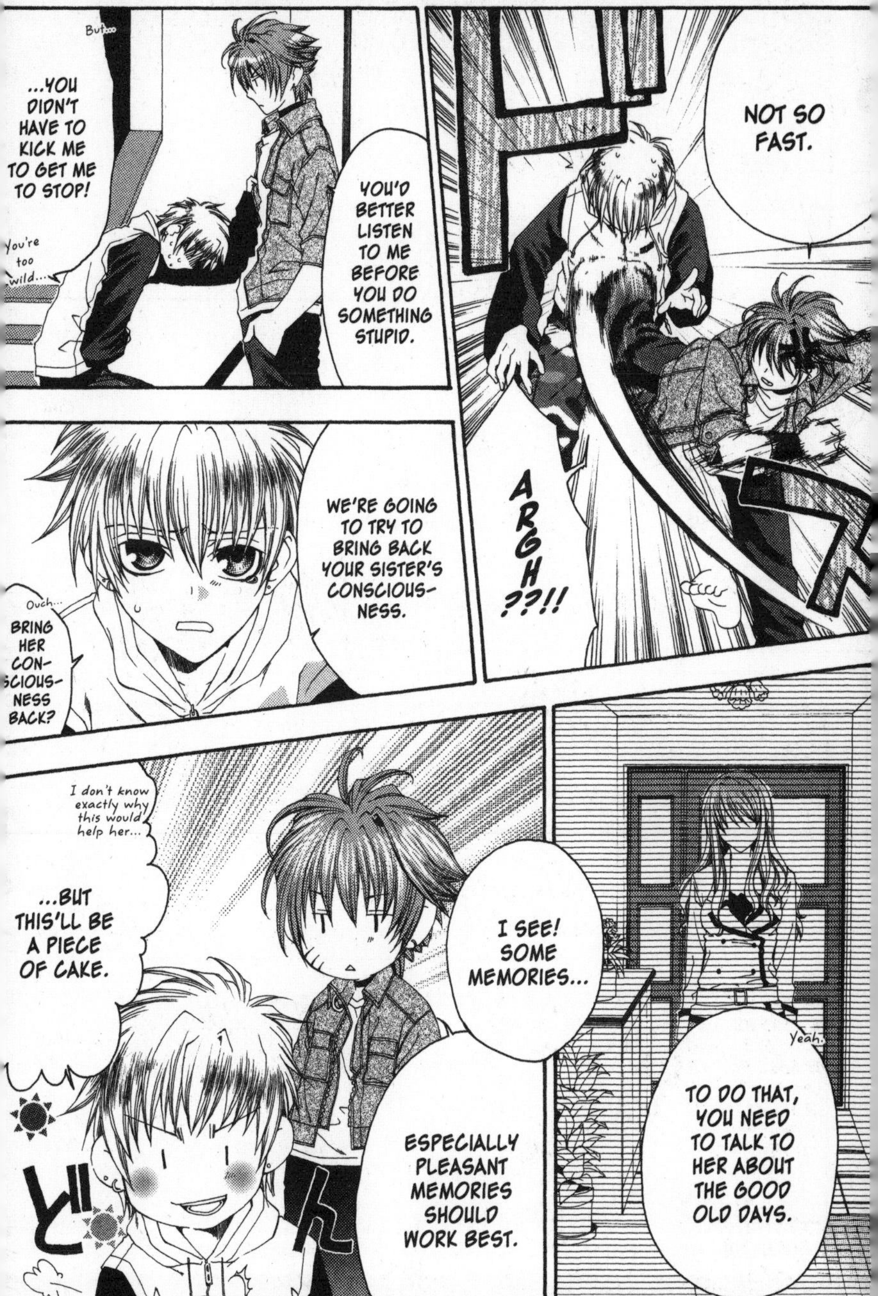
NOT SO FAST.
ARGH??!!
YOU'D BETTER LISTEN TO ME BEFORE YOU DO SOMETHING STUPID.
But...
...YOU DIDN'T HAVE TO KICK ME TO GET ME TO STOP!
You're too wild...
WE'RE GOING TO TRY TO BRING BACK YOUR SISTER'S CONSCIOUS-NESS.
Ouch...
BRING HER CON-SCIOUS-NESS BACK?
Yeah.
TO DO THAT, YOU NEED TO TALK TO HER ABOUT THE GOOD OLD DAYS.
I SEE! SOME MEMORIES...
ESPECIALLY PLEASANT MEMORIES SHOULD WORK BEST.
I don't know exactly why this would help her...
...BUT THIS'LL BE A PIECE OF CAKE.
どん

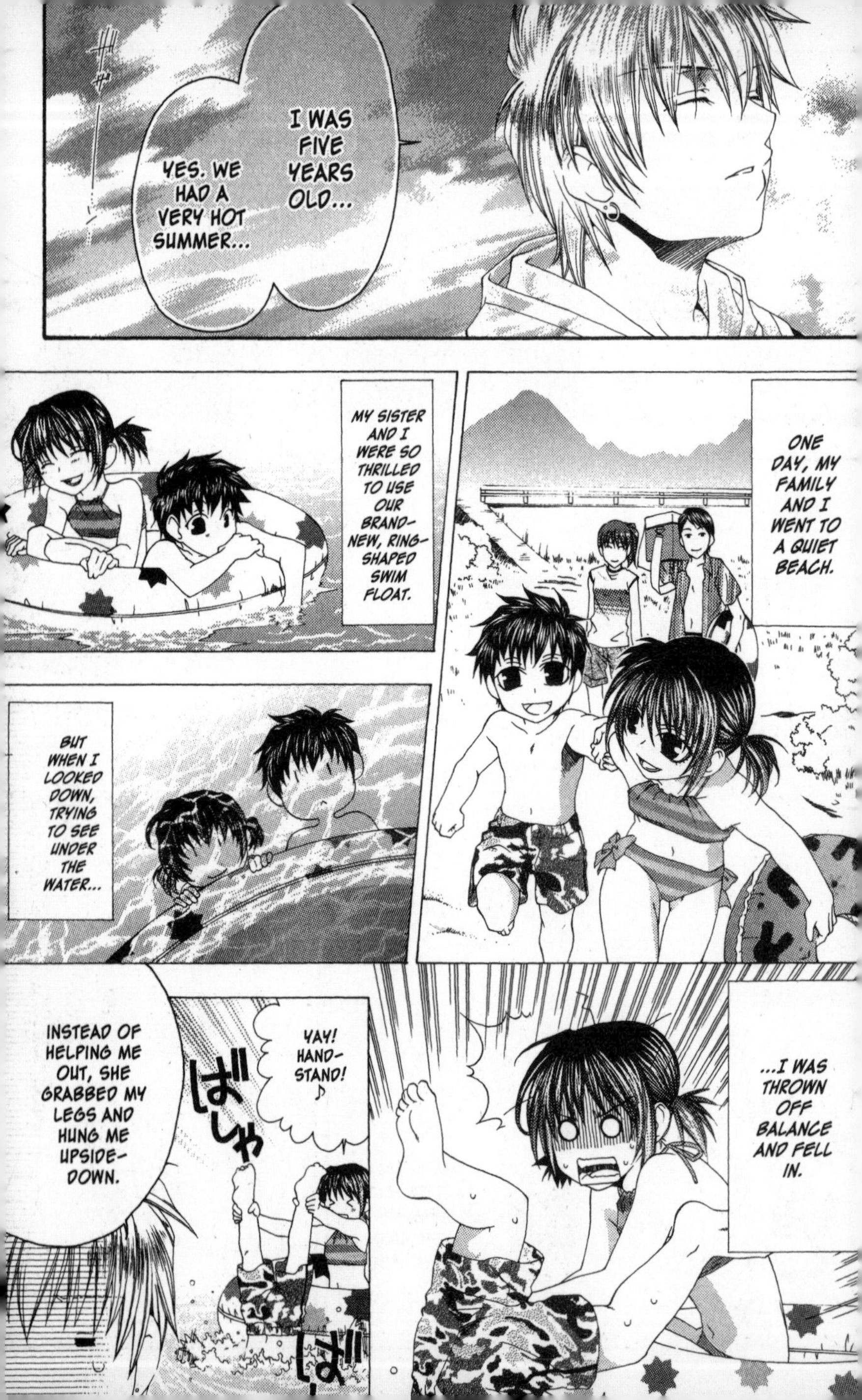
I WAS FIVE YEARS OLD...
YES. WE HAD A VERY HOT SUMMER...
ONE DAY, MY FAMILY AND I WENT TO A QUIET BEACH.
MY SISTER AND I WERE SO THRILLED TO USE OUR BRAND-NEW, RING-SHAPED SWIM FLOAT.
BUT WHEN I LOOKED DOWN, TRYING TO SEE UNDER THE WATER...
...I WAS THROWN OFF BALANCE AND FELL IN.
YAY! HANDSTAND! ♪
INSTEAD OF HELPING ME OUT, SHE GRABBED MY LEGS AND HUNG ME UPSIDE-DOWN.
ばしゃ

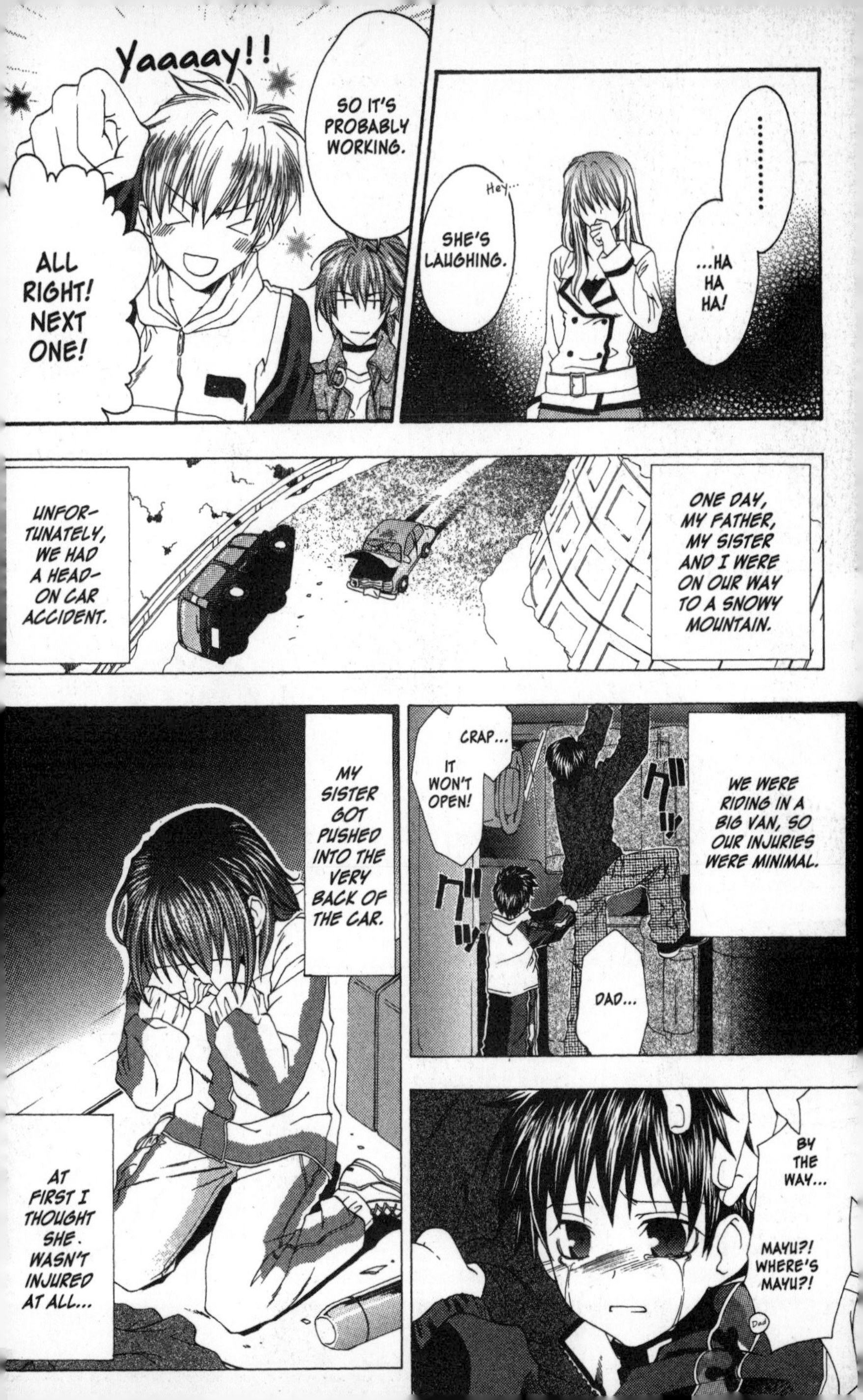
......
...HA HA HA!
Hey...
SHE'S LAUGHING.
SO IT'S PROBABLY WORKING.
Yaaaay!!
ALL RIGHT! NEXT ONE!
ONE DAY, MY FATHER, MY SISTER AND I WERE ON OUR WAY TO A SNOWY MOUNTAIN.
UNFORTUNATELY, WE HAD A HEAD-ON CAR ACCIDENT.
WE WERE RIDING IN A BIG VAN, SO OUR INJURIES WERE MINIMAL.
CRAP...
IT WON'T OPEN!
DAD...
BY THE WAY...
MAYU?! WHERE'S MAYU?!
MY SISTER GOT PUSHED INTO THE VERY BACK OF THE CAR.
AT FIRST I THOUGHT SHE WASN'T INJURED AT ALL...

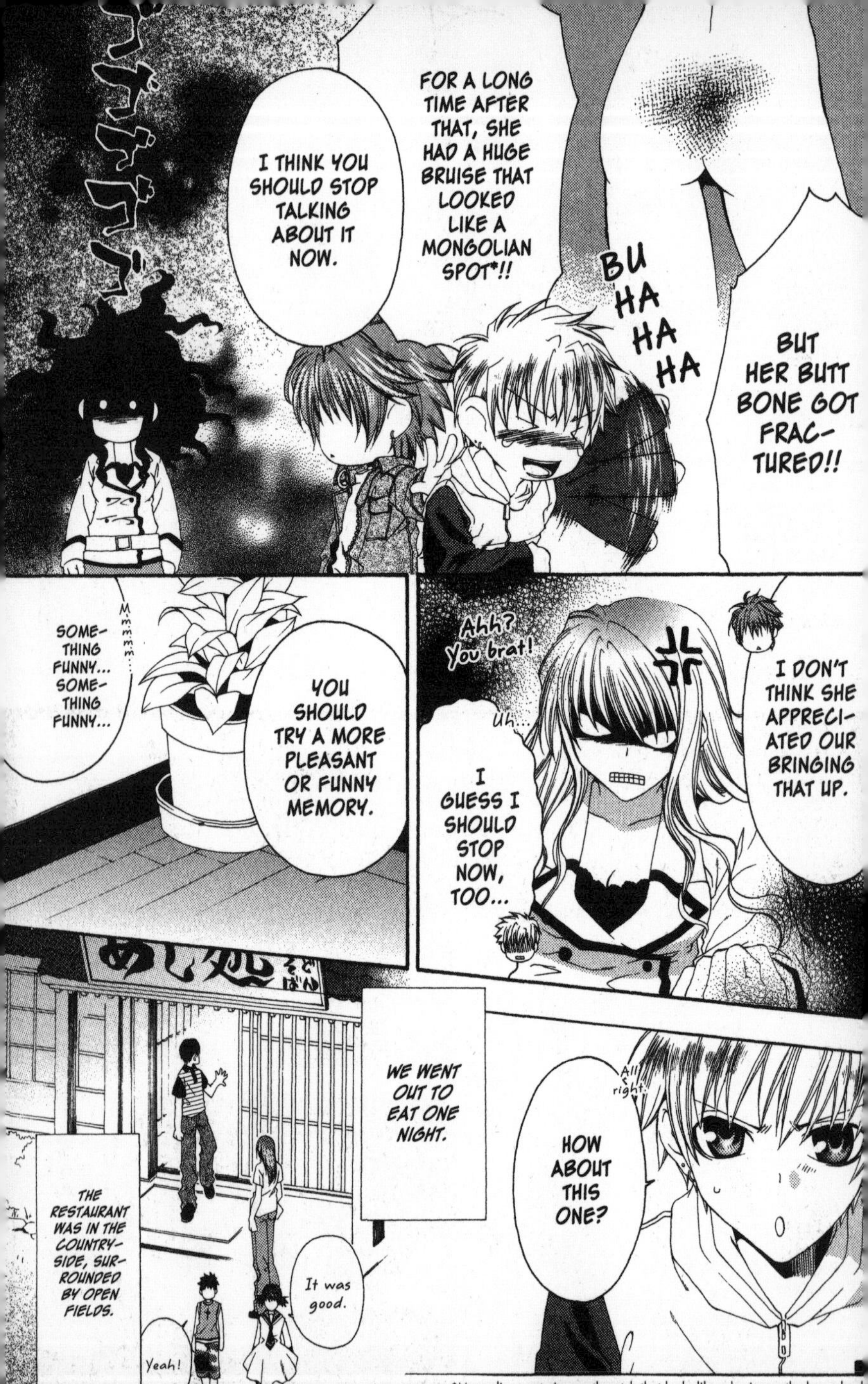
FOR A LONG TIME AFTER THAT, SHE HAD A HUGE BRUISE THAT LOOKED LIKE A MONGOLIAN SPOT*!!
BUT HER BUTT BONE GOT FRAC-TURED!!
BU HA HA HA
I THINK YOU SHOULD STOP TALKING ABOUT IT NOW.
I DON'T THINK SHE APPRECI-ATED OUR BRINGING THAT UP.
Ahh? You brat!
Uh...
I GUESS I SHOULD STOP NOW, TOO...
YOU SHOULD TRY A MORE PLEASANT OR FUNNY MEMORY.
SOME-THING FUNNY... SOME-THING FUNNY...
Mmmmm...
All right.
HOW ABOUT THIS ONE?
WE WENT OUT TO EAT ONE NIGHT.
THE RESTAURANT WAS IN THE COUNTRY-SIDE, SUR-ROUNDED BY OPEN FIELDS.
It was good.
Yeah!

*Mongolian spot: A smooth patch that looks like a bruise on the lower back

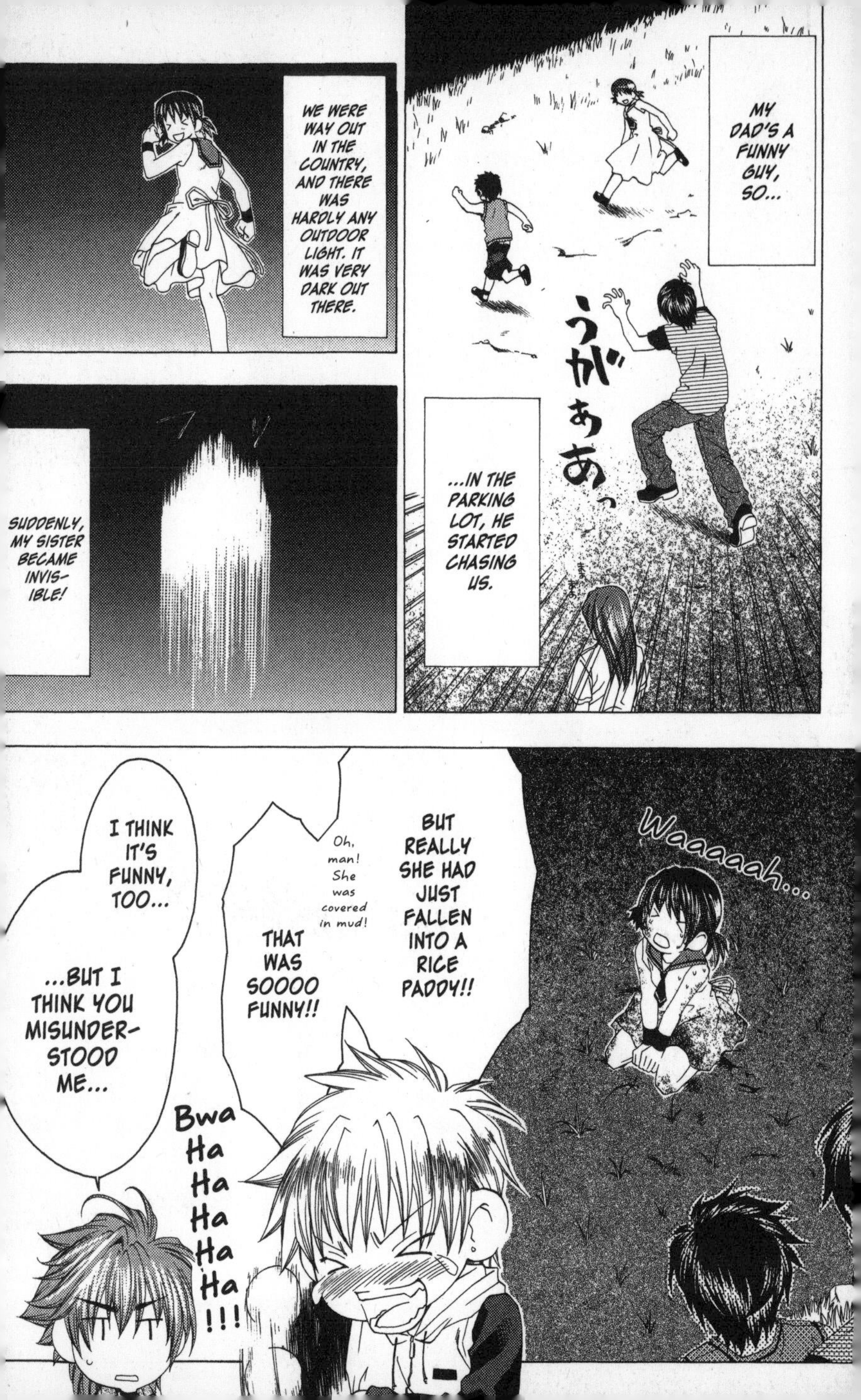
MY DAD'S A FUNNY GUY, SO...
うがあぁっ
...IN THE PARKING LOT, HE STARTED CHASING US.
WE WERE WAY OUT IN THE COUNTRY, AND THERE WAS HARDLY ANY OUTDOOR LIGHT. IT WAS VERY DARK OUT THERE.
SUDDENLY, MY SISTER BECAME INVIS-IBLE!
Waaaaaah...
BUT REALLY SHE HAD JUST FALLEN INTO A RICE PADDY!!
Oh, man! She was covered in mud!
THAT WAS SOOOO FUNNY!!
Bwa Ha Ha Ha Ha Ha!!!
I THINK IT'S FUNNY, TOO...
...BUT I THINK YOU MISUNDER-STOOD ME...

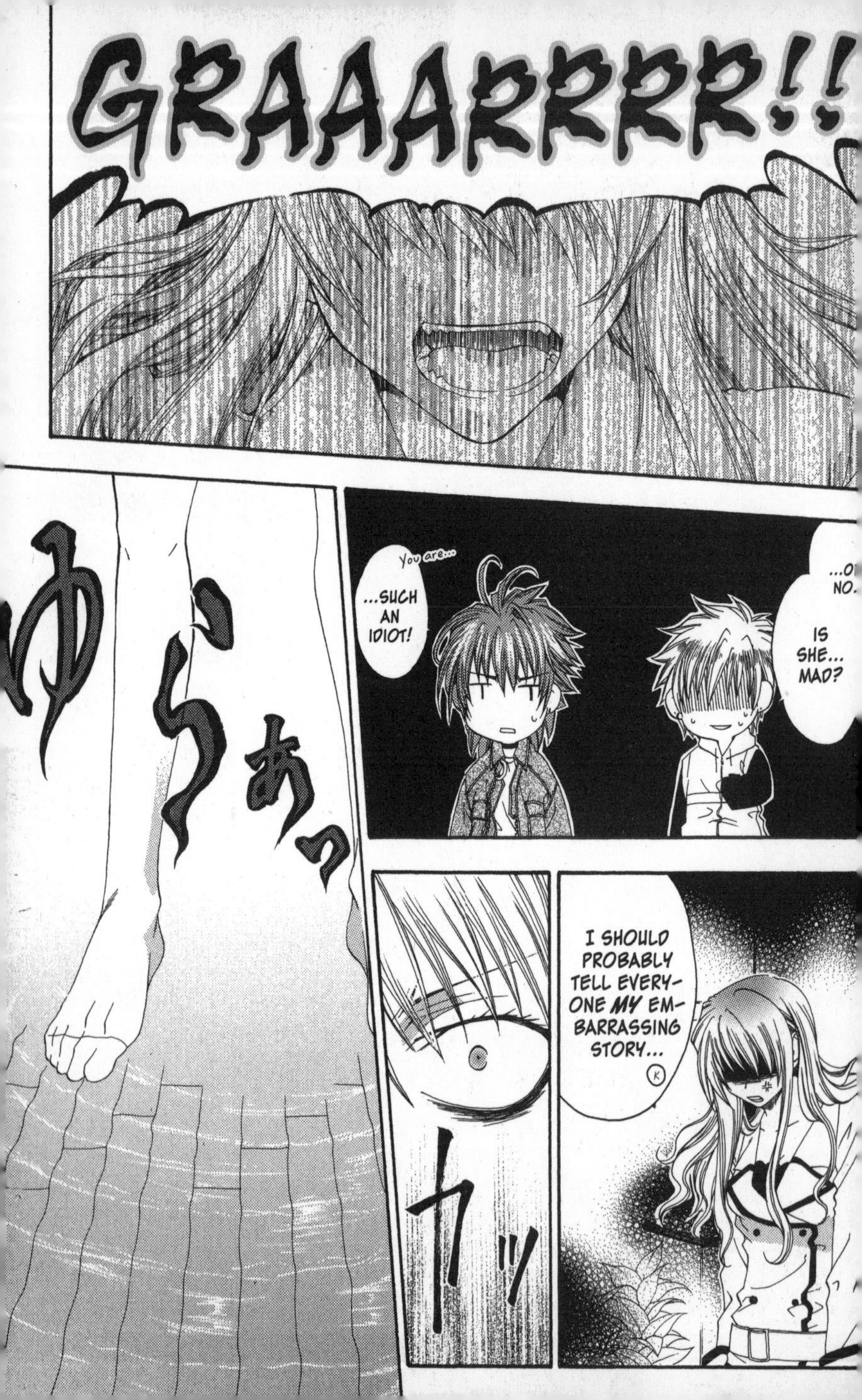
GRAAARRRR!!
...O NO.
IS SHE... MAD?
You are...
...SUCH AN IDIOT!
I SHOULD PROBABLY TELL EVERY-ONE MY EM-BARRASSING STORY...
カッ
ゆらあっ

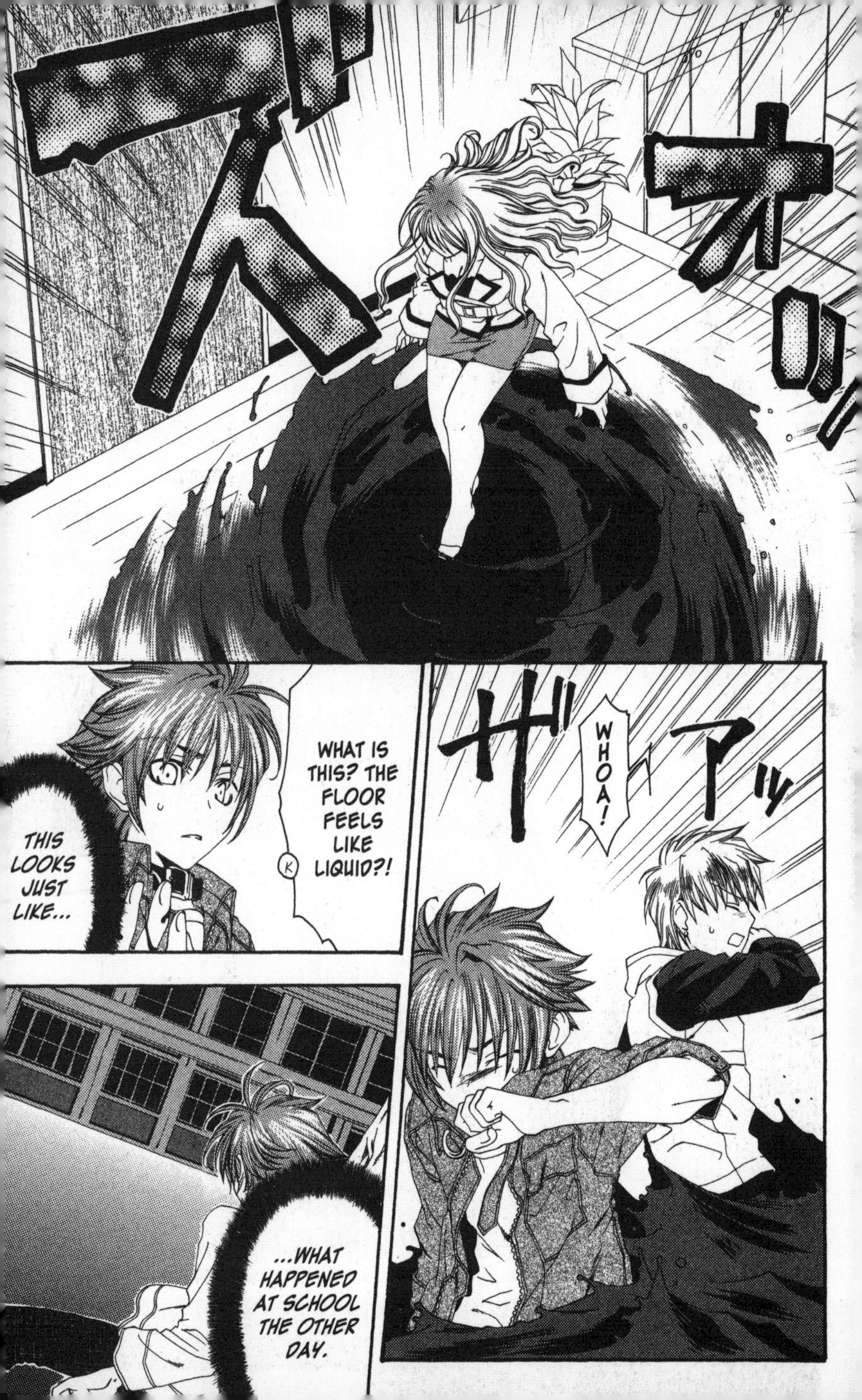
ズオッ
ザアッ
WHOA!
WHAT IS THIS? THE FLOOR FEELS LIKE LIQUID?!
THIS LOOKS JUST LIKE...
...WHAT HAPPENED AT SCHOOL THE OTHER DAY.

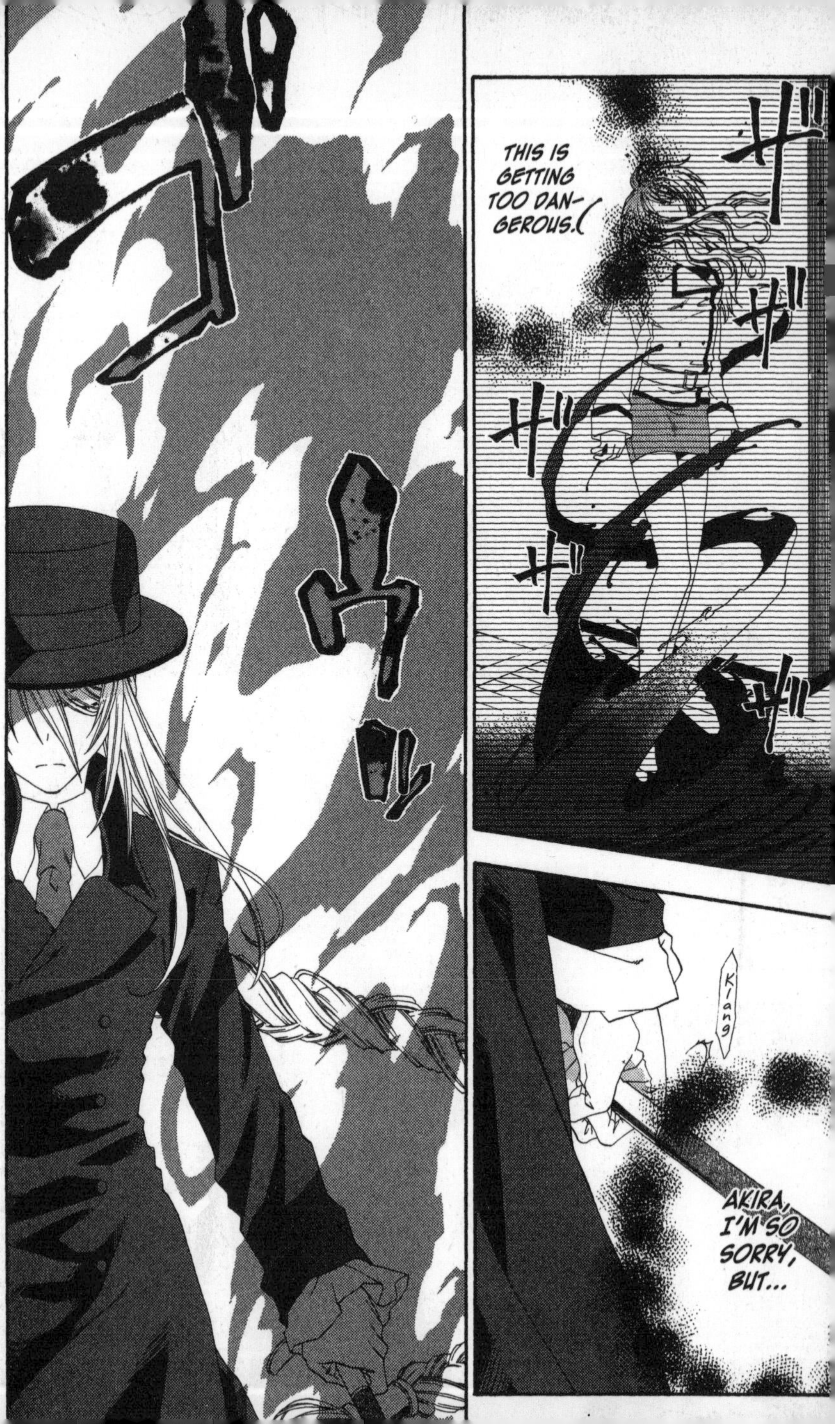
THIS IS GETTING TOO DAN-GEROUS.
Klang
AKIRA, I'M SO SORRY, BUT...

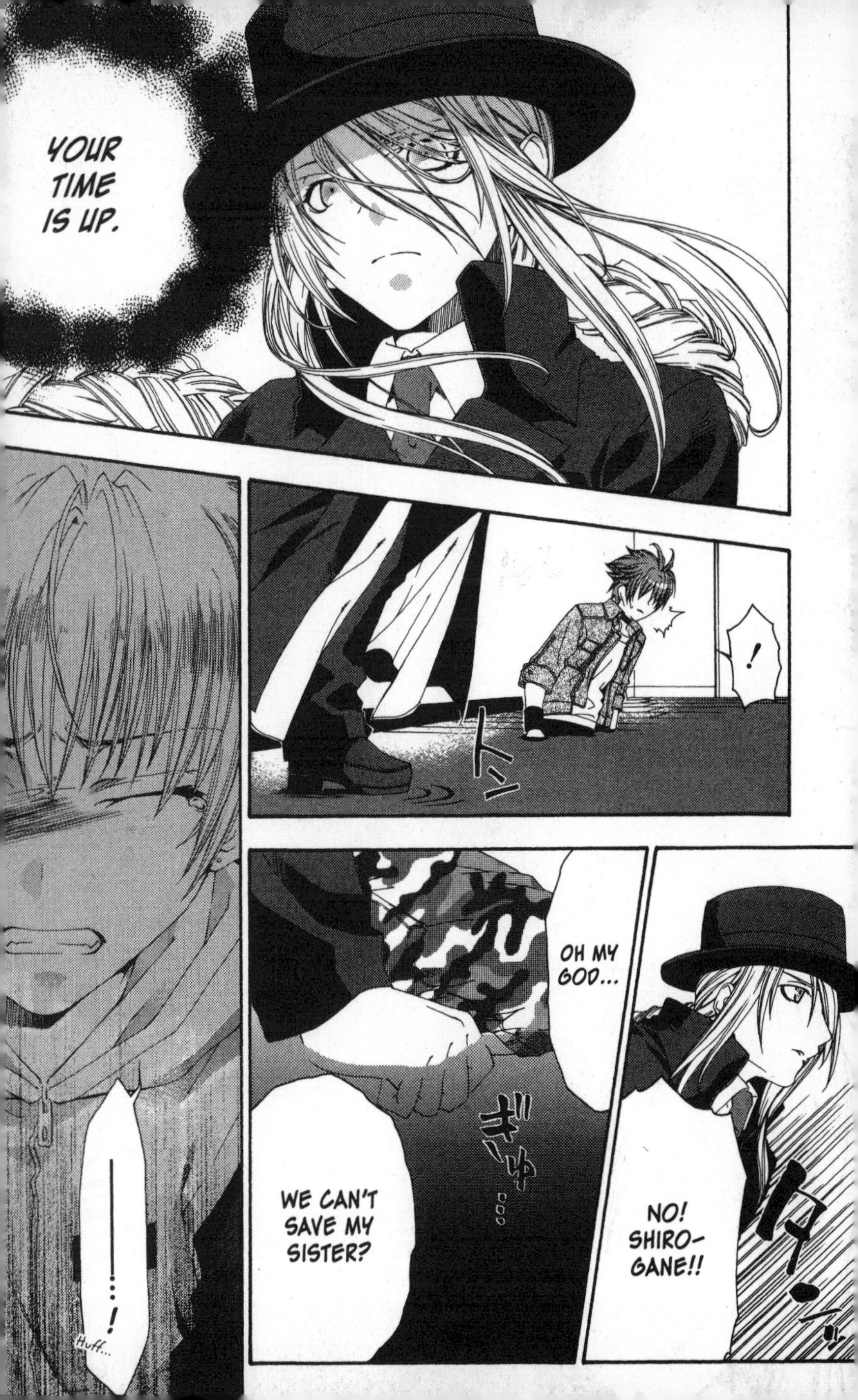

YOUR TIME IS UP.
!
トン
NO! SHIRO-GANE!!
OH MY GOD...
WE CAN'T SAVE MY SISTER?
ぎゅ…
——...!
Huff...

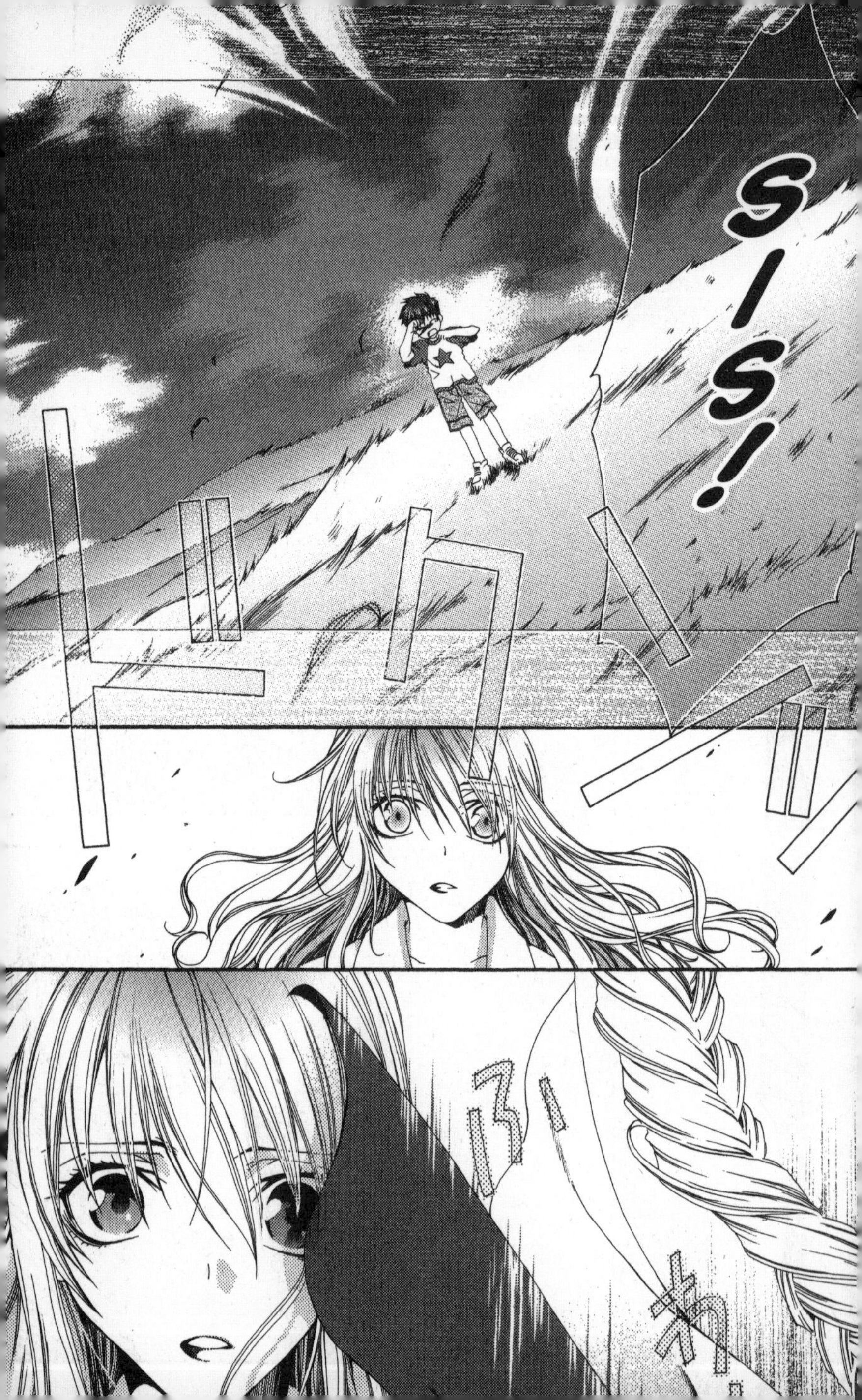
S-I-S!

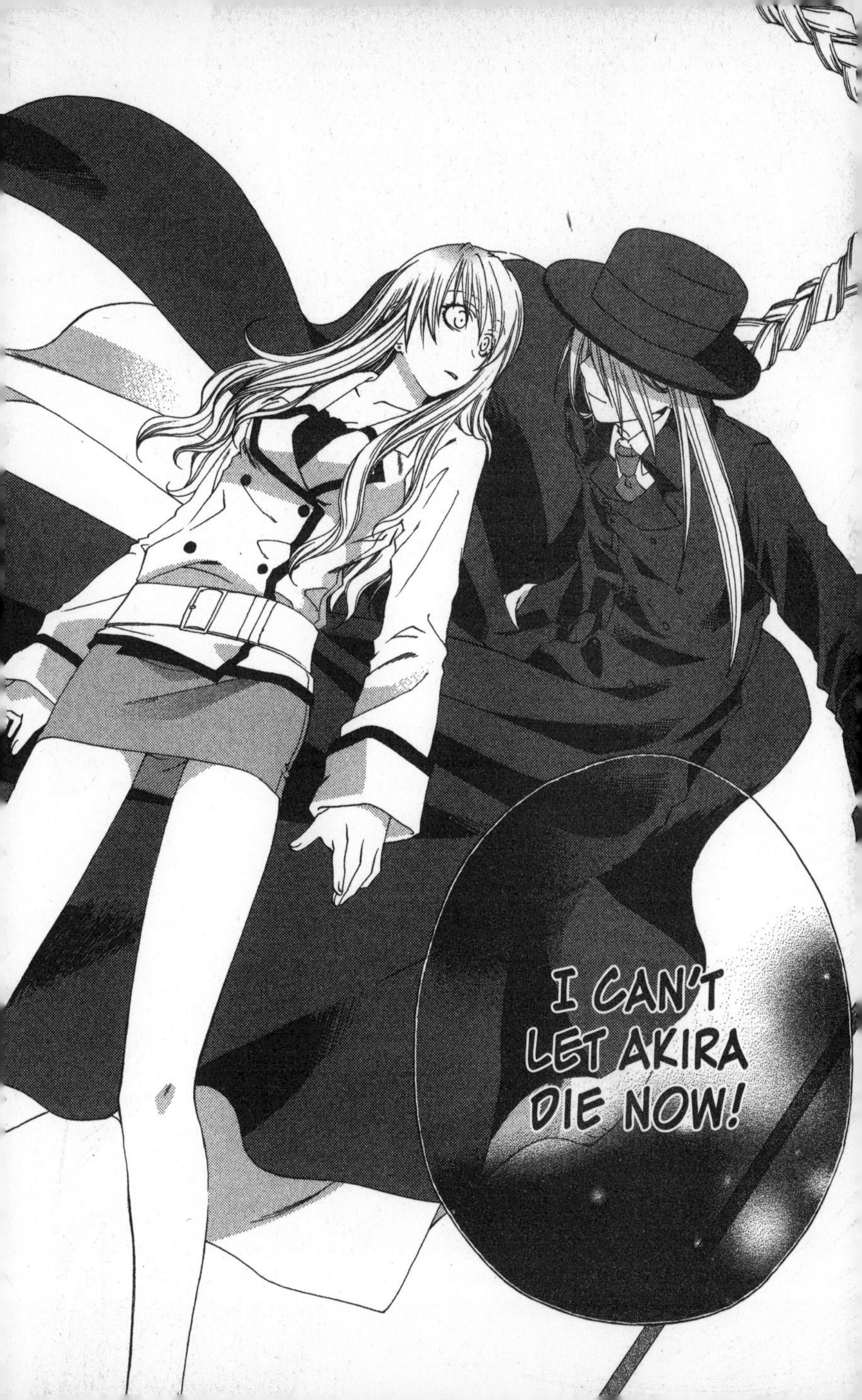
I CAN'T LET AKIRA DIE NOW!

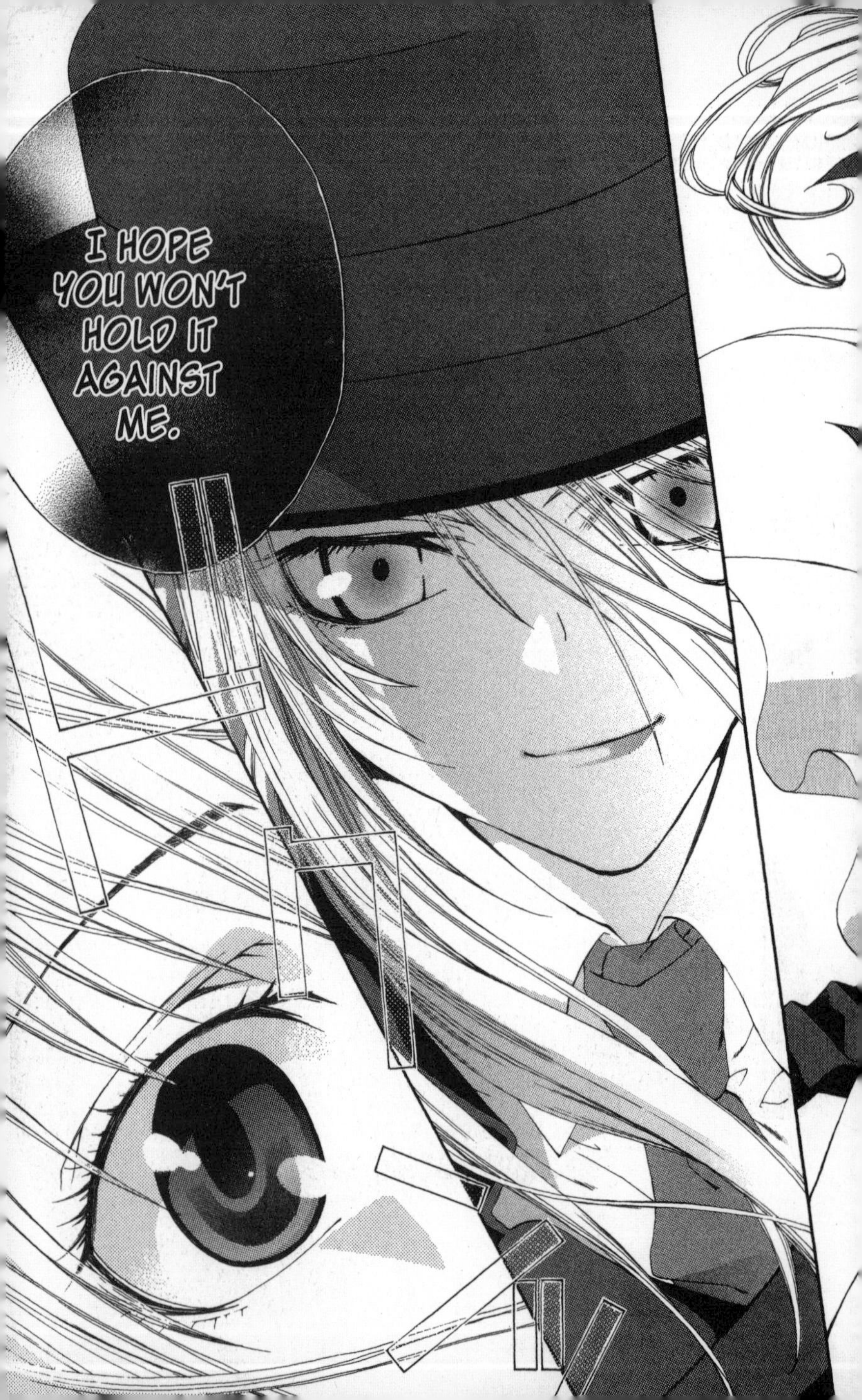
I HOPE YOU WON'T HOLD IT AGAINST ME.

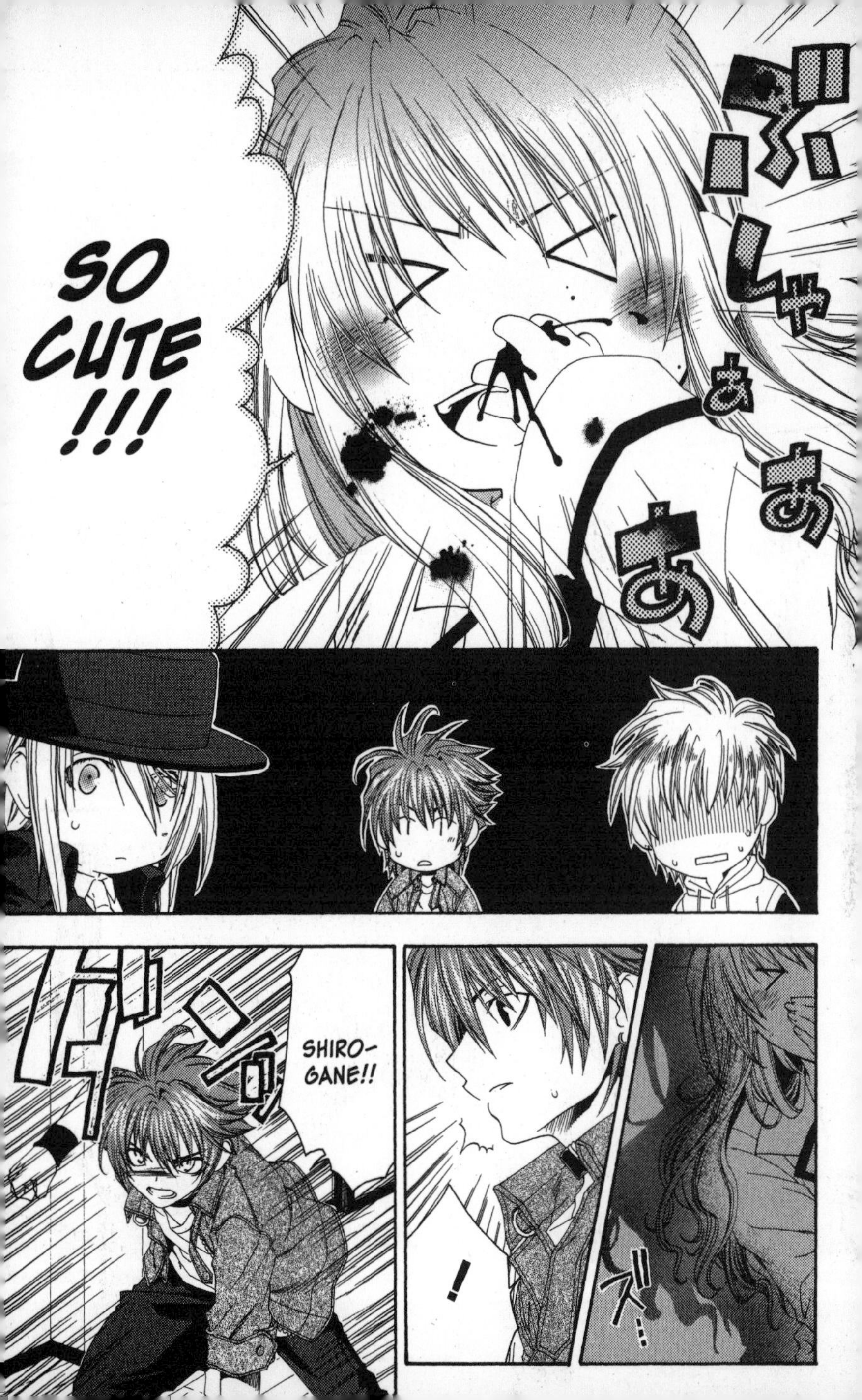
ぶしゃぁああ
SO CUTE!!!
ズ…
!
SHIRO-GANE!!

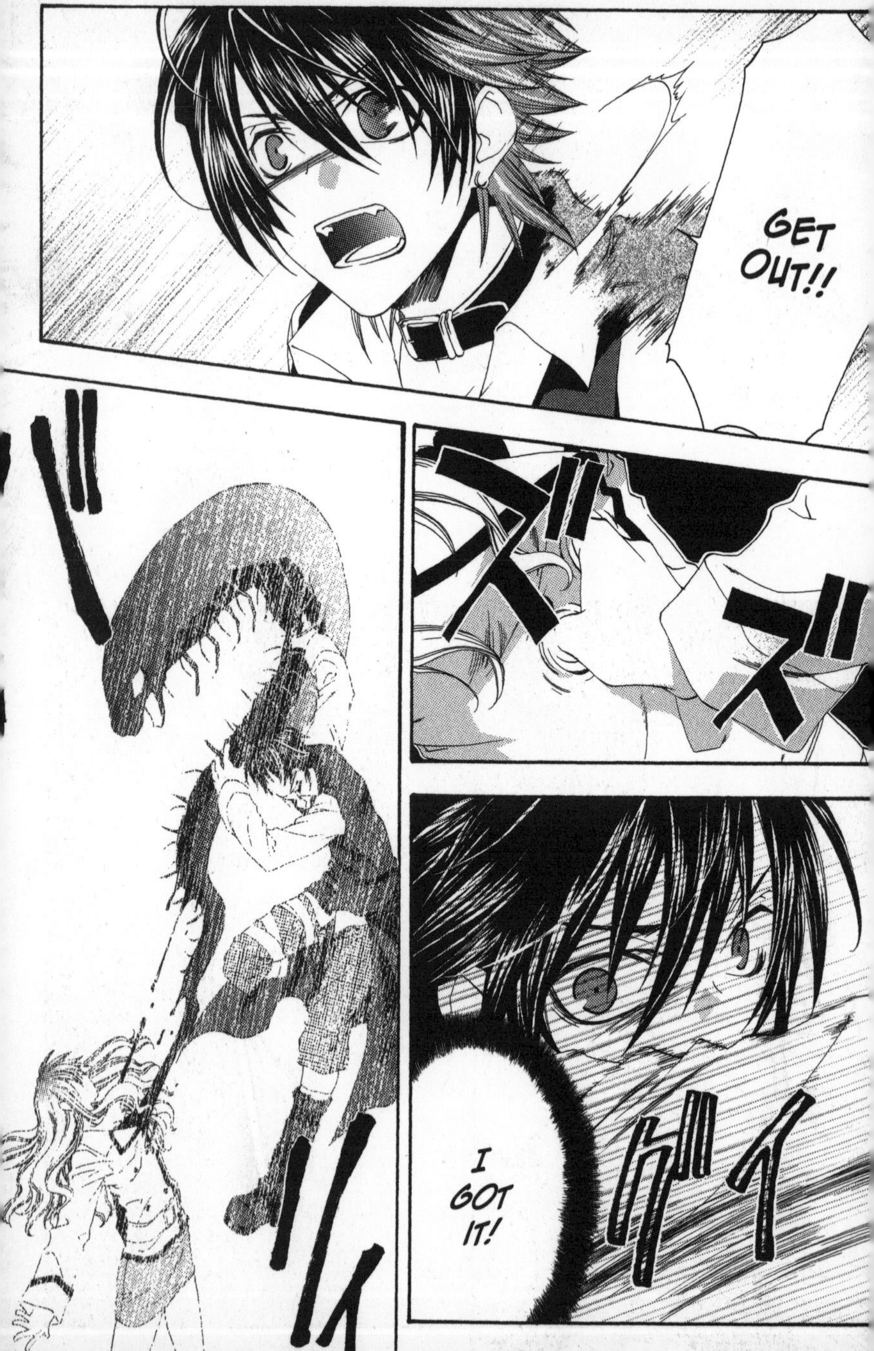
GET OUT!!
ズズ
I GOT IT!

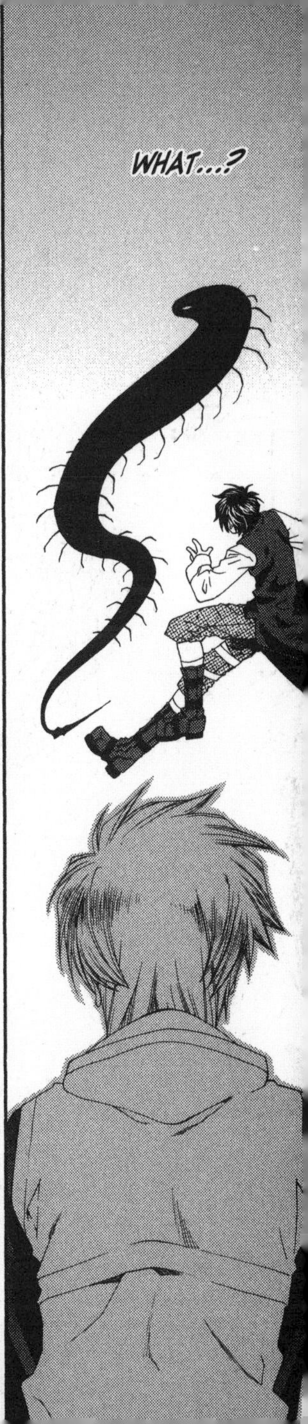
WHAT...?

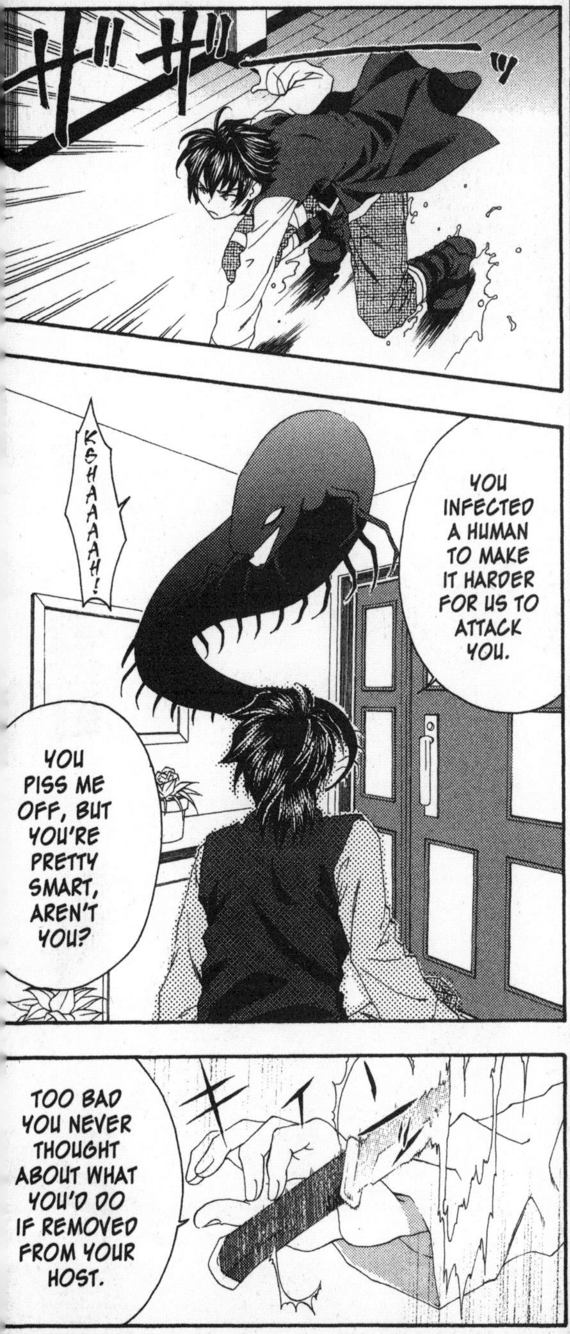
ザッザッ
YOU INFECTED A HUMAN TO MAKE IT HARDER FOR US TO ATTACK YOU.
KSHAAAAAAH!
YOU PISS ME OFF, BUT YOU'RE PRETTY SMART, AREN'T YOU?
TOO BAD YOU NEVER THOUGHT ABOUT WHAT YOU'D DO IF REMOVED FROM YOUR HOST.

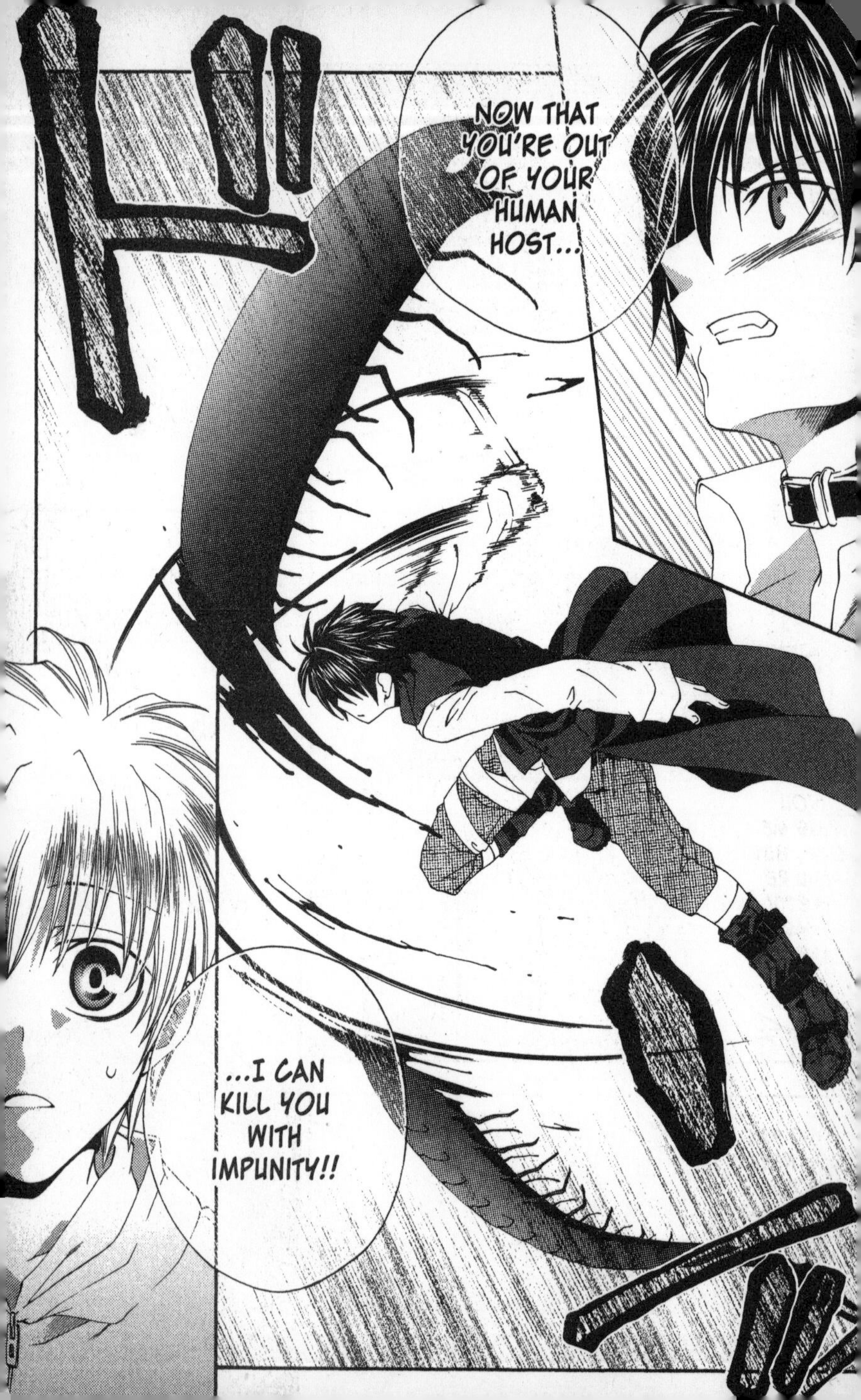
NOW THAT YOU'RE OUT OF YOUR HUMAN HOST...
ド!!
...I CAN KILL YOU WITH IMPUNITY!!

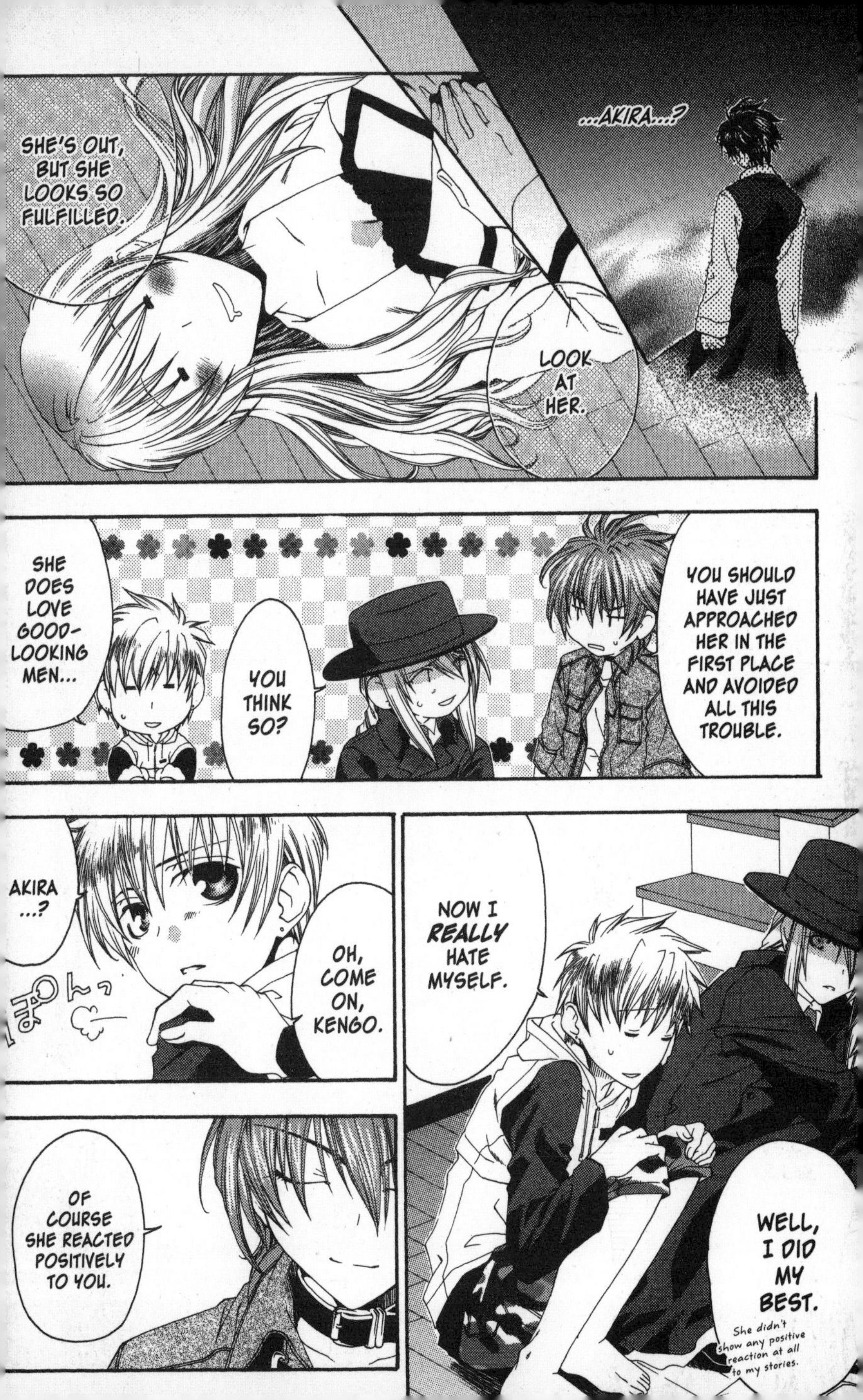
...AKIRA...?
LOOK AT HER.
SHE'S OUT, BUT SHE LOOKS SO FULFILLED.
YOU SHOULD HAVE JUST APPROACHED HER IN THE FIRST PLACE AND AVOIDED ALL THIS TROUBLE.
YOU THINK SO?
SHE DOES LOVE GOOD-LOOKING MEN...
NOW I **REALLY** HATE MYSELF.
WELL, I DID MY BEST.
She didn't show any positive reaction at all to my stories.
OH, COME ON, KENGO.
AKIRA ...?
OF COURSE SHE REACTED POSITIVELY TO YOU.

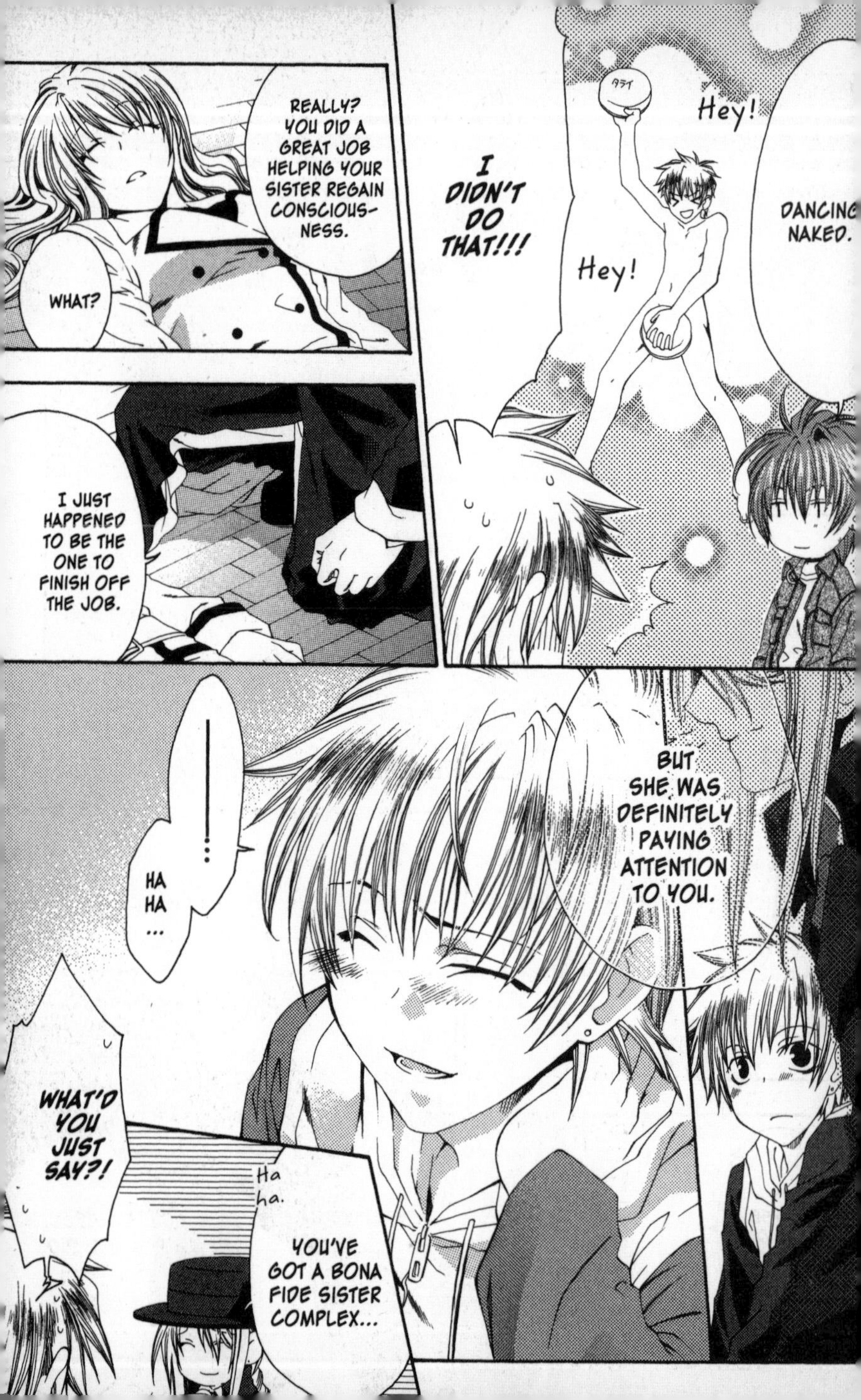

DANCING NAKED.
Hey!
Hey!
I DIDN'T DO THAT!!!
REALLY? YOU DID A GREAT JOB HELPING YOUR SISTER REGAIN CONSCIOUS-NESS.
WHAT?
I JUST HAPPENED TO BE THE ONE TO FINISH OFF THE JOB.
BUT SHE WAS DEFINITELY PAYING ATTENTION TO YOU.
—...!
HA HA...
Ha ha.
YOU'VE GOT A BONA FIDE SISTER COMPLEX...
WHAT'D YOU JUST SAY?!

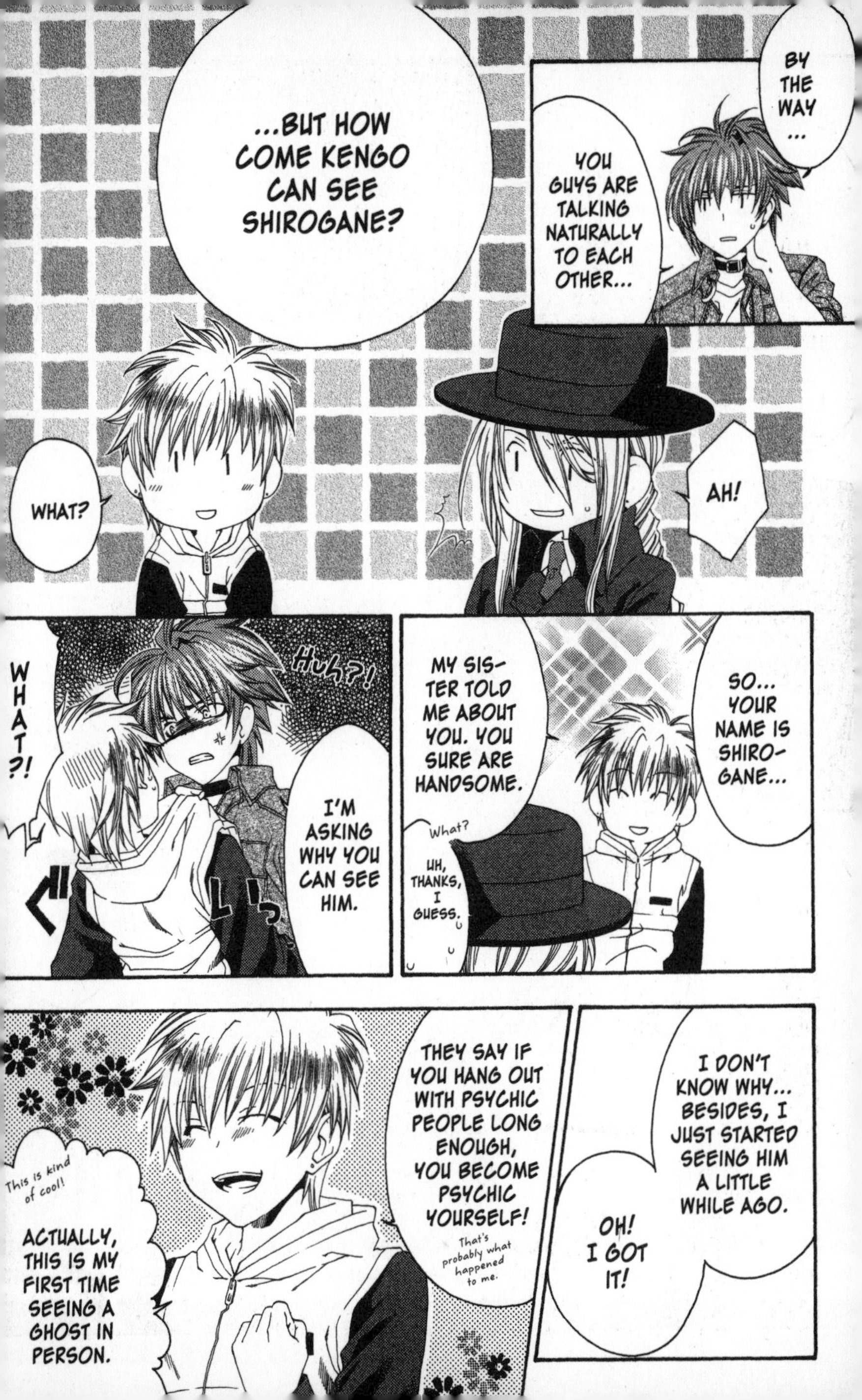

BY THE WAY...
YOU GUYS ARE TALKING NATURALLY TO EACH OTHER...
...BUT HOW COME KENGO CAN SEE SHIROGANE?
AH!
WHAT?
SO... YOUR NAME IS SHIROGANE...
MY SISTER TOLD ME ABOUT YOU. YOU SURE ARE HANDSOME.
What?
UH, THANKS, I GUESS.
Huh?!
WHAT?!
I'M ASKING WHY YOU CAN SEE HIM.
I DON'T KNOW WHY... BESIDES, I JUST STARTED SEEING HIM A LITTLE WHILE AGO.
OH! I GOT IT!
THEY SAY IF YOU HANG OUT WITH PSYCHIC PEOPLE LONG ENOUGH, YOU BECOME PSYCHIC YOURSELF!
That's probably what happened to me.
This is kind of cool!
ACTUALLY, THIS IS MY FIRST TIME SEEING A GHOST IN PERSON.

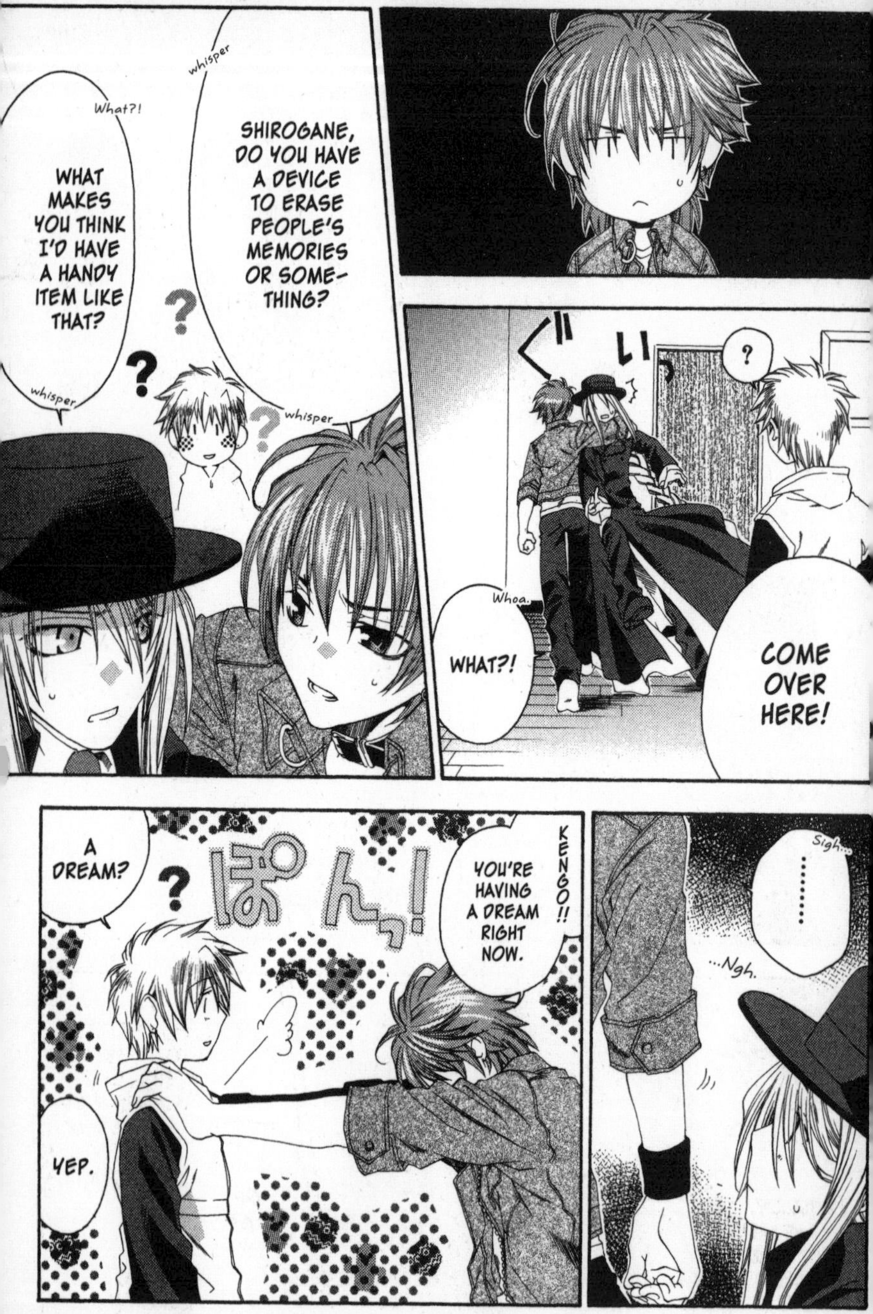
?
COME OVER HERE!
ぐい
Whoa.
WHAT?!
whisper
SHIROGANE, DO YOU HAVE A DEVICE TO ERASE PEOPLE'S MEMORIES OR SOMETHING?
whisper
What?!
WHAT MAKES YOU THINK I'D HAVE A HANDY ITEM LIKE THAT?
whisper
Sigh...
......
...Ngh.
KENGO!!
YOU'RE HAVING A DREAM RIGHT NOW.
ぽんっ!
A DREAM?
YEP.

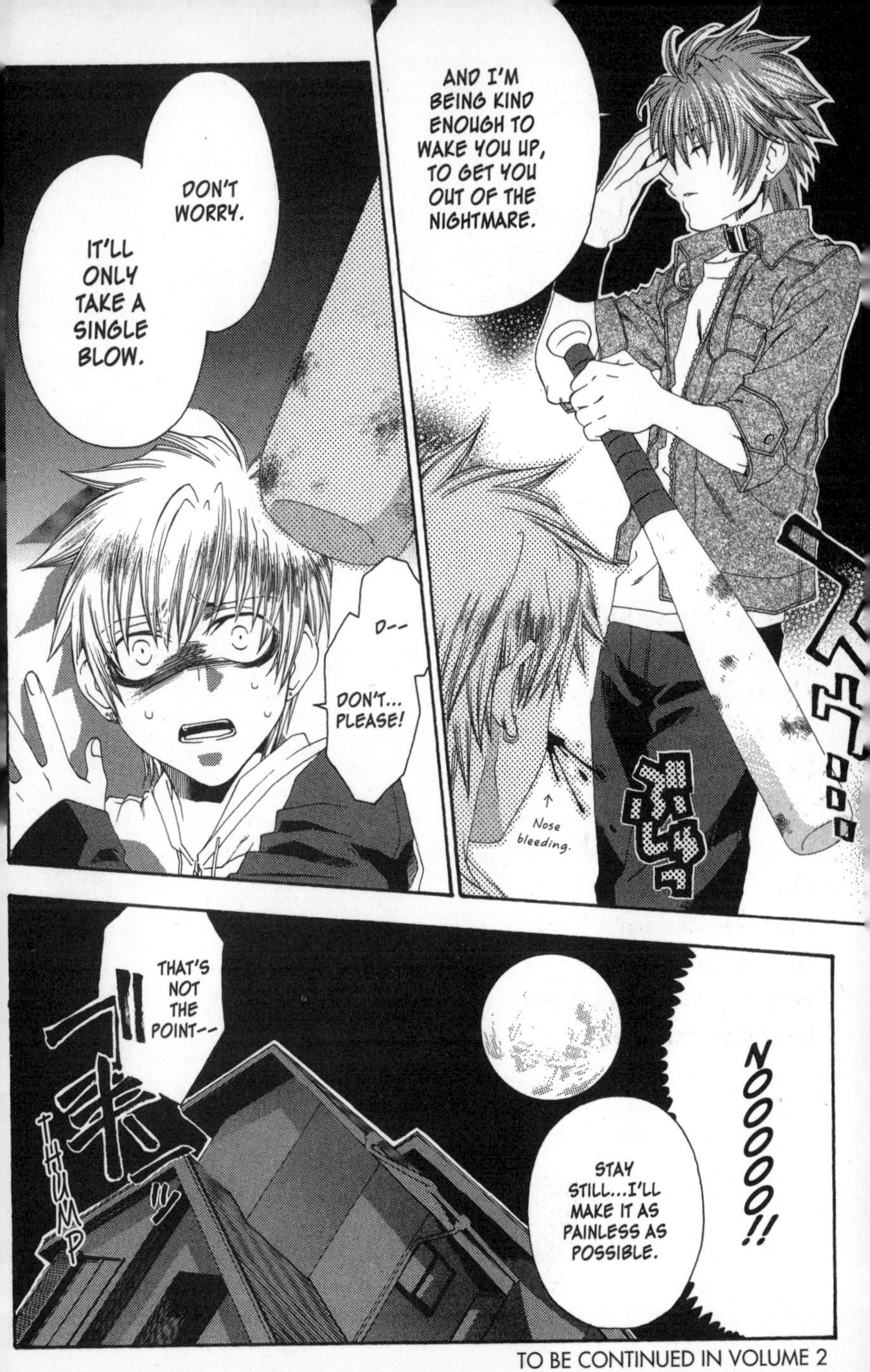
AND I'M BEING KIND ENOUGH TO WAKE YOU UP, TO GET YOU OUT OF THE NIGHTMARE.
↑ Nose bleeding.
DON'T WORRY.
IT'LL ONLY TAKE A SINGLE BLOW.
D--
DON'T... PLEASE!
NOOOOOO!!
STAY STILL...I'LL MAKE IT AS PAINLESS AS POSSIBLE.
THAT'S NOT THE POINT--
THUMP

TO BE CONTINUED IN VOLUME 2

In the next

Monochrome factor

The fact that Shingo, Aya, and many other ordinary people are gaining the ability to see shin and other shadow creatures indicates a serious disruption in the balance between the worlds! When a serial killer slaughtering the locals left and right turns out to be a shin himself, Shirogane and Akira learn that a sinister shadow world power is about to make its move...

Humidity

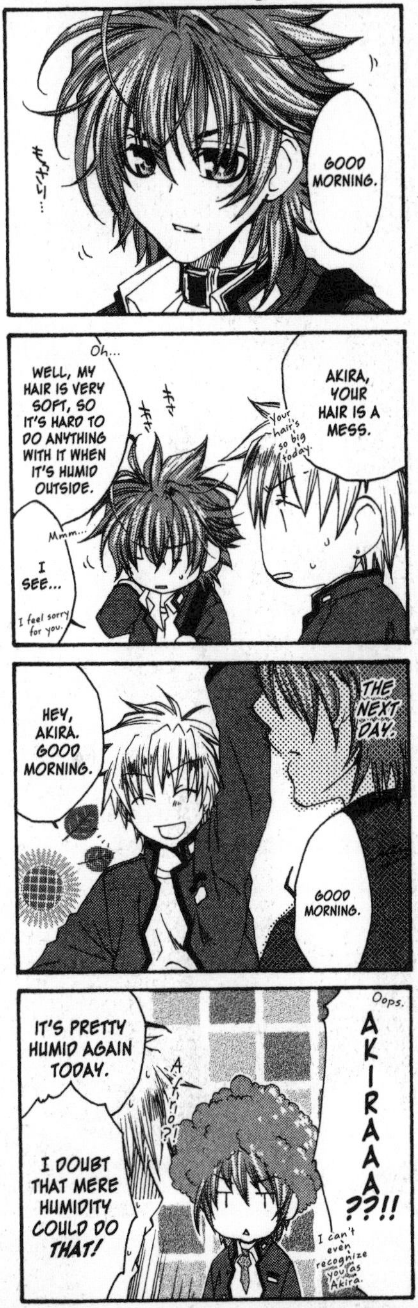
GOOD MORNING.
AKIRA, YOUR HAIR IS A MESS.
Your hair's so big today.
Oh...
WELL, MY HAIR IS VERY SOFT, SO IT'S HARD TO DO ANYTHING WITH IT WHEN IT'S HUMID OUTSIDE.
Mmm...
I SEE...
I feel sorry for you.
THE NEXT DAY.
HEY, AKIRA. GOOD MORNING.
GOOD MORNING.
Oops.
AKIRAAAA??!!
I can't even recognize you as Akira.
A-Akira?!
IT'S PRETTY HUMID AGAIN TODAY.
I DOUBT THAT MERE HUMIDITY COULD DO THAT!

In My Way

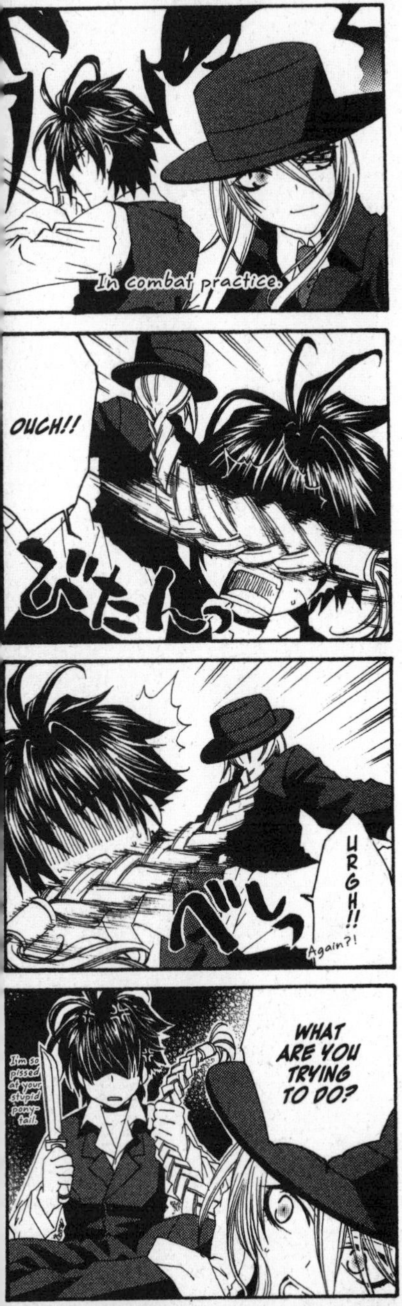
In combat practice.
OUCH!!
ぴたんっ
URGH!!
Again?!
べしっ
WHAT ARE YOU TRYING TO DO?
I'm so pissed at your stupid ponytail.

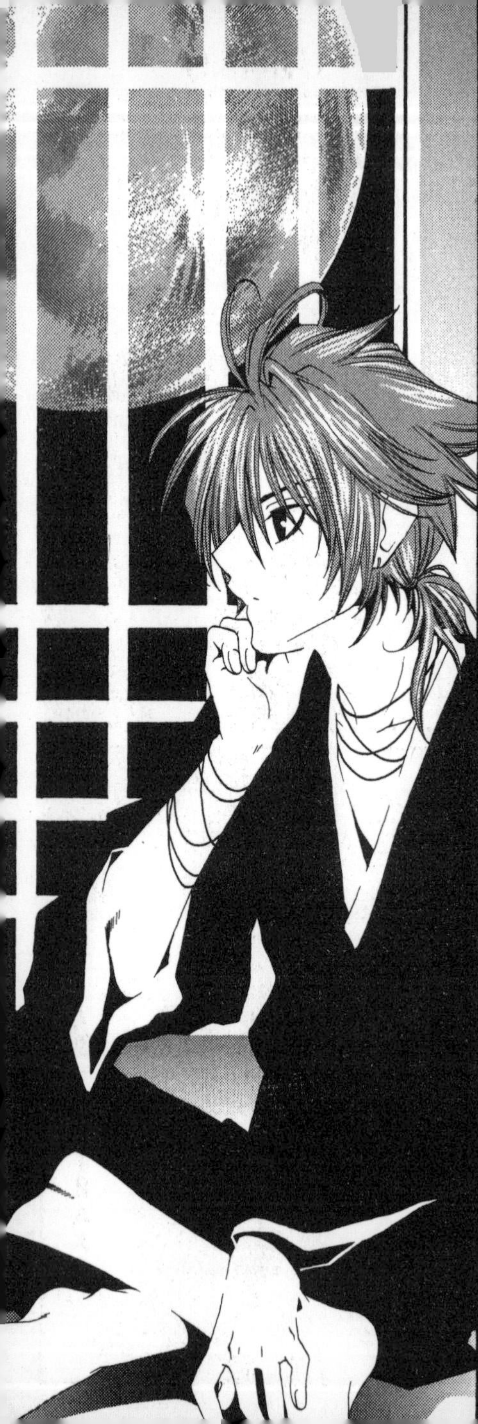

Talk

Hi, this is Kaili Sorano. *Monochrome Factor* volume 1 is finally here!! At last... really! I'm slow at drawing, so I feel sorry for those who have been waiting for this book to come out... (sweat drop) In any case, I truly appreciate the readers who purchased a copy of this volume!!

Monochrome Factor is based on a story I had in mind when I was in high school. I made a lot of changes to the characters and time period, but the basic story plot remains the same. I was quite intense back then and had a "do-it-all-the-way" attitude... (LOL). The appearances of Shirogane and Akira, when transformed into shin, can be traced to a certain extent to the characters I made up back then. The story will reveal my personal interests as you continue to read the title...so please stay with me.

I regret that there are almost no extra pages to write a good postscript, and I am writing this in my bad handwriting. This sure is hard to read, isn't it? Despite that, thank you so much for reading this postscript.

Hope to see you in the next volume.

Separation Sky

Thanks

Editor ... Mr. Iida
Assistants ... Muffy, Koike, Yuka, Suii, Mayu

...Thanks to all of you...and sorry! I know I can be quite a burden at times... (sweat drop)

二海堂 昶(にかいどう あきら)
Akira Nikaido

Monochrome Factor Character Profiles 1

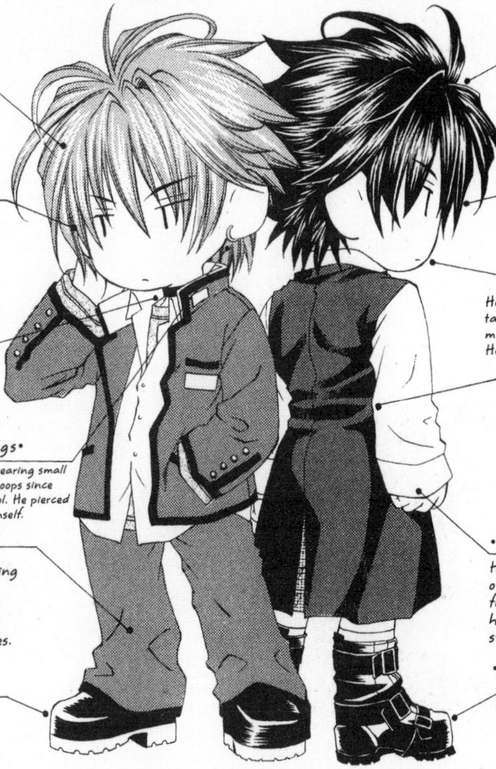
•Hair•
Very soft and unruly. Naturally light brown.
•Ear•
Some hearing loss from listening to loud music.
•Choker•
His favorite accessory. He always wears it.
•Earrings•
He's been wearing small clutchless hoops since grade school. He pierced his ears himself.
•Fashion•
He likes tight clothing and white shirts. His favorite pants are straight jeans, especially black ones.
•Shoes•
He likes black boots, especially manly looking ones such as combat boots.
•Brain•
He's pretty bright. He taught himself English and has successfully mastered it. But he hates school, so his academic grades suck.
•Vision•
Left: 0.8, Right: 1.0
•Language•
His speech is rough. He always talks in a straightforward manner, and is often rude. He's a good singer.
•Frame•
Slim, with a well-balanced figure that lets him move very quickly. He has good muscle tone.
•Fighting skills•
He's pretty strong. He often gets involved in fights and knows how to handle them, but he never starts fights himself.
•Alertness and agility•
He has quick reaction time, but not much endurance. He tends to get sleepy when worn out.

Age: 16 years old	Birthday: December 11	Blood type: B
Height: 175 cm (5' 7")	Weight: 57 kg (126 lbs)	Shoe size: 25 cm (size 7)
Weapons: Two hunting knives. They're 21 cm (8") long and the blade is transparent.		

Hobbies Sleeping, watching movies, buying CD's, teasing Kengo, Reading (books written in English)	Special skills Guitar, piano, conversational English, fighting, sleeping all day, making unreasonable requests (of Kengo)

His likes	His dislikes
Color: Black, white, red, silver	Color: Pink, yellow, pastels
Food: He says he likes "not-too-heavy" dishes, but he often doesn't know what he's talking about when it comes to food.	Food: Sweets (HATES sweet stuff)
Books: Novels (especially science fiction and mysteries)	Books: Self-improvement books such as "How to get rich," "How to be successful," etc.
Music: American and British music (hard rock, punk, electronica)	Music: Love songs
Games: Action games, music games	Games: RPGs (bore him easily)
TV: Doesn't watch TV often, but likes variety shows.	TV: Soap operas
Movies: Movies from the '70s through the '90s. Any genre, as long as it's interesting.	Movies: Long, boring movies
Animals: Felines	Animals: Smelly animals
Others: sleeping, high places, conversational English, British comedy, spring, fall	Others: School, teachers, kids, smoking, winter, summer, crowds, exercise, fights

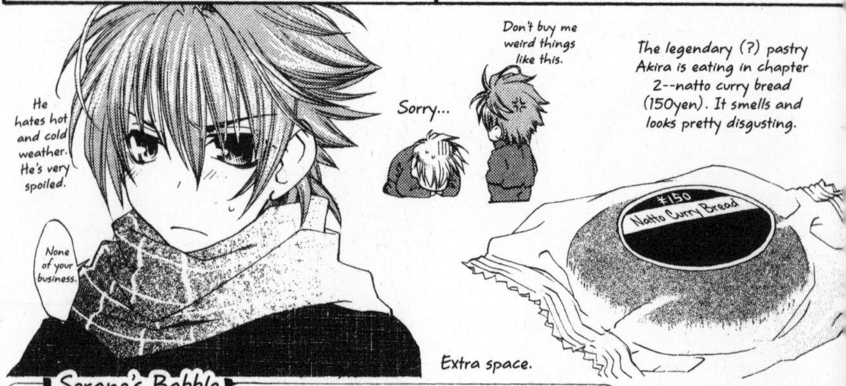
The legendary (?) pastry Akira is eating in chapter 2--natto curry bread (150yen). It smells and looks pretty disgusting.
¥150
Natto Curry Bread
Don't buy me weird things like this.
Sorry...
He hates hot and cold weather. He's very spoiled.
None of your business.
Extra space.

Sorano's Babble

Akira, the main character, is one of the hardest to draw. My assistants tend to have a hard time with his complicated hairdo. I feel kind of sorry for them. Some of the problems with his hairdo are: 1) Although it's very soft, his hair won't flap in the wind. 2) His hair tends to be big, so when he's drawn next to a character with smaller hair, Akira tends to stand out too much. 3) Inking his hair takes a long time...and so forth. He tries to act cool (?), but he is a big cat lover. But cats don't like him for some reason, and he often gets heartbroken. He always talks in a straightforward manner that reminds me of my own sister's. He's also as arrogant as my sister. ...Does that mean my position is similar to Kengo's?

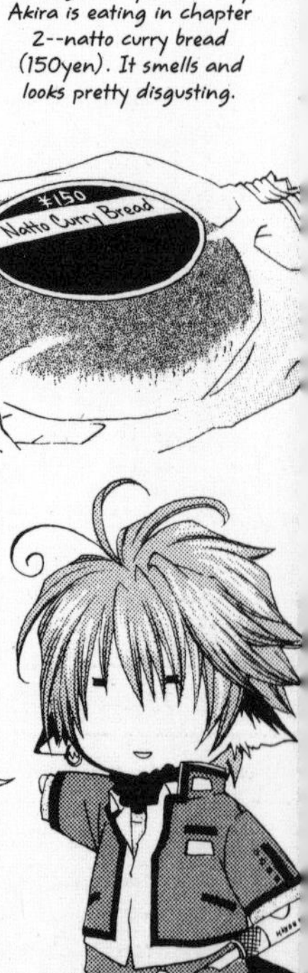

Kaili Sorano

Showy hairdo

I'm not wearing a toupee.

Monochrome Factor volume 1 is finally published! It was almost a mission impossible...(in many ways). This is my very first published manga! There are a lot of other things I've never done before that I'd love to try. Next time, I hope to carry out a certain project I have in mind. (I sound so passive now...)

Akira

Meow!!

The cat doesn't like him.

. . . .

The cat likes him.

HELLO, KITTY!

You're so cute.

Purrr...

!!!

↑ The same cat.

AKIRA! KNOW WHAT? THIS KITTY'S——

April 18-20, 2008

at the Jacob Javits Center, New York City

New York Comic Con is Coming!

Find the best in **Anime, Manga, Graphic Novels, Video Games, Toys, and Movies!** NY Comic Con has hundreds of **Celebrity Appearances, Autographing Sessions, Screenings, Industry Panels, Gaming Tournaments, and Much More!**

Go to **www.nycomiccon.com** to get all the information and **BUY TICKETS!** Plus, sign up for special New York Comic Con updates to be the first to learn about Guests, Premieres, and Special Events!

Reed Exhibitions

TOKYOPOP MANGA SUPPLEMENT

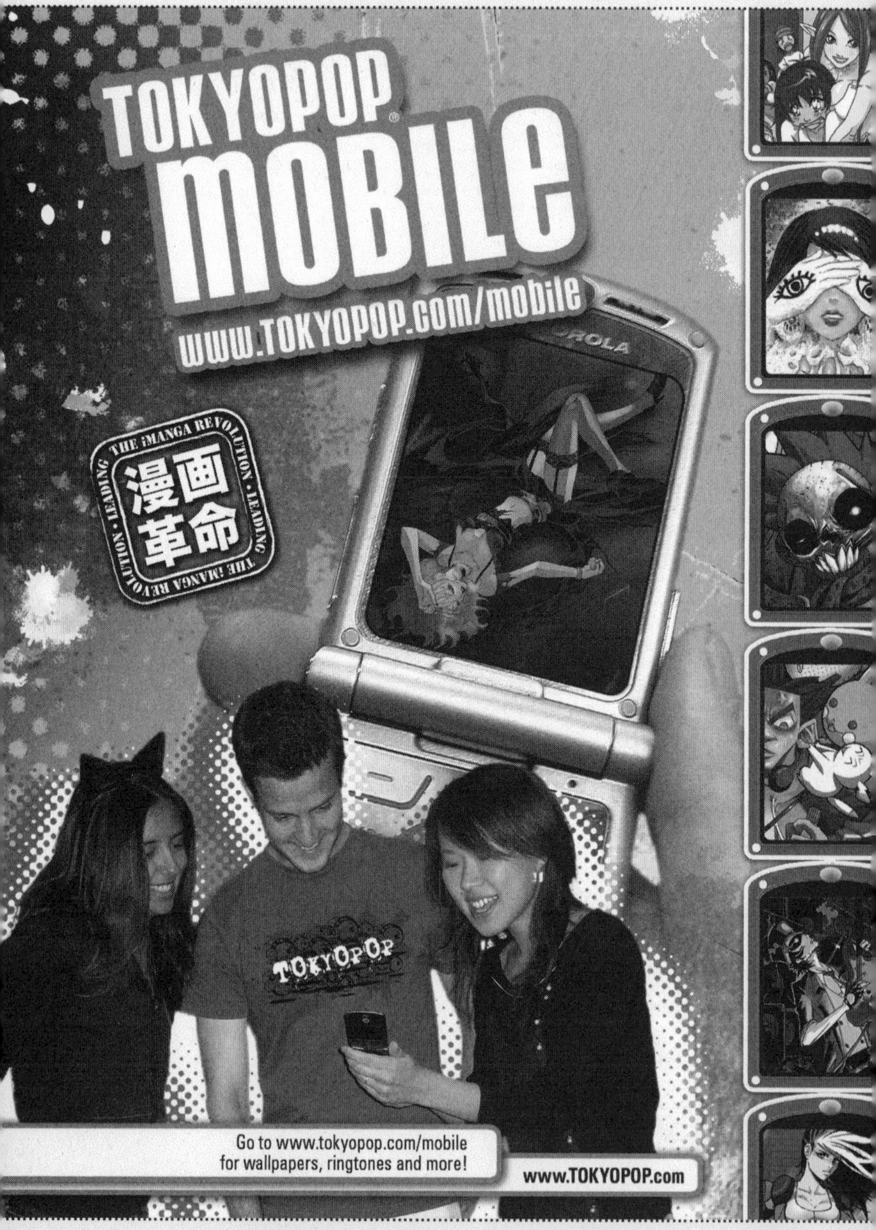
TOKYOPOP MOBILE
www.TOKYOPOP.com/mobile
THE iMANGA REVOLUTION · LEADING THE iMANGA REVOLUTION · LEADING
漫画革命
TOKYOPOP
Go to www.tokyopop.com/mobile
for wallpapers, ringtones and more!
www.TOKYOPOP.com

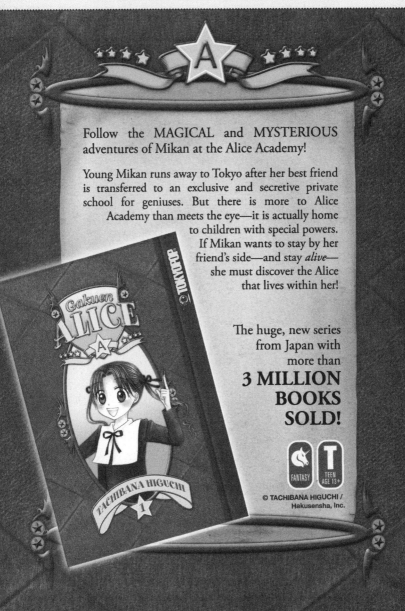

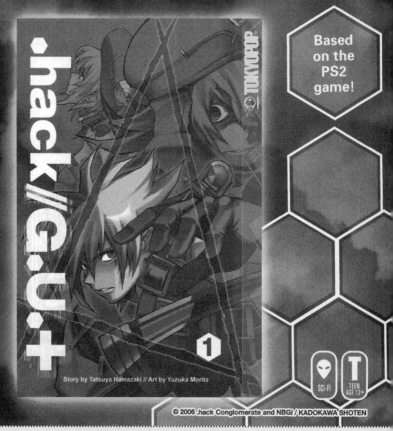

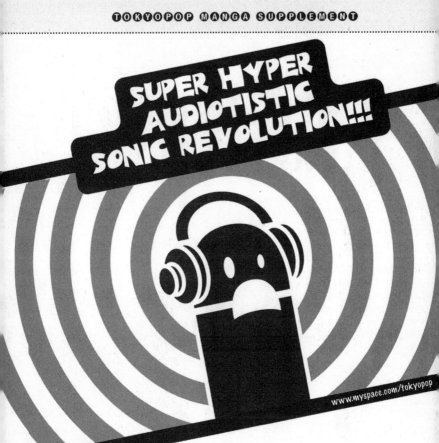
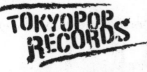

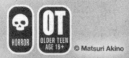
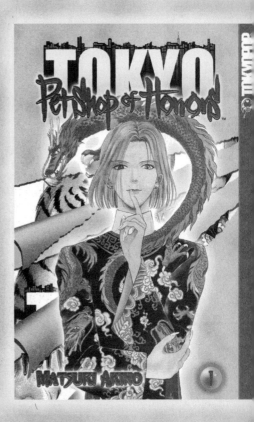
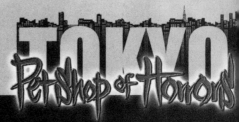

D0805148

STOP!

This is the back of the book.
You wouldn't want to spoil a great ending!

This book is printed "manga-style," in the authentic Japanese right-to-left format. Since none of the artwork has been flipped or altered, readers get to experience the story just as the creator intended. You've been asking for it, so TOKYOPOP® delivered: authentic, hot-off-the-press, and far more fun!

DIRECTIONS

If this is your first time reading manga-style, here's a quick guide to help you understand how it works.

It's easy... just start in the top right panel and follow the numbers. Have fun, and look for more 100% authentic manga from TOKYOPOP®!

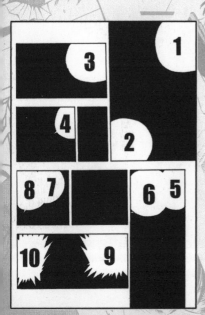